Using
Statistics
to Make
Educational
Decisions

To Dad, who is a problem-solver nonpareil

Using
Statistics
to Make
Educational
Decisions

David Tanner
California State University, Fresno

Los Angeles | London | New Delhi
Singapore | Washington DC

Los Angeles | London | New Delhi
Singapore | Washington DC

FOR INFORMATION:

SAGE Publications, Inc.
2455 Teller Road
Thousand Oaks, California 91320
E-mail: order@sagepub.com

SAGE Publications Ltd.
1 Oliver's Yard
55 City Road
London EC1Y 1SP
United Kingdom

SAGE Publications India Pvt. Ltd.
B 1/I 1 Mohan Cooperative Industrial Area
Mathura Road, New Delhi 110 044
India

SAGE Publications Asia-Pacific Pte. Ltd.
33 Pekin Street #02-01
Far East Square
Singapore 048763

Executive Editor: Diane McDaniel
Assistant Editor: Theresa Accomazzo
Production Editor: Brittany Bauhaus
Copy Editor: Amy Rosenstein
Typesetter: C&M Digitals (P) Ltd.
Proofreader: Dennis W. Webb
Indexer: Molly Hall
Cover Designer: Bryan Fishman
Marketing Manager: Katharine Winter
Permissions Editor: Adele Hutchinson

Copyright © 2012 by SAGE Publications, Inc.

Printed in the United States of America

Library of Congress Cataloging-in-Publication Data

Tanner, David.

Using statistics to make educational decisions / David Tanner.

p. cm.
Includes bibliographical references and index.

ISBN 978-1-4129-6977-2 (pbk.)

1. Educational statistics–Study and teaching.
2. Educational tests and measurements. I. Title.

LB2846.T29 2012

This book is printed on acid-free paper.

11 12 13 14 15 10 9 8 7 6 5 4 3 2 1

CONTENTS

DETAILED CONTENTS

PREFACE

Perhaps the major justifications historically to educators for a course in statistics were to put students in a position to understand the professional literature and to prepare them to conduct their own research for a thesis or some other culminating project. Although those two purposes remain important, the educational landscape has changed for those who work in schools and colleges. Government scrutiny and intensified oversight of institutions that were once governed almost exclusively at the local level have changed education. Observers are curious about how schools compare, about which district is best, about which states are spending the most per student on education, about whether reforms are making a difference, and about why so many students are failing.

Some of these questions require quite technical answers, answers which educators historically redirected to the "experts." The district's tests and measurements person or the college's institutional researcher was the authority on intricate questions, particularly when they involved any level of quantitative analysis. But the questions leveled at all educators have become so acute and so persistent that they can no longer be deferred to someone else. Besides, beyond the learners themselves, who has a more direct interest in figuring out which reading curriculum works best than the reading teacher? What school principal wouldn't profit from knowing how to determine how much of the difference in students' mathematics achievement can be explained by the amount of homework the student completes? Accountability advocates want to make these questions every educator's domain, and it's at least disingenuous to embrace the task of delivering a curriculum, for example, and then duck the companion responsibility to determine whether it's more effective than whatever program it replaced. This book was written to help educators develop the tools and the conceptual understanding they need to deal with such questions.

Our Common Purpose

As a point of departure, I note that we share a desire to help students learn a discipline that precious few would pursue of their own accord. That reality means that in some measure, we proselyte for quantitative analysis. But the task is larger than nurturing and encouraging a few converts since *all* of our students must develop some confidence with statistics. Absent that ability, meaningful change in education is unlikely because educators can't provide definitive answers to the most substantive questions.

Chapter Coverage and Organization

Several things will distinguish the book from other introductory statistics textbooks. If not entirely unique, they at least make this work unlike many of the mainstream books.

First, the title makes it apparent that the book is written for educators. Of course statistics concepts aren't any different for educators than they are for anyone else, but at least the examples here should feel familiar to people in K–12 or higher education. This emphasis reflects a complaint by my fellow graduate school students many years ago who found it difficult to relate to analyses of crop yields.

To help students rise above the initial trepidation, we will start very simply. Part I begins with a first chapter that is entirely nonmathematical. It serves as a platform for introducing some of the terminology and explaining some of the emphases. The order of the other chapters in Parts I and II is largely predictable. From the introduction, the progression is to data presentation, data distributions, and then z scores.

Part III of the book comprises Chapters 5–9 and is focused on tests of significant differences for interval/ratio scale data, from the z test to the factorial *ANOVA*. Because many first courses don't include factorial *ANOVA*, that procedure and one-way *ANOVA* have separate chapters. Factorial *ANOVA* is included because for some there will be a second course, and even when there isn't the topic is so common in the research literature and so fundamental to research design that I thought it irresponsible to leave it out. Part III ends with a chapter on repeated measures designs for interval scale data— the before/after t and the within-subjects F.

The Part IV chapters are all related to correlation. Chapter 10 is on the Pearson Correlation without Spearman's *rho,* which is reserved for Chapter 14, and several other tests for ordinal data. Chapter 11 covers bivariate regression, with multiple regression treated separately in Chapter 12.

Although not often a first-term topic, multiple regression, like factorial *ANOVA*, is so important to research design that I thought it a disservice to the student to exclude it. In addition, it's there for those who have the luxury of a second course.

Chapters 13 and 14 in Part V are devoted to nonparametric procedures. Chapter 13 is based on the *chi*-square topics and nominal data, and Chapter 14 to procedures for ordinal data, with both independent and dependent groups, including Spearman's *rho*. First-term courses often don't cover Mann-Whitney and Friedman's *ANOVA*, but there's an important harmony in showing students some of the procedures that are available for each of nominal, ordinal, and interval/ratio data.

Part VI includes two chapters that are a little unusual in an introductory statistics text. Government involvement in K–12 and postsecondary education and the associated emphasis on standardized testing is much of the reason for Chapter 15, where some of the more basic measurement issues are introduced. They seem particularly relevant to this most tested generation of students. Although it isn't common to cover score reliability or perhaps any of the testing issues in a statistics text, those topics provide a ready application for concepts such as correlation (for test/retest reliability and concurrent validity, for example) and for a discussion of measurement error, which is related to the many standard error discussions in a statistics book. Including the chapter encourages educators to recognize the important and logical connection between statistical analysis and the formal testing that has become the hallmark of contemporary education.

As important as they are as a point of statistical departure, much of the data analysis that will occupy this generation of educational scholars will involve something more advanced than z scores and one-sample t-tests. Students won't read much of the research in their areas of concentration without encountering analysis of covariance, multivariate analysis of variance, and several other advanced topics. Although some of it is beyond even a second statistics course, I thought an introduction, on a conceptual level only, to a few of the more common, advanced topics would be helpful to students. Chapter 16 certainly isn't comprehensive. I expect many instructors will review the list and wonder why some other topic wasn't added to the list, but at least the careful reader can know how a stepwise regression solution differs from a direct solution, or how discriminant function analysis differs from *MANOVA*, or what Spearman had in mind when he designed factor analysis. Most of the topics are fleshed out with at least some SPSS® output, but for all of them there is enough of a discussion that students will have a working knowledge of the kinds of questions each procedure was designed to answer.

PARTICULAR CONTENT EMPHASIS

Effect size calculations and confidence intervals often get short shrift in introductory textbooks. In addition to their value in understanding the published research, many of the more important educational journals now require that potential authors submit them. Whether they publish their research (and I recognize that most won't), or just consume the published literature, students will encounter both effect sizes and confidence intervals so they need to have at least a working knowledge of what they do. Those topics are addressed in several places.

Confidence intervals are introduced initially in Chapter 5 with the z test, and then are reinforced in Chapter 6 for the independent t-test, in Chapter 11 with bivariate regression, and finally in Chapter 12 with multiple regression. These multiple applications give students the opportunity to view confidence intervals from several angles.

To accommodate their different applications, effect sizes also come up in several chapters. Cohen's d and *omega*-squared are both introduced in Chapter 6 for the independent t-test, with some discussion about the advantages of each. Because it's the effect size that SPSS offers, the focus shifts to partial *eta*-squared in Chapter 7 for one-way *ANOVA*, in Chapter 8 for factorial *ANOVA*, and again in Chapter 9 for the repeated measures *ANOVA*. The coefficient of determination in Chapters 10 and 11 allows students to examine effect sizes from the correlation point of view, with its equivalent for more than two variables, multiple R squared in the Chapter 11 discussion of multiple regression. Although they must be interpreted differently than the other effect sizes, *phi* coefficient and Cramer's V are also often treated in this category. They're introduced with the *chi*-square test of independence in Chapter 13. All of these discussions will help education students determine whether their nonrandom outcomes also have practical importance.

Rather than a chapter devoted entirely to research design, I elected to introduce the basic issues in Chapter 6 in the context of the independent t-test, and then integrate design concepts with each of the other procedures thereafter. There are references to research issues again in Chapters 7 and 8 with the *ANOVA* chapters, in the regression chapters, and in the chapters on nonparametric procedures. My feeling was that students would understand best by placing design into multiple contexts this way.

There is also no chapter devoted entirely to probability. The issue is fundamental, certainly, but can seem unnecessarily esoteric to students when it's treated separate from the statistical tests of which it is so much a part. So probability issues are introduced briefly in Chapter 3 in the discussion of data distributions, more thoroughly in Chapter 4 with z scores and particularly in

Chapter 5 with the z test and the concept of statistical significance. It's discussed frequently thereafter, generally in the context of interpreting statistical outcomes.

PEDAGOGICAL ELEMENTS

In addition to examples that are based on educational issues, each chapter begins with the kinds of problems that educators face and an outline of how one faced with such a problem can respond. The development of the chapter is an exploration of solving the problem. In the chapter summary the problem is revisited and some of the steps toward solving it are retraced.

Particularly in the early going, statistics books tend to be concept intensive. As an aid to the reader, each important new term is in boldface, is defined in text, and then defined again in a margin note. All of these terms also appear in the end-of-book **Glossary**.

In each chapter where it's relevant, there is SPSS output for some of the problems that are worked in text. This allows students to compare long-hand results to computer-generated output. There's also an SPSS appendix at the back that contains detailed steps for completing each of the procedures that are featured in the chapters. Where they can be helpful, screenshots of what SPSS looks like are included. Certainly SPSS isn't the only statistical package available, but it's probably common enough to make the exposure helpful, and as it turns out, other programs like Systat and SAS use quite similar command structures.

Part of the task for a statistics instructor is to introduce the student to how some new concept or idea can be elaborated. Once the reader has worked with the mechanics of how the procedure works and what it was designed to explain, there can be a wider application of the subject. These occasional broader applications occur in relevant chapters in a feature titled Through a Wider Lens.

There is great value in repetition. Examples in text are followed by more examples, and then yet more opportunities in the end-of-chapter problems. Following the usual pattern, the answers for the odd-numbered exercises will be available in the back of the book.

ANCILLARIES

Additional ancillary materials further support and enhance the learning goals of the third edition of *Effective Instructional Strategies: From Theory to Practice*. These ancillary materials include the following:

Instructor Teaching Site:
www.sagepub.com/tanner

The instructor teaching site provides an integrated source for all instructor materials, including the following key components for each chapter:

Chapter Outlines: Carefully crafted outlines follow the structure of each chapter, providing an essential reference and teaching tool.

Course Syllabi: Sample syllabi—for semester, quarter, and online classes—provide suggested models for instructors to use when creating the syllabi for their courses.

PowerPoint Slides: Chapter-specific slide presentations offer assistance with lecture and review preparation by highlighting essential content, features, and artwork from the book.

Test Bank (Word): This Word test bank offers a diverse set of test questions and answers for each chapter of the book. Multiple-choice, true/false, short-answer, and essay questions for every chapter help instructors assess students' progress and understanding.

Discussion Questions: Chapter-specific questions help launch discussion by prompting students to engage with the material and by reinforcing important content.

Student Study Site:
www.sagepub.com/tanner

The student study site provides an integrated source for all student study materials, including the following key components for each chapter:

E-flashcards: These study tools reinforce students' understanding of key terms and concepts that have been outlined in the chapters.

Web Quizzes: Flexible self-quizzes allow students to independently assess their progress in learning course material.

ACKNOWLEDGMENTS

Even when but a single author is listed, a book is never the product of just one individual's work. Several people who teach the course for which this book was designed provided wonderful suggestions about what was working and what needed to be modified. If the book has strengths, in substantial measure they reflect input from (listed alphabetically):

Amy Atwood,
University of Wisconsin-Madison

David Coffland,
Idaho State University

John Huss,
Northern Kentucky University

Todd E. Johnson,
Washington State University

Pui-Wa Lei,
Pennsylvania State University

Ratna Nandakumar,
University of Delaware

Laura L. Onafowora,
North Carolina Central University

John J. Pantana,
Liberty University

Carolyn Pearson,
University of Arkansas, Little Rock

Jennifer Reeves,
Nova Southeastern University

Mack C. Shelley, Iowa State
University

David A. Tanner, University of North Texas, Dallas, also reviewed early drafts of some of the material and offered helpful guidance for how it might be strengthened.

I owe a great debt to my students both at California State University, Fresno, and at Alliant International University. After many years of teaching statistics, I find myself more interested than ever in discovering the most productive approach to teaching students and doing justice to the discipline.

Suzanna Nielson developed the cartoons that appear in each chapter. She did an excellent job of capturing some of the problems, missteps, and confusion we witness if we spend any time with statistics. All of the cartoon scenarios have some basis in the author's experience, by the way, although the connections are more tangential in some situations than others.

By their nature, statistics books involve a myriad of ideas and calculations, and the attendant potential for error is substantial. Tom DeHardt did a wonderful job of detecting many of the minor gaffes that would otherwise haunt a finished work. I appreciate his careful attention to detail.

Several at SAGE Publications have been closely associated with the book, of course, and each has made an important contribution. Steve Wainwright showed initial interest in this project and nurtured it in the early going. I am very grateful for his support and encouragement. Upon Steve's departure, the project fell to Diane McDaniel and Leah Mori, who have both been stellar in their suggestions and in their instincts for what the manuscript needed. It has been an honor to work with all three.

No one has enjoyed a steadier partnership or more consistent support from a companion than I. Susan's encouragement has been integral to my completing this project, and I am deeply grateful to her.

—*David Tanner*

PART I

Developing a Context for Statistical Analysis

Chapter 1

A CONTEXT FOR SOLVING QUANTITATIVE PROBLEMS

THE PROBLEM

Phil is an academic counselor at the local community college where he's been a member of the staff for several years. He hopes one day to work in the office of institutional research, perhaps as its director. It's been years since he took a class but he recognizes that some of the questions that he and others ask about how they're doing at the college require some ability with quantitative analysis. He picks up a statistics text in the bookstore, leafs through the pages, and wonders whether he's ready to pursue an advanced degree.

QUESTIONS AND ANSWERS

❏ What does this book have to do with my career as an educator?

From kindergarteners to graduate students, today's learners belong to the most scrutinized and indeed the most tested generation of students. Many of the questions asked about the quality of their education and about their educational progress require some quantitative analysis. This book is designed to help with just such problems.

❏ How much of a mathematician will I need to be to navigate this textbook?

The answer is not a mathematician at all in the usual sense of that description. A little introductory algebra will help but you will need nothing beyond. It's far more important to think logically than it is to have an extensive background in mathematics.

❏ Since computers and software are available for statistical analysis, do I have to perform the calculations myself?

For two reasons, the answer is yes. Those who can work solutions understand the analysis more readily than those who cannot, and it's actually quite satisfying to complete a solution longhand, although you may have to trust me on this for now.

✦ – ✦ – ✦

About Statistics

When things are important to us, we often create a record of them. When a piece of music is particularly moving, a meal is outstanding, or a friendship is unusually meaningful, we at least create memories that serve as a more-or-less permanent record of the experience. Some of the other things that we wish to remember are important not because they involve the emotions that the foregoing evoke, but because they are a record of the choices made in the past and may become elements in the decisions that are yet to come. This seems particularly likely at a time when educators at all levels are scrutinized more carefully than perhaps they ever have been. Ours is an age of educational accountability.

Numbers offer a great economy in record keeping. Although certainly there are some things that can't be readily reduced to numbers, this book is about describing and analyzing things that can. Some numbers are nothing more than convenient labels to indicate a category to which an individual belongs. This is the case when summaries are made of something like students' academic majors, and for convenience, the majors are numbered. At other times, the number indicates how much of some quality an individual possesses, as with a verbal aptitude gauge where higher scores indicate that the individual measured possesses more of, or a higher level of, some characteristic than one with a lower score. In either example, the numbers allow one to reduce what could be lengthy verbal descriptions to a relatively compact record. Whether we're gathering information about a second language speaker's reading comprehension, the dropout rate in a particular school district, or the number of units for which entering freshman students typically register, someone is relying on their ability to quantify several important outcomes. Efforts to discover more effective teaching, curb the dropout rate, or evaluate trends in student registration often depend on educators' abilities to manipulate and analyze quantitative data.

This is the reality that Phil faces in the chapter introduction. He, and all educators and decision makers, needs to be able to answer questions about differences and about relationships, about the way things are and how they might be improved. Questions about the average age of entering freshmen, or the changing attitudes of entering freshmen, or about whether there have been changes in students' level of preparation for college-level study over time may involve quite intricate quantitative analyses. Equipping readers to deal with such issues is the point of this book.

REGARDING THE MATH

To be straightforward about a couple of things as we begin, note that by its nature statistical analysis is mathematical and a good deal of basic math is involved in some of the things we will do as we progress, but it is *basic* math. Because the issues educational decision makers face are complex and involved doesn't always mean that the analytical techniques used to confront those issues need to be.

Does that sound inconsistent? Perhaps only continuing in the book will be convincing, but in a number of years of teaching statistical analysis, your author has come to two conclusions:

1. Students often have very little background in quantitative analysis generally, and little experience with mathematics specifically beyond an introductory algebra course.

2. The lack of mathematics needn't be an impediment to statistical analysis and decision making.

Perhaps like the aspiring institutional researcher in the chapter introduction, that last (first?) algebra class was as long ago as somewhere in secondary school, but he, and you, can flourish nevertheless.

By the way, if the reader has *more* than a little algebra that's terrific, but that hasn't been assumed. The more advanced students among us will just need to be a little patient during the early chapters while those who have had less math, or a longer interruption, get up to speed.

If it *has* been a while since formal mathematics coursework, one of the more important things to do by way of beginning is just to review things like the order in which multiple mathematical operations must occur. Many of the mistakes that students make when there are multiple calculations required stem from forgetting that, in order, the student works

- in parentheses first,
- then with exponents,
- then with multiplication and division, working from left to right, doing whichever comes first, and
- then addition, and subtraction, again working the leftmost problem first.

If "please excuse my dear Aunt Sally" still helps one remember, great. If it doesn't, find something else to use as a guide because some of the formulae involve several calculations. It's important to be clear about whether we subtract or divide first when the formula calls for both.

For students whose earlier forays into some sort of quantitative analysis were, well, modest in outcome, a course like this can be about redemption. With some persistent study and practice, even those whose prior experiences prompt trepidation at the prospect of a statistics class can excel.

ANSWERS THE OLD-FASHIONED WAY

The truth of the matter is that in the present age, beyond balancing your checkbook (and perhaps not even that), relatively little quantitative analysis is carried out without using a computer. Sometimes there is just too much information to deal with to make avoiding the computer practical. Even when there aren't mounds of data to absorb, computers are very convenient. Business-oriented spreadsheets such as Microsoft's Excel, to say nothing of dedicated statistical packages like SPSS, have built-in statistical procedures that address most of the problems we'll tackle in an introductory statistics textbook. Indeed, statistical packages provide analyses of extremely complex and involved problems. And yet there is a good deal of emphasis in this book on hand calculation. Why? The question deserves some attention.

It isn't just the aspiring institutional researchers such as Phil who wish to answer questions that involve some data analysis. We all have questions that require some "number crunching," but when we rely entirely on a computer to do the work a problem emerges. In an effort to be user-friendly, software developers have made generating solutions very easy, so easy in fact that you and I can run elaborate statistical procedures without really understanding whether we have satisfied the assumptions that the procedure requires, or whether we even understand the implications of the output. The user is not only the beneficiary, but sometimes also the victim of the software developer's ability to make complex analyses accessible.

To counter this problem, we'll do some pencil-and-paper work. With the exception of some of the procedures in Chapter 16, we'll work each new type of problem longhand before leaning on the computer for answers. The beauty of longhand calculations is that every step is visually discrete. Instead of just trying to understand what the solution means, we can consider why each calculation is made and also note its impact. How and why everything is done is usually more transparent working longhand than it is when peering at computer output. If the "it's good for you" argument makes all of this sounds like eating oatmeal when you'd really rather have waffles, longhand calculations have an ancillary benefit. Working solutions can actually be quite satisfying; they can prompt quite a feeling of accomplishment.

IT'S GREEK TO ME!

A little statistical notation is going to help us. Although sigma (Σ), rho (ρ), mu (μ), and other Greek symbols can be intimidating at first glance, there's no need to worry. We're making no forays into Sir Isaac Newton's calculus. For us the symbols are components of a mathematical shorthand. They're

SOURCE: Created by Suzanna Nielson.

"When do we learn to calculate the over and under on football games?"

symbols for values we'll either calculate without much difficulty or abbreviations for mathematical procedures you probably already know how to complete. They really aren't going to be a problem. Each symbol will be explained before it's pressed into service. Besides, think of the mileage you'll get from casually mentioning to your colleagues that $\mu = 85.437$ for eighth-grade language arts students on the district's benchmark math test!

Different Kinds of Statistics

■ **Descriptive statistics** summarize a data set.

■ **Inferential statistics** reveal the larger group through the smaller group's characteristics.

If he is to work in his college's Office of Institutional Research, Phil will need to be able to both describe and analyze data. In fact, describing and analyzing define the bulk of statistical tasks. The **descriptive statistics** we'll begin working with in Chapter 2 allow one to summarize the characteristics of a data set. Sometimes the descriptive task employs graphs and figures to represent the data. Developing the tools for these show-and-tell descriptive tasks are the subjects of Chapters 2 and 3.

Beginning with Chapter 5, and then carrying on through the balance of the book, the focus will change from describing data to drawing inferences about data. There we will learn how to understand large groups by examining smaller groups. That's the domain of **inferential statistics,** and it allows anyone dealing with quantitative data to have a great economy in her or his analysis. When we observe certain conventions about the way the smaller group is formed, it can tell us a good deal about the nature of the larger group, which brings us to the next topic.

Samples and Populations

■ A **population** is all members of a defined group.

■ A **sample** is any subset of a population.

Statistical analysis involves two kinds of groups, all possible members of any specified group that defines a **population**, and any subset of the population, which is called a **sample**. When noting just above that one can view the larger group through the lens that a smaller group provides, we were talking about understanding the population by analyzing the sample. If we're careful about the way the sample is selected, we can come to know a great deal about the aptitude for college study among *all* freshman students (the population) by examining the aptitude that a smaller number (the sample) possess, as long as they're representative. The reader will always know which group we're talking about because we'll use Greek letters to indicate the characteristics of populations, and more familiar Roman letters for samples.

The symbol μ (mu) mentioned above is the symbol for the arithmetic average (the mean) of some characteristic in a population, verbal ability for example. As long as he's referring to just his institution, all students at Phil's school represents a population. If the mean age for all students in that group is 24.545, he could indicate that as $\mu = 24.545$. The corresponding symbol for the mean of the sample is M, which although not universally used, is increasingly common. (It used to be common to use x-bar, an ex with a bar over it, to signify the mean, but many of the major research journals have adopted M.) If instead of everyone, Phil selects a sample of 30 students from his institution and determines their average age to be 22.916, he would represent that value as $M = 22.916$.

THE CONNECTION BETWEEN QUANTITATIVE ANALYSIS AND RESEARCH DESIGN

Educational decision makers have little interest in **constants** precisely because they don't vary. How interesting would it be to study the weather if everyone had the same weather and it was the same every day? **Variables**, conversely, have that name because they have different manifestations. **Qualitative variables** include such characteristics as an individual's gender, ethnicity, political affiliation, or school site. Differences in variables like those are indicated not by the amount of the characteristic one possesses, but by the category to which an individual belongs. We may use numbers to code the site at which one teaches, for example, but as is the case with all such variables, the number only indicates the category and has no mathematical significance.

By contrast, for **quantitative variables** there are measurable differences in whatever is gauged. For characteristics such as age, spelling ability, or intelligence, differences in the amount of what is measured are indicated by the numbers that are assigned. Examining something like achievement differences between primary English speakers and English learners involves both a qualitative and a quantitative variable. The group into which one falls (primary English or English learner) is a qualitative variable. The individual's score on a reading test is a quantitative variable.

So constants hold no allure for us, but variables pique our curiosity. We all have questions and perhaps theories about why things vary. When we put together a formal plan for gathering and analyzing data so that we can answer those questions, we have developed a **research design**. Part of the purpose of a research design is to specify what the researcher believes to be the

■ **Constants,** which never vary, hold little analytical value.

■ **Variables,** however, are interesting precisely because they have different manifestations.

■ **Qualitative variables** differ by category rather than by amount, but there are measurable differences in **quantitative variables**.

■ **A research design** is a formal plan for gathering and analyzing data.

- The variable thought to affect another is called the **independent variable**.

- The variable influenced is the **dependent variable**.

relevant variables. We'll deal with this in more detail in Chapter 6, but when one variable is thought to have an effect on another, that antecedent variable is termed an **independent variable** and the one upon which it is judged to have an effect is called the **dependent variable**. If homework is thought to have a facilitative effect on students' grades, homework is an independent variable and grades, the dependent variable. We raise the issue now because part of the point of a book like this is to put us in a position to answer such questions. Although this isn't a research design text *per se*, the topics we will study are all topics intimately related to design issues.

TESTING ISSUES

For any K–12 educator and to some degree also for higher educators, there seems to be little refuge from testing. If Phil is successful in his pursuit of the Office of Institutional Research, managing and analyzing test data will be a significant part of his task. With questions about student admissions, students' disabilities, mandated educational goals, and so on, testing issues pop up everywhere. As it turns out, many of those testing issues have important statistical components, and the tools we can develop in a course such as this will help us to understand the issues better. For that reason, a section on Test and Measurement Topics has been included. In Chapter 15, we'll use some of the descriptive and analytical procedures developed earlier in the book to examine issues such as score reliability and detecting testing bias.

Historically, test and measurement issues were almost exclusively the domain of the testing experts. Certainly testing issues sometimes require a highly technical and esoteric set of skills and knowledge, but testing issues have becomes so pervasive that educators who develop some ability with analyzing testing data are in a unique position to bring about improvement. Part of what drives the testing movement is the realization that it isn't enough to deliver curriculum and instruction. One must be able to document how well it was done. Educational testing has implications for educators and learners that are too important for the educators not to be more directly involved, so we'll develop some statistical tools that will allow us to tackle at least some of the fundamental testing questions.

CHAPTER ORGANIZATION

Just as was the case for this chapter, each of those that come after will begin with a *Problem* to provide a context for the material we're going to cover, accompanied by some questions and tentative answers to focus the reader on particular issues that an educator is likely to face. Periodically in the chapter, text boxes titled "Key Terms" such as those in this chapter will provide brief definitions of the technical terms that are introduced in each chapter. All of those concepts and definitions appear again in a Glossary at the back of the book.

All of the procedures we'll explore have applications beyond those which are suggested in the chapter. That's part of their value, of course. Although there are examples for each procedure in text and, frequently, *Another Example* thrown in for the value of the practice, there are also occasional boxes titled *Through a Wider Lens* to suggest a the broader application for the concepts. Study them for the suggestions they make about the more general uses there are for what we're doing.

Most of the chapters introduce new formulae. Each one is numbered and explained, and then listed at the end of each chapter. The end-of-chapter listing also repeats a brief explanation of each formula's purpose.

Except for this first chapter, each chapter also ends with a list of practice problems to supplement those worked longhand earlier in the chapter. According to the usual practice, solutions for half of the end-of-chapter problems are provided in a section at the end of the book.

SOFTWARE AND HARDWARE

With all of the matter of fact about the importance of working longhand solutions, even your author, who is very fond of calculating paper-and-pencil solutions, recognizes that it isn't practical with large data sets. The idea is to get you comfortable with computer applications as well, which brings us to SPSS, the "Statistical Package for the Social Sciences."

In the interest of student familiarity, many of the longhand problems in the chapters also have output from SPSS solutions. At the end of the book, there's an Appendix for SPSS procedures. It provides a step-by-step sequence for completing the problems worked in the chapters.

Several dedicated statistical software packages are available that will handle the problems we'll take up, and people who do a great deal of analysis probably each have their own favorite. However, among educators and social scientists generally, SPSS may be the most popular, which is one reason why a version of this book is available with a trial version of that software. Like many software publishers, the versions change from time to time, but don't be too concerned about obsolescence. The commands involved in the analyses and the appearance of the output have changed very little in the several most recent versions of the software.

One of the educational decision maker's assets is a hand calculator. Many of them have statistical functions built in, and some are very sophisticated in the solutions they can generate. Your instructor will probably have a recommendation about the particular type she or he wishes you to use. In an age of inflating prices in many areas, happily for us, electronic devices are relatively inexpensive. Your local discount supermarket probably has all the calculator you will need for this class for less than $15. Get one, and develop some familiarity with how the memories work and how to access the statistical functions. The more elaborate graphing calculators will also perform the statistical functions we need, but we aren't going to use the graphing function, and those more expensive tools probably represent calculator overkill for an introductory statistics class.

Studying for Statistics

Without wishing to sound paternal, a comment on how to study statistics seems appropriate. Part of the beauty of language arts instruction is that learners are obliged to practice the content whether or not class is in session. Ordinary day-to-day communication almost makes it impossible *not* to generalize much of the language learning. Because statistical analysis isn't nearly as commonplace as ordinary language communication, it doesn't offer the same advantage. Many opportunities exist to use statistics in the normal course of events to be sure, but we have to look for them. To minimize that limitation it's important to think about the material when *not* in class, which yields (drum roll, please) a rationale for homework. Doesn't advocating homework in a book for educators have a satisfying consistency? The work *out* of class is about more than practice. It's very much about learning to generalize new abilities beyond the classroom environment.

Between the reading and the homework, this material will take some time. As a practical matter, an hour each day during the week is going to pay greater learning dividends than a marathon the night before class. The statistical analyses we're going to tackle here aren't particularly difficult, but they may be different from the way you usually think and analyze problems. The kind of logic we're trying to cultivate seems to come more readily when we work at it often than when we occasionally work for long sessions.

AND FINALLY

The Phil referred to in the "Problem" at the beginning of the chapter is intended to appeal to each of us, of course. It isn't that we necessarily aspire to head some institution's Office of Institutional Research, but the fact is that, like Phil, some of the really pressing questions every educator faces require some understanding of quantitative analysis. Developing solutions to those problems often doesn't require highly sophisticated mathematics. The skills and procedures we need to be effective in our educational careers are within the reach of the typical university student. To develop the grounding we need to be successful, we'll do some things that may seem a little old-fashioned, like producing longhand calculations that could more quickly be done by computer, but it's all part of the plan for your progress. Be clear about the overarching goal. It isn't that you will perhaps "weather," or survive the course, but that you will succeed, and in grand fashion. So let's begin in earnest.

STUDENT STUDY SITE

Visit the Student Study Site at **www.sagepub.com/tanner** for additional learning tools.

Chapter 2

DESCRIBING DATA

THE PROBLEM: HOW TO DESCRIBE LARGE AMOUNTS OF DATA

Almost by default, Mr. Garcia has become the district's data analyst. His mathematics background and the district's need to make sense of the data they collect on everything from students' language and economic status to their test scores have pressed him into service. He knows that there are differences both in the *amount* and the *kind* of information that various measures provide. He will need to find a way to summarize the data and explain the differences to a variety of audiences.

QUESTIONS AND ANSWERS

❑ When analyzing a thing sometimes we are interested in *what kind* it is, and sometimes in *how much* of it there is. What descriptive will accommodate both the quality and the quantity of things?

The answer brings us to the scale of the data. Data scale will be an important consideration in statistical decision making.

❑ What's the best way to describe the characteristics of a group without having to describe each member individually?

This is the domain of descriptive statistics.

I t's Chapter 2 and you're still with us, which is good news. As you continue to work with and think about the concepts we raise, you'll find that they come more easily. Using statistics for educational decisions isn't difficult but the logic involved *is* different from the way most people usually think. Sometimes it takes a little while to adopt the statistician's mind-set. Those who make this transition most readily don't make occasional forays into the topics. They study a little each day, rather than a great deal once a week or so.

Whether describing the performance of eighth-grade students on a history test or the leadership qualities that most teachers prefer in a principal, the tasks contain common elements. In

15

either case, one must find a way to reduce the information that comes from multiple sources to a set of clear and manageable findings. Otherwise, those who wish to know the results are left to review all of the data themselves, gather their own information, or maybe just guess. The first two choices are simply too uneconomical. The last option, which isn't unknown unfortunately, too easily compromises accuracy. Although people guess about things all the time (there was word of a school principal who judged teachers' classroom management by the tidiness of the Venetian blinds in their windows), when the outcome is important we usually want something more reliable than a random pick, intuition, or folk wisdom to guide us.

The task of describing data assumes that the data vary, by the way. If they're uniform, there's no need for analysis. If everyone in the senior class passes the high school exit exam, in terms of that outcome, differences in students' ethnicity, gender, or elementary schools are unimportant because none of those differences is related to the outcome.

■ Different "kinds" of measures gauge different qualities referred to as **data scales**.

But with educational data, uniformity is rare. We find that some students do better on tests than others, and that not all teachers admire the same leadership qualities in their principals, and that there can be important differences in students' learning from school to school. Indeed, it is variability that makes data interesting. Our initial task is to outline a process educational decision-makers can use for describing data, which brings us to **data scale**.

THE SCALE OF THE DATA

■ **Measurement** involves using rules to assign numbers.

Technically speaking, **measurement** is assigning numbers according to rules. It's a dry definition but serviceable. Sometimes the measurement is simply a matter of counting, as it is when one "measures" the number of words the student spells correctly on a spelling test. Data scale refers to the way different kinds of measures are categorized. For example, students' ethnicity data are a different category of measure than students' verbal abilities.

Different characteristics have different qualities, and measuring them calls for different approaches so that we avoid the apples-to-oranges comparisons that your sage fifth-grade teacher warned you of when you were introduced to fractions (Although comparing apples to oranges is actually pretty logical since both are tree fruits, wouldn't it make more sense to caution against comparing apples to sheep?). Anyway, as we will see later, the scale of the data is one of the factors that dictates how one should analyze the data.

■ **Nominal** data indicate a category.

■ **Ordinal** data allow ranking.

■ **Interval** data indicate degree of difference, and **ratio** data include a meaningful zero.

Four scales of measurement exist: **nominal**, **ordinal**, **interval**, and **ratio**. Nominal scale data yield the least amount of information about the object, and ratio scale data yield the most. Your mnemonic device for remembering the scales in order is the French word for black, "noir." The first letter refers to nominal, the second ordinal, and so on.

Nominal Scale Data

With nominal data, individual cases in the data set are defined by the category into which the case either fits or does not fit; a characteristic held or not held. Sometimes there are several categories, as there are when people are classified according to their political affiliation. Sometimes there are just two, such as gender.

By definition, nominal categories, are independent; an individual fits into a particular category or does not. There are no "partial" memberships. For us, there aren't *degrees* of feminineness or masculinity. Subjects are either male or female.

To simplify tabulation it's common to assign a number to the category. If Mr. Garcia (from the chapter introduction) surveys students to see which postsecondary institution they applied to, he might tabulate the responses by assigning a "1" to those who select the local private liberal arts college, a "2" to those who prefer State U, and so on. *When numbers indicate a nominal data category, they have no mathematical meaning beyond identifying that category*. Mr. Garcia is just trying to keep track of who wants to go where. The "2" for those planning on State U doesn't mean that those who made this choice are twice as much as the "1s" in some way.

Another Example

Although gender is perhaps the most frequently used example, many kinds of nominal data are used in educational decision-making. Whether students in a school are urban, suburban, or rural calls for nominal data as does asking the student's major or marital status.

Ordinal Scale Data

Ordinal data add the ability to compare individuals in "greater-than" or "less-than" terms; they allow rankings. Classifying participants in an academic competition according to gender represents nominal data. Indicating who finished first, second, third in the competition is ordinal measurement. Ordinal data don't indicate how well anyone did in absolute terms, only how they compare with others.

Ordinal measurement is quite common in education. When we ask,

Who is the *slowest* reader?

Did they do *better* than last time?

Are you *more anxious* than you were before the last test?

We're asking for ordinal data.

■ **Percentile scores** indicate the percentage of all scores that occur at, or below, a point.

Percentile scores are a common type of ordinal data. Percentile scores indicate the percentage of individuals who scored at (technically, it's possible that all scores could have the same value) or below a point. They indicate that someone scoring at the 73rd percentile has a higher math score than someone at the 72nd percentile. But percentile scores don't indicate the size of the interval between those two points. One can't know from the percentile scores whether the difference between the 73rd and 72nd percentiles was one correct answer on the test, two, or several. If Mr. Garcia is asked to develop a list for graduation with each student's class ranking, the data are ordinal.

Another Example

Ordinal data are everywhere in education. Because developmental differences can be so pronounced, kindergarten teachers ask who the *oldest* or *youngest* students are. The track coach is anxious to recruit to her sport the *best* athletes. Students recognize which homework problems are the *easiest* to solve. Although the formality of the measurement may vary, these all involve ordinal data.

Likert-type surveys employ a format where a series of statements, such as "I enjoy studying statistics" are followed by choices such as "strongly agree," "agree," and so on down to "strongly disagree." One who answers "strongly agrees" feels more strongly than if the response was only "agrees," although it isn't clear *how much* stronger.

Interval Scale Data

Interval data indicate *how much* greater or less there is of whatever is measured by providing consistent intervals between consecutive data points. A lower score indicates less of the measured quality, like ordinal scale data, but we know how much less when the data are interval. When the data are interval, the performance gap between someone who scored 37 and someone who scored 43 is the same as that between one who scored 50 and another who scored 56. Interval data provide a good deal more information than ordinal data provide.

One needs to take care about how a zero score is treated, however. With interval data, zero is a point along a scale, but the zero doesn't indicate the absence of the quality measured.

Consider Fahrenheit measures of temperature. If the thermometer reads 0, it doesn't indicate the absence of heat, but only that the mercury has reached that point on the scale midway between +1 and −1 degrees. There are much colder temperatures possible, as anyone who has experienced subzero knows. Zero on the Kelvin scale is a different matter, of course, since for that measure, zero is the coldest temperature possible.

Ratio Scale Data

The meaning of zero changes with ratio data. Unhappily, if you know this from personal experience, a 0 in your bank balance really *does* mean there is no money in the account; bank statements contain ratio measures. But there's another component to ratio data. They allow meaningful ratio comparisons. Measures of height are ratio data and someone who is 6 feet tall is actually twice as tall as a child of 3 feet.

Ratio data are relatively uncommon in educational measurement. To understand this we need to distinguish between the test score and the trait measured. A spelling test is used to gauge students' spelling abilities. Should someone score 0 on a standardized spelling test, for example, it is accurate enough to say that the student missed every item. The number of items spelled correctly is a ratio measure. It doesn't follow, however, that the student has no spelling ability. The number of words missed is in ratio scale, but the measure of the student's spelling ability is not.

Consider some other examples:

- The major intelligence tests have a mean of 100 points for the population. Probably no one wishes to suggest that someone who scores 75 on an intelligence test is half as intelligent as someone who scores 150, and three-fourths as intelligent as someone who scores 100. Intelligence scores are not ratio measures. Some will argue that neither are they interval measures.
- Scores on the verbal subtests of the Graduate Record Exam range from 200 to 800. The difference in performance from 600 to 625 is viewed as the same improvement as from 515 to 540, which indicates interval data, but there is no "0" score on the GRE-verbal, no score indicating the absence of verbal ability. The data aren't ratio scale.

From the standpoint of statistical decision making, there is little need to distinguish between interval and ratio measures because statistical procedures that work for one work also for the other. Indeed, the SPSS, the statistical package lists nominal data, ordinal data, and then "scale" data, the group covering both interval and ratio data. From this point we'll distinguish only between nominal, ordinal, and interval/ratio data.

THROUGH A WIDER LENS

Although the language of data scale may be new, the concepts probably aren't. In the (very) small southern Alberta high school the author attended, there was one school-sponsored sport, basketball for boys. (This was before Title IX, and it was Canada in any case.) Those who played were guards, forwards, and so on, nominal descriptions. The starters were *better* players (ordinal measurement) than the substitutes. The scoring sheet at the end of the game indicated how many points each player scored. Those data were ratio. The intervals were equal, suggesting interval data, but if the scoring sheet indicated zero (not uncommon), it actually meant that the individual did not score.

It's common to gather data that involve more than one scale, by the way. If Mr. Garcia is asked to determine which of two classes did better on a particular test, the test scores probably represent interval data, but the class to which a particular student belongs is a nominal classification.

DESCRIPTIVE STATISTICS

■ Many statistics can be descriptive, but descriptive statistics usually refers to what is typical and how much data variation there is.

Descriptive statistics are calculated so that one can know the essential characteristics of data sets without having to refer to each individual measure.

Our introduction to data scale leads logically to this section because determining the proper descriptive statistic to use is partly dictated by the scale of the data involved.

The most common descriptive statistics are those that measure

(a) central tendency and

(b) variability.

Central tendency statistics indicate what is most typical in a data set. The variability statistics are companions to central tendency and indicate how much individual cases tend to deviate from what is typical. Educators often need to know what's most characteristic of the group in a set of reading scores and then how much individuals' scores stray from that most typical score.

Measures of Central Tendency

To accommodate the different kinds of information provided by data of different scales, there are three different central tendency statistics, the **mode**, the **median**, and the **mean**.

The Mode

The most frequently occurring measure in a group of data is the mode. If one is gathering data on the ethnicity of students at a particular elementary school and Hispanic students are the most numerous, Hispanic students are the mode for ethnicity. If the issue is the state of origin among students at a major university and there are more Kansans than students from any other state, Kansans are the mode. If the physics exam produces more 65 scores than any other, 65 is the mode.

■ The most frequent value in a group is the **mode**.

One can determine the mode for data of any scale. With ordinal, interval, and ratio data, one has choices about which measure of central tendency is best, but not with nominal data. For those data the mode is the *only* appropriate measure of central tendency.

The reason for this is that the data scales are cumulative. Ordinal data include the information that nominal data provide, plus something more. Interval data provide what ordinal and nominal data provide, but with nominal data, all we have is how many there are in each category, so which category has the most is the only calculation we can make.

Although the mode is a relatively crude measure, it can be quite helpful. To analyze and improve recruitment efforts, for example, an admissions officer at a college might be interested in the data Mr. Garcia gathered on students' preferences for postsecondary study, along with similar data from the other high schools in the area. They might look like those in Figure 2.1.

At a glance, it's apparent that the Metro district produces the greatest number of applicants. Perhaps it's because Metro is the largest, or the closest, but for whatever reason, the mode is students from Metro.

Remember that mutually exclusive characteristics define nominal data. In this example, the applicants from the local service area are graduates of

Figure 2.1 Which Is Most Common? Determining the Mode

School Districts in the Service Area	Applicants
Countryside	78
Metro	320
Mountain View	148
Oakdale	237
Community	212

Countryside, or Oak Dale, or Metro, or one of the other districts, but only one. To keep the example simple, we conveniently ignored the possibility that a student might have attended high schools in two or more of the districts. Since measurement is counting, nominal data are also sometimes called "count" data.

■ Data may be **unimodal** (one mode), **bimodal** (two modes), or . . . .

The data in Figure 2.1 have just one mode—they're **unimodal**. If Metro and Oakdale both had had the same, or a reasonably similar, number of applicants, we would say the data are **bimodal**.

Consider another example of bimodality. If a teacher in a language arts program administers a verbal comprehension test to a group of new students who are evenly divided between those who speak English as a second language and those who are honors students attending the school because of its music program, the scores might be bimodal. Those struggling with the language will likely score near the lower end of the distribution. The honors students, if they are more fluent in English, will probably bunch at the upper end.

The Median

■ The **median** is a set of scores' midpoint.

When ordinal, or interval, or ratio data are arranged in order, the median (M_{dn}, said "M, sub d, n") is the point below which half the scores in the group occur. Suppose special education teachers are surveyed regarding their level of job satisfaction, maybe with a Likert-type instrument using statements like, "I enjoy coming to work each day." The possible responses and a numerical code might be as follows:

5 "strongly agree"

4 "agree"

3 "neither agree nor disagree"

2 "disagree"

1 "strongly disagree"

If there are 20 statements, and all of the items are framed in positive terms ("positive terms" means that "strongly agreeing" with the statement always indicates high satisfaction—this isn't always the case in surveys. If one of the statements stated "I find the work very frustrating," a "strongly agree" response means something very different from a "strongly agree" to "I find being a special educator very satisfying"), a median score of 78 suggests that most people are pretty happy with their jobs since if everyone had answered "agree" to each statement, the score would have been 80 (4×20). A median score of, say, 32 suggests a good deal of discontent.

The median isn't usually calculated as much as it is identified. For an odd number of cases, the median is the middlemost number. Perhaps seven student body officers have the following rankings in their respective classes: 35, 29, 44, 47, 33, 32, 33. What's the median class ranking for the student body officers?

1. Arrange the rankings in order. From lowest to highest they are:

    29, 32, 33, 33, 35, 44, 47.

2. Identify the middle most number. Since there are 7 values, the median is the 4th value, which is **33**.

If the number of rankings is even, the median is the average of the *two* middle numbers. If there is an eighth student with a class ranking of 39, the median class ranking is as follows:

1. Inserting the new ranking in the appropriate place:

    29, 32, 33, 33, 35, **39,** 44, 47.

2. Determine the middle *two* numbers in the distribution, which will be the 4th and 5th numbers, 33 and 35.

3. The median is the average of these two numbers; $(33 + 35)/2 = 34$

    $M_{dn} = 34$.

It's probably obvious, but if the two middle numbers in an even-numbered distribution have the same value, the median is that number.

Another Example

Students at a community college create an online "How do you like your instructor?" forum. The four members of the math department are ranked 1st, 3rd, 12th, and 15th among all instructors. What is the median ranking for the math instructors?

   The scores are already arranged in order from highest to lowest finish and with an even number of scores, the median is going to be the average of the 3rd and 12th rankings. Therefore, the $M_{dn} = 3 + 12 = 15 \div 2 =$ **7.5.** The median ranking is 7.5. Comparing that value with the median ranking in other departments will indicate how instructors from the different departments stack up against each other, according to those who ranked them.

The Mean

The most commonly used measure of central tendency is the arithmetic average of the numbers in a group, the mean. The symbol we will use is *M*, and the formula for calculating means is,

$$M = \frac{\Sigma x}{n} \qquad\qquad 2.1$$

What looks like an odd E is the uppercase Greek letter *sigma* (pronounced with a hard "g"), and for us it always indicates the summation of what follows. In this case, that's the sum of all the individual scores signified by *x*. The formula is said "*M* equals sigma *x* divided by *n*," and the terms mean the following:

- ■ The **mean** is the average, and more affected by extreme scores, or **outliers**.

M = the mean, or the arithmetic average for the group

Σ = the summation, or the total of

x = each individual number in the set so that

Σx = the sum or total of all the individual values in the group

n = the number of scores in the group

In statistics as in mathematics generally, Greek letters are often used to represent frequently used terms or procedures like summation.

The mean may be the most commonly reported statistic of *any* kind. Although the calculation is simple, it is also unusually informative because it includes information from every number in the group. Incidentally, its meaning as an average value would make little sense if it didn't require data of at least interval scale.

Note that the median and mode can also be calculated for interval (or ratio) data and the information the three measures of central tendency provide together is complementary. The mode indicates which measure is the most frequent. The median indicates the midpoint in a distribution, and the mean indicates the average of the numbers.

For seven administrators whose ages are 35, 38, 43, 47, 47, 54, 57, verify that

the mean or average age is 45.857,

the median age is 47, and

the mode is also 47 (although this isn't much of a mode and one might conclude that there isn't one).

It isn't uncommon to see the mean calculated for data like those from the Likert-type survey for special educators above, or the "I like statistics" example in the ordinal data section. Although common enough, it shouldn't be done. Implicit in a mean score is the assumption that the change in whatever is measured is the same between any two consecutive scores—from 2 to 3 is the same increase as from 11 to 12. Hopefully, you can see the flaw in that related to ordinal data. There's no way to assure that the interval between "strongly agree" and "agree" is consistent with any other two consecutive points in the scale. At the very least, it would be very difficult to demonstrate. For such data the median is a more appropriate measure.

THE EFFECT OF OUTLIERS

Sometimes a few individual measures in a group are so high or so low compared with the others that they have an undue effect on the statistics. Such scores are called **outliers,** and they alter the mean more than either the mode or the median. For that reason, when there are outliers in a data set, it's helpful to report all three measures of central tendency. When the mean has a dramatically different value than the median and the mode, it's often because of the effect of outliers and may be a poor guide to what is typical in a data set.

Back to the ages of the seven administrators, perhaps we decide to include the principal of an alternative high school. She sold insurance for 40 years before becoming an educator, and she's now 80. Note how her age affects each measure of central tendency.

For our (now) 8 administrators whose ages are, 35, 38, 43, 47, 47, 54, 57, **80,** the mode for age remains 47. Because there were two 47-year-olds the median doesn't change either, the M_{dn} remains 47:

$$\text{the mean } M = \frac{\Sigma x}{n}$$

$$\Sigma x = 35, 38, 43, 47, 47, 54, 57, 80 = 401$$

$$n = 8$$

$$\frac{401}{8} = 50.125$$

In this case, neither the mode nor the median is affected by the eighth number, in spite of its extreme value, but the eighth number does affect the value of the mean, changing it from 45.857 to 50.125. Particularly in small data sets an outlier can affect the three statistics quite differently.

THROUGH A WIDER LENS

The strength of the mean as a measure of central tendency is that it includes data from every member of the group. But that can also be a problem. Among the six or eight students in the class of 1966 who took the government-required exam for 12th-grade physics in the author's high school, one student produced a perfect exam, which was unprecedented. Assuming that the other 11 or so test-takers manifested a more pedestrian level of talent, what do you think the impact would be on the average physics score in the group?

One of the reviewers of this manuscript noted that in a particular school district locked in salary negotiations, the local newspaper reported a higher-than-expected average salary for teachers, which weakened their argument that they were underpaid. An investigation revealed that the salaries of superintendents, principals, and other 12-month personnel had been averaged in with the more modest salaries of classroom teachers. Technically they are all educators, of course, but comparing 9-month classroom teachers and administrators' salaries inflated salaries beyond what would have been the mean for just teachers. If the ratio of administrators to teachers is fairly high, the distortion could be substantial.

Measures of Variability

Measures of variability, or dispersion, are the statistical companions to central tendency values. They indicate how much scores tend to differ from one another. Small measures of variability indicate that scores are generally quite similar. Larger measures of variability indicate more difference among the scores. How spread out the data are has an important influence on the way we analyze and understand them.

The Range

■ The **range** is the difference between the highest and lowest values in a group.

The easiest measure of variability to calculate is the **range** (R), which measures the distance from the largest to the smallest number in the group by simple subtraction. For the age data (without the 80-year-old), $R = 22$ ($57 - 35 = 22$). All of the ages in this group of teachers occur over an interval of 22 years.

The range doesn't take into consideration how many scores there are in the group, where those scores occur, or how evenly they are distributed. If more extreme scores are added to the group the range can increase, but no number of additional scores will decrease R.

Perhaps a school counselor has set up three different peer-group mentoring programs, each following different guidelines. After a year, the counselor comes to Mr. Lopez for help analyzing the grade-point averages of students who are involved in each of the three programs. The data are as follows:

A: 2.1, 3.7

B: 2.1, 2.35, 2.87. 3.0, 3.1, 3.45, 3.46, 3.5, 3.65, 3.7

C: 1.0, 1.2, 1.33, 1.5, 2.6

Verify that for all the groups $R = 1.6$. This is in spite of differences in the number of values in each group and differences in the number of values involved. Those factors don't affect the range. Mr. Lopez cautions the counselor that although the range doesn't reveal it, the students in group C have grade averages generally lower than those in A or B.

Dividing Up the Range

Although the range is a fairly coarse measure of variability, subdividing it makes it more precise. The median (M_{dn}) occurs at the midpoint in a distribution of scores and so divides the data into halves. If the halves are themselves divided into halves, the result is **quartiles,** or quarters of the distribution. The quartiles are determined by those percentile scores that specify the point below which the 25%, 50%, and 75% of the distribution occurs.

Since the median occurs at the midpoint of the distribution, by definition it is the 50th percentile, the point at or below which half the scores occur. Percentile scores are used to divide a range of scores into quartiles, portions of the range that each contain one-fourth of the scores. In summary, then,

The 25th percentile, P_{25} is the point below which 25% of the scores occur. It's the first quartile (Q_1). (This will be slightly different on SPSS.)

The 50th percentile, P_{50} (which is also the median) marks the second quartile (Q_2).

The third quartile (Q_3) occurs at P_{75}.

The interval from Q_1 to Q_3 (from P_{25} to P_{75}) is the **interquartile range**. Since it's the middle half of the distribution, it excludes the highest and lowest scores. The **semi-interquartile range** (Q) is more commonly reported, perhaps because it excludes even more of the extreme scores. It's *half* the interquartile range:

$$Q = \frac{(P_{75} - P_{25})}{2} \qquad 2.2$$

■ Fourths of the range are called **quartiles**.

■ The **interquartile range** stretches from the 25th to the 75th percentile in a distribution.

■ Half the interquartile range is the **semi-interquartile range**.

As with any measure of variability, large values of Q indicate relatively greater variability, but with Q, the reference is to the variability in the middle of the distribution. A small value for Q indicates homogeneous scores in the middle. If two sets of data both have scores that range from 20 to 60 so that $R = 40$, but for the first set $Q = 8$ and the second $Q = 20$, scores in the second set are much more variable than those in the first.

At least with relatively small data sets like we have in this chapter, the simplest way to identify the quartiles is to arrange the scores from left to right, smallest to largest, stacking the multiple occurrences of repeated scores vertically to indicate their repetition. The result is Figure 2.2, where the quartiles are indicated for a set of 20 test scores. It's called a frequency distribution because the frequency with which individual scores occur is reflected in the height of the columns in the figure. (Frequency distributions are discussed more fully in Chapter 3.)

Figure 2.2 Creating a Frequency Distribution and Identifying the Quartiles

The students' science test scores are the following:

13, 14, 8, 16, 17, 13, 16, 14, 20, 14, 12, 15, 17, 15, 14, 15, 13, 16, 14, 15

If scores are arranged from smallest to largest and repeated scores are stacked vertically, the result is a frequency distribution.

```
                    14
                    14  15
           13  14  15  16
           13  14  15  16  17
   8  12  13 │14 │15  16  17  20
   ─────────────────────────────
           Q1  Q2    Q3
```

There are five scores in each quartile (20/4).

    The 5th score is a 13 and the 6th a 14. Q_1 occurs at 13.5 [(13 + 14)/2].

    The 10th score is a 14 and the 11th a 15. Q_2 (M_{dn}) occurs at 14.5.

    The 15th score is a 16 and the 16th score is also a 16, so Q_3 occurs at 16.

The interquartile range is 2.5, that interval from 13.5 to 16.
The semi-interquartile range is 1.25 [(16 − 13.5)/2].

If instead of 20 there were 60 scores in the set, $Q1$ = the midpoint between the 15th and 16th scores (60/4 = 15), and so on. It's important to remember that quartiles are based on the number of scores occurring at various points, when the scores are placed in order.

Another Example

Students seeking vocational guidance completed a test of mechanical ability for which their scores are 31, 37, 42, 44, 46, 49, 51, 55, 59, 66, 73, 76. Although quartiles are ordinarily calculated only for entire populations, for this group:

M_{dn} = 50, the midpoint between the 6th and 7th scores. This is also Q_2.

The IQR is the difference between Q_3 and Q_1.

Q_3 is midway between scores 9 and 10: 59 and 66. That value is 62.5.

Q_1 = 43, the midpoint between 42 (the 3rd score) and 44 (the 4th score). This makes the IQR = 19.5 (62.5 − 43).

The horizontal axis in a frequency distribution like the one in Figure 2.2 displays the different score values in order from the lowest on the left to the highest score on the right. As we noted, the height of the data on the vertical axis indicates the frequency with which particular scores in the set occur.

Figure 2.2 also illustrates that quartiles are not necessarily equidistant from each other. This is a reminder that the percentile scores upon which quartiles are based are not interval scale data. If percentile scores were interval scale, the difference between each of the quartiles would be constant because the difference between consecutive percentile scores would likewise be constant. Clearly, it isn't.

Recall that one reason for examining the interquartile range is to get a better picture of what is most representative in a data set. However, excluding half the distribution, as the interquartile range does, is rather extreme. Many of the excluded scores are probably *not* uncharacteristic. An alternative is to divide the distribution into tenths, called **deciles,** and calculate the **interdecile range,** which includes the middle 80% of a distribution of scores. Excluding only the top and bottom 10% of scores retains more of the original distribution than the interquartile range and, when data are fairly variable to begin with, it's probably a better representation of what is typical.

■ An alternative to the interquartile range is the **interdecile** range that excludes the top and bottom **deciles** or tenths of the range.

The Variance

■ The **variance** is the sum of the squared score-to-mean differences divided by n − 1.

■ The **standard deviation** is its square root.

It appears in research reports and general analyses less often than the standard deviation discussed below, but the **variance** is a good way to gain another perspective on data variability. Our symbol for the variance of the scores in a sample is s^2, and the formula we will use is the following:

$$s^2 = \frac{\Sigma(x_i - M)^2}{n - 1}$$ 2.3

Where,

s^2 = the variance

Σ = the sum of

x_i = each score from the 1st to the "*i*th," or last score

n = the number of scores in the sample

The formula indicates that one sums up all of the squared differences between individual scores and the mean, and then divides that sum by the number of scores, minus one. In order, the steps are (1) determine the mean for the group, M; (2) determine the difference between each individual score and the mean, from the first number (*x*), to the last or "*i*th" number, x_i (the "*i*" just indicates the last value, however many there are); (3) square the difference between each individual score and the mean of the sample sum the squared differences, and divide by the number of scores, $n - 1$.

The −*1* part of that denominator is a correction made when dealing with samples (which is nearly all of the time). For the variance for a population, the denominator would be N. The uppercase N signifies the number in the entire population. Without data from *all* students in Bannock County, or *all* teachers in West Virginia, the sample variance, with the $n - 1$ correction, is more appropriate.

We often rely on samples for what they reveal about the related population. The −*1* in the variance formula is there to correct for the tendency for the sample to underestimate how much data variability there is in the population; the −*1* is a "correction for a biased estimator." We'll make the same correction below with the standard deviation. Note that the $n - 1$ change is greatest for small samples. As sample sizes increase, the impact of the correction diminishes, which makes sense since larger samples are likely to be increasingly like the population.

The way the variance is calculated is quite revealing. The first issue is how much individual scores vary from the mean—that's the $\Sigma (x_i - M)$ part of the formula. But why square the differences before summing them? Why not just sum them and divide by $n - 1$ to get a mean measure of score variability?

If you think through this for a minute, you'll figure it out. About half of the scores in a group are going to have values less than the mean and the other half, of course, higher. As a result, the positive and negative differences would offset and sum to 0. So instead, the differences are squared, which does away with the negative values, and the squares summed. To turn this value into something like an average, the total is divided by the number of scores, minus one for that correction noted above. Figure 2.3 provides an example of calculating the variance for five spelling-test scores.

Figure 2.3   Calculating the Variance

$$s^2 = \frac{\Sigma(x_i - M)^2}{n - 1} \qquad\qquad 2.3$$

In words, the formula means the following:

1. determine the mean
2. subtract the mean (M) from each of the scores (the first x to the last, or ith x) in the group
3. square the difference between M and each x
4. sum the squared differences
5. divide the result of step 3 by the number of scores, minus 1 ($n - 1$)

A group of second-grade students take a spelling test, and we wish to know the variance in five of the scores (6, 7, 9, 11, 14).

$M = \Sigma X/N = 47/5 = 9.4$

1. $6 - 9.4 = -3.4,$
   $7 - 9.4 = -2.4$
   $9 - 9.4 = -.4$
   $11 - 9.4 = 1.6$
   $14 - 9.4 = 4.6$

2. $-3.4^2 = 11.56, -2.4^2 = 5.76, -.4^2 = .16, 1.6^2 = 2.56, 4.6^2 = 21.16$

3. $11.56 + 5.76 + .16 + 2.56 + 21.16 = 41.2$

4. $41.2/4 = 10.30$

$s^2 = \mathbf{10.30}$

The variance can be a little difficult to interpret in isolation, and in truth it's the near relative to the variance, the standard deviation, which tends to get more use. Large variance values occur when individual numbers differ substantially from the mean of the group. In such cases, either several numbers differ from the mean or at least a few differ substantially.

SOURCE: Created by Suzanna Nielson.

"I think my aptitude is actually higher than the tests show. I need a correction for a biased estimator."

DEGREES OF FREEDOM

■ **Degrees of freedom** refers to the number of scores in a group that are free to vary when the value of some related statistic is known.

Any calculated statistic, in this instance the variance, has **degrees of freedom**. Abbreviated *df*, the degrees of freedom are the number of scores in the group from which the statistic is calculated that are free to vary independently when the final value of the statistic is known. In the case of the variance, and for many statistics, *df* = the number of scores in the group, *−1*. That's our denominator in Formula 2.3. As an illustration, earlier we noted that if all the deviation scores in a group are summed, but not squared, they equal zero. That is, $\Sigma(x_i - M) = 0$.

- If we have a group of four scores, say 3, 4, 5, and 6, then $M = 4.5$.
- The deviation scores for the first 3 values will be -1.5, $-.5$, and $.5$.
- Without even calculating, we know that the last value must be 1.5 in order for $\Sigma(x_i - M) = 0$.
- That fourth number isn't free to vary, which is to say that this sum of square differences has $df = 3$ (which of course is $n - 1$).

Degrees of freedom will come up again in Chapter 6.

The Standard Deviation

If the most frequently cited measure of central tendency is the mean (M), then the companion for variability is the standard deviation (s). Like the variance, the "anchor" for this statistic is the mean of the group. Calculating the standard deviation indicates what the standard, or "typical" deviation is of individual scores from the mean. As their respective s^2 and s symbols suggest, the variance (s^2) is the square of the standard deviation (s), or alternatively, squaring the standard deviation yields the variance. How easy is that?

Because the standard deviation is so often a part of our effort to view the population through the sample, we make the same "$n - 1$" correction for a *sample* standard deviation. The formula is the following:

$$s = \sqrt{\frac{\Sigma(x_i - M)^2}{n - 1}}$$

2.4

Like Formula 2.3 for the variance,

Σ = the sum of

x_i = each individual score from the 1st to the "ith", or last score

n = the number of scores in the sample

The formula indicates that one sums up all of the squared differences between individual scores and the mean, divides that sum by the number of scores, minus one, and then takes a square root of the result. The discrete steps are (1) determine the mean for the group, M; (2) subtract the mean from each individual, from the first number (x), to the last or "ith" number, x_i; (3) square the difference between each score and the sample mean; (4) sum the squared differences, divide by $n - 1$, and take a square root of the result.

Conceptually, the standard deviation is the square root of the average of the squared deviations of measures from the mean of the group. There's a standard deviation example in Figure 2.4.

Other formulae exist for calculating sample standard deviations, by the way. Some of them are called "calculation formulae" because they're easier to use when working longhand, particularly with large data sets. However, the logic of standard deviation is less clear in those versions, and we'll stick with Formula 2.4 for standard deviation and Formula 2.3 for the variance. As long as the "$n - 1$" adjustment is made when the data are from samples, the different formulae all provide the same answer.

Figure 2.4   A Sample Standard Deviation Example

A Sample Standard Deviation Example

$$s = \sqrt{\frac{\Sigma(x_i - M)^2}{n-1}} \qquad 2.4$$

Example:

We have the following English placement scores for a sample of college entrants and wish to know how much scores typically vary from the mean of the sample.

	$x_i - M$	$(x_i - M)^2$
12	−1.7	2.89
	.3	.09
	1.3	1.69
17	3.3	10.89
12	−1.7	2.89
11	−2.7	7.29
9	−4.7	22.09
15	1.3	1.69
14	.3	.09
18	4.3	18.49
$M = 13.7$		$\Sigma = 68.10$

1. $x_i - M$ is the difference between each individual score and the mean

2. $(x_i - M)^2$ is the square of each difference

3. $\Sigma =$ the sum of the squared differences

$$s = \sqrt{\frac{68.10}{9}}$$

$$s = \sqrt{7.567} = 2.751$$

The standard deviation of English placement test scores is 2.751.

Although there are variations, the calculator key for sample standard deviation is often identified with something like σ_{n-1}, and the key for population standard deviations, σ_n. What looks like an "o" with a tail on top is the lowercase Greek letter *sigma*, the symbol for standard deviation. Don't be distracted when both keys use the sigma symbol. It's the $n - 1$ versus the n in the notation that we're interested in.

Besides hand calculators, dedicated statistical packages for the computer provide the calculations, of course, as do spreadsheets programs like Microsoft's Excel. They all have statistical functions built into them, and virtually all of them calculate *sample* standard deviations (with the $n - 1$ correction) as the default.

Like the variance, the standard deviation statistic answers the question, "How varied are individual scores from the mean of the group?" Some statistical tests require the standard deviation as a measure of data variability and others call for the variance; just remember that having calculated one, it's easy to get to the other.

Another Example

A classroom teacher has scores on writing assignments completed by a dozen honors students. He is sensitive to the tendency those scoring essays sometimes manifest of settling into a scoring pattern where there is little variation. He provides a set of scores to Mr. Garcia and asks him to analyze the scores in terms of some measure of variability. Mr. Garcia decides to calculate a standard deviation. The scores are 3, 3, 4, 5, 5, 6, 6, 6, 7, 8, 8, 10.

$$s = \sqrt{[\Sigma(x_i - M)^2]/n-1}$$

1. The $M = 5.917$.

2. Verify that the squared individual *x*-minus-*M* differences are: 8.509, 8.509, 3.675, .841, .841, .007, .007, .007, 1.172, 4.339, 4.339, 16.671.

3. Verify that the sum of the squared differences is 48.917.

4. Dividing by 11 ($n - 1$) yields 4.447.

5. Finally, taking the square root gives us $s =$ **2.109**.

Certainly one could glance at the 12 "raw" scores in the box above and note that there is some variety in the scoring, but the standard deviation helps reveal more precisely how the data are distributed, as Chapter 3 will indicate.

Looking at SPSS Output

In the SPSS Primer in the Appendix, there are directions for completing descriptive statistics, but it might help to see the output here. If we run the problem in the box above (*Another Example*), asking only for the mean and standard deviation, the output is as follows:

Descriptive Statistics

	N	Mean	Std. Deviation
scores	12	5.92	2.109
Valid N (listwise)	12		

The figure indicates how many scores there were, 12 (and unfortunately, it's the uppercase N), and provides the calculated values of the sample mean and the sample standard deviation. The mean is rounded to two decimal points, the standard deviation is rounded to three. They both match our longhand calculations, as long as we round similarly.

A Reminder

Sometimes we get so preoccupied calculating statistics that we forget to use a little logic. Note that the smallest value any range, or variance, or standard deviation can have is zero. If every student has the same homework score s (and for that matter, s^2, and R) $= 0$. *But no measure of variability can be less than zero.* If the calculations yield a negative value, start looking for an arithmetic error.

Other Measures of Variability

The range, variance, and standard deviation do not constitute an exhaustive list of the measures of variability. Sum of squares (*SS*), for example, will come up in Chapter 7. It's a measure of variability important to analysis of variance, regression, and other statistical procedures. Other measures of variability, such as the coefficient of variation, your author has elected not to introduce. He assumes that the reader is as grateful as he was as a statistics student for such considerations. Just recognize that there is a longer list, although those most germane to the more common analyses and tests are here.

Another Word About Samples and Populations

Earlier we distinguished between standard deviations and variances for samples and population by the denominator in the calculation. Ordinarily there is more than the $n − 1$ in the formula to visually separate them. As we briefly mentioned in Chapter 1, Greek letters are often used in statistical discussions to indicate population values. For example, M symbolizes the mean of a sample. Its companion for the mean of a population is μ, the Greek equivalent of the lowercase m. (It's usually pronounced "mew.")

For the standard deviation and variance values, the Greek sigma (σ) indicates a *population* standard deviation and σ^2 the *population* variance. Such population values are called **parameters**. Parameter values (σ, σ^2) are rarely calculated in the work educators do. Occasionally parameters are available from a national testing agency or something like a government census, but more often we do without them, relying instead on the estimates of their value that statistics represent.

■ The Greek letters mu and sigma in statistical notation indicate population characteristics called **parameters**.

SUMMARY

Mr. Garcia's task was to organize and summarize data. He needed a way to classify data according to the type of information they provide and according to what is typical in a group. Those are every educator's tasks. We're all awash in information. Having a systematic way to organize and describe data is an important component of educational decision making.

Scale describes the kind of information that different data provide. Nominal scale data allow one to sort individuals into categories. Ordinal data allow one to rank individuals according to whether one has more or less of some measured characteristic than another such as the best speller, the fastest reader, or the most analytical thinker. Interval data have consistent intervals between data points. One can rank interval data, certainly, but one also can know how much greater or less one case is compared with another—how *much* faster she reads, how *far* below the mean for the class he spells. Ratio data add a zero that indicates the absence of the measured characteristic. Ratio data also allow one to make ratio comparisons such as determining that one student earned twice as many credits as another or missed only half as many days because of sickness. Since the statistical tests that are appropriate for ratio scale also work with interval data, the two are often lumped together in statistics discussions.

Descriptive statistics allow one to summarize data. Measures of central tendency, variability, and association are all descriptive statistics, although we won't get to association until later.

The appropriate descriptive statistic depends partly on the scale of the data one wishes to describe. The mode is the only measure of central tendency that makes sense for nominal data. The median is a central tendency measure for data of at least ordinal scale. The mean requires at least interval data.

Measures of central tendency are often accompanied by some measure of data variability. The range is the simplest measure of variability. The standard deviation and its square, the variance, contain much more information about how data are distributed. Those two statistics are based on all measures in the distribution rather than just the highest and lowest scores.

Because Chapter 1 was largely introductory, this chapter is the first that is really substantive. This is a good time to be a little self-congratulatory. With the Chapter 2 concepts "under your belt," you've gained important access to the statistical decision maker's hallowed precincts. If some of the concepts seem less than crystal clear, give yourself time to work the end-of-chapter problems. Statistical analysis involves a different kind of thinking than we do in many circumstances and sometimes it takes a while to become comfortable with it, but what is important is that you've begun.

EXERCISES

1. When people are classified according to whether they are right- or left-handed, what is the scale of the data?

2. If the school psychologist calculates percentile scores for 50 students who have been administered a measure of achievement motivation, the scores will represent data of what scale?

3. If the data allow one to conclude that one subject has twice as much of a characteristic as another subject, the data must be at least of what scale?

4. A group of students tested for a learning disability have the following intelligence scores: 95, 110, 100, 105, 105, 90, 95, 115, 90, 100.

   Calculate:
   a. the mean
   b. the median
   c. the range
   d. the standard deviation

5. Students receive the scores below on an in-class mathematics test. The scores represent the number of items scored correctly.
   a. The data are of which scale?
   b. Determine the mean, median, mode, range, and standard deviation for the scores.

15	15
13	17
16	14
15	13
12	15
10	17

6. As the district's human resources specialist, you have been asked to analyze data on the ages of special education teachers in the district. For a sample of 10 you find them to be as follows: 24, 25, 28, 28, 31, 36, 39, 40, 53, 54.

   a. Calculate the mean, standard deviation, and range.
   b. If a new teacher with age 30 is added, what happens to the standard deviation?
   c. What happens to the range?

7. A group of high school students have the following scores on a history essay:

   8, 9, 9, 10, 10, 10, 11, 11, 12. Before doing the calculation, answer the following questions, and then do the calculations and check your answers.

   a. What will be the impact on the value of the standard deviation of these scores of adding another 10? Why is the impact not greater?
   b. What will be the impact on the value of the standard deviation of adding a 5? Why is the change to the standard deviation greater than adding a 10?

8. Determine the scale of each of the following:

   a. Teachers are ranked from greatest to least according to teaching ability.
   b. A group of track athletes is timed in the 100-meter run.
   c. College students are grouped according to major.
   d. Reading students are scored according to how many words per minute they can read at their grade level.
   e. Graduating students are classified according to how strongly they feel about attending college.

   For each of the above, what is the most sophisticated measure of central tendency that can be calculated?
   For which would one be able to calculate a standard deviation?

9. Using your recently developed "AssessmeNt Gauging Student Tension" instrument (ANGST, for short), you gather anxiety data from statistics students about to take their first test. Their scores are as follows:

   23, 19, 17, 18, 22, 28, 20, 25, 11, 20, 21, 19, 14, 19, 21
   What are the values of the following?

   $$n$$
   $$M$$
   $$M_{dn}$$
   $$s$$

10. Use SPSS to generate mean, standard deviation, and range for these data.

    23   19   17
    18   22   28

20 25 11
20 21 19
14 19 21
19 21 14
27 24 25
21 24 26
15 17 23
16 17 28

11. A group of students have completed a history test and answered the following number of test items correctly: 23, 27, 31, 33, 34, 34, 35, 37, 40, 45. What is the

    a. scale of the data?
    b. the range?
    c. the mean?
    d. the standard deviation?
    e. the median?

12. If a 35 were added to the data in item 11, explain what would happen to the value of the standard deviation (answer without calculating). How would that additional number affect the range (answer without calculating)?

THE FORMULAE AND THEIR SYMBOLS

Formula 2.1: The mean of a set of scores:

$$M = \frac{\Sigma x}{n}$$

Formula 2.2: The semi-interquartile range:

$$Q = \frac{(P_{75} - P_{25})}{2}$$

Formula 2.3: The variance of a set of scores:

$$s^2 = \frac{\Sigma(x_i - M)^2}{n-1}$$

Formula 2.4: The standard deviation of a set of scores:

$$s = \sqrt{\frac{\Sigma(x_i - M)^2}{n-1}}$$

STUDENT STUDY SITE

Visit the Student Study Site at **www.sagepub.com/tanner** for additional learning tools.

PART II

Presenting Data

Chapter 3

DATA DISTRIBUTIONS

Picturing Statistics

THE PROBLEM: HOW TO DISPLAY COMPLEX DATA SETS

For several years, the superintendent has budgeted funds to support English learners with reading tutors in the elementary school classrooms. Facing a tight budget, he has asked Ms. Rivers, who is an elementary school principal, to prepare a data presentation that will justify continued funding. Her task is to illustrate the reading tutors' impact to nonprofessionals.

QUESTIONS AND ANSWERS

❑ What is an effective way to illustrate the performance of many students relative to each other?

There isn't just one answer to this question. The principal can use frequency distributions, stem-and-leaf displays, pie and bar charts, histograms, or frequency polygons. Several options exist for data presentations.

❑ Can simple tables and figures provide answers about important data relationships without further analysis?

Although figures and tables are often precursors to more elaborate analytical procedures, they needn't be. Sometimes what we seek is revealed by nothing more elaborate than a careful arrangement of the data.

The focus in Chapter 2 was on classifying and describing data. The concept of data scale provided a framework for organizing data according to the kind and amount of information they provide. In turn, data scale helps one determine the descriptive statistics that are appropriate. We noted, for example, that calculating a mean requires data of at least interval scale.

Having been introduced (or more likely reintroduced) to these classification and description tools, the focus shifts to displaying and presenting data. If you have a penchant for organizing things and find yourself creating visual displays to clarify large amounts of information, you'll be right at home in this chapter. The treatment will be quite brief by necessity. Entire books have been written on arranging and presenting data (see Friendly, 2000; Tufte, 2001, for example) but we'll make at least a beginning.

The Frequency Distribution

■ In a **frequency distribution**, data are displayed so that their variety and their frequency of occurrence are both apparent.

Most data sets of any size include several of the same measure. Whether they are engineering students' analytical ability scores or vocabulary scores for county fourth graders, some of the scores will be repeated, perhaps many times. In a **frequency distribution** (Chapter 2), scores are displayed in terms of both their variety and the frequency of their occurrence.

Perhaps the Department of Education for the state requires that students' test results in Ms. Rivers' school be grouped according to whether the student is Advanced, Proficient, Basic, Below Basic, or Far Below Basic in reading ability. In a table designed to indicate reading results, such categories take the place of individual scores and the frequency will indicate the number of students in each category. Among students in a particular fifth-grade class not participating in the tutoring program mentioned in the chapter introduction, Table 3.1 indicates the following reading results:

The f symbol indicates the number of times a score is repeated in a frequency distribution. It's at the heart of this particular table, which is one kind of *grouped* frequency distribution. Were the data not grouped, we would just have a list of 30 different students' reading classifications—a very long table. If individuals were listed one at a time from either Advanced down or from Far Below Basic up, we would have *an ordered array* (which since they are rankings would provide ordinal data, by the way). If the list isn't organized, the array is *disordered*. Unlike Table 3.1, every measure is independently represented in either an ordered or a disordered array.

Table 3.1   A Frequency Distribution for Fifth-Grade Reading Scores From Students Not Participating in a Tutoring Program

Reading Performance Classification	f
Advanced	2
Proficient	3
Basic	8
Below Basic	13
Far Below Basic	4
Total	30

Grouped frequency distributions are extremely common. Examples are classifying people by the number who fall into lower, middle, and upper social classes, or by the number who are high school graduates, the number with some college, the number who are college graduates, and so on.

The "groups" in a grouped frequency distributions are **class intervals.** They make the data much easier to absorb visually, but there's a sacrifice of detail because the scores that make up the class interval don't appear in the table. It isn't apparent from just examining Table 3.1, for example, what scores make up the "Advanced" class interval. We just know how many individuals fall into that group.

If there were 24 items on a spelling test, and students' scores ranged from 0 to 24, we could simplify the data with a different grouped frequency distribution. Perhaps the following are the class intervals:

■ Grouping the data in a frequency distribution rather than listing them individually creates **class intervals.**

0–4

5–9

10–14

15–19

20–24

Here the class intervals include actual test scores but without indicating exactly what the scores were. Although that is so, a grouped frequency distribution still allows one to approximate the mean of the group. It's calculated by multiplying the midpoint of each class interval by the frequency of the scores in that interval, summing the results, and then dividing the total by the number of class intervals. The steps are

1. Determine the midpoint of each class interval. Add the two extreme scores in the interval and divide by two for a midpoint value.

2. Multiply the midpoint value by the number of scores in the interval.

3. Sum the products from each interval.

4. Divide the sum of the midpoint products by the number of intervals.

For the spelling data, perhaps we have the following scores:
3, 4, 6, 6, 7, 7, 8, 10, 11, 15, 16, 24

The mean for the original spelling scores then is:

$$M = \Sigma x/n$$

$$= 117 / 12 = 9.75$$

When the spelling scores are arranged in a grouped frequency distribution employing the class intervals we used above, the data look this way:

Interval	f
0–4	2
5–9	5
10–14	2
15–19	2
20–24	1

Using the grouped frequency distribution to approximate the mean it would be as follows:

Int. mid pt $* f$

$$((0 + 4)/2) * 2 \quad = \quad 4$$

$$((5 + 9)/2) * 5 \quad = \quad 35$$

$$((10 + 14)/2) * 2 = \quad 24$$

$$((15 + 19)/2) * 2 = \quad 34$$

$$((20 + 24)/2) * 1 = \quad \underline{22}$$

$$\Sigma = 119$$

$$119/12 = 9.917$$

There will generally be some discrepancy between this measure and the actual value of the mean. The variation usually won't be large, and the value can be very helpful in data summaries when the original scores aren't available. Because there *will* usually be some variation from the actual mean of the sample, any reporting should distinguish between this calculation and the actual mean of the sample.

Apparent Versus Actual Limits

Above we used only integers, whole numbers, to create the class intervals but often they must accommodate scores that can have *any* value along a continuum. For the spelling data, the **apparent limits** of each interval are indicated by the highest and lowest integers in each interval. As long as the scores are only integers this works fine but truly continuous data (consider students' grade-point averages, for example) require something more comprehensive.

The **actual limits** of a class interval extend from half a point below the lowest integer in the interval (the lower *apparent* limit) to a half point above the highest integer (the higher *apparent* limit). So for the 5 to 9 spelling interval, the actual limits are 4.5 to 9.5. The width of the interval is the difference between the upper and lower actual limits. The value of this difference will be the same as the number of integers between the apparent limits: $9.5 - 4.5 = 5$, and we have 5 integers in the interval from 5 to 9 (Sheskin, 2004).

If the upper actual limit of the 5 to 9 class interval is 9.5 (9 +.5), what is the actual lower limit of the 10 to 14 interval? Oops, it's also 9.5 (10 − .5). Should decimal scores be included in the summary, which interval should include a score of 9.5? Sheskin's (2004) solution is the following: When a number could fit in either of two class intervals, create a rule. If the first digit in the number is odd, for example, the number goes in the lower of the two class intervals. If it's even, the value is assigned to the higher of the two class intervals.

Guidelines for Developing a Grouped Frequency Distribution

A frequency distribution must follow some conventions:

- The groups must all have equal ranges. In the spelling test where all the scores are whole numbers, each group includes five possible scores. But even if the scores include decimals, the ranges must be equal.
- A particular score or observation can fit into just one group. This is simple enough for intervals with apparent limits. Actual limits that include decimal values may require a rule such as the odd/even guideline above to restrict a score to one group.

■ Data displays employ categories with **apparent limits**, represented by the lowest and highest integers in the category, and **actual limits**, which extend the interval up and down ½ point.

SOURCE: Created by Suzanna Nielson.

"It looks like continuous data have apparent limits. My parents won't send me any more money."

There aren't hard-and-fast rules about the number of groups in a frequency distribution, although Sheskin (2004) suggested the square root of the number of scores as a guide. By that standard, if there are 40 scores to summarize, $\sqrt{40} = 6.325$, or about 6 class intervals might be appropriate, but this represents a very rough guideline. We want a balance between economy and clarity. It's easier to manage data in relatively few categories, such as rural versus urban schools. The trade-off for that economy, however, is that the results can be too broad to help much with any analysis. If schools of all different locations are placed into just two groups, rural and urban, the differences between suburban schools and inner city schools are obscured. So are the differences between rural and semirural schools (however they are defined). Conversely, too many class intervals diminish the value of grouping the data in the first place as the groupings would no longer provide a concise data summary.

Increasing the number of categories certainly increases the information provided, but any time individual scores are collapsed into a category, there's a penalty. Some of the information regarding the exact value of the original observation is lost to anyone who doesn't have the original data set.

Frequencies, Relative Frequencies, and Cumulative Relative Frequencies

If a *frequency* count indicates how many times a particular score occurs, the *relative* frequency indicates the *fraction* of times a score occurs. It may be reported as a common fraction, or more commonly as a decimal value. As the name suggests, a *cumulative relative* frequency totals the data from the particular interval with those from the previous intervals. Earlier we arranged spelling scores in a frequency distribution. Adding the relative frequency and cumulative relative frequencies results in the following:

Interval	Frequency	Relative Frequency	Cumulative Relative Frequency
0–4	2	.167	**.167**
5–9	5	.417	**.583**
10–14	2	.167	**.750**
15–19	2	.167	**.917**
20–24	1	.083	**1.0**

- The second column contains the same frequency values as the earlier table.
- The fraction of the total that occur in the particular interval are the values in the third column.
  - Two of the 12 total scores occur in the first (0–4) interval; 2/12 = .167.
  - Five of the 12 scores occur in the second interval; 5/12 = .417, and so on.

- In the fourth column the frequencies accumulate.
  - In addition to the 5, 5 – 9 scores, the second interval includes the 2 scores from the first interval: $(2 + 5)/12 = .583$.
  - The third cumulative relative frequency includes those from the first interval (2), the second interval (5) as well as the third (2); $9/12 = .750$, and so on.

Stem-and-Leaf Displays

■ **Stem-and-leaf displays** list all values according to stem (the numbers preceding the final value), and leaf (the final digit).

If Ms. Rivers wishes not to lose the information provided by the original scores, but still needs a way to summarize the data, **stem-and-leaf displays,** or stem plots, are an alternative to grouped frequency distributions. They retain all the individual scores but in an altered format. Perhaps for a particular test we have the scores in Table 3.2.

Table 3.2   Spelling Scores

2	11	15	17	20
5	12	15	17	21
5	12	16	18	21
6	12	16	18	22
10	13	16	18	22
11	14	17	20	24

Arranged in a stem-and-leaf display, the Table 3.2 data look this way: (stem) (leaves)

0 | 2556

1 | 0112223455666777889

2 | 0011224

The stem-and-leaf display indicates each number in a set starting with the smallest value at the top of the display. Each score has two parts, a *stem* and a *leaf.*

- The *stem* is made up of all the digits in each score that precede the final digit in each score.
  - o If the score consists of just a single digit score, as do the first four spelling scores, the stem is 0.
  - o If the score is in the teens, the stem is a 1.
  - o It is a 2 for scores in the 20s. If the score is 115, the stem is 11, and so on.

- The stem scores are arranged with the stem for the smallest number at the top of the display and then the balance of the stem scores in order below it.
- The *leaf* is the last digit in the original score.
  - o The values are arranged from smallest to largest beginning at the top of the display.
  - o Each digit represents a separate leaf from a separate original score.

Reading from the top down, the display indicates that the values in the stem and leaf display above were a 2, two 5s, and so on down to the highest value in the display, a 24. Nothing from the original score is lost in a stem-and-leaf display. Repeated scores are reflected in repeated "leaf" values. The advantage of these data presentations is that they are both compact and complete, which is unusual in data displays.

Another Example

An assistant principal is collecting data on the ages of the teaching staff at her school in an effort to anticipate future hiring needs. What would a stem-and-leaf display look like for classroom teachers of the following ages? 22, 23, 23, 25, 28, 35, 36, 37, 38, 38, 45, 46, 46, 55, 59, 62, 63, 65. Working from the youngest to the eldest, it should look like this:

2 | 23358

3 | 56788

4 | 566

5 | 59

6 | 235

Observation: Although one can see at a glance that there are three people in their 60s, the teaching staff is comparatively young. Most of the staff are in their 20s and 30s.

INTERPRETING TABLES AND FIGURES

Tables and figure can offer analytical advantages. The data in Table 3.1 indicate that, for example, there are half as many Advanced readers (2) as there are Far Below Basic readers (4). As a proportion of the whole, advanced and proficient readers together constitute 1/6th of all readers (5/30 = 1/6). Or advanced and proficient readers are 16.7% of the whole (5/30 = .167 × 100 = 16.7). The point is that working from a grouped frequency distribution, other characteristics of the data are easier to recognize and often easier to explain to an audience than they might be in some other presentation.

Tabular data can be adapted to a variety of ancillary questions. In addition to listing fifth-grade students' reading by performance level, it wouldn't be difficult to add another variable such as gender, which might result in a table like the following:

	Students' Performance Level				
	Advanced	Proficient	Basic	Below Basic	Far Below Basic
Female	1	1	5	6	1
Male	1	2	3	7	3

This is a "cross-tabular" data arrangement that accommodates *two* class intervals. The student's performance level (the original class interval) is in the columns and the new variable, the student's gender, is indicated in the row. When it's done in SPSS using the "cross tabs" option under "descriptive statistics," the result is Figure 3.1. (The steps for completing this procedure in SPSS(R) are in the SPSS Primer in Appendix B.)

Figure 3.1 A Cross-Tabular Presentation of Students' Gender and Their Level of Reading Proficiency

1 = female, 2 = male * 1 = advanced, 2 = proficient, 3 = basic, 4 = below basic, 5 = far below basic cross-tabulation

Count	1 = advanced, 2 = proficient, 3 = basic, 4 = below basic, 5 = far below basic					
		1	2	3	4	5	Total
1 = female 2 = male	1	1	1	5	6	1	14
	2	1	2	3	7	3	16
	Total	2	3	8	13	4	30

Note that the table produced by SPSS is virtually the same as the table we created except that it also includes row and column totals.

PREPARING DATA FIGURES

Sometimes data figures offer an advantage over tables. The story is told of a British analyst during World War II whose task was to determine where to position armor plating in fighter aircraft to best protect the pilots. He observed several aircraft that had been exposed to enemy fire and then plotted on a figure the points where all the observed damage had occurred. His solution was then to place the armor near the pilot, where there had been *no* bullet holes! At first blush this seems counterintuitive, but his reasoning was that none of the observed holes had been fatal for pilot or machine or they would not have returned. He concluded that it was damage elsewhere that proved fatal. Analyzing data from figures isn't usually a life-or-death proposition, but the related questions are important nevertheless.

Pie Charts

When the task is to clarify proportions between different classes or groups, a pie chart is often more helpful than a table of numbers, however they are organized. Ms. Rivers could use the data in Table 3.1 to indicate how 30 students not participating in a tutoring program were classified according to reading ability. In Figure 3.2A, she has used the same values to create a pie chart. Figure 3.2B is a pie chart for a group of 32 fifth-grade students who did participate in a tutoring program and for whom reading classifications were as follows:

■ Pie charts and bar charts are both used to represent proportional differences in data categories, either by triangular wedges or with bars of different sizes.

  5 Advanced

  7 Proficient

  13 Basic

  5 Below Basic

  2 Far Below Basic

In the figure the exact mathematical proportions aren't stated, although they're often added, but the figure alone gives suggests how the different categories compare. Because the figure is based on proportions of the particular whole, pie charts provide for easy comparisons across groups that may have entirely different totals.

Figure 3.2 Pie Charts

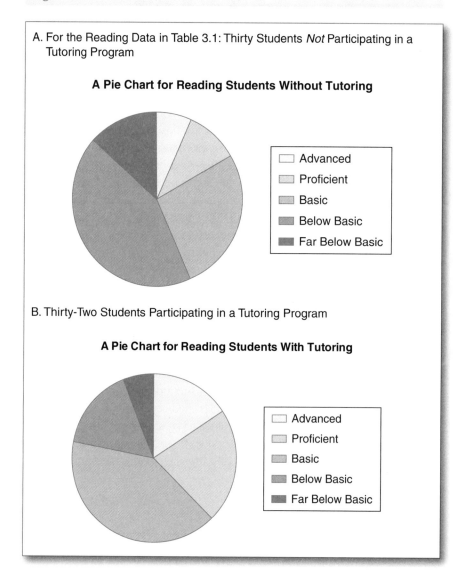

A. For the Reading Data in Table 3.1: Thirty Students *Not* Participating in a Tutoring Program

A Pie Chart for Reading Students Without Tutoring

- Advanced
- Proficient
- Basic
- Below Basic
- Far Below Basic

B. Thirty-Two Students Participating in a Tutoring Program

A Pie Chart for Reading Students With Tutoring

- Advanced
- Proficient
- Basic
- Below Basic
- Far Below Basic

This particular presentation responds to one of the issues raised at the beginning of the chapter. The pie chart is a figure that allows Ms. Rivers to quickly illustrate the difference in reading performance between students that are tutored and those that are not. Note the differences in proportions on the two tables for any category.

Bar Charts

Consider an alternative to the pie chart. If Ms. Rivers creates a column for each category for the data in Table 3.1 and represents the frequency in each category by the height of the column, she has the **bar chart** in Figure 3.3. The frequency can also be reflected in horizontal bars.

Recall that the reading data categories ranged from Advanced down to Far Below Basic. Those categories are essentially rankings, and the way the categories are arranged in the figures reflects this. Note that the pie charts and bar charts indicate the differences in the proportions of individuals falling into the different categories, but in this instance, there's no way to know how much better Advanced students performed than Proficient students.

If a bar chart were created for nominal data, ethnicity for example, the order in which the bars appear is generally unimportant. This changes when there is a logical order as there is for the Advanced, Proficient, Basic, and so on ordinal classifications of students' reading. When there's an inherent order to the categories, the arrangement of the figures should reflect it.

Figure 3.3   A Bar Chart of Reading Performance Based on the Table 3.1 Data

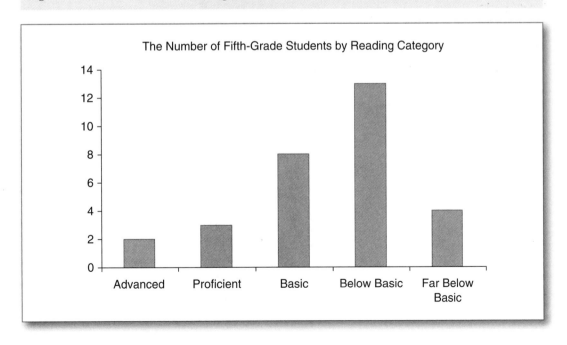

Histograms

■ A **histogram** is a graph in which the frequency of individual measures is indicated by the height of the bars.

With ordinal, interval, or ratio scale data, the values are often continuous, and it's common to use a **histogram** to present them. Histograms look like bar charts except that there are no gaps between columns, indicating that the data continue without interruption in the next category. The limits between categories are actual limits rather than apparent limits. In addition, the *order* of the bars or columns is always significant in a histogram. Figure 3.4 is a histogram illustrating the reading comprehension scores for 15 students.

In this histogram, created in SPSS (there are directions in the SPSS Primer in Appendix C for completing a histogram), the odd-numbered columns (30s, 50s, and so on) aren't labeled, but you can see them represented.

Figure 3.4 A Histogram of Reading Comprehension Scores

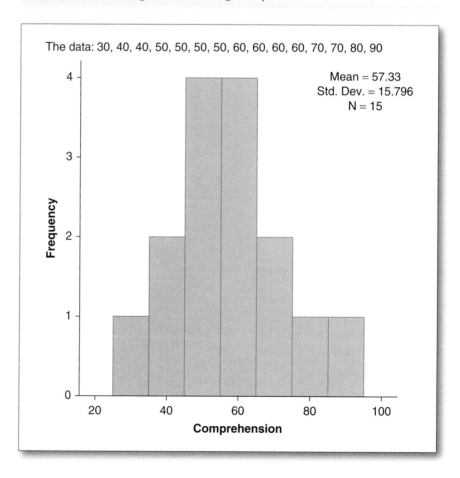

The data: 30, 40, 40, 50, 50, 50, 50, 60, 60, 60, 60, 70, 70, 80, 90

Mean = 57.33
Std. Dev. = 15.796
N = 15

The vertical (y) axis is labeled "frequency" to indicate that the height of columns indicates the number of values in each category. Note also that SPSS automatically prints the values for mean, the sample standard deviation, and the number of values that, unfortunately for us since we're dealing with sample data, is labeled "N," rather than "n."

Frequency Polygons

Although the histogram relies on columns for data presentation, the **frequency polygon** employs discrete points at the middle of each group or class interval. Once the points are connected, the frequency polygon is a graph of a frequency distribution. Like bar charts and histograms, scores in a frequency polygon graduate from the lowest number in the distribution on the left to the highest values on the right of the horizontal axis. Also like the vertical bar chart and the histogram, the frequency with which a score occurs is indicated by the height of the point on the vertical axis.

■ **Frequency polygons** are plotted according to values along a horizontal **abscissa** and a vertical **ordinate** that are Cartesian coordinates.

Cartesian coordinates give frequency polygons their structure. In that first algebra class, you plotted points along two lines at right angles. The horizontal line was the x axis, or the **abscissa**, and the vertical line was the y axis, or **ordinate**. The lines intersect at the **point of origin** where $x = 0$ and $y = 0$.

We can use Cartesian coordinates to create a frequency polygon based on either class intervals or individual scores. If we had spelling results for 30 students to go with the class intervals we spoke of earlier, the data might be as follows:

■ Both coordinates = 0 at the **point of origin**. The figure usually represents the graph's upper right hand quadrant.

0–4..........1

5–9..........3

10–14.......8

15–19......11

20–24.......7

Plotted on a frequency polygon the data look as they do in Figure 3.5. Because the points that the lines join are plotted at the middle of each class interval, individual within-group differences are lost and the best estimate of an individual's score becomes the mean of the class interval.

In a frequency polygon, the points indicating the frequency of the scores are connected with straight lines. The series of connected lines in Figure 3.5

Figure 3.5 Spelling Data Arranged in a Frequency Polygon

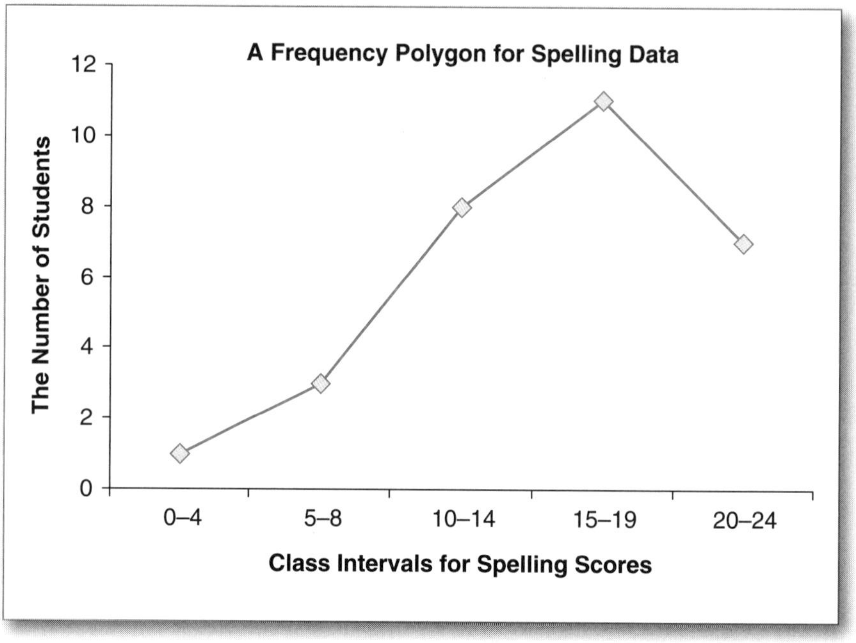

A Frequency Polygon for Spelling Data

look like so many "dogs legs" and reflect, among other things, that we don't have a very large number of scores, just those fitting into five class intervals. Still, they give one a sense of where the most frequently occurring scores are. As the amount of data and the number of intervals increase, the straight lines get shorter and the entire plot begins to look increasingly like a curve.

One of the most enduring uses of a frequency polygon, at least in books like this, is to display the normal (bell-shaped) curve. The normal curve is a frequency polygon. In order for the graph to reflect the bell shape, however, individual scores are plotted. With many different scores and a data set of substantial size, the straight lines between data points become imperceptible, and the shape takes on the character of a continuous curving line.

In Figure 3.6, note that the numbers to the right and above the point of origin are all positive. If all the scores in a frequency polygon are positive, only this upper right **quadrant** is involved. The other three quadrants are typically omitted.

As with all frequency polygons, the *x* axis indicates the range of scores possible, the lowest near the point of origin to the highest on the extreme right. The highest *y* value indicates the score on the *x* axis, which has the

■ Graphs are created by vertical and horizontal lines which intersect at right angles. The four sections which result are each called a **quadrant**.

Figure 3.6   Cartesian Coordinates

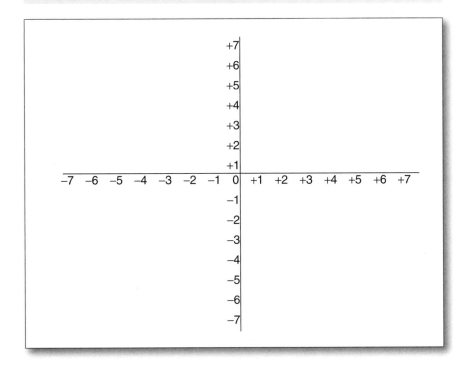

greatest number of repetitions (greatest frequency). If there are enough scores, say the reading results for all fifth-grade students in Los Angeles County (128,913 in 2007, which probably meets the "enough" criterion), there's a good chance that the curve will take on a bell shape.

The Normal Distribution

When the data for a large group are arranged in a frequency polygon it takes on a predictable shape. That is, we often know before we even collect or plot the data how the resulting frequency polygon will look.

This foreknowledge is because of the work of people like Karl Gauss, a gifted German mathematician of the 18th and 19th centuries who was also something of a child prodigy and demonstrated early his keenness for detecting patterns in data. The story is told that during his primary school years, his teacher tried to keep his students busy by directing them to add up all the integers from 1 to 100. In a flash of insight, young Karl recognized that the lowest and highest numbers in the set sum to 101 (1 + 100), as do the next lowest

■ A **normal**, or **Gaussian distribution** takes on the bell shape because it is symmetrical, unimodal, and the standard deviation is about 1/6th of the range.

and next highest numbers $(2 + 99)$, as well as the next $(3 + 98)$. Extrapolating this conclusion to the 50 possible pairs, he knew that the 50 pairs times the 101 total for each pair $= 5,050$. Although the story may be apocryphal, at least it fits the intellectual gifts of someone who helped others recognize the consistency in data sets. The contribution that's most relevant here, however, is Gauss's description of the **normal**, or in his honor, the **Gaussian distribution**.

Central Tendency and Normality

The concept of normal distributions didn't originate with Gauss, but his work verified that large numbers of measures of a particular characteristic (such as the reading scores of all fifth-grade students in L.A. County) tend to have certain consistencies that we associate with normal distributions. Frequency polygons based on large groups are often:

- Symmetrical; each half mirrors the other,
- Unimodal, which is to say that the distribution has just one most frequently occurring value, just one peak in the frequency distribution, and
- The standard deviation value is about 1/6th of the range.

The fact that the data are symmetrical and unimodal indicates that the mean, median, and mode all have the same value. They all occur at the middle of the distribution. As one moves in either direction away from the mean, the scores occur with diminishing frequency although, as we will see, that decline isn't steady.

Normality is a characteristic of large groups. Even when the individuals are selected from populations known to be normal, it isn't possible for small groups' measures to constitute a normal distribution.

When a data distribution isn't symmetrical it is said to be **skewed**. The symbols, $sk = 0$ indicate a symmetrical distribution. Skew is created when scores on one side of the distribution aren't counterbalanced by scores a similar distance from the mean on the other side. For example, Ms. Rivers has reading scores for nine of the English learners referred to at the beginning of the chapter. From lowest to highest they are:

30, 40, 40, 50, 50, 50, 60, 60, 70

For these values:

$$M = 50$$

$$M_{dn} = 50$$

$$M_o = 50$$

The mean, median, and mode have the same value because scores of 40 are exactly offset by scores of 60. The 30 is countered by the 70.

Relying on a visual perception of balance would be cumbersome with a large data set. A more practical indicator of a symmetrical distribution is how the mean compares with the median and mode since, as we noted, in a symmetrical distribution these three measures of central tendency have the same value.

If a tenth student takes the reading test and scores 95, we have the following:

30, 40, 40, 50, 50, 50, 60, 60, 70, **95**

This score of 95 can be considered an **outlier**, because it is a more extreme score than any of the others in the sample. Note the impact that the outlier has on each measure of central tendency. The median and mode remain unchanged:

$M_{dn} = 50$

$M_o = 50$

But the recalculated mean becomes:

$M = 54.5$

Although the median and mode can also be affected by extreme scores the impact is less than it is for the mean. Here the outlier creates positive skew ($sk+$), or "right skew." In effect, the mean gets "pulled" away from the other measures of central tendency in the direction of the outlier, defining the type of skew. If the mean is a higher value than the M_{dn} and the M_o, there is positive skew as it is here. If it's lower, the skew is negative.

Although comparing the mean to the median and mode will usually provide a sufficient estimate of skewness, we can actually calculate the value directly. The formula is:

$$sk = \frac{3(M - M_{dn})}{s} \qquad\qquad 3.1$$

Where,

sk = skew

M = the mean of the values

> ■ When a data distribution isn't symmetrical it is **skewed** in the direction of the **outliers**, the extreme, least characteristic scores.

M_{dn} = the median of the values

s = the standard deviation of the values

Positive values indicate positive skew, of course, and negative values, negative skew.

For the sake of illustration, assume that Ms. Rivers wants to describe the group of 10 English students' scores more precisely. Suspecting that data tend to reflect some skew she determines what we already know:

$M = 54.5$

$M_{dn} = 50$

She calculates the standard deviation and finds:

$s = 18.326$

Now applying Formula 3.1 she determines that:

$$sk = \frac{3(M - M_{dn})}{s}$$

$$sk = \frac{3(54.5 - 50)}{18.326}$$

$sk = .737$

Values within +/− 1.0 indicate modest skew. This fits with what we already noted to be some modest skew in the 10 reading scores.

Why Do We Care?

The discussion of normality is about more than describing data, as we'll note in the box immediately below. In addition to describing data, we'll see in later chapters that whether a particular analysis is appropriate may depend upon the normality of the data. If data are badly skewed, for example, some statistical tools shouldn't be used. Determining normality is not just an academic discussion nor is it undertaken just for descriptive purposes.

In Chapter 2, we learned to associate the mean with central tendency for interval data, the median with central tendency for ordinal data, and the mode with central tendency for nominal data. As we see here, however, the median and mode can be very helpful as indicators of skew with interval data. If data are interval, unimodal, and fairly well-balanced (symmetrical), one calculates the mean. If interval or ratio data are skewed, one adds the median. If interval or ratio data cluster at more than one point, one adds the mode. It isn't uncommon for researchers to cite all three measures of central tendency for interval/ratio data because they can provide some reassurance that data are symmetrical and unimodal. They can also indicate the direction of any skew and list the multiple modes.

If instead of 95 the 10th person had scored 5 or 10 (or anywhere lower than 50), the effect would be to create some negative skew ($sk-$) or "left skew"; the more extreme the score, the greater the skew. A few English learners still struggling with the language in a class of otherwise good readers will likely score poorly on any reading test until they overcome the language difficulty. Until that time, the distribution of the class's reading scores will probably reflect negative skew. Figure 3.7 provides exaggerated examples of both positive and negative skew.

Although symmetry ($M = M_{dn} = M_o$) is a condition for normality (not "normalcy," by the way, which you can blame on Warren G Harding), it doesn't assure normality. A symmetrical distribution could have any shape, so long as the left half mirrors the right. If we added three more scores of 95 and four scores of 5 to the 10 numbers above, the distribution would be symmetrical but definitely not normal. We'd have a "*bi*modal" distribution, as the bar graph in Figure 3.8 suggests.

Dropping the scores of 5 and 95 to return to the original nine reading scores, we have the symmetrical and unimodal distribution of scores, but the frequency polygon certainly isn't bell shaped, as Figure 3.9 makes clear. In fact, the nine history scores appear, well, triangular. Like a normal distribution, they indicate a decline in the frequency of numbers moving away from the mean in either direction, but in contrast to a normal (Gaussian) distribution, the decline in this case is completely consistent.

Figure 3.7 Positive and Negative Skew in Data Distributions

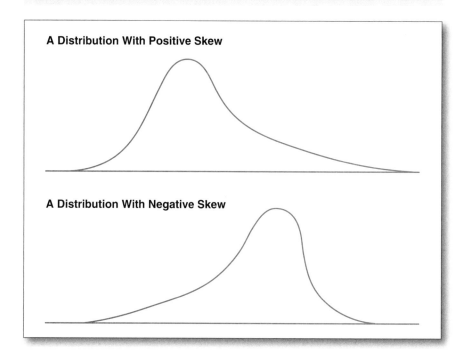

Figure 3.8 Data Indicating a Bimodal Distribution of Scores

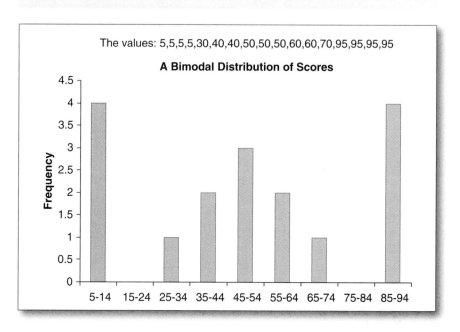

Figure 3.9   A Frequency Polygon for the History Test Scores

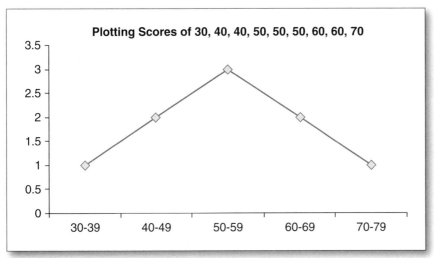

The Standard Deviation and Normality

Like Figure 3.9, the data nearest the middle of the normal distribution have the greatest frequency in a normal distribution. Also like the figure, the frequency diminishes as one leaves the center of the distribution, but in normal distributions the decline isn't constant. It is most precipitous nearer the mean/median/mode and then tails off with values more distant from the center of the distribution. One standard deviation from the mean in either direction marks what is called the **point of inflection**. It is the point at which, if one continues to move farther from the mean, the curve moves to the left or right more rapidly than it falls toward the abscissa. The angle of approach to the abscissa diminishes as the distance from the mean increases.

Regardless of whether the data are anxiety measures among adults in West Virginia or mathematics scores for fourth graders in Idaho, it's quite likely that if one gathers enough scores, both distributions will be bell shaped. This is a big deal to those analyzing quantitative data because in a normal distribution specified percentages of the scores will consistently fall in particular regions. These regions are determined by their distance from the mean of the distribution in standard deviation units. In a normal distribution, from the mean to either

■ The **point of inflection** where a normal curve moves outward more quickly than downward occurs at +/− one standard deviation from the mean.

- Plus or minus one standard deviation always includes about 34.13% of the data.

- Plus or minus two standard deviations always includes about 47.72% of the data.
- Plus or minus three standard deviations always includes about 49.87% of the data.

Consider the implications. As long as data are normally distributed, and we have access to the mean and standard deviation, we know before we begin approximately where particular portions of scores will occur. If a major intelligence test has a mean of 100 and a standard deviation of 15, we know before we gather any of the scores that about 34% of the entire population will fall between 100 and 115. Extending this, 68%, or a little over two-thirds will have intelligence scores between 85 (from the mean to $-1s$) and 115 (from the mean to $+1s$). Figure 3.10 illustrates these relationships.

Note from the figure that there isn't some point at which one has accounted for 100% of the distribution. Particularly with something like intelligence, there is always at least the theoretical possibility of a yet higher or lower score than any yet measured. Certainly the probability of yet more extreme scores declines as one moves farther from the mean in either direction, but the tails of the distribution are said to be "asymptotic to the abscissa." That two-dollar phrase means that, in theory at least, the tails

Figure 3.10   The Percentage of a Normal Distribution Under the Curve

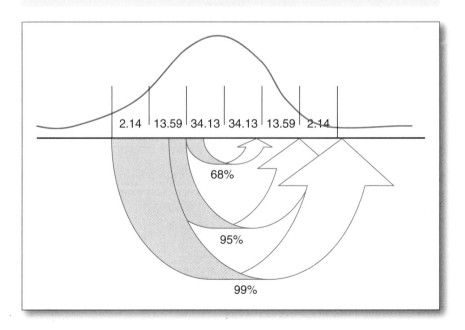

extend out infinitely in either direction, coming closer and closer to the horizontal axis but never touching.

s = 1/6th R

Earlier, we noted that one of the criteria for a normal distribution is a standard deviation that is about 1/6th of the range. Like the other criteria for normality, this applies primarily to large data sets, and although educators spend most of their time with relatively small groups, the concept deserves some amplification. The range/standard deviation relationship provides an index for evaluating the **kurtosis** of distributions. It may sound like an ailment, but kurtosis describes the degree to which the data are bunched around the middle of the distribution.

- When the standard deviation is about 1/6 R, the data are said to be **mesokurtic**. Normal distributions are mesokurtic.
- Data for which the $s > 1/6\ R$ are **platykurtic** (think of "plat" like flat), too spread out to be normal.
- And data for which $s < 1/6\ R$ are **leptokurtic** ("lep" is a little like leap), too bunched together to be normal.

An English composition test is administered to all 11th-grade students in the county. If scores range from 10 to 35 with $s = 8.450$, what can be said about kurtosis?

- If $R = 25$ (35 − 10)
- $s = 8.450$
- The standard deviation is too great given the range (or the range is too small given the standard deviation).

Whichever way it is said, there is too much variability for the distribution to be normal. Such a platykurtic distribution is represented in Figure 3.11A.

It is quite common for smaller samples to be platykurtic. The issue came up initially in Chapter 2 where we noted that standard deviations tend to shrink as the number in the group increases. In order for something approximating a normal curve to emerge, there has to be a certain amount of redundancy among scores, particularly among those nearest the mean. This is unlikely to happen in any consistent way when there are relatively few scores in the set to begin with.

If for the test results described above:

- $R = 25$
- $s = 2.500$
- The standard deviation in this case is too *small* given the range (6 × 2.500 = 15.00)

> ■ **Kurtosis** describes how much spread there is in a distribution.
>
> ■ Normal distributions are **mesokurtic**.
>
> ■ Distributions with too much variability are **platykurtic**, and distributions with too little variability are **leptokurtic**.

This distribution is leptokurtic (Figure 3.11B).

When the data are normal, for $R = 25$, s will be about 4.166. If that were the case, the distribution would be described as mesokurtic, literally "*middle*kurtic." The distribution in Figure 3.11C is mesokurtic. Like we said about symmetry, a mesokurtic distribution is necessary but by itself not sufficient for normality.

The 1/6th rule provides a rather coarse way to determine whether data are mesokurtic. In fact, data could be rather like they are in Figure 3.8 above and still meet the 1/6th criterion, but it's a serviceable way to describe a distribution nevertheless.

Figure 3.11   Platykurtic (A), Leptokurtic (B), and Mesokurtic (C) Distributions

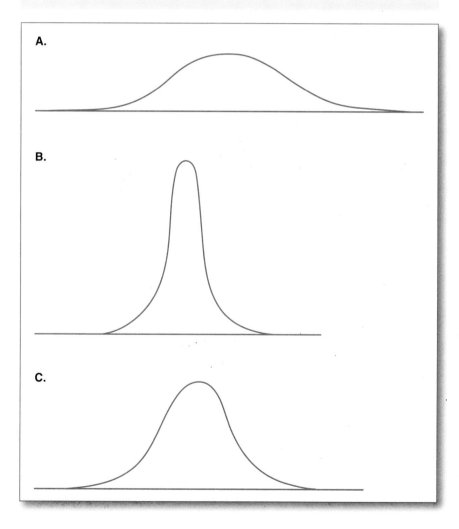

A.

B.

C.

If you're compelled to actually calculate a kurtosis value, the formula is as follows:

$$kur = \frac{\Sigma(x_i - M)^4 - 3}{(n-1)s^4}$$ 3.2

Where,

kur = the kurtosis value

x_i = each value in the sample

$(x_i - M)^4$ = take the difference between each number and the mean

^{4} = raise each difference to the 4th power (rather than just squaring them as we did with the variance and standard deviation)

Σ = sum the differences raised to the 4th

n = the number in the sample

s^4 = the sample standard deviation, also raised to the 4th power

Recall that the reading scores for the group of English learners Ms. Rivers was trying to describe, with that 10th, outlying score were 30, 40, 40, 50, 50, 50, 60, 60, 70, 95.

When she calculated skew, Ms. Rivers found modest positive skew. Applying Formula 3.2 we find that:

$$M = 54.5$$

$$s = 18.326$$

and that:

$$\Sigma(x_i - M)^4) = 3,199,910.625$$

$$(n - 1)s^4 = 9 \times 112,790.034 = 1,015,110.309$$

$$kur = 3,199,910.625 \div 1,015,110.309 = 3.152 - 3 = .152$$

A distribution which is too peaked is leptokurtic. This is indicated by positive kurtosis values. A too-flat distribution is platykurtic, for which the value will be negative. This value here indicates that this group is very slightly leptokurtic. By the 1/6th rule, it looks a bit platykurtic. For one with the patience to do the calculations, the formula gives a more accurate answer than the 1/6th rule, which is an estimate.

The final "−3" in the formula makes a distribution with kur = 0 neither platykurtic nor leptokurtic. Some formulae omit that final term to make values greater than 3 indicate a leptokurtic distribution and values from 0 to 3, leptokurtic. The SPSS calculations include that final term.

Although skewness and kurtosis can both be calculated directly, they rarely are for two reasons. First, using the measures of central tendency to determine skew, and using the 1/6th rule for an estimate of kurtosis usually lets one determine normality well enough to satisfy most statistical requirements for normality. Second, the formulae for determining skewness and kurtosis (especially the latter with its 4th-power requirements) are quite tedious. So absent masochistic tendencies, we generally either use the estimation procedures outlined here, or use computers and statistical software to do the work.

If skewness and kurtosis *are* actually calculated with SPSS, the resulting values of +/− 1.0 for skewness and for kurtosis indicate that the related data are ideal for statistical analysis; that is, they're essentially normal. However, because some departure from strict normality is tolerated by most statistical applications, values of +/−2.0 are usually acceptable.

DETERMINING WHAT IS REPRESENTATIVE

Recall from Chapter 2 that the section of the distribution from the 25th percentile (P_{25}) to the 75th percentile (P_{75}) marks the interquartile range, *IQR*, for short. Recall also that the *IQR* can serve as a guide to what is most representative in a set of scores. The problem with unrepresentative scores, as we noted when we discussed skewness, is that they have the greatest potential to distort data and the statistics that we calculate to describe them. The more extreme they are, the greater their distorting effect. Because all scores are squared in standard deviation calculations, extreme scores affect the standard deviation out of proportion to their number. Recall that the standard deviation is based on the square of the difference between individual scores and the mean of the distribution. Large differences, therefore, have a relatively greater impact on the standard deviation value because they not only contribute the largest differences between the score and the mean, they are then squared in the bargain.

There are a couple of ways to respond. When reporting the sales of new homes the measure of central tendency used most often is the "median price." This is because of the distorting effect a relatively few very expensive homes can have when calculating the mean. Salary data also tend to reflect positive skew. One way to respond is simply to avoid using the mean when there are outliers. However, that's only a partial solution since some analyses require the mean rather than the median (or the mode).

A second option is to identify and then eliminate the offending scores. To do this first one must have some way to determine which scores are outliers, or to say it another way, to determine the point at which a score should be considered an outlier. A subjective component always exists to making such a decision, but there are procedures that at least yield a consistent answer. Lockhart (1998) references outliers to the interquartile range. By his approach, outliers are values outside the interval stretching from 1.5 times the *IQR* below Q_1 to 1.5 times the *IQR* above Q_3. Put more succinctly, an outlier is

$$\text{any score below } Q_1 - (1.5 \times IQR), \text{ or} \qquad\qquad 3.3$$

$$\text{any score beyond } Q_3 + (1.5 \times IQR) \qquad\qquad 3.4$$

Figure 3.12   Creating a Frequency Distribution and Identifying the Quartiles

A group of students' test scores are as follows:
13, 14, 8, 16, 17, 13, 16, 14, 20, 14, 12, 15, 17, 15, 14, 15, 13, 16, 14, 15

If scores are arranged from smallest to largest and repeated scores are stacked vertically, the result is a frequency distribution.

Since $n = 20$ and $20/4 = 5$, the quartiles will occur between

    the 5th and 6th scores (Q_1),

    the 10th and 11th scores $(Q_2,$ the $M_{dn})$, and

    the 15th and 16th scores (Q_3)

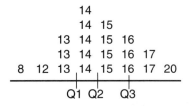

The data in Figure 3.12 first appeared as a frequency distribution with quartiles indicated in Figure 2.2:

$$Q_1 = 13.5$$
$$Q_3 = 16$$

Therefore, $IQR = 2.50$ $(16 - 13.5)$.

Because $1.5 \times 2.5 = 3.75$, outliers are

values lower than $Q_1 - 3.75 = 13.5 - 3.75 = \mathbf{9.75}$, and

values higher than $Q_3 + 3.75 = 16 + 3.75 = \mathbf{19.75}$

For the scores in Figure 3.12, the only score lower than 9.75 is 8, and the only score higher than 19.75 is 20. By Lockhart's (1998) definition, these two scores are outliers.

Lockhart's (1998) approach is a procedure that will provide consistency to decisions about outliers. It isn't a rule. The task of deciding when to exclude data is going to be determined by the size of the data set, the number of extreme scores involved, and the type of decisions one is trying to make. If SPSS output indicates that a data set is non-normal and that ordinary analyses are, therefore, not appropriate (skewness and/or kurtosis values are beyond +/− 2.0), one might consider eliminating the most extreme scores. The process outlined above is at least one way to approach the task.

With all our matter-of-fact about quartiles, deciles, IQRs, outliers, and so on, don't forget that these are all just descriptive tools. We're usually just trying to gain a sense of "the lay of things," so don't abandon reason and basic logic in favor of a lot of elaborate calculations. For example, it makes no sense for someone who is trying to decide about the value of an advanced placement curriculum in an honors program to exclude extremely high scores simply because they skew the distribution.

SUMMARY

Ms. Rivers, and any educator who needs to make data understandable to an audience, particularly an uninformed audience, will find that they are often easier to understand when they're presented as tables or figures. Whether we're trying to make a case for the continuation of a reading program or just attempting to organize information so we can appraise it more accurately, statistical analysis often begins with placing the data into a table or a graph.

Perhaps the primary criterion for producing good figures and tables is that they require very little additional explanation. The two pie charts in Figure 3.2 respond to the superintendent's request for a presentation that clarifies the value of a tutoring program threatened by the budgetary chopping block. Good presentations shouldn't need much interpretation, but if they're carefully done, they can also suggest secondary questions about why the frequencies or proportions are what they are.

For data analysts few concepts emerge as persistently in data presentation and analysis as the concept of normality. Whether one is gathering data on the number of years of experience the educators in a school district have or attempting to digest the latest standardized test scores, normality tends to have a presence. Any computer statistical package worth its salt will calculate skewness and kurtosis, but these indicators of normality can usually be estimated reasonably well. Comparing the measures of central tendency provides ready evidence about whether data are symmetrical (and gives one a chance to determine whether the data are unimodal in the bargain), and comparing the standard deviation to the range is a way to estimate kurtosis. However user-friendly a statistical software program might be, your author is a staunch advocate of using these estimates. Often examining and comparing descriptive statistics is more revealing than staring at a skew number on a computer printout.

When data *are* normal, one knows what will be characteristic of the group and something about what to expect in the population as a whole. Such distributions allow us to know what percentage of the population will occur between particular standard deviation units, for example. In Chapter 4, we'll use this information to determine the probability that an individual might score in *any* region of a population, something that can be very helpful to an educator.

This chapter was intended to provide tools for data description. It's been a bit term-intensive, but don't worry too much about committing them to memory. The point of the Glossary is to provide a reference source. The more frequently used terms will become an integral part of your statistical vocabulary just because they come up so often. So have another look at them, consider the examples again, and soldier on. You're doing fine!

EXERCISES

1. What guidelines must one follow to create a grouped frequency distribution?

2. For the following scores on the verbal portion of the Graduate Record Exam, create a stem-and-leaf display: 240, 275, 290, 295, 340, 380, 385, 450, 450, 495, 560, 570, 620, 625, 680, 700.

3. If the data in item 2 are listed as they are presented, what type of array do they represent?

4. What advantage does a pie chart offer over a bar chart when data from two different distributions have different numbers of scores?

5. How is a bar chart using vertical columns to represent frequency visually different from a histogram?

6. If one were to plot several scores that all occurred at least once according to Cartesian coordinates but they all had negative values, in which quadrant would the graph appear?

7. A data distribution of history test scores has $M_o = 24$, $M_{dn} = 27.5$, and $M = 29.0$. What can be said about skew?

8. A group of 10 students are selected for a study of height. One of them happens to be the center on the basketball team. What will the most likely affect be on skew of including that person?

9. For a distribution of population data, $R = 43$ and $s = 3.756$, what can be said about kurtosis?

10. The following are measures of achievement motivation (AchMot) among remedial mathematics students: 12, 13, 15, 16, 18, 21, 21, 22, 24, 25, 25, 26. How should skew and kurtosis be described?

11. Using the data in item 10, one wishes to identify outliers.
    a. What is the value of the interquartile range (IQR)?
    b. Values outside what two points would be considered outliers according to Lockhart's (1998) procedure?

12. How is it possible to have a symmetrical distribution that isn't normal?

13. Using the stem-and-leaf display in item 2:
    a. $M_{dn} = ?$
    b. $Q_1 = ?$
    c. $Q_2 = ?$
    d. $Q_3 = ?$

14. Using the item 2 data, are there any outliers?

15. According to what we know of normal distributions, if the item 2 data represented a normal distribution, what two points would include approximately 68% of the distribution?

16. A school psychologist has the following scores from a measure of students' verbal aptitude: 33, 35, 37, 37, 43, 48, 49, 52, 57, 58, 58, 60.
    a. Arranged in a stem-and-leaf display, what evidence is there that if these data reflect the population from which they're drawn, the population isn't normal?
    b. Calculate the measures of central tendency. What can be said about skewness?
    c. Compare the standard deviation to the range. What can be said about kurtosis?

REFERENCES

Friendly, M. (2000). *Visualizing categorical data.* Cary, NC: SAS Institute Inc.

Lockhart, R. S. (1998). *Introduction to statistics and data analysis for the behavioral sciences.* New York, NY: W.H. Freeman and Company.

Sheskin, D. (2004). *Handbook of parametric and nonparametric statistical procedures* (3rd ed.). Boca Raton, FL: Chapman and Hall/CRC Press.

STAR. (2007). *California standardized testing and reporting.* Retrieved from http://star.cde.ca.gov/star2007/index.asp

Tufte, E. R. (2001). *The visual display of quantitative information* (2nd ed.). Cheshire, CT: Graphics Books.

THE FORMULAE AND THEIR SYMBOLS

Formula 3.1: $sk = \dfrac{3(M - M_{dn})}{s}$

is the formula for determining a value for skew.

Formula 3.2: $kur = \dfrac{\Sigma(x_i - M)^4}{(n-1)s^4}$

is the formula for calculating a kurtosis value.

Formula 3.3: $Q_1 - (1.5)\,(IQR)$ is the formula for determining which values in the lower end of the distribution are outliers.

Formula 3.4: $Q_3 + (1.5)\,(IQR)$ is the formula for determining which values in the upper end of the distribution are outliers.

STUDENT STUDY SITE

Visit the Student Study Site at **www.sagepub.com/tanner** for additional learning tools.

Chapter 4

WORKING WITH THE NORMAL CURVE

z Scores

THE PROBLEM: HOW TO COMPARE DATA FROM DISSIMILAR MEASURES

Ms. Washington is a secondary school counselor who tries to help students qualify for college admission. She spends a good deal of time prepping them for the admissions tests. Since different colleges require different tests, and students often apply to more than one, many take multiple tests. Ms. Washington wonders if there's a way to compare a student's results from one test to another.

Like a competent counselor should, Ms. Washington knows the minimum scores the different colleges require. She also knows how students have performed in the past. She needs to know how likely students are to score in the required ranges.

QUESTIONS AND ANSWERS

❑ When tests have different means and standard deviations, is there a way to compare them directly?

This is the "apples and sheep" problem we raised in Chapter 2. We'll solve it by transforming the "raw" test scores into what are called "standard" scores that all have the same mean and standard deviation.

❑ How can one determine the probability of scoring in a particular area of a distribution?

When data are normal, particular areas of the distribution always include the same percentage of the population. Applied to admissions test scores, this will allow Ms. Washington to determine the probability that individual students will score in specified ranges.

Much of the Chapter 3 discussion revolved around normal (Gaussian) distributions. Now it's time to apply the normal distribution to some educational problems.

Probably many of the characteristics in which educators have an interest are normally distributed. The verbal ability of all seventh-grade students in the district, the grade averages of all high school seniors in the state, and the mechanical ability of all secondary students in the county each refer to characteristics of populations that are likely to be normally distributed. There's no way to be certain of normality without examining the distributions more closely, but when we have data for the entire population, many populations are likely to be normal.

The z Distribution

Many normal distributions exist, which is to say that there are many populations for which the mean, median, and mode occur near the same point and for which the standard deviation is about 1/6th of the range. But each of these normal distributions represents different characteristics. With their different means and standard deviations, comparisons of one to another aren't easy to make. That's one of Ms. Washington's problems at the beginning of the chapter. Scores for two different admissions tests might both be normally distributed, but with different ranges, means, and standard deviations, how does one compare them?

- Among normal distributions there is one **standard normal (z) distribution.**

Among the many normal distributions the **standard normal distribution** stands apart. This distribution, often called the **z distribution**, has the same symmetry, unimodality, and mesokurtic shape that all normal distributions have, but the mean and standard deviation values are fixed at 0 and 1.0, respectively. This distribution presents an opportunity. If data from other distributions are fitted to the z distribution, comparisons of dissimilar data sets are much easier to make, but there are other advantages, as we shall see.

- The **z transformation** creates scores with mean = 0, and standard deviation = 1.0.

The first step is to turn the scores from their original distributions into scores that fit the z distribution. We need the z **transformation**. It has this form:

$$z = \frac{(x - M)}{s} \qquad\qquad 4.1$$

Where,

z = the z equivalent of the original "raw" score

x = the raw score

M = the mean of the raw scores

s = the standard deviation of the raw scores

Before using the z transformation, there are two issues. First, although this transformation turns any set of scores into z scores, it doesn't "normalize" them. Data that are skewed and platykurtic to begin with will still be skewed and platykurtic after the z transformation. This is important for reasons we'll get to below.

Second, the "M" and "s" symbols indicate that this transformation is for sample data. If they were population data, the symbols in the formula would be the Greek letters μ and σ for the mean and standard deviation, and the formula would be:

$$z = \frac{(x - \mu)}{\sigma}$$ 4.2

The mechanics of using the formula are the same in either case, but we're much more likely to have sample than population data. Formula 4.1 will generally be our formula.

Calculating z Scores

The z transformation isn't difficult. To determine the z values for any set of scores one must

1. calculate the mean (M) and standard deviation (s),

2. subtract the mean from each score ($x - M$), and

3. divide the result by the standard deviation.

A group of secondary-school students in their junior year take a college admissions exam and have the following scores: 16, 17, 18, 20, 21, 22, 24. What is the value of 20 as a z score? The calculations are in Figure 4.1.
So, for $x = 20$, $z = .100$.

Interpreting z

The z score can be very informative. Since the mean of the standard normal distribution is 0, the z scores for any raw score lower than its mean will be negative. Without wanting to sound like the guy who hawks those forever-sharp knives on TV, wait, there's more. Because z is a ratio of difference (the raw score minus the mean in the numerator) to variability (the standard deviation in the denominator), z reveals how far the original raw score is from the mean in standard deviation units. A z value of -1.3, indicates 1.3 standard deviations *below* the mean. The $z = .100$ from Figure 4.1 indicates that for this group of scores, 20 is 1/10th s *above* the mean.

Figure 4.1 Calculating the *z* Score

1. Calculate the mean:

   $M = \Sigma x/n = (16 + 17 + 18 + 20 + 21 + 22 + 24)/7 = \mathbf{19.714}$

2. Calculate the standard deviation:

   $$s = \sqrt{\Sigma(x-M)^2 / n-1}$$

x	x − M	(x − M)²	Σ(x − M)²	Σ(x − M)²/n − 1	$\sqrt{\Sigma(x-M)^2 / n-1}$
16	−3.714	13.794			
17	−2.714	7.366			
18	−1.714	2.938			
20	.286	.082			
21	1.286	1.654			
22	2.286	5.226			
24	4.286	18.370			
			49.430	8.238	2.870

   $s = \mathbf{2.870}$

3. Calculate *z*,

$$z = (x - M)/s$$
$$z = (20 - 19.714)/2.870$$
$$z = .100 \text{ (.0996 rounded up)}$$

Determining the "Best" Performance

At the beginning of the chapter, we noted that sometimes we need to compare results from different tests. Comparisons are simple when scores come from the same test, but what if there are different tests with different ranges, means, and so on? Transforming them into *z* scores creates a common standard.

Suppose a college freshman takes reading and math placement tests and scores 43 and 67, respectively. With the means and standard deviations, we have the following:

	Reading	Math
$x =$	43	67
$M =$	38.75	65.00
$s =$	4.56	6.97

Once they're converted to z values, both scores fit a distribution where $M = 0$ and $s = 1.0$. At that point we can compare them directly, and the highest z will represent the measure where the student performed best.

$$z = \frac{(x - M)}{s}$$

$$z_{43} = \frac{(43 - 38.75)}{4.56} = .932$$

$$z_{67} = \frac{(67 - 65.00)}{6.97} = .287$$

Both scores are positive, indicating that this student scored above the mean on both tests, but we knew that as soon as we calculated M. The z values indicate that the reading score is .932 above the mean, while her math score is .287 standard deviations above the mean. She did better on the reading test.

Another Example

An applicant to a professional training program took admissions tests A and B, for which he wishes to compare results. Because national data are available, to calculate z he'll trade the M and s statistics for the parameters μ and σ. Test A has $\mu = 22$ with $\sigma = 5.0$. Test B has $\mu = 1000$, with $\sigma = 200$. If the student scores 19 on A and 900 on B, on which has he performed best?

$$z = (x - \mu)/\sigma$$

$$z_{19} = (19 - 22)/5 = -.60$$

$$z_{900} = (900 - 1000)/200 = -.50$$

Be cautious with the interpretation of these z scores. The z for test A is more extreme, and since both scores are negative, the more extreme score is the one farthest below the mean. The student performed better on Test B.

We may not be able to compare apples to sheep, but when data from different sources are in interval form and we can find means and standard deviations for each group, the z transformation allows us to compare scores from different sources.

Providing a common score for dissimilar measures has many applications. A psychologist may have scores for both a client's motivation to succeed and her motivation to avoid failure. Since the motivation to succeed suggests more creativity and risk-taking and the motivation to avoid failure indicates a very orthodox approach to tasks, knowing which is stronger might help explain behavior.

Perhaps a child is taller than his peers. Calculating z scores for his height and weight will indicate whether he is similarly heavier than his peers.

z AND THE PERCENT OF THE POPULATION UNDER THE CURVE

In Chapters 2 and 3 we noted the connection between how much one deviates from the mean of a normal distribution and the percent of the population included. Since $z = 1.0$ indicates one standard deviation above the mean, from the mean to $z = 1.0$ includes 34.13% of the population. It follows that from $z = $ 1.0 to $z = 1.0$ (plus *and* minus one standard deviation from the mean) includes 68.26% of the population, and so on. This will hold for all normal distributions.

But what good is this for samples like that in Figure 4.1, where there are too few measures for anything approaching a normal curve? Although sample data are unlikely to be normal, when the sample is drawn from a population of measures that *is* normal, we can still use the z transformation. Note that when we speak of data normality, we're referring to the population from which a sample was drawn rather than to the sample itself.

TABLE A

Not only do we have the percentage of the population under the curve at 1, 2, and 3 standard deviations from the mean referred to in Chapter 3, but more detailed tables are available. Table A in the Tables of Critical Values appendix indicates that percentage of a normal population for values of z from .01 to about 3.00. Since $+/- z = 3.00$ includes more than 99% of the distribution, we'll rarely need the percentage for a more extreme z value.

Not all z tables are arranged the same way. Our Table A indicates the percentage of the distribution *between a value of z and the mean* of the distribution. If z is positive, the table indicates the percentage of the population on the right half of the distribution from between the z value and the mean. If z is negative, the table indicates the percentage on the left half of the distribution from z to the mean. The z tables in other texts may be different.

Although we've been calculating to three decimals (thousandths), the table only shows to hundredths. A table indicating the percentages for every value of z from .000 to 3.000 would be impossibly large, so we'll round z values to 2 decimals.

Table A begins with $z = 3.00$, for which the percentage of the distribution is 49.87. It indicates that, in a normal distribution, 49.87% occurs between $z = 3.00$ and the mean, $z = 0$. The next value is $z = 2.99$, for which the percentage between that point and the mean is 49.86, and so on. The table percentages for particular values of z are easier to keep track of if you write them in parentheses next to the z value as follows:

$$z = .10 \ (3.98)$$

This indicates that 3.98% of a normal population occurs between $z = .10$ *and the mean of the distribution* (where $z = 0$).

Although half the values of z will be negative (the lower half of the distribution), there are no negative z values in the table. Can you guess why? Because normal distributions are symmetrical, the percentage of the distribution between $z = .10$ and the mean is the same as the percentage between $z = -.10$ and the mean. When z values have the same number but different signs, they include the same percentage of the distribution.

EXTENDING z SCORES

Now back to Ms. Washington and the college applicants. Perhaps she knows that 21 is the minimum acceptable score at one of the colleges, and her question is, what percent of the student population (those scoring 20 or lower) does such a score exclude.

- Our value of z for $x = 20$ was .10.
- Table A indicates that 3.98% of the population is between $z = .10$ and the mean.
- With 50% of the population below the mean, 3.98% between the mean, and $z = .10$, $50 + 3.98 = 53.98\%$ of the student population is excluded if 21 is the minimum acceptable score.

To Underscore the Point: Normal Distribution

What Table A provides is the proportion of a normal distribution between any value of z and the mean of the distribution. Because normal distributions are symmetrical, whether the value of z is positive or negative won't change the percentage of the distribution between a point and the mean. A table value of $z = 2$ indicates that 47.72 of the distribution occurs between that point and the mean. Adding the 50% for the negative half of the distribution indicates that 97.72% occurs *below* the point at which $z = 2.0$. If the $z = -2.0$, however, only 2.28% occurs below that point (50 − 47.72).

FROM z TO PERCENTILES

Chapter 2 taught that percentile scores indicate the point at, or below, which the specified percentage of the group occurs. Seventy-three percent of the distribution occurs at, or below, the point defined by the 73rd percentile, and so on. Because the table values associated with z scores can be used to determine the percentage of the distribution occurring below a point, it's easy to go one more step and turn that percentage into a percentile score. The table indicates that 34.13% of the distribution occurs between $z = 1.0$ and the mean of the distribution. If we add in the negative side of the distribution, we can say that $z = 1.0$ occurs at the 84th percentile (50 + 43.13, rounded to the whole number). The median, of course, occurs at the 50th percentile, the point below which 50% of the distribution occurs. Minus one standard deviation occurs at the 16th percentile (50 − 34.13), and so on. Once the percentage of the distribution below a point is determined, we also have the percentile score, which, by the way, is always rounded to a whole number.

In a normal distribution, the locations of the 25th percentile (P_{25}) and the 75th percentile (P_{75}) mirror each other on the abscissa (the horizontal line in the frequency distribution indicating the different score values). In a skewed distribution they won't, as Figure 4.2 illustrates.

As is the case with standard scores, much of the percentile score's value is the normative reference it provides, but be careful with the interpretation. Ordinarily, someone with a ranking of "1" possesses the highest score, but a percentile rank of "1" indicates a low score, the point below which the *bottom* 1% of scores occur. A score in the 1st quartile is a score in the *lowest* fourth of the distribution, not the highest. It isn't uncommon for these values

Figure 4.2   Locating the 25th, 50th, and 75th Percentile Scores in Different Distributions

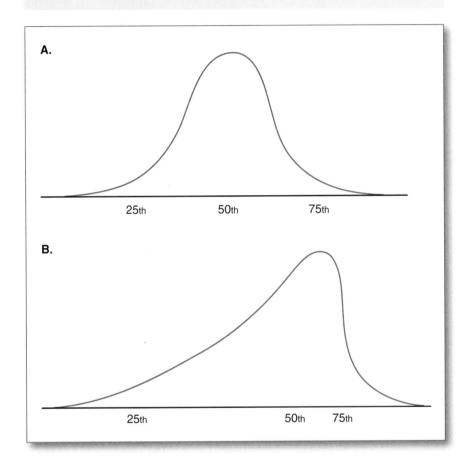

to be interpreted incorrectly. The author once had a dean who hoped for the time when students in area schools would score in the 1st quartile on state-mandated tests . . . !

Percentile scores provide rankings and remember that ranks are ordinal (Chapter 2) rather than interval data. One shouldn't assume that the interval between P_1 and P_5 is the same as that between P_{39} and P_{43}, for example, even though the difference is 4 percentile points in either case. Whether populations are normal or not, extreme scores tend to be less common than scores closer to the middle of the distribution. Because there are more scores in this area, the interval between P_{39} and P_{43} will usually cover a smaller portion of the abscissa than the interval between P_1 and P_5. Be careful when an audience might equate percentile ranks with percentages. Percen*tages* are interval scale data and on an achievement test indicate the portion of the total the student answered correctly. Percen*tiles,* conversely, are transformations of raw scores that are used to determine a ranking for the individual compared with the normative group. They provide no direct evidence of how many items the individual scored correctly but only how the individual compares with others (Anastasi, 1976).

Probabilities and Percentages

This is a good time to consider the connection between percentages and probabilities, two concepts that are often bound together in statistics. Probability values range from 0 to 1.0 and deal with the likelihood of an occurrence. An event with zero probability ($p = 0$) is one with no likelihood of occurring. Although "hope springs eternal," the probability that this book will ever be ranked above one of the *Harry Potter* books on the *New York Times* best-seller list is *near* 0, possible perhaps, but profoundly unlikely. An event with $p = 1.0$ always happens. Note that probability values cannot be negative. Nothing has a $p < 0$ likelihood of occurrence.

We have no interest in certainties (events with $p = 0$, or $p = 1.0$); they leave us nothing to analyze. In the northern hemisphere, daily temperatures have a higher average in July than in January. No one discusses the probability that they will be otherwise because it is either $p = 0$, or so near to it that the discussion is a waste of time absent a meteor collision or a nuclear explosion serious enough to alter atmospheric conditions.

Once we have calculated z scores and used Table A to determine the percentage below or above a point, we can also speak of the *probability* of an outcome by dividing the percentage by 100. Since the percentage of the distribution at or below a raw score of 20 on the college admissions test was 53.98%, the probability that one student selected at random from the population will score 20 or lower is 53.98/100 = .5398. Rounded to thousandths, the probability is $p = .540$. So the percentage under the normal curve divided by 100 indicates the probability that an event will occur in that region of the normal distribution. The probability that someone selected at random will score below the mean on any measure that's normally distributed is $p = .500$ (the 50% of the distribution below the mean, divided by 100).

SOURCE: Created by Suzanna Nielson.

"Did he say something about 'M minus meow over sickma?'"

Another Example

Some years ago, an acquaintance offered that he had scored 165 on an intelligence test (one wonders what level of insecurity prompts someone to volunteer such information). If intelligence is normally distributed with a mean of 100 and a standard deviation of 15 (technically, those values would be indicated by $\mu = 100$ and $\sigma = 15$, since they're population values), what's the probability that someone selected at random will have an intelligence score of 165, or higher? Note that we can only answer questions about the probability of a score occurring in a defined range rather than about the probability of a particular score. Technically, a discrete point has no width and so takes up 0% of the distribution.

$$z = (x - \mu)/\sigma$$
$$z = (165 - 100)/15$$
$$z = 4.333$$

Our table only goes to $z = 3.0$ (49.87), which is a substantially lower z value, but even with that value only .13% (50 − 49.87) of the distribution is beyond. The probability that someone selected at random from the general population might have an intelligence score $z = 3.0$ or higher, therefore, is $p = .0013$, or said a different way, there are just 13 chances in 10,000 of such a score. Without wishing to doubt the man's veracity or his accuracy, a score that is *yet an additional* 1 1/3 standard deviations higher would be very improbable indeed; more likely than the Harry Potter example certainly, but very unlikely.

The Probability of Scoring Between Two Points

In addition to calculating the percentage below or above a particular score, we can determine the percentage *between* two points. Back to the data in Figure 4.1, perhaps Ms. Washington has spent some time analyzing admissions test scores and has concluded that most of her focus should be on students who score between 17 and 23. Her reasoning is that those who score below 17 will either not attend a conventional college or university or they'll opt for the local community college, which has an open admissions policy. Those who score beyond 23 are likely to be sought out by more prestigious schools and will need very little help getting admitted. Her question is, what's the probability that students will score between those two points?

Note that the two scores are on either side of the mean. If we:

- Transform 17 and 23 into z scores, and then
- Look up the Table A values for each,
- Adding the table values together will indicate the percentage of the distribution under the curve between those two points, and
- Dividing the percentage by 100 will indicate the probability that a student will score between the two scores.

Two Values on Opposite Sides of the Mean

1. Using Figure 4.3 as a guide, draw something approximating a normal curve to help you picture what's asked.

2. Turn both 17 and 23 into z scores.

   a. $z = \dfrac{(x - M)}{s}$

   $z_{17} = \dfrac{(17 - 19.714)}{2.870} = -.945$, or $-.9$

   b. $z_{23} = \dfrac{(23 - 19.714)}{2.870} = 1.144$ or 1.14

   c. Plot the z values on your curve, noting the approximate distance each value is from the mean on either side—just under one standard deviation below the mean for z_{17} and just slightly more than one standard deviation above the mean for z_{23}.

3. Check the table values for each score.

   a. $z_{17} = -.95$ (32.90)
   b. $z_{23} = 1.14$ (37.29)

The z scores for 17 and 23 and the relevant percentages have been plotted in Figure 4.3A.

Figure 4.3 Determining the Probability of Scoring Between Two Points

A. The Percent of the Population Under the Curve Between Scores on Opposite Sides of the Mean

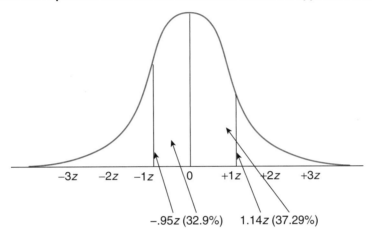

$-.95z$ (32.9%) $1.14z$ (37.29%)

The area from $-.95z$ to the mean accounts for 32.9% of the area under the curve. From $1.14z$ to the mean accounts for 37.29%. Since those two areas adjoin but do not overlap, we can add them to determine the total: $32.9 + 37.29 = 70.19\%$ of the population under the curve between those two points.

B. The Percent of the Population Under the Curve Between Scores on the Same Side of the Mean

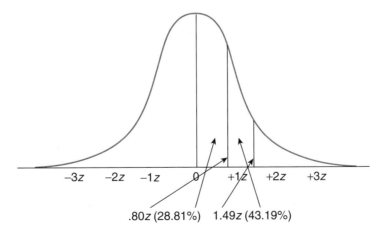

$.80z$ (28.81%) $1.49z$ (43.19%)

The area from $.8z$ back to the mean accounts for 28.81% of the area under the curve. From $1.49z$ to the mean accounts for 43.19% but that includes the area covered by $.8z$. We must subtract that portion: $43.19 - 28.81 = 14.38\%$ of the area between those two points.

4. Because Ms. Washington's question is of the probability of scoring between those two points, the sum of the two table values gives us the percentage of the distribution between the two points: 32.90 + 37.29 = **70.19**%.

5. The probability is the percentage divided by 100: 70.19 ÷ 100 = **.702**.

The probability that a randomly selected student will score anywhere from 17 to 23 is $p = .702$.

Two Values on the Same Side of the Mean

When two scores are on the same side of the distribution, we subtract the smaller table value from the larger to determine the percentage of the distribution between them. Perhaps two applicants have virtually identical grades, but slightly different admissions scores of 22 and 24. Ms. Washington's question is about how different those scores are—what percentage of the distribution is between them. The process is as follows:

1. Determine the z values for the two scores.

   a. $z = \dfrac{(x-M)}{s}$

   $z_{22} = \dfrac{(22-19.714)}{2.870} = .796$, or .80

   b. $z_{24} = \dfrac{(24-19.714)}{2.870} = 1.493$, or 1.49

2. Check the table values for each value of z.

   a. $z_{22} = .80$ (28.81)
   b. $z_{24} = 1.49$ (43.19)

3. Because 22 and 24 both occur above the mean of the distribution, the table value for the larger score (z_{24}) also includes the portion of the distribution between the smaller score (z_{22}) and the mean. To determine just the percentage *between* their two points, (Figure 4.3 B), subtract the smaller table value from the larger:

   43.19 − 28.81 = 14.38
   14.38% of the population of all students taking the test will score between 22 and 24.

Stated as a probability, $p = .144$ (14.38/100, rounded) that someone will score from 22 to 24. Although the two students have very similar grades, their levels of aptitude for college level work (assuming that this is what the test measures) differ somewhat. The admission scores of more than 14% of the population will occur in the interval from the lower score to the higher.

The Percentage of the Distribution Outside an Interval

The school counselor might be curious about how her group compares with the population who take the test. In particular, maybe she's interested in the percentage who score below or beyond the range represented by her group. Be careful here. At first glance one may be tempted to say, "But no one is below 17 or above 24. Shouldn't the percentage below 17 and above 24 be 0?" Although no one in the *sample* scored in that area, we're interested in the larger population.

We begin by calculating z scores for 17 and 24.

$$z = \frac{(x-M)}{s}$$

$$z_{17} = \frac{17-19.714}{2.870} = -.95(32.90)$$

$$z_{24} = \frac{24-19.714}{2.870} = .1.49(43.19)$$

- The region from $-.95\,z$ to $1.49\,z$ includes $32.90 + 43.19 = 76.09\%$ of the area under the normal curve. Those values are plotted in the distribution in Figure 4.4.
- That 76.09% leaves $100 - 76.09 = 23.91\%$ outside that area; thus, 23.91% of all scores in the population will occur either below 17 or above 24.

Rules for Determining the Percentage of the Population Under Areas of the Curve

1. To determine the percentage of the distribution below a particular z score:
   a. If the z score is positive, add the table value to 50 (to account for the half of the distribution below the mean).
   b. If the z score is negative, subtract the table value from 50.

Figure 4.4 Determining the Percentage of the Distribution Outside Two Points

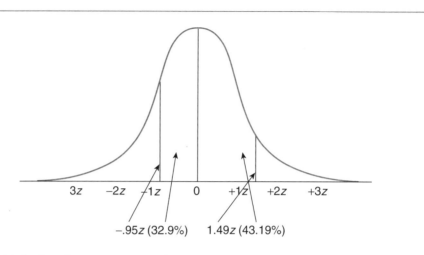

The area from −.95z back to the mean accounts for 32.9% of the area under the curve. From 1.49z to the mean accounts for 43.19%. Therefore the area between the two z scores accounts for 32.9 + 43.19 = 76.09% of the population. To determine the percentage outside those two points, we simply subtract the area accounted for from 100: 100 − 76.09 = 23.91% of the population falls in the area outside those two points.

2. To determine the percentage of the distribution above a z score:
   a. If the z score is positive, subtract the table value from 50.
   b. If the z score is negative, add the table value to the half of the distribution (50) above the mean.

3. If the question is of the percentage of the population between two points:
   a. If they are on opposite sides of the mean, determine z for each and add their table values.
   b. If they are on the same side of the distribution, determine z for each, and subtract the smaller table value from the larger.

4. If the question is of the percentage of the population outside two points:
   a. If they are on opposite sides of the mean, determine z for each, subtract both table values from 50, and add the results.
   b. If they are on the same side of the distribution, determine z for each, subtract the table value for the smaller z value from that for the larger, and subtract that result from 100.

Although these directions will work fine, the better course is to diagram the distribution, calculate the z values and then plot them on the diagram, indicating the areas under the curve designated by the table values. Then think about what's asked and you'll usually be able to reason your way to a solution. In the long term, this approach is going to be more helpful than memorizing a rule.

USING SPSS

Using the computer and SPSS to generate z scores is quite simple. The same window that provides for descriptive statistics provides a box titled "save standardized values as variables." If checked, it produces a column in the "Data View" window in which the score from any variable for which descriptive statistics are being calculated has a corresponding z value. Using the data from Figure 4.1 and requesting descriptive statistics for an analysis we have the following in the output window:

Descriptive Statistics

	N	Minimum	Maximum	Mean	Std. Deviation
Zscores	7	16	24	19.71	2.870
Valid N (listwise)	7				

It indicates that there were 7 values entered, that the lowest was 16 and the highest 24, that the mean was 19.71, and the standard deviation was 2.870. Back in the "Data View" window, there is now a second column titled "Zscores" appearing beside the first which we entered:

scores	Zscores
16	−1.29408
17	−.94568
18	−.59727
20	.09954
21	.44795
22	.79636
24	1.49317

The first column will be titled whatever name you gave it, "scores," in our example. The second column, containing the z scores, will insert a "Z" before the name for the first column so that in our example it is headed "Zscores." In A Primer in SPSS at the back of the book, there is a primer with the step-by-step procedure for completing this procedure.

FROM PERCENTAGES TO z SCORES

In addition to using z scores to determine the percentages of the population in specified areas, we can reverse the process and work from percentages back to z. Note, for example, that one could determine which values of z include the middle 95% of the distribution.

Recall that Table A indicates the percentage of the distribution between z and the mean. Since the table provides values for only half the distribution, to determine the z that includes the middle 95%:

- First we halve the percentage. Half of 95% is 47.5%.
- Check the table for the z value that includes to 47.5% of the distribution between z and the mean of the distribution.
- That value is . . . $z = 1.96$.
- Since 1.96 includes 47.5%, then + *and* −1.96 includes 95%.

Another Example

What value of z excludes the extreme 1% of the distribution? As before, first we divide the included portion of the distribution (99%) in half, 49.5% as it turns out, and then look for the z value that includes that percentage.

There's a bit of snag with this one. The table indicates that +/− $z = 2.57$ includes 49.49% of the distribution, and +/− $z = 2.58$ includes 49.51% of the distribution. What we really need is the percentage for $z = 2.575$, but most z tables stop at 2 decimals. Traditionally, statisticians use the more conservative value, so we'll settle on $z = 2.58$ as the value that includes the middle 99% of the distribution.

and a Related Point

These values of z that include the middle 95% and 99% of the distribution weren't selected randomly. As we move to significance testing they become very important to determining when outcomes are statistically significant. More on this in chapters to come.

WORKING BACKWARD FROM z

Sometimes the z score is available (perhaps they are published with other standardized test results, for example), but what we really want is one of the other values in the z transformation. Note that the formula for z involves four values. Although it's usually z we're interested in, given any three of the values, we can always determine the fourth. It involves a little algebra (thus vindicating your ninth-grade algebra teacher who told you it would be valuable some day), but it isn't difficult.

If we wish to know the raw score:

1. $z = (x - M)/s$, so

2. $(x - M)/s = z$, then

3. Multiplying both sides by s yields $x - M = z(s)$

4. Adding M to both sides we have $\boldsymbol{x = z(s) + M}$

For example, a student's z score $= -.95$ on a vocabulary test. For the same test $M = 22.500$ and $s = 3.450$. What was the student's raw score?

$x = z{\cdot}s + M$

$x = -.95(3.450) + 22.500$

$= 19.223$

If it's the standard deviation we need:

1. $z = (x - M)/s$, so

2. $(x - M)/s = z$, then

3. The reciprocal of both sides yields $s/(x - M) = 1/z$, and

4. Multiplying both sides by $(x - M)$ yields $s = (x - M)/z$

For example, on the vocabulary test, a student's raw score $(x) = 19.223$, the z score $= -.95$ and $M = 22.500$. What was the standard deviation for the test?

$s = (19.223 - 22.500)/-.95$

$= 3.449$ (the difference is because of round-off differences).

Although it's unlikely that one would have the other values but not the mean, it too can be derived from the others.

1. $z = (x - M)/s$, so

2. Multiply both sides of the equation times s: $z(s) = X - M$

3. Add the mean to both sides yielding $z(s) + M = X$

4. Subtract $z(s)$ from both sides of the equation yielding $M = x - z(s)$

For example, on the vocabulary test, a student's raw score $(x) = 19.223$, the z score $= -.95$ and $s = 3.449$. What was the mean for the test?

$$M = x - z \cdot s$$

$$M = 19.223 - (-.95)(3.50)$$

$$M = 22.548 \text{ (the difference between this mean and the value with which}$$
we began is due to round off).

OTHER STANDARD SCORES

■ The various **standard scores** all indicate a raw score's distance from the mean in standard deviation units.

The z score is actually one of a family of scores called **standard scores**. Just as z always has the same mean and standard deviation, so do each of the others, which makes them easy to interpret because they don't rely on a particular set of circumstances for their meaning. In the case of z, a score of 1.5 means that the raw score from which z was calculated was 1.5 standard deviations beyond the mean for the group. Although the means and standard deviations differ for each, this is so for all standard scores. Whether the results are from Broward County, Florida, or Beaver County, Montana, the interpretation is the same.

The *T* Score

A fact of life when dealing with z scores is that about half of all values will be negative. Although the reader may be not bothered by a negative score, explaining them to those unfamiliar with them can be complicated. If a student scores slightly below the mean for the group, say $z = -.1$, the student's performance is actually quite representative of all who took the test, but students and parents, and perhaps too many educators, can get nervous at the mention of "negative." The T score addresses these circumstances.

A T distribution looks like a standard normal (z) distribution, except that the mean is 50 and the standard deviation is 10. A z of $0 = $ a T score of 50. If $z = -1$, $T = 40$, and so on. Once z scores are calculated, it's easy to determine the equivalent value of T as follows:

$$T = z \cdot 10 + 50 \qquad\qquad 4.3$$

If a student's score on a nationally standardized test is reported as $z = 1.73$, what is the equivalent T value?

$T = z \cdot 10 + 50$

$T = 1.73(10) + 50$

$T = 67.30$

If a score is $-.84$, what is the equivalent T value?

$T = z \cdot 10 + 50$

$T = -.84(10) + 50$

$T = -8.4 + 50 = 41.6$

With a mean $= 50$, T scores are, perhaps, more comfortable to educators and to parents. Except in the most extreme situations, the T distribution eliminates the possibility of a negative score. To see how T, z, and the other standard scores covered here compare, consider Figure 4.5 where they are all presented in reference to the same normal distribution.

The Normal Curve Equivalent

Like T scores, *normal curve equivalent (NCE)* scores use $M = 50$, but *NCE* scores are also connected to percentile scores. We noted earlier that percentile scores aren't equal interval scores and, therefore, aren't among the standard scores, but *in normal distributions* one can predict where particular percentile scores will occur. This is a key to understanding *NCE* scores that equate to some percentile scores in a normal distribution. An *NCE* score of 1 occurs at the same point as a percentile rank of 1 in a normal distribution, and an *NCE* of 99 occurs at the same point as the 99th percentile. The middle of the distribution, which of course is the median or 50th percentile, is also $NCE = 50$. These relationships occur because of the *NCE* standard deviation, which is a rather odd-sounding $s = 21.06$. Beyond the 1st, 50th, and 99th, *NCE* scores do not occur at the same point as the numerically same percentile ranks.

With a mean of 50 and scores from 1 to 99, *NCE* values sound like common scoring systems based on percentages. The 1 to 99 range of scores was scaled to cover that portion of the distribution where scores are most likely to occur. For example, recall that the interval between -2 and $+2$ standard deviations includes about 95% of a normal distribution. In the *NCE* distribution that corresponds to $50 - (2 \times 21.06)$ and $50 + (2 \times 21.06)$ or the range from about 8 to 92 (see Figure 4.5).

Because we know the mean and standard deviation of *NCE* scores, we can calculate *NCE* scores from z scores, just as we did for T.

Figure 4.5 Standard Scores, Percentile Scores, and the Normal Distribution

	2.15%	13.59%	34.13%	34.13%	13.59%	2.15%	

s

−3	−2	−1	0	1	2	3

z

−3	−2	−1	0	1	2	3

T

20	30	40	50	60	70	80

NCE

1	10	20	30	40	50	60	70	80	90	99

stanine

1	2	3	4	5	6	7	8	9

percentile*

1	10	20	30	50	70	80	90	99

*Percentile scores are not standard scores, lacking equal intervals between data points, but they are frequently used to report standardized test data.

$$NCE = z(21.06) + 50 \qquad 4.4$$

The Standard Nine-Point Scale

Called "stanines" for short, these scores were originally based on percentile scores. Rather than discrete points, the stanines are 9 contiguous bands, and except for the first and last stanine, which must extend to include extremely low and extremely high scores, each stanine is ½ standard deviation in width. These 9 bands make up the abscissa of a normal distribution (see Figure 4.4). The stanines were positioned so that they include fixed percentages of scores in a normal distribution from the lowest 4% of scores in the 1st stanine to the highest scores 4% of scores in the 9th stanine (Table 4.1).

Table 4.1   The Percentage of Scores in a Particular Stanine

1st Stanine	2nd Stanine	3rd Stanine	4th Stanine	5th Stanine	6th Stanine	7th Stanine	8th Stanine	9th Stanine
4%	7%	12%	17%	20%	17%	12%	7%	4%

Regarding stanine scores, note that:

- The mean of the distribution occurs in the middle of the 5th stanine so that half of the interval is either side of the mean.
- Stanines 2 through 8 are each ½ standard deviation wide.
- The 1st stanine has no lower bound as it must include all possible scores from the 4th percentile down.
- Likewise, the 9th stanine has no upper bound. It includes all scores from the 96th percentile and higher.

Note that the 5th stanine has the largest percentage of scores. This is consistent with what we know about normal distributions; the greatest number of scores is in the middle of the distribution.

Like the other standard scores, stanines are equal-interval scores, although we'll qualify that a little for the 1st and 9th stanines. Recall that the percentile scores upon which stanines are based are not equal interval, however.

Much of the appeal of the stanine is that we're less likely to make an issue of inconsequential differences. Using z scores as an example, a parent or a teacher might be inclined to view the performance of someone who scores $z = -.15$ on aptitude test quite differently from another who scores $z = +.2$, but the difference is probably quite minor, and as it turns out, both scores are in the 5th stanine. Stanines keep us grounded by reminding us that some score differences don't matter very much.

As with the other standard scores, we can get from z to the stanine as follows:

$$\text{stanine} = 2 \cdot z + 5, \text{ rounded} \qquad 4.5$$

Perhaps someone scores 84 on a test of analytical ability for which the mean is 72.461 and the standard deviation is 5.683. What is the person's stanine score?

First, the z score:

$z = (x - M)/s$

$\quad = (84 - 72.461)/5.683$

$\quad = 2.030$

Next, the stanine score:

$\text{stanine} = 2 \cdot z + 5$

$= 2 (2.030) + 5$

$= 9.060, \text{ rounded} = 9\text{th}$

Someone who scores 84 on this test of analytical ability scores in the highest stanine, the 9th.

The stanine's advantage is also its weakness. Although we might be less likely to read too much into minor raw score differences, in order to accomplish this we must sacrifice some precision. Look back at Table 4.1, which displays the percentile scores in a given stanine. Note that in a normal distribution, scores at the 40th percentile (the upper bound of the 4th stanine) and the 41st percentile (the lower bound of the 5th stanine) occur in separate stanines. Conversely, all scores from the 41st to the 60th percentiles occur in the same stanine, the 5th. The difference between scores in different stanines may be smaller than the difference between scores in the same stanine.

Another Example

A test of mechanical aptitude has been designed for industrial arts students. For the population, $\mu = 17.375$ and $\sigma = 2.450$.

1. What is the z score for someone who scores 22 on the test?

    $z = (x - \mu)/\sigma$

    $z_{22} = (22 - 17.375))/2.450 = 1.888$

2. What is the equivalent T score?

    $T = z \cdot 10 + 50$

    $= 1.888(10) + 50 = 68.88$

3. What is the equivalent NCE score?

    $NCE = z \cdot 21.06 + 50$

    $= 1.888(21.06) + 50 = 89.761$

4. What is the equivalent stanine?

    stanine $= 2 \cdot z + 5$

    $= 2 (1.888) + 5$

    $= 8.776$, rounded $= $ 9th stanine

An initial test score of 22 on a test with mean $= 17.375$ and standard deviation $= 2.450$ is equivalent to a z score of 1.888, a T score of 68.88, an NCE score of 89.761, and the 9th stanine.

The Nonstandard Grade Equivalent Score

The grade equivalent score isn't a standard score although it's a very common reporting tool. Read many score reports from an educational testing agency or a state department of education and one encounters something like "5.3" for a reading score. Instructions often urge one to interpret such a score to mean that the reader is performing at the fifth-grade, third-month level—it's interpretation suggesting a precision the score can't deliver. They imply that those analyzing the test data have precise measures of the typical reading performance for any month in any grade for a student performing at grade level.

If a test is administered to third-grade students and one of those students scores 5.3, *on this third-grade test*, technically what that means is that if a group of typical fifth-grade students in their third month took the test, this student's score would be their average, but that's a far cry from presuming that the student is reading on a fifth-grade level. Remember, it's a third-grade test. Furthermore, it would be hugely expensive to administer a test to enough different samples of students that one could equate with exactness a particular score with a precise age, down to the month. Grade equivalent scores *will* provide an estimate of whether a student is generally performing above or below grade level, but *they shouldn't be treated as placement scores*. Their format usually suggests an exaggerated level of precision.

Standard Scores With Specified Characteristics

Our discussion of *z, T, NCE,* and stanine scores really suggests that any distribution can be manipulated so that it has preselected values for its mean and standard deviation. To do so is to produce a ***modified standard score*** (*MSS*). Actually, any set of scores can be adjusted so that they have a predetermined mean and standard deviation. Working from the *z* score, the formula for a modified standard score follows the pattern used with the other standard scores. It is:

■ A **modified standard score** is a score created so that it has a prespecified mean and standard deviation.

$$MSS = s_{spec} \cdot z + M_{spec} \qquad\qquad 4.6$$

Where,

MSS is the modified standard score

s_{spec} = the standard deviation specified for the modified standard score

M_{spec} = the mean specified for the modified standard score

Perhaps the junior high school mathematics instructors in a school district collaborate to create a benchmark math test. They recognize that the test and the individual items will need to be updated from time to time, but they wish for the instrument to have constant characteristics. They decide to create a test with a mean of 25 and a standard deviation of 5. That makes M_{spec} = 25 and s_{spec} = 5.

The process is to

- Transform each of the students' scores into z scores, then
- Perform the second transformation so that M_{spec} = 25 and s_{spec} = 5.

For example, a particular student scores 73 on the test that, for all students for the year, has M = 75 and s = 7.450.

First the z score.

$$z = (x - M)/s$$

$$= (73 - 75)/7.450$$

$$= -.268$$

Now, to alter the mean and standard deviation to the specified values:

$$MSS = s_{spec} \cdot z + M_{spec}$$

$$= 5(-.268) + 25$$

$$= 23.658$$

In a distribution standardized so that M = 25 and s = 5, the student's score is 23.658. By taking this approach, individual items can be modified slightly from year to year, but the mean and standard deviations will remain constant—25 and 5, respectively in this case.

Is this cool or what? *You* get to specify what the mean and standard deviation will be in the distribution. This process allows major test developers to have constant characteristics for their tests even as the particular instruments are revised from time to time. For many years, the SAT tests administered for college and university admission have had means and standard deviations of 500 and 100, respectively. Several of the major intelligence tests maintain means of 100 and standard deviations of 15. One can do likewise for a measure given in a classroom, a district, a county, in spite of the fact that the instrument may change modestly from time to time.

Another Example

A school district has contracted with a testing agency for a "progress assessment" (PA), which district officials use as a gauge of what to expect when students take state-mandated tests. The contract calls for the agency to make improvements to the test from year to year, but the district officials wish to maintain a mean of 50 and a standard deviation of 15 so $M_{spec} = 50$ and $s_{spec} = 15$. By taking this approach, individual items can be modified slightly from year to year, but the mean and variability measures will remain constant. The process is to

  a. transform each of the students' scores into z scores, and then

  b. perform the second transformation, so that $M_{spec} = 50$ and $s_{spec} = 15$.

For example, a particular student scores 73 on the test that, for all students for the year, has $M = 75$ and $s = 7.450$.
First the z score:

$$z = (x - M)/s$$
$$= (73 - 75)/7.450$$
$$= -.268$$

Now, to alter the mean and standard deviation to the specified values

$$MSS = s_{spec} \cdot z + M_{spec}$$
$$= 15(-.268) + 50$$
$$= 45.980$$

In a distribution standardized so that $M = 50$ and $s = 15$, the student's score is 45.980.

SUMMARY

Normal distributions certainly aren't always the case in data analysis. A lack of normality is common enough that different analytic procedures exist for just such contingencies, and we'll examine what are called nonparametric procedures later in the book. Happily, however, many of the things educators must measure and analyze *are* normally distributed in populations.

   The characteristics of normal distributions are known well enough that the educator can make predictions with some confidence about what to expect in future distributions, which scores are most likely to occur, and what the probability is of scoring in a specified area. This is what allowed Ms. Washington to answer the questions she had about the students she was helping with college admissions.

The business of reporting, interpreting, and analyzing performance is simplified with the use of standard scores. The z scores, T scores, stanines, and *NCE* scores that we reviewed here have descriptive statistics that vary some, but they also have a great deal in common. Their intervals are all based on the standard deviation of the scores in the distribution, which permits one to derive one standard score from another, but it is the z score that is used most commonly in statistical analysis.

Standard scores are normative scores. A particular score indicates where that individual is positioned relative to all of the others who were also measured. Once a raw score is transformed into a standard score, besides making the predictions and probability statements that we made using z scores, one can make direct comparisons of scores from distributions with very different descriptive characteristics.

As valuable as z scores are for both conceptual and practical reasons, we're usually more interested in the performance of groups than of individuals. In the next chapter we'll apply what we have learned about z to groups and begin to make references to that touchstone of quantitative analysis "statistical significance." If you can calculate a z score and determine the probability of scoring below, or above, or between two points, you'll be fine with the next chapter. If those topics seem not quite settled in your imagination, work the examples again, look at the explanations, and work through the exercises at the end of the chapter (yes, *all* of them). You're going to be fine!

EXERCISES

1. The large urban school district creates a benchmark spelling test for sixth-grade students. A random sample of scores yields the following: 20, 22, 23, 23, 25, 28, 28, 29, 29, 32, 33, 35, 36, 39, 42. For the district as a whole, determine the percentage of the distribution
   a. lower than 34?
   b. lower than 26?
   c. between 30 and 38?

2. The Reasoning Ability Test (RAT) has $\mu = 38.00$ and $\sigma = 4.50$.
   a. What is the z score for someone with RAT = 33?
   b. What is the z score for someone with RAT = 39?
   c. What proportion of scores will occur between scores of 33 and 39?
   d. What proportion will occur above RAT = 40?

3. For a particular individual, we have RAT = 41, with group characteristics, $M = 38.00$ and $s = 4.50$. For the same person we have Comprehensive Aptitude Test (CAT) score of 72, with $M = 64.00$ and $s = 7.75$. According to these test scores, which is the stronger measure, reasoning, or computation ability?

4. The ANxiety General Stress Test (ANGST, for short) has been developed as a measure of psychological stress for classroom teachers. For a random sample of teachers the scores are as follows: 47, 49, 53, 53, 54, 58, 61, 64, 75, 81:

a. What is the z score equivalent of 81?
b. What is the probability that someone selected at random will score 81 or lower?
c. Why is that probability not 100%, since 81 is the highest group in the sample?

5. What are the equivalent T scores for the person in item 3 who had RAT = 41 and CAT = 72?

6. Using the data from item 4, what are the equivalent z, T, NCE, and stanine scores for someone with ANGST = 78?

7. If the data in item 4 represented a normal distribution, what is the probability of each of the following ANGST scores?

a. lower than 50
b. higher than 65
c. between 40 and 85

8. For any normal distribution of scores, what percentage of scores will fall between the following z scores?

a. z = −.5 and z = .5
b. z = −1.96 and z = 1.96
c. z = 1.0 and z = 2.0
d. z = −2.0 and z = −3.0

9. What percentage of z scores will occur in the following ranges?
a. Outside (either side) of the range z = −1.0 to z = 1.0
b. Outside (either side) of the range z = 1.17 to z = 2.15
c. Outside (either side) of the range z = −1.35 to z = −.35

10. What is it that sets percentile rankings apart from z, T, NCE, and stanine scores?

11. An industrial arts instructor has designed a test of mechanical aptitude (MechA) and having investigated its properties, finds that students with scores lower than 8 tend to do poorly in the class. Those with scores higher than 12 excel. Administering it to a random sample of industrial arts students reveals the following scores: 7, 5, 9, 13, 12, 10, 14, 10, 11, 10.

a. What percentage of the distribution will fall in the area of the distribution expected to do poorly?
b. What percentage of the distribution will fall in the area of the distribution expected to excel?
c. A score of 12 occurs at what percentile?

12. An associate superintendent for personnel has gathered data on the ages of area principals in an effort to anticipate retirements. She finds the following ages: 38, 39, 43, 45, 45, 47, 49, 53, 55, 56, 56, 59. For an age of 53:

a. What is the z score equivalent?
b. What is the T score equivalent?
c. What is the NCE equivalent?
d. What is the stanine equivalent?

13. A schoolwide vocabulary test for fifth-grade students yields the following scores for a random sample: 14, 16, 17, 17, 18, 21, 21, 24, 25, 26. If the intent is to maintain $M_{spec} = 20$ and $s_{spec} = 2.50$ on the test, what are the modified standard scores for students who score 15 and 22?

REFERENCE

Anastasi, A. (1976). *Psychological testing* (4th ed.). New York: Macmillan Publishing.

THE FORMULAE AND THEIR SYMBOLS

Formula 4.1: $z = z = \dfrac{x - M}{s}$

This is the formula for transforming "raw" scores into z scores, giving them a mean of zero and a standard deviation of one; x is the score to be transformed and M and s are the mean and standard deviation of the group of scores.

Formula 4.2: $z = z = \dfrac{x - \mu}{\sigma}$

If instead of a sample there are population data involved, this is the z score formula. The μ and σ are the mean and standard deviation, respectively, of the population of scores.

Formula 4.3: $T = z \cdot 10 + 50$

The T transformation converts scores from a z distribution into one where $M = 50$ and $s = 10$.

Formula 4.4: $NCE = z \cdot 21.06 + 50$

This formula is the *NCE* transformation from z. In the *NCE* distribution, scores range from 1 to 99; $M = 50$ and $s = 21.06$.

Formula 4.5: stanine $= 2 \cdot z + 5$, rounded

This is the stanine, or "standard nine-point scale" transformation from z.

Formula 4.6: $MSS = s_{spec} \cdot z + M_{spec}$

The modified standard score (MSS) transforms z scores into distributions with any specified mean (M_{spec}) and standard deviation (s_{spec}).

STUDENT STUDY SITE

Visit the Student Study Site at **www.sagepub.com/tanner** for additional learning tools.

PART III

Examining Differences

Chapter 5

Probability and the Normal Distribution

THE PROBLEM: HOW TO DETERMINE WHEN A DIFFERENCE IS SIGNIFICANT

Mr. Forsythe has spent several years at a low-performing elementary school. Three years ago, frustrated with poor performance, he organized educators and parents who would reform mathematics instruction and boost test scores. With some initial inertia overcome, the team feel that the time has come to compare their students with those in the district as a whole. Mr. Forsyth wonders how much difference between his students and those in the rest of the district will constitute a "significant" difference. Further, he wonders how large his sample must be in order to have a reasonable picture of how all students are performing.

QUESTIONS AND ANSWERS

❑ How does one determine whether a sample is characteristic of a population?

How much difference is a "significant" difference? These questions will bring us to the distribution of sample means and the z test.

❑ How large must the sample be to represent the population with fidelity?

The answer depends upon how confident we want to be of the results, but we'll explore a procedure for determining needed sample size.

To this point we have learned to use a variety of statistics to describe data, to organize them for presentation, and to transform them into scores that conform to distributions with specified means and standard deviations. We've also determined what data characteristics indicate normality. These represent no small accomplishment in the (statistical) pilgrim's progress. As important as they are for those purposes, they're also components of procedures that will let us answer Mr. Forsythe's questions.

A LITTLE REVIEW

In Chapter 4, we found that when a characteristic is normally distributed, we can calculate z scores (Formula 4.1: $z = (x - M)/s$), consult Appendix Table A, and predict how likely it is that individuals will score in specified domains. The normality requirement is important. There's no making "silk purses out of sow's ears" here. The z transformation doesn't "normalize" scores, but if the distribution is normal to begin with, one can use the z scores to determine how likely it is to score below this point, between those two points, and so on.

Recall that the z score is a ratio of the difference between the raw score and the mean of the group (in the numerator) to the standard deviation of the group (in the denominator). As a matter of interpretation, a score of $z = 1.25$ is 1.25 standard deviations above the mean. Our Table A is organized accordingly. The z values reflect the percentage of the distribution from a particular value of z to the mean of the distribution.

The reason for reminding us of our ground is that in this chapter, we'll do for groups what we did for individuals in Chapter 4. We want to be able to determine how likely it is that a *group* will score in a particular domain of the distribution, or between two points, and so on. The procedure for these analyses will be our first statistical test, the **z test**. It's going to look like the z score transformation used in Chapter 4, and also like the one-sample *t*-test that we'll use in Chapter 6, so it's important that we're comfortable with the thinking involved.

THE DISTRIBUTION OF SAMPLE MEANS

■ The **distribution of sample means** is a population based on the means of samples rather than on individual scores. It allows one to determine whether a particular sample is likely to have been drawn from the specified population, which is the z test.

For the sake of illustration, assume that Mr. Forsythe's district is a large suburban school district and that he has mathematics scores for all sixth-grade students in the district. If he had the inclination and the time, he could create from that population, a population based on the means of samples from that population. From the population of sixth-grade students he could randomly select 30 students (or some other sample of reasonable size), determine the mean math score for the group, and then plot the mean in a frequency distribution. If this were done until the population was exhausted, the result would still be a population frequency distribution, but one based on *mean* scores rather than individual scores. It's called a **distribution of sample means**, or the sampling distribution of means, and for reasons we'll discuss in a moment its data are normal.

Don't let the fact that we don't sample one student at a time diminish the fact that this is still a population. All a population requires is all possible members. Whether they're represented as individual (*x*) values or in group means (*M*) is unrelated to whether it's a population.

The Central Limit Theorem

Part of the logic behind creating a population based on sample means is the desire to evaluate groups rather than individuals, but there's another reason. Recall that using Table A to make probability statements about the likelihood of particular outcomes is possible because all normal distributions are unimodal, symmetrical, and so on. Table A is appropriate only when data are normal. However, *when a population is created with sample means as the distribution of sample means is, the resulting population will be normal even if the original population of individual scores was not.* This principle is according to **the central limit theorem**.

    Are you skeptical? In a preliminary sort of way we can illustrate the workings of the central limit theorem. Perhaps there's a remedial spelling class for which the entire population consists of 6 students. They each take a test on which there are 10 spelling words, and their scores range from 2 though 7, each student with a different score. Figure 5.1 is a bar chart of the frequency of their scores:

■ The **central limit theorem:** A population of sample means will be normal, even if the distribution of individual scores wasn't.

Figure 5.1   A Frequency Chart for the Scores 2 Through 7

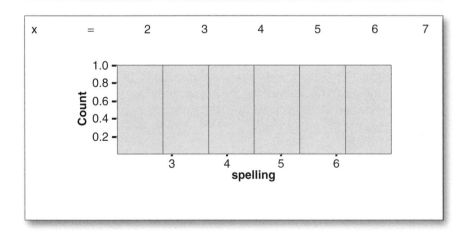

Doesn't reflect much of a normal curve, does it? But from those individual scores, let's create a distribution of sample means. If we:

- draw samples of *two* scores at a time,
- "sample with replacement," which means that each time a score is selected it is replaced before the second score in the pair is selected so that it's possible to select the same score twice,
- calculate the 21 possible mean scores,
- and then plot the means,

we begin to see, as Diekoff (1992) demonstrated, how a distribution of sample means differs from a raw score distribution. The list of 21 possible mean score combinations is the content of Table 5.1.

Table 5.1 illustrates that some mean scores can be repeated and some can occur only once. When sampling "with replacement," a mean of 2.0 can occur only one way, of course. It comes from drawing a 2, replacing it and then drawing the 2 again. Likewise, there is only one possibility of selecting numbers that result in means of 2.5, 6.5, or 7.0. But there are two possibilities of means of 3.0, 3.5, 5.5, and 6.0, and three possibilities that drawing two numbers would result in means of 4.0, 4.5, or 5.0. If we create another bar chart to represent the frequencies with which the mean scores in Table 5.1 can occur, the result is Figure 5.2.

This SPSS graph illustrates the sort of frequency distribution that can occur when some scores are more likely than others. It makes it clear, for example, that even when sampling with replacement, the most extreme mean scores are also the least likely to occur, and that the mean scores that have the middle-

Table 5.1   Sampling With Replacement: All Possible Combinations of 2 Scores for the Numbers 2 Through 7

2, 2	3, 3	4, 4	5, 5	6, 6	7, 7
2, 3	3, 4	4, 5	5, 6	6, 7	
2, 4	3, 5	4, 6	5, 7		
2, 5	3, 6	4, 7			
2, 6	3, 7				
2, 7					

Figure 5.2 A Frequency Distribution of the Means of All Possible Pairs of Scores, 2–7

The mean scores for all possible pairs are as follows:

M =   2.0   2.5   3.0   3.5   4.0   4.5   5.0   5.5   6.0   6.5   7.0

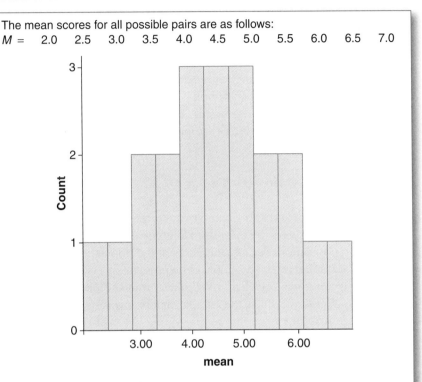

(Note. To create this figure in SPSS, create a data file with one variable for the first score and a second for the second score. Enter the data and then for each pair of scores, have SPSS calculate the mean. The commands for doing this in the menu line across the top are as follows:

Transform→Compute

After which one must type in a name for the "Target Variable." I've called it "mean." In the box labeled "Numeric Expression" indicate that the mean is to be calculated by adding the values for the other two variables together and dividing the result by 2.

To create the histogram, then, the commands are:
Graphs→Interactive→Histogram

The default for the vertical (y) axis indicates "count," which is fine. For the horizontal (x) axis, click and drag "mean."

Click the "Histogram" tab at the top, and click the "Number of intervals" box. Indicate 11 since there are 11 different possible mean scores ranging from 2.0–7.0. Click "OK."

most values tend to be the most common. There are simply more possibilities for middle-of-the-distribution scores than there are for extreme scores. Clearly, the distribution of means from samples of $n = 2$ (Figure 5.2) has a different look than the distribution of the six raw scores (Figure 5.1).

It's a stretch to call the distribution in Figure 5.2 normal, but it's certainly closer than the distribution in Figure 5.1. This is in spite of the fact that this distribution of sample means is based on *very* small samples. With a population of $N = 6$, we're quite restricted in terms of possible sample sizes. With larger populations, larger samples can be used, and the larger the samples upon which the mean scores are based, say $n = 30+$, the more normal the resulting distribution of sample means will be.

Sampling Error and the Law of Large Numbers

■ **Sampling error** is the difference between characteristics of the sample and those of the population.

Because they're more accessible, samples are often used for what they reveal about populations. This is the essence of inferential statistics. A sample is any subset of the population. Because elements of the population are missing in the sample, it can never exactly emulate the population's characteristics, but if a sample is randomly selected, it will differ from the population only by chance. The *degree* to which the sample differs from the population is a measure of **sampling error**.

Note that sampling error doesn't mean that there was an error in the usual sense of making a mistake. It just means that there is some variation between the sample and the population. As the size of a random sample increases, the probability that sample characteristics will differ substantially from the population diminishes. The fact that sampling error is smallest when random samples are largest is related to another fundamental theorem of probability called the **law of large numbers**. This "law" outlines one of the bedrock principles in statistical analysis: Error resulting from random variability diminishes as sample size increases. It's a statement of the obvious, but other things equal, large samples tend to be more like the population than small samples.

■ The **law of large numbers** indicates that error diminishes as sample size increases.

Sampling error is minimized when the scores that make up the sample have values similar to the population—the means are similar, for example. Conversely, error increases when cases with extreme scores are selected out of proportion to their representation in the population.

The Effect of Extreme Scores

When a college's institutional researcher wants to determine how a particular population of students is performing, he or she probably doesn't sample with replacement as we did to create Figure 5.2. It's much simpler to just sample without replacement and not return an individual to the population before selecting the next subject. Returning to our population of 6, when sampling without replacement, what is the chance of selecting any sample of $n = 2$ for which $M = 2$, or $M = 7$. Of course it's zero. Since there is only one of each, if either 2 or 7 is randomly selected, whatever its companion number is will moderate the value of M. This just reminds us that values of 2 or 7 are possible when selecting $n = 1$, but not if $n = 2$; individual scores tend to be more extreme than sample means. The effect of extreme scores is minimized when groups are selected. The larger the group size, the more modest the impact that outliers have on the shape of the distribution.

DESCRIBING THE DISTRIBUTION OF SAMPLE MEANS

In Chapter 4, we used Greek symbols to designate the characteristics of populations. We called them "parameters" and used μ as the symbol for the parameter mean of a population. Actually, μ represents the mean of a population based on *individual* scores. In the distribution of sample means, the mean of the population is actually a "mean of sample means" rather than a mean of individual scores. We indicate it as μ_M.

How does μ compare to μ_M? We can check by comparing (a) the mean of our six original scores to (b) the mean of all 21 possible pairs of scores in Table 5.1.

a. $(2 + 3 + 4 + 5 + 6 + 7)/6 = \mathbf{4.5}$

b. $(2 + 2.5 + 3 + 3.5 + 4 + 4.5 + 3 + 3.5 + 4 + 4.5 + 5 + 4 + 4.5 + 5 + 5.5 + 5 + 5.5 + 6 + 6 + 6.5 + 7)/21 = \mathbf{4.5}$

> ■ The **standard error of the mean** is a measure of variability in the distribution of sample means. It is the standard deviation of all the sample means that constitute the distribution of sample means.

As it turns out, the value of the mean of the distribution of individual scores will have the same value as the mean of the distribution of sample means. That is, $\mu = \mu_M$. Whether it's the mean of a population of individual scores or the mean of a distribution of sample means doesn't affect the value.

What about variability? Calculating the standard deviations of both sets of scores allows us to continue the comparison. Just as σ indicated the standard deviation of all individual scores in a population, appending M as a subscript to σ, gives us σ_M, formally the **standard error of the mean**, which gauges variability in the distribution of sample means. Comparing σ with σ_M is quite revealing.

First σ, the standard deviation of the original raw scores:

For 2, 3, 4, 5, 6, 7

$\sigma = \mathbf{1.708}$ (check this one—the value of practice and so on, but beware of the adjustment to a population standard deviation. The $n - 1$ in the denominator of the formula becomes N since these are population data.)

Now σ_M, the standard deviation of the mean scores, or standard error of the mean:

2, 2.5, 3, 3.5, 4, 4.5, 3, 3.5, 4, 4.5, 5, 4, 4.5, 5, 5.5, 5, 5.5, 6, 6, 6.5, 7

$\sigma_M = \mathbf{1.291}$ (you can trust your author on this one)

Plainly, individual scores vary more than mean scores. Although $\mu = \mu_M$, $\sigma \neq \sigma_M$, and this isn't surprising. We already noted that extreme scores have a greater impact on variability when treated as individuals than they do when they are components of a sample mean, so evidence that $\sigma > \sigma_M$ isn't news.

When creating samples by "sampling without replacement" (that is, not replacing the score chosen before choosing the next score), and using relatively large sample sizes, of course some of the most extreme scores that occur with individuals aren't possible as group means.

Measuring variability by calculating the standard deviation of the sample means was to make a point about how variability values compare. When populations are larger, this approach is impractical and below there's a less tedious way to determine σ_M.

Be a little careful with the language we use with "the standard error of the mean." In subsequent chapters, we'll calculate multiple "standard error" values. In statistics, the *standard* errors are, like standard deviation, measures of score deviation. The standard error of the mean is a gauge of how much the means of individual samples in the distribution of sample means vary from μ_M. Perhaps the following will be helpful:

The Reference Group	Mean	Variability Measure
A sample:	M	s
A population of individual scores:	μ	σ
The distribution of sample means:	μ_M	σ_M

THE *z* TEST

With the parameters that indicate central tendency and variability in the distribution of sample means, we're ready for the z test. The formula looks much like the z score transformation from Chapter 4:

$$z = \frac{(M - \mu_m)}{\sigma_m}$$

5.1

SOURCE: Created by Suzanna Nielson.

"And I pledge a retreat from normality. I'll work for salary distributions with negative skew!"

Where,

z = the test value

M = the sample mean

μ_M = the mean of the distribution of sample means

σ_M = the standard error of the mean

Deriving the Values for the *z* test

What we needed for z scores we could calculate from the data. For the z test, all the sample yields is M. Because the means of populations (μ) are often published, and $\mu = \mu_M$, μ_M isn't too difficult to determine, but outside the statistical community, people don't deal often with σ_m. Where does that leave Mr. Forsythe? As it turns out,

$$\sigma_m = \frac{\sigma}{\sqrt{N}}$$

5.2

Where,

σ_M = the standard error of the mean

σ = the population standard deviation

N = the number in the group

If the population standard deviation (σ) is available, the standard error of the mean (σ_m) can be calculated from sample data.

Calculating the z test

Perhaps parents are interested in how well a group of English language (EL) learners in Mr. Forsythe's class perform in mathematics when there is a heavy emphasis on word problems. For an instrument designed by the district the mean is 50 (the value of μ and therefore μ_M) and the standard deviation for students in this particular grade throughout the district (σ) is 11.874. A sample of EL students has the following scores:

31, 33, 36, 36, 38, 41, 43, 48, 54, 55

What is the probability that a group selected at random will perform at or below the level of these EL students?

1. Verify from the sample that $M = 41.50$

2. Since $\sigma = 11.874$ and $\sigma_m = \frac{\sigma}{\sqrt{N}}, = \frac{11.874}{\sqrt{10}} = 3.755$

3. $z = \frac{(M - \mu_m)}{\sigma_m} = \frac{(41.5 - 50)}{3.755} = -2.264$

4. The table value for $z = -2.264$ is 48.81 indicating that in a normal distribution (which is what we have with the distribution of sample means), 48.81% of the population will occur between 41.50 and the mean of the population, 50.

5. By subtraction we can determine that 50 − 48.81 = 1.19% of the population will occur *below* this point.

6. Dividing the percentage by 100 indicates the probability of scoring in this range. In this case, 1.19/100 = .0119 and with rounding, $p = .012$.

Compared with the population of all students, Mr. Forsythe's sample is a very low-performing group (which might be expected of EL students dealing with a heavily text-based test). The z test makes the same analysis available for groups that the z score provides for individuals.

Although the z score is important for what it reveals about individuals, because they can vary so widely individual performances often shed little light on what is occurring in the group as a whole. The z test examines the relative performance of the group.

REPRESENTATIVENESS AND STATISTICAL SIGNIFICANCE

The z test offers another bonus. It allows one to judge what is representative. By comparing the mean of the sample (M) with the mean of some known population (μ_M) in the numerator of the test statistic, with Table A we have what we need to determine whether the population represented by the sample is significantly different from the population to which it is compared.

One of Mr. Forsythe's questions at the beginning of the chapter is whether students in a low-performing elementary school have made significant progress. The initial problem was that students at this school were performing at a lower level than students elsewhere in the district. As such, they originally represented a population functioning at a lower level than the rest of the students. After 3 years of the special mathematics curriculum, how do they compare?

For a district test the mean (and also μ_M) = 35.450, and the standard deviation (σ) = 7.943. A random sample of Mr. Forsythe's students have the following scores:

23

26

29

32

33

34

35

35

36

37

37

39

1. Verify that $M = 33.000$ and that $\sigma_M = \dfrac{7.943}{\sqrt{12}} = 2.293$

2. $z = \dfrac{(M - \mu_m)}{\sigma_m} = \dfrac{33 - 35.450}{2.293} = \mathbf{-1.068}$

Obviously, there is a difference between the two means and furthermore, a negative z indicates that the mean of the sample is lower than the mean of the population. However, some of the difference is probably just sampling error. At what point is the difference so great that sampling error no longer plausibly explains it? When is the difference between sample and population "significant"?

The primary application for the z test is to examine whether the sample in question is likely to be one of the samples making up the distribution of sample means for which μ_M is the mean. When the sample *is* representative, any difference between M and μ_M can be attributed to sampling error.

■ **Statistically significant** means that an outcome isn't likely to have occurred by chance.

But sometimes the differences are too great to be explained by sampling error. When that occurs the sample must belong to some population *other* than the one with which it is compared. That's the point at which the difference is **statistically significant,** which begs the question, where is that point?

"Statistical significance" is a term coined by Ronald Fisher (later when he was knighted, *Sir* Ronald) whose work we'll examine more closely in Chapter 7. One of Fisher's many contributions is a standard for determining when something is statistically significant. He suggested that when an outcome occurs among the most probable 95% of outcomes, it should be considered characteristic of those outcomes, or *not* statistically significant. Correspondingly, the most extreme 5% of outcomes are so improbable that they should be considered statistically significant, or *not* representative. Don't let the negatives be confusing:

not statistically significant = representative = a random occurrence

statistically significant = not representative = a nonrandom outcome

So just to repeat, when a difference occurs among the 95% of most likely outcomes, it is *not* statistically significant. In a z test, when a sample *is* statistically significant it means that there is something at work besides sampling variability. The sample is different enough that it likely represents some population other than the one with which it is being compared.

Back to the Gaussian Distribution

How do we know what outcomes are the most characteristic 95%? Appendix Table A will help us. Recall that the way the table is formatted one can determine the percentage of a normal distribution occurring between any value of z and the mean of the distribution, whether μ or μ_M. Note the following:

- Because normal distributions are symmetrical, Table A provides the values for only half of the distribution because the percentage between $z = -1$ and the mean, and $z = +1$ and the mean are the same.
- The middle 95% of the distribution divided in half leaves 47.5% on either side of the distribution.
- The value of z for 47.5% of the distribution between that point and the mean will indicate the point at which the difference can no longer be explained by sampling variability.

Scanning Table A for 47.5% and then working backward to the corresponding value of z reveals . . . 1.96! This is a number worth remembering. Anytime the absolute value (the value without regard to the sign) of $z = 1.96$, or greater, by Fisher's 95% criterion, the result is statistically significant. When a z test yields a z value less than 1.96, the difference can be explained by sampling variability; such a result isn't statistically significant.

Mr. Forsythe's Question

Looking back at the data for Mr. Forsythe's students, we found that $z = -1.068$. If we round that value to $z = -1.07$ and check Table A, we find that such a

z value includes 35.77% of the distribution between that point and the mean. The 35.77% on either side of the distribution (35.77 × 2 = 71.54%) is well within the most typical 95% of outcomes. This group is not significantly different from the population.

This is actually the longer road to the statistical decision because we just noted that any z value less than +/–1.96 indicates that the sample isn't statistically significant. The population represented by the sample—the fourth graders from the low-performing school—has a mean not significantly different from the population with which it was compared—all fourth graders in the district.

Did the sample group appear to perform less well than the population? Yes, they had a lower mean score, but a difference ($z = -1.068$) could reflect sampling error. Whoever collected the data may have just randomly selected 12 students who are predominantly from the lower half of the distribution.

Is this good news or bad? From the point of view of the people connected with Mr. Forsythe's school, it is very good news. Students who have historically been low performers are now scoring at a level that isn't significantly different from students in the district as a whole. There appears to have been important progress. The scores for the students in the sample have improved relative to their predecessors at this school.

Another Example

A group of juniors have just taken the SAT in anticipation of college admissions. Published data indicate that population mean (μ) and standard deviation (σ) for the SAT-M are 500 and 100, respectively. Since $\mu = \mu_M$, μ_M will also be 500, of course. Eight students take the verbal section of the test and score as follows:

450, 475, 530, 550, 580, 600, 610, 630.

Are they characteristic of the population of all who take the SAT?

1. Verify that $n = 8$ and calculate the standard error of the mean.

$$\sigma_m = \frac{\sigma}{\sqrt{n}} = \frac{100}{\sqrt{8}} = 35.355$$

2. Calculate the mean of the sample

Verify that $M = 553.125$

3. Calculate the z test value

$$z = \frac{(M - \mu_m)}{\sigma_m} = \frac{553.125 - 500}{35.355} = \mathbf{1.503}$$

Comparing the sample mean with the population mean indicates that these eight students did better than the national average, but is the difference significant? At $z = 1.503$ (less than 1.96), the result is *not* significantly different from the population. These students are characteristic of the population of all students taking the SAT-M.

Another Example

A superintendent in a large urban school district wonders whether a coaching program will affect students' performance. She arranges for an outstanding teacher to work with a newly hired teacher. On a national test for ninth-grade students, the mean is 55.683 with a standard deviation of 16.943. After 16 weeks, the new teacher's students have these scores: 43, 49, 57, 59, 64, 66, 67, 67, 73, 79, 84, 88.

1. Verify that $M = 66.333$

2. Verify that $\sigma_M = 4.891$ ($16.943/\sqrt{12}$)

3. Calculate z

$$z = (M - \mu_m)/\sigma_m$$

$$z = (66.333 - 55.683)/4.891 = 2.177$$

By Fisher's standard, for whatever reason, the new teacher's students are performing significantly better than students in the nation as a whole. Note, by the way, that we can't be sure that it's coaching that's making the difference. Perhaps it's the new teacher's enthusiasm and creativity that's the explanation, or perhaps these are better-than-average students to begin with, but for whatever reason their performance on this test is significantly higher than the performance of students nationwide.

PROBABILITY, THE ALPHA LEVEL, AND DECISION ERRORS

Probability values (p) range from 0 to 1.0.

- Events that have a probability of $p = 0$ never occur.
- Events with $p = 1.0$ always happen.

We're interested in neither of those extremes. They're certainties that leave us nothing to analyze. Our domain is outcomes with probabilities between $p = 0$ and $p = 1.0$.

■ **Alpha level** is the probability of incorrectly determining a statistically significant result, a **type I error**.

In a distribution of outcomes from statistical testing, events that occur with $p = .05$ have an important place. They represent perhaps the most common standard for statistical significance. The significance standard also indicates what is called a test's **alpha (α) level**.

Recall that for the z test, a z value that is statistically significant indicates that the sample isn't representative of the particular population; it's beyond the middle 95% (by the most usual standard) of the population of all possible outcomes. But isn't that extreme 5% still part of the population? Won't some of those results declared significant actually represent the population in question, albeit the most extreme part of that population? The answer is, absolutely.

■ An **alpha error** occurs if when the null hypothesis is erroneously rejected. If further testing with new data indicates that the initial finding of statistical significance was in error, an alpha error occurred with that first test.

When that happens, one has committed what is called an **alpha error**. The standard adopted for determining statistical significance indicates the probability that such a decision error will occur. If the criterion for significance is the extreme 5% of the distribution, then $\alpha = .05$. The alpha level reminds us when a test result matches or exceeds the value indicating the middle 95% of the distribution, and the sample is declared to represent some different population, about 5 times in 100, we'll be wrong.

Statistical decisions are about probabilities, not certainties. Chances are that if $z = 1.96$ or larger, the sample *is* characteristic of some population other than the one with which it is compared, but occasionally the decision is an error. The test's alpha level defines the probability of making such an error. Also called **type I errors**, or also "false positives," they occur when further testing would reveal that what was thought to be a statistically significant result actually wasn't.

Perhaps a group of 10th-grade students is randomly selected and administered a standardized test of problem-solving ability. A z test compares their performance with the performance of all students nationally. If the calculated value of z is, say $z = 2.01$, it appears that according to the 95% criterion, the sample is performing significantly better than the population of all test-takers since +/− 2.01 excludes *less than 5%* of the distribution. Consider a number of reasons why a sample might perform better than the population generally, but still be a part of it:

- Maybe these students were lucky enough (granting them the benefit of the doubt) to have recently solved some of the very problems used in the test, but are otherwise typical 10th-grade students.
- Perhaps, although randomly selected, the sample was randomly drawn from what turned out to be the upper end of the distribution.
- Perhaps the students were lucky guessers.

If any of these explained the results, concluding that the sample of students belongs to some population other than typical 10th-grade students would be an alpha, or type I, error. The z value may suggest that the sample belongs to some other population, but if further testing with new data reveals that they aren't, we've committed an alpha (type I) error.

Every time an education researcher or analyst concludes that a result is statistically significant there is a chance that the conclusion is erroneous. The catch is that in the moment, there's no way to know whether an error is present. We know that errors occur, but we don't know precisely when.

So in summary, events which have a probability of occurrence of $p = .05$ are, by the most common standard, statistically significant. Such a standard excludes as characteristic of the population in question, events which occur only 5% of the time, or less. But some events in any normal population occur only rarely. Testing at $p = .05$, or any other p value, defines the likelihood of an alpha error. If one tests at $p = .05$, then α also $= .05$.

Decision Errors Continued

In the effort to have more certainty about results, there are some options. The first is to simply collect new data and run the analysis again. Consistent results reinforce the initial finding. Another alternative is to apply a more rigorous standard for statistical significance. Although adopting a .05 level for alpha error is common, it certainly isn't universal, and testing with alpha at .01, or .001 dramatically reduces the probability of type I errors. As the alpha value shrinks, the z value that one must meet in order to be considered significant grows so that at $\alpha = .01$, the probability of alpha error becomes 1/5th the error probability incurred when $\alpha = .05$. As alpha shrinks, the z value, indicating significance, grows. At $\alpha = .01$, $z = 2.58$ (or 2.57, but 2.58 is the value usually quoted). Although the probability of an alpha error can be whatever the analyst specifies before conducting the test, values of .05, .01, and .001 are probably most common.

If $\alpha = .001$, the potential for an alpha error is just 1 in 1,000! Why not always test at that level and all but eliminate the potential of alpha error? The answer is that alpha error has a companion. Just as one can declare a result to be statistically significant in error, one can also fail to detect a statistically significant result that is present. This constitutes a **type II or beta (β) error** (or yes, a "false negative"). In z testing one commits a beta error when the sample *does* represent a population different from the one to which it's compared, but the z value suggests that it doesn't. In this case the sample

■ A **type II** or **beta error** occurs when one incorrectly concludes that a result isn't statistically significant.

actually represents, for example, a population of remedial readers rather than the population of all sixth-grade students, and because the calculated value of z is less than 1.96, the difference isn't apparent.

In terms of beta or type II error, not all tests are created equal. A *powerful* test is one that detects significant results when they are present. Powerful tests have relatively few β errors. For example, such tests are more likely to find significant differences in the scores of 10th-grade honors students compared with other 10th-grade students than a less powerful test.

On the Horns of a Dilemma

Although the probability of a type I error is set at .05, .01, or whatever, there is no pre-established level for type II errors, but the probability of type I error affects the probability of type II errors. Including more of the most extreme parts of the distribution into what is considered characteristic of the population correspondingly makes it more likely that one will miss identifying a sample that actually represents some other population. If we diminish type I errors with a more rigorous standard, we increase the potential for type II errors so that to some degree we're obliged to "pick our poison." Which of the decision errors we opt for is based on which of alpha or beta error poses the greater threat.

If you're establishing a standard for certifying airline pilots or surgeons, the choice is fairly straightforward—test at a conservative alpha level and guard against type I error; we don't want to certify as competent someone who may not be. In fact, we're probably willing to exclude some who may be marginally competent to avoid turning loose on the public someone who isn't.

If you're the "education czar" responsible for certifying teachers, you lower the standard for certification to guard against type II error and make sure that no one who is competent is excluded. Conversely, if you insist on competency, you guard against type I error by raising the standard so that no one who is not competent is accidentally included. Someone has the chore of deciding which error poses the greater threat.

To sum up, the alpha value reminds us of the probability of a type I error. Indeed, because they indicate probability values, the level at which one conducts a test is often listed as a p value rather than an α value. It's a convention we'll follow from this point on in the book. Just remember that when a statistical test is conducted at $p = .05$, the potential for type I error, an alpha error, in the event of a statistically significant finding is .05.

WHO DECIDES? DETERMINING STATISTICAL SIGNIFICANCE

Rather than adopting preset standards for statistical significance, a statistics professor the author once had voiced a different view. His position was that what is significant depends upon circumstances and that to adopt .05, for example, is arbitrary. He argued that one ought to determine the probability that a calculated outcome could have occurred by chance and then let audiences make their own determinations about whether it is statistically significant.

This is more feasible than it once was. The statistical tables in textbooks can't indicate the probabilities for *all* possible outcomes, but statistical packages like SPSS calculate precisely the probability associated with any outcome. Professor Smith's approach was to leave the burden of deciding what is significant with the consumer.

We'll adopt a middle ground. When we do longhand calculations, we'll use the tables in the back of the book, which restrict us to testing at .05 or .01. When we do problems on SPSS, we'll make a statement about whether the result was statistically significant, but also note the exact probability that the value could have occurred by chance.

CONFIDENCE INTERVALS

For z tests, the issue is whether the sample mean is likely to represent the population with which it's compared. When z is statistically significant, the inference is that the mean of the population from which the sample was taken is different from the mean of the population with which it was compared. However, the z test doesn't reveal what the value of that other population mean is. This is where the **confidence interval** comes in.

When z is statistically significant, a range of values can be calculated around the sample mean (M) within which the population mean (μ_M) represented by M will occur with a specified probability. In the confidence interval:

- M provides a "point estimate" of the value of the new population, μ_M.
- The confidence interval provides a range of values within which the mean of the distribution represented by M will probably occur.

■ **Confidence intervals** for z are intervals within which the population mean represented by a sample will probably occur.

Calculating the Confidence Interval

A sample mean (M) provides one estimate of the mean of the population from which it comes (μ_M), but with all we know about sampling error, even large samples are sometimes poor estimates. Confidence intervals indicate how precisely M estimates μ_M, by indicating a range of values within which μ_M is likely to occur. The formula for a confidence interval for a significant value of z is,

$$CI = +/-z(\sigma_M) + M \qquad\qquad 5.3$$

Where,

CI = the confidence interval

z = the value from the z table (A) corresponding to the level of confidence one specifies

σ_M = the value of the standard error of the mean from the z test

M = the value of the sample mean

A .95 confidence interval provides a range of values within which the mean of the population represented by M will occur 95% of the time. For a .95 confidence level, the corresponding value of z in the equation will be 1.96. For .99 confidence, it's z = 2.58, and so on.

The size of the interval is a function of the level of probability required, and the amount of variability in the distribution of samples means, indicated by σ_M. If one wishes to be more certain of capturing the population mean, the value of z that corresponds with larger portions of the distribution must increase and the width of the interval must also expand. Likewise, if data variability increases perhaps because sample size shrinks, the value of the standard error of the mean will increase, and this too stretches the confidence interval.

In a box example earlier in the chapter, a superintendent examined the impact that coaching teachers have on student achievement. We found that

z = 2.177

The sample mean (M) was 66.333 and the standard error of the mean (σ_M) was 4.891. Since we tested at p = .05, the z value for the confidence interval is z = 1.96. To calculate a .95 confidence interval:

$$CI = +/-z(\sigma_M) + M$$

$$CI = +/-1.96(4.891) + 66.333$$

$$CI = 9.586, -9.586 + 66.333$$

$$CI = 75.919, 56.747$$

Interpreting the Confidence Interval

With 95% confidence, the population mean from which the sample in the z test (M) was drawn is between 56.747 and 75.919.

If we need more confidence that we've captured μ_M, say .99 confidence, we substitute 2.58 for 1.96 and the interval becomes

$$CI = +/-2.58(4.891) + 66.333$$

$$CI = 12.619, -12.619 + 66.333$$

$$CI = 78.952, 53.714$$

Moving from .95 to .99 confidence increased the interval from 19.172 points (75.919 − 56.747), to 25.238 points (78.952 − 53.714). We noted earlier that because the standard error of the mean reflects data variability (σ), and sample size ($\sqrt{n}$), it too affects the size of the interval. As the size of the group increases (the divisor in the standard error of the mean formula), the value of the standard error of the mean will decrease. Recall from Chapter 2 that overall variability typically decreases as group sizes increase. In summary then, confidence intervals tend to be largest when data variability is great, group sizes are relatively small, and level of confidence must be high.

SAMPLE SIZE AND CONFIDENCE

The questions that structured our discussion in this chapter reflect the comparison of M to μ_M:

- Why did the students in Mr. Forsythe's school initially lag behind the other students in the same grade?
- What happened to close the gap?

Comparing a sample with a population involves some risks, as we've noted, but under certain circumstances the sample can provide a reliable indicator of the parent population's characteristics. In fact, a randomly selected sample will differ from the population only by chance. Although that's a help, in small samples, even chance differences can be profound. So how large must the sample be in order for one to have confidence that it's large enough to emulate the important characteristics of the population it represents?

One approach is to make the sample large enough that its standard deviation is similar to that of the population (Sprinthall, 2000). This is what Formula 5.4 accomplishes. It is as follows:

$$n = \left[\frac{(z)(\sigma)}{allowed\ variation\ from\ \sigma} \right]^2 \qquad\qquad 5.4$$

Where,

n = the required sample size

z = the value of z corresponding to the required level of certainty, or confidence. Since $z = +/-1.96$ includes 95% of the distribution of outcomes, if one wishes to be .95 confident, one adopts $z = 1.96$

σ = the population standard deviation of the measure

Allowed variation from σ = the variability between sample and population standard deviations one is willing to tolerate

The allowed variation from σ is essentially a value judgment. The more certain one must be about emulating the population, the smaller the variation allowed from σ.

Perhaps a community college adviser works with students who are preparing to teach. She wishes to know how her aspiring teachers compare with students statewide on a competency test for teacher candidates. If

a. The standard deviation on the required test is $\sigma = 10$

b. She wishes to have 95% confidence that her sample will reflect the population (so $z = 1.96$, since + and − 1.96 includes 95% of the distribution)

c. She is willing for her sample to diverge from the population standard deviation by 2 points

$$n = \left[\frac{(z)(\sigma)}{allowed\ variation\ from\ \sigma} \right]^2 \qquad 5.4$$

$$= \left[\frac{(1.96)(10)}{2} \right]^2$$

$$= \left[\frac{(1.96)}{2} \right]^2$$

$$= 96.04$$

Randomly selecting about 96 subjects will provide a sample that will have a standard deviation within 2 points of the population standard deviation (σ) 95 times out of 100.

If the advisor is willing to diverge from the population standard deviation by 3 points and she decides that .90 confidence is sufficient, she can dramatically reduce the required sample size. In that case, the result is as follows:

$$n = \left[\frac{(z)(\sigma)}{allowed\ variation\ from\ \sigma} \right]^2$$

$$= \left[\frac{(1.65)(10)}{3} \right]^2$$

$$= 30.25$$

Nine times out of 10, a randomly drawn sample of about 30 will have a standard deviation within 3 points of the standard deviation of the population from which it was drawn. But 3 points off a population standard deviation of 10 may be more difference than one wishes to accommodate. The trade-off that comes from relaxing requirements, of course, is the greater risk of a sample that's unlike the population from which it was drawn, a factor in any subsequent analyses.

The potential problem in sample size estimation is the value of the population standard deviation, σ. If population data for the standard deviation are simply not available, one can estimate it from a sample standard deviation, s. After all, we keep arguing that s is an estimate of σ. Remember, however, that overall variability tends to shrink as sample size increases, and inordinately small samples may provide little helpful information regarding the standard deviation of the population.

Another Example

A college admissions officer has questioned the performance of new students on an entry-level mathematics test for freshman students. He wishes to compare this year's entering students with those of the past. Accumulated scores show a standard deviation of 12.755. He wishes to be .99 confident of being within 2.50 points of the population standard deviation. How large must his sample be?

$$n = \left[\frac{(z)(\sigma)}{allowed\ variation\ from\ \sigma} \right]^2$$

$$= \left[\frac{(2.58)(12.755)}{2.5} \right]^2$$

$$= \left[\frac{32.908}{2.5} \right]^2$$

$$= 173.269$$

Ninety-nine times out of 100, a randomly selected group of about 175 freshman students will provide a sample within 2.5 points of the population standard deviation. If it's a very small college, and 175 students create difficulty, he can reduce the requirement by either allowing more divergence from the population or reducing the required level of certainty. At .95 the calculations become:

$$n = \left[\frac{(z)(\sigma)}{allowed\ variation\ from\ \sigma} \right]^2$$

$$= \left[\frac{(1.96)(12.755)}{2.5} \right]^2$$

$$= \left[\frac{24.0}{2.5} \right]^2$$

$$= 100$$

If the sample is too small, the results may provide little useful information about differences in performance. If the sample is too large, the researcher is probably wasting resources on results that would have been accurate enough with fewer subjects.

How can the sample be too large, you may ask; doesn't a sample become increasingly like the population as n increases? Well it does, but there is a point of diminishing returns. Other things equal, a sample of 80 will generally provide much more useful information than a sample of 40, and a sample of 120 will generally provide more informative data than a sample of 80, but the improvement in the quality of information is less dramatic with very large numbers of subjects. A good researcher won't discard data already collected, but sometimes the cost in time and money of gathering additional data isn't justified.

CONVENIENCE SAMPLES

In this discussion of determining sample sizes, we've made a point of noting the need for random sampling, or random selection of the subjects. Random samples provide an important safeguard to the researcher. At the other end of the sampling spectrum, we have **convenience samples,** which are used because they're accessible. But sometimes they're handier than they are helpful.

■ Calling a sample a **convenience sample** reflects the fact that the sample was probably an intact group chosen because of its accessibility rather than because it manifests the statistical properties of the population.

If an enterprising ninth-grade classroom teacher wishes to see whether increasing the amount of positive reinforcement affects students' English scores, perhaps she'll use her own class out of convenience. If she faithfully provides positive reinforcement every 5 minutes of the period for the entire semester and then uses a z test to check the performance of her students against those in the district at large, she has no assurance that they were characteristic of the population of all ninth-grade students to begin with. If there are significant differences, perhaps they were there before she began. Perhaps her students were performing less well than those in the district initially so that the difference at the end of term is greater than the z test suggests. There are many obstacles to random selection, and some of them are difficult to surmount, but there is a good deal of safety in random selection when it's possible.

SUMMARY

In this chapter, we tackled our first statistical test, the z test. It's a relatively simple test with much in common with the z scores we calculated in Chapter 4, but the form of the z test is very important. Like the z score, it is a ratio of the difference between the means (the sample versus the population) to a measure of variability (the standard error of the mean). When the absolute value of that ratio is beyond the z values indicating the most representative outcomes, typically the middle 95%, we conclude that the difference is significant. In such cases, the difference between sample and population means is too great to attribute the outcome to chance; the sample likely represents a population with a different mean value.

This is a very important concept in educational analysis. When new programs or strategies are instituted we often look for ways to determine whether the program "makes a difference." In the language of statistics the question becomes whether the innovation has so transformed the sample that the population it represents is different from the population with which it was compared.

Because statistical testing is based on probabilities rather than certainties, there is the potential for error. Alpha errors occur when we conclude that a result is statistically significant when further testing would reveal that it isn't. Beta errors occur when further testing would reveal that a nonsignificant finding was erroneous. The complication for the educator is that the two errors are related and diminishing the potential for one magnifies the risk of committing the other. Decision errors are a fact of life for the educational decision maker, which is why replicating research is so important.

A sample mean is one of the possible values of the mean of the related population. In the case of the z test, M is a point estimate of μ_M. When z is statistically significant, an indicator of how accurate that point estimate is can be determined by calculating a confidence interval around M within which the value of the population mean (μ_M) will occur with specified probability. The more certain one wishes to be about containing the value of μ_M, the wider the accommodating interval must be.

When samples emulate the important characteristics of populations, we can understand the population via the sample. But there's a natural relationship between the size of the randomly selected sample, and the fidelity with which it represents the population. Formula 5.3 provides a way to estimate how large a sample must be in order for one to have confidence that the sample has about the same variability as the population.

For much of the last two chapters the normality of data distributions has been a central issue. We have learned how to estimate normality and we know that a distribution based on sample means can be normal even when its individual scores are not. However, the fact remains that small samples, even when they're randomly selected, fall short of normal distributions and many of the questions we wish to answer about education and educational issues depend on our use of samples that have fairly limited sizes. This was a point of dispute between two famous English statisticians, Karl Pearson and Ronald Fisher. Pearson advocated relying only on populations in statistical analysis and Fisher argued that smaller samples can work. We'll see how a third statistician, William Sealey Gosset, solved the problem in the next chapter.

EXERCISES

1. If all the teachers and clerical personnel in a school district have an average age of 37.5 years, what will be the value of the mean of the distribution of sample means (μ_M) created from such a population?

2. If the standard deviation of the ages of the educators in item 1 is calculated, how will that value compare to the standard error of the mean (σ_M) based on the same population? Explain any difference.

3. The assistant vice president for personnel at a college has job performance scores for all clerical staff with a mean value of 32.956 and a standard error of the mean of 5.924. What is the probability of randomly selecting a sample with a job satisfaction mean of 35.0 or higher?

4. The clerical staff in the college of sciences have the following job performance scores: 35, 37, 38, 42, 47, 48, 51. Based on the parameters in item 3, and at $p = .05$, are they significantly different from students in the college as a whole?

5. The standard deviation for a particular population is $\sigma = 13.755$. For a group of 65, what is the standard error of the mean?

6. The admissions officer at a graduate school notes the following scores on the quantitative portion of the Graduate Record Exam (GRE): 425, 450, 480, 510, 510, 550, 550, 560, 590, 600, 625, 650. If the national mean is 500 with a standard deviation of 100

   a. At $p = .05$, is this group characteristic of the national population?
   b. What's the probability that a group of applicants to graduate school would score at the level of this sample or higher?

7. Given the mean and standard deviation for GRE scores among the population of students aspiring to graduate school, noted in item 6

   a. How large must the sample be in order to vary no more than 10 points from the standard deviation of the population, with .95 probability?
   b. How large must the sample be to be within 5 points of the standard deviation with a probability of .99?

8. A group of 11th-grade students are involved in a debate program. Their scores on a verbal aptitude test are as follows: 26, 28, 28, 31, 33, 33, 34, 36. If the national mean for verbal aptitude among 11th-grade students is $\mu = 27.846$ and $\sigma = 4.50$

   a. At $p = .05$ are these students significantly different from the national population?
   b. Are they significantly different at $p = .01$?
   c. Regarding the first question (a), what's the probability of alpha error?

9. A university sponsors a re-entry program for students who have been away from the institution for a year or longer and are re-enrolling. The director of the program knows that the average age of students at the university is 23.830 years, with a standard deviation of 5.0. The ages of a sample of re-entry students are as follows:

   19, 22, 23, 25, 26, 27, 27, 28, 32, 37

   At $p = .05$, are their ages significantly different from the ages of students at the university generally?

10. A nationally administered reading test has $\mu = 55.849$ and $\sigma = 8.492$.
    a. How large would a sample need to be in order to be within 2 points of the standard deviation with .95 confidence?
    b. At $p = .05$, are students whose scores are the following characteristic of students nationwide? 38, 42, 45, 46, 49, 52, 55, 57

11. On a test of motor dexterity for kindergarten children, the national mean is 14.557, with $\sigma_M = 1.754$. A group of kindergarten students who manifested fetal alcohol syndrome in infancy have the following scores: 6, 6, 7, 7, 8, 10, 10, 11, 12, 12, 14, 14, 15, 16, 18.
    a. At $p = .05$, are their measures of motor dexterity significantly different from the dexterity of children nationally?
    b. If the sample represents a population significantly different from the population with $\mu = 14.557$, calculate a .95 confidence interval.

12. A sample of college freshman with $M = 73.428$ and $\sigma_M = 5.391$ are found to have significantly higher scores on the math placement test than is true of all college freshman students.
    a. Calculate a .95 confidence interval for the mean of the population represented by this sample.
    b. How would increasing the sample size impact the breadth of the confidence interval? Why?

REFERENCES

Diekoff, G. (1992). *Statistics for the social and behavioral sciences: Univariate, bivariate, and multivariate*. Dubuque, IA: William C. Brown, Publishers.

Sprinthall, R. C. (2000). *Basic statistical analysis* (6th ed.). Boston, MA: Allyn & Bacon.

THE FORMULAE AND THEIR SYMBOLS

Formula 5.1: $z = \dfrac{M - \mu_m}{\sigma_m}$

This is the formula for the z test. It allows one to determine whether a sample is characteristic of, or significantly different from, a population.

Formula 5.2: $\sigma_m = \dfrac{\sigma}{\sqrt{N}}$

If a value for the population standard deviation (σ) is available, one can calculate the standard error of the mean (σ_m) with this formula.

Formula 5.3: $CI_z = +/\text{-}z(\sigma_M) + M$

This is the formula for calculating a confidence interval when z is statistically significant in a z test.

Formula 5.4: $n = \left[\dfrac{(z)(\sigma)}{allowed\ variation\ from\ \sigma} \right]^2$

This formula allows one to estimate the sample size needed so that the sample has a standard deviation similar to a particular population, with a specified level of probability.

STUDENT STUDY SITE

Visit the Student Study Site at **www.sagepub.com/tanner** for additional learning tools.

Chapter 6

t FOR ONE, OR TWO

THE PROBLEM: HOW TO COMPARE GROUPS

By checking his state's department of education website, Mr. Valero can see how his eighth-grade math students compare with other eighth graders. The mean for his students' math scores is a little higher than the state average. Is the difference worth noting? With much energy and no small amount of district money committed to the new math program, much rides on the answer.

There are also some comparisons *within* his school that interest him. Another teacher supplemented her math program with a good deal of computer work. Has it had an impact? Do her students perform differently than Mr. Valero's?

QUESTIONS AND ANSWERS

❑ Is there a statistically significant difference between a group at one school and students statewide?

This is the same question we addressed with *z* test in Chapter 5, but now we're asking with only a mean for the statewide data. This will bring us to the *one-sample t-test*.

❑ Is the performance of *two* separate samples significantly different?

The *independent* t-*test* answers this question.

❑ What procedures let one observe the influence that one variable has on another?

A plan to study and analyze particular effects is a *research design*.

A LITTLE HISTORY

In the last chapter we had our first look at "significant" differences with the *z* test. Recall that when an outcome is among the most extreme 5% of possible outcomes, by convention, it's no longer a random outcome but is *statistically significant*. That extends to *t*-tests and the work of William Sealy Gosset.

Gosset was a chemist who worked for the brewing giant Guinness in the early 20th century. His task was to ensure consistency between the brewer's standard and the individual batches of beer brewed daily. To do this he invented the *t*-tests. Appreciating their more general application, Gosset wanted to publish his work but was thwarted by a Guinness policy forbidding publication. It was enacted because an earlier employee had published trade secrets. Feeling that Guinness wouldn't be harmed by his publication, Gosset wrote under the pen name "Student." Traditional statistics texts still refer to "Student's *t*."

The pseudonym "Student" reveals something of Gosset's unassuming nature. He maintained friendships with two other statistical luminaries of the time, Karl Pearson and Ronald Fisher, men of substantial ego who felt professional and probably personal animosity toward each other. Gosset maintained good relations with both. He published in *Biometrika*, which Pearson founded and edited, and was heard on one occasion to deflect attention from his own accomplishments by saying something like, "Oh, Fisher would have come to it had I not."

FROM THE *z* TEST TO THE ONE-SAMPLE *t*-TEST

In the beginning chapter problem, Mr. Valero has a mean for the state (μ) and for his students (M), but he has neither the standard deviation for the population of individual students (σ), nor a standard deviation of the means of all the schools in the state (the standard error of the mean, σ_m). He lacks the denominator he needs for a *z* test.

This isn't uncommon with on-line data. Means for populations and specific samples are easy to come by but population standard deviations are often not published. To determine whether the performance of a particular group is significantly different from the state average requires that we move from *z* test to the **one-sample *t*-test**.

■ Like the *z* test, **one-sample *t*-test** compares a sample with a population to determine significance, but without the need for σ_M.

Both tests answer the same question: Is a particular sample likely to have been drawn from a population that has a specified mean? The logic behind both tests is related to the distribution of sample means (Chapter 5) where the mean of the population (μ_m) is the mean of all the sample means (M) and data variability (σ_m) is gauged by the standard deviation of the sample means. Mr. Valero lacks the variability measure.

The Estimated Standard Error of the Mean, SE_m

Population characteristics (μ, σ, μ_M, σ_M) are the parameters we spoke of in Chapter 2. The *M*, *s*, and *n* values, conversely, are statistics from samples. In fact, statistics are *estimates* of parameter values.

Just as we calculated the parameter standard error of the mean with $\sigma_m = \sigma/\sqrt{N}$ (Formula 5.2), we can *estimate* the standard error of the mean by substituting statistics for parameters. To distinguish between the **estimated standard error of the mean** and the population standard error of the mean (σ_m), we'll designate the estimate as SE_m. It's calculated as follows:

$$SE_m = \frac{s}{\sqrt{n}}$$ 6.1

■ The **estimated standard error of the mean** gauges variability in the distribution of sample means for the one-sample *t*-test.

Where,

SE_m = the estimated standard error of the mean

s = the sample standard deviation

n = the number in the sample

Enjoy the harmony here. Just as we calculated the population standard error of the mean by dividing σ by the square root of *N*, we determine the *sample* standard error of the mean, SE_m, by dividing the sample standard deviation, *s*, by the square root of the number in the sample, *n*.

Now back to the problem. Perhaps Mr. Valero has a rather small math class and his students' scores on the state-required test are as follows:

47

36

39

27

52

55

43

40

49

45

To calculate the estimated standard error of the mean, first verify that for this sample of students, $M = 43.300$, which we will need later, and $s = 8.233$. Using Formula 6.1, we can then calculate the estimated standard error of the mean:

$$SE_m = \frac{s}{\sqrt{n}}$$

$$SE_m = \frac{8.233}{\sqrt{10}} = 2.604$$

Because it is based on data from a sample of all eighth graders, the 2.604 represents one of the possible values of the standard error of the mean for the population, σ_m. Mr. Valero's math students *are* a sample of the larger population. What we're trying to determine is whether they are a *representative* sample. We'll see later that how representative they are depends upon how large the sample is and how it is selected.

The One-Sample *t*-test

The one-sample t looks like the z test, except that the denominator is SE_m rather than σ_m:

$$t = \frac{M - \mu_m}{SE_m}$$

6.2

If the state mean for math scores is $\mu = 38.180$, then $\mu_m = 38.180$ as well (Chapter 5). Mr. Valero can now determine whether his students are performing at a significantly different level than the students in the state as a whole. Substituting into the formula the values he has yields the following:

$$t = \frac{M - \mu_m}{SE_m}$$

$$t = \frac{43.300 - 38.180}{2.604} = \mathbf{1.966}$$

Interpreting the *t* Value

So the calculated value of t is 1.966. Remember that with z tests, +/– 1.96 indicated a statistically significant result. So with $z = 1.966$, Mr. Valero's class is performing at a significantly different level than students statewide are performing, right? There's one more thing.

Degrees of Freedom and the *t* Distribution

A $z = +/-1.96$ indicates a statistically significant result in *any z* test because there is just one *z* distribution. Its data are always normal and the mean and standard deviation are always 0 and 1.0, respectively. In contrast to *z, there are many* t *distributions*, each with different characteristics defined by their degrees of freedom.

We first raised degrees of freedom in Chapter 2 with the variance. Remember that if there are 10 scores in a sample with a known mean, 9 of the scores are free to have any value at all. Their numbers don't matter as long as that last number makes the mean come out right. For the variance and for the one-sample *t*, if $n = 10$, $df = 9$. Each change in *df* indicates a different *t* distribution, each with its own critical value, unlike *z* for which there is just one critical value for $p = .05$, which was $z = +/- 1.96$.

Recall that large samples tend to have smaller standard deviations than small samples; they're less variable. So the +/– standard deviation value required to capture the middle 95% of a large sample is smaller than the value that capture the middle 95% of a smaller sample. This is reflected in the critical values for the different *t* distributions—larger distribution, smaller critical value. Table B in the Tables of Critical Values appendix has the critical values for *t* and reflects this:

Critical Values for a Two-Tailed t-test

df	level of significance	
	.05	.01
1	12.706	63.657
2	4.303	9.925
3	3.182	5.841
.	.	.
.	.	.

The heading indicates that the first column is for degrees of freedom, 1, 2, and 3 . . . in this case. The second column is the value at which *t* becomes statistically significant when testing at $p = .05$. Anything within +/– this value indicates outcomes that occur somewhere in the middle 95% of the distribution. The third column is the critical value for testing when the decision is to treat only the extreme 1% of outcomes as statistically significant. If $df = 1$ (which would mean that the sample size was $n = 2$), and one is testing at .05, the calculated value of t from the t-test would have to be equal to or larger than 12.706 to be statistically significant.

Note that the values decline precipitously at first, and then less dramatically as df increase throughout the table. What's the critical value when we have an infinite number of df? Ignoring the fact that an infinite sample size isn't possible, that 1.96 ought to look familiar! As df (sample sizes) increase, the t distribution becomes increasingly like z. If $df = \infty$, critical values for z and t-tests are the same.

And the Answer Is . . .

The t-test comparing Mr. Valero's class to the population yielded $t = 1.966$. Because $n = 10$, $df = 9$ and the critical value is **2.262**, written this way:

$$t_{.05\ (9)} = 2.262$$

The subscripts indicate that 2.262 is the *table value* for $p = .05$ when $df = 9$. If we draw a distribution and mark where the t value we calculated occurs ($t = 1.966$) compared with the table value ($t = 2.262$), it's easier to interpret the result (see Figure 6.1).

At $p = .05$ level and $df = 9$, no value of t between -2.262 and $+2.262$ is going to be statistically significant as long as we're unconcerned about the direction of the difference. When we become more particular about whether the sample mean is *larger* or *smaller* than the population mean rather than just *different* this will change, but for now the issue is just whether the absolute (*absolute* values are symbolized by vertical lines either side of the value. $|1.96|$ indicates that the sign of 1.96, + or –, doesn't matter) t value, is less extreme than the absolute table value.

Is the students' mean score different than the mean for students throughout the state? It is. Is the difference statistically *significant*? At $p = .05$ and $df = 9$, it isn't. Because the calculated t is less extreme than the table value the difference between sample and population might be just a random difference. Mr. Valero's students are characteristic of students statewide, although perhaps they represent the upper portion of that population.

Figure 6.1   The Critical and Calculated Values of *t*

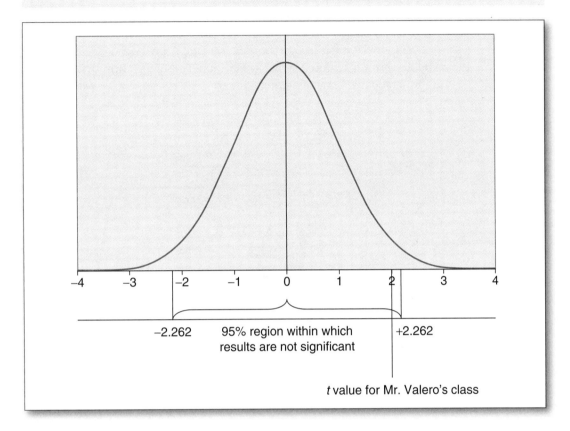

-2.262   95% region within which
results are not significant   +2.262

t value for Mr. Valero's class

INFERENTIAL STATISTICS

If requirements such as random selection and sample size are satisfied, the mean of a sample can provide a fairly accurate estimate of the mean of the population. That is, we can understand the population which is often not accessible by examining the sample. This is the substance of inferential statistics, a concept we first raised in Chapter 1; we infer the population from the sample. But Mr. Valero's group remind us that samples, even large samples (of which this was *not* one), are never exactly like the populations from which they are drawn.

Conversely, had the calculated value of *t* been equal to or larger than the table value, it would have indicated that the class had characteristics different from the population. If Mr. Valero's group had significantly higher math performance than students statewide, we couldn't have understood the population very well through the lens the sample provided since the sample would have represented some other population, perhaps that of gifted eighth-grade mathematics students.

"I don't see it as a larger allowance. I see it as more degrees of freedom."

Another Example

To gauge students' progress against state-required standards, school districts often create their own "benchmark" tests to provide feedback before administering the state test.

Students in a continuation high school have just completed the district benchmark test for reading and produced the following scores: 23, 25, 33, 34, 34, 35, 36, 36, 38, 42, 47, 49. The mean for the district as a whole is 41.515. Are these continuation students performing at a significantly different level than all students in the district?

In this case, the population is the district and the mean level of performance for the district is 41.515. So μ and therefore $\mu_m = 41.515$.

1. Verify that our sample statistics are as follows: $M = 36$, and $s = 7.616$

2. Verify that the value of $SE_m = 2.198$

$$SE_m = \frac{s}{\sqrt{n}}$$

$$SE_m = \frac{7.616}{\sqrt{12}}$$

Calculate the value of t

$$t = \frac{M - \mu_m}{SE_m}$$

$$t = \frac{36 - 41.515}{2.198}$$

$$= -2.509$$

1. Compare calculated t to the table value.

$$t_{.05\,(11)} = 2.201$$

The absolute value of the calculated t is greater than the table value. The performance of the continuation students is significantly different from students in the district as a whole.

LOOKING AT SPSS OUTPUT

At the end of the chapter, there's a tutorial for a one-sample t on SPSS but in the meantime the output below is how the results would look if we completed the problem comparing Mr. Valero's 10 students to all eighth-grade students on SPSS.

One-Sample Statistics

	N	Mean	Std. Deviation	Std. Error Mean
math	10	43.30	8.233	2.604

One-Sample Test

	Test Value = 38.180					
					95% Confidence Interval of the Difference	
	t	df	Sig. (2-tailed)	Mean Difference	Lower	Upper
math	1.966	9	.081	5.120	−.77	11.01

- The descriptive statistics for the problem are listed in the first table.
- In the second table the "test value =" indicates the value of the population mean—the value with which our sample mean was compared.
- In the "t" column is the calculated t and degrees of freedom in the next column.
- In the "Sig." column SPSS indicates the probability that $t = 1.966$ with $df = 9$ could have occurred by chance. Since anything that occurs in the extreme 5% of the distribution is statistically significant, the usual standard is that a probability of .05 or less indicates significance. The smaller the Sig. value, the less likely the t value is to have occurred by chance.
- For now, ignore the last two columns in the second table (which SPSS provides whether one wants them or not). We'll come to confidence intervals below.

THE INDEPENDENT *t*-TEST

■ The **independent *t*-test** analyzes whether two samples are likely drawn from populations with the same mean.

Rather than whether a sample represents a population, the issue with the *independent t*-test is whether two samples come from populations with the same mean. The "independent" in **independent *t*-test** indicates that subjects in one group cannot also be subjects in the other. The groups have to be mutually exclusive. We'll modify the independence requirement in Chapter 8 with the before-after *t*-test, but for now people in one group can't also be in the other.

The Distribution of Difference Scores

Perhaps achievement motivation is the same for populations of both women and men. If we drew samples of the same size from each population, calculated the mean of each, and subtracted one mean from the other the result could be called a "difference score." If this were done repeatedly for all possible pairs of samples and the differences plotted in a frequency distribution the result would be a *sampling distribution of difference scores.* Its mean would be $\mu_{m1\text{-}m2}$ with the subscripts a reminder of how the difference scores are determined.

Since some difference scores are positive ($M_1 > M_2$), some negative ($M_1 < M_2$), and occasionally some zero ($M_1 = M_2$), what's the mean of the sampling distribution of differences? Because positive and negative differences balance out $\mu_{m1\text{-}m2} = 0$.

Variability in this distribution is gauged by the **standard error of the difference,** $\sigma_{m1\text{-}m2}$, which is the standard deviation of all difference scores, although in practice we estimate the value with a statistic.

■ The **standard error of the difference** is the denominator in the independent *t*. It measures within-groups variability.

The Logic of the Independent *t*-Test

Consider an example of an independent t-test. An investigator wishes to examine the impact that coaching teachers in instructional best practices may have on student achievement. In the resulting study, subjects are randomly selected for two groups, one from each of two schools. Upon examination, the researcher finds that the means of the two groups on a particular achievement test are very similar. The two groups appear to belong to populations with the same mean.

The researcher randomly selects school A and assigns "coaches" to help those teachers adopt instructional best practices. The school B teachers continue without extra help. After 16 weeks, the two groups are tested and their performances compared. At issue is whether two groups, initially drawn from populations with the same mean, still belong to populations with the same mean after the 16 weeks. A significant *t* will indicate that they don't and that coaching (assuming that the other relevant variables are controlled) has prompted achievement changes in one group of students.

The Test Statistic

The numerator in the independent *t*-test statistic is $M_1 - M_2 - \mu_{m1\text{-}m2}$, the mean of the first sample, minus the mean of the second, minus the mean of the distribution of differences. Since $\mu_{m1\text{-}m2} = 0$, that expression is usually deleted leaving just $M_1 - M_2$. The test statistic is

$$t = \frac{(M_1 - M_2)}{SE_d}$$

6.3

Where,

M_1 = the mean of group 1

M_2 = the mean of group 2

SE_d = the estimated standard error of the difference

The denominator, SE_d, is the *estimate* of $\sigma_{m1\text{-}m2}$, the standard error of the difference and we can calculate SE_d from the samples. Its formula *when sample sizes are equal*, is,

$$SE_d = \sqrt{(SEm_1^2 + SEm_2^2)}$$

6.4

Where,

SE_d = the estimated standard error of the difference

SE_{m1} = the standard error of the mean from group 1

SE_{m2} = the standard error of the mean from group 2

For SE_d,

1. Calculate SE_m for each sample (Formula 6.1)

2. Square those SE_m values

3. Sum the squared SE_m values

4. Determine the square root of the sum

After 16 weeks, the achievement scores for students whose teachers were coached and not coached are:

Coached teachers' students: 34, 44, 47, 54, 64, 73

Noncoached teachers' students: 29, 31, 46, 48, 51, 64

Calculating the Independent *t*

1. Calculate the two means.
   a. Verify that for the coached group, $M_1 = 52.667$, and for the
   b. Noncoached, $M_2 = 44.833$

2. Calculate the standard deviations. Verify that for the
   a. Coached group it is $s_1 = 14.137$, and for the
   b. Noncoached group it is $s_2 = 13.106$

3. Calculate the standard errors of the mean ($SE_m = s/\sqrt{n}$). Verify that for the
   a. Coached group it is $SE_{m1} = 5.771$, and for
   b. Noncoached it is $SE_{m2} = 5.350$

4. Calculate the estimated standard error of the difference:
   a. $SE_d = \sqrt{(SEm_1^2 + SEm_2^2)} =$

   b. $\sqrt{5.771^2 + 5.350^2} =$

   c. $\sqrt{61.927}$

   d. **7.869**

5. Now the *t* value (Formula 6.3):

$$t = \frac{(M_1 - M_2)}{SE_d} = \frac{52.667 - 44.833}{7.869} = \textbf{.996}$$

Interpreting the *t* Statistic

The larger the *t* value, the less likely that the two samples represent populations with the same mean. The "critical value" upon which our decision is based is in Table B.

- For the independent *t*-test degrees of freedom are $n − 1$ *for each group*, so

$$df = n_1 + n_2 - 2$$

   o For two samples of $n = 10$, for example, $df = 18$
   o For a sample of 13 and a sample of 11, $df = 22$, and so on

In our example, there were two groups of $n = 6$, so $df = 10$ ($6 + 6 = 12 − 2 = 10$). In Table B, the critical value for 10 *df*, and $p = .05$ is **2.228**; $t_{(.05, 10)} = 2.228$.

Our calculated $t = .996$. With $t_{(.05, 10)} = 2.228$, the coaching does ***not*** have a significant impact on student achievement.

SE_d for Unequal Samples

Formula 6.4 treats the two standard errors of the mean equally, which is fine when sample sizes are equal. When they *aren't*, we use the Formula 6.5:

$$SE_d = \sqrt{\left[\frac{(n_1 - 1)s_1^2 + (n_2 - 1)s_2^2}{(n_1 + n_2 - 2)} \right] \left[\frac{1}{n_1} + \frac{1}{n_2} \right]} \qquad 6.5$$

It's certainly longer than Formula 6.4 but it isn't difficult. The only values are the sample sizes (n_1 and n_2) and the variances (s^2) for each group. Just be careful with math order of operations and remember that s^2 is just the square of the standard deviation.

For SE_d and unequal samples with n_1 = the number in Group 1 and s_1^2 = the variance in Group 1:

1. Calculate the variance (s^2) for each group

2. Multiply $n_1 - 1$ by the variance for group 1 (s_1^2)

3. Multiply $n_2 - 1$ by the variance for group 2 (s_2^2)

4. Sum the results of steps 2 and 3 and divide by $n_1 + n_2 - 2$

5. Divide 1 by n_1, divide 1 by n_2 and add those two results together

6. Multiply the Steps 4 and 5 results

7. Take a square root of the result of Step 6

Another *t*-Test Example

Mr. Valero and his colleague both use the same mathematics curriculum, but his colleague supplements her students' work with computer exercises. Are the two groups significantly different? We already have Mr. Valero's data.

$M_1 = 43.300$

$s_1 = 8.233$

$n_1 = 10$

The colleague's students' scores are 41, 45, 59, 61, 59, 58, 49, 55, 63, 57, 64
Verify that

$$M_2 = 55.545$$

$$s_2 = 7.448$$

$$n_2 = 11$$

For the standard error of the difference

$$SE_d = \sqrt{\left[\frac{(n_1-1)s_1^2 + (n_2-1)s_2^2}{(n_1+n_2-2)}\right]\left[\frac{1}{n_1}+\frac{1}{n_2}\right]}$$

$$SE_d = \sqrt{\left[\frac{(10-1)8.233^2 + (11-1)7.448}{(10+11-2)}\right]^2\left[\frac{1}{10}+\frac{1}{11}\right]}$$

$$SE_d = \sqrt{\left[\frac{(610.041)+(554.727)}{19}\right][.191]}$$

$$SE_d = \sqrt{(61.304 \times .191)} = \sqrt{11.709} = \mathbf{3.422}$$

Now the *t* statistic: $t = \dfrac{M_1 - M_2}{SE_d} = \dfrac{43.300 - 55.545}{3.422} = \mathbf{-3.578}$

For *t* at $p = .05$ and 19 *df* $(10 + 11 - 2)$, the critical value is, $t_{(.05, 19)} = 2.093$.
The calculated *t* exceeds the table value. The difference between the two groups is statistically significant at $p = .05$; the two groups now represent populations with different means. The computer supplement appears to help. (We know they did better because their mean score is higher than the mean for Mr. Valero's group. What *t* verifies is that they did *significantly better*.)

The Sign of *t*

The fact that *t* is negative isn't relevant to significance, as long as the issue is just whether there is a *difference*. We made no judgment about whether computers benefit students, or impede them (perhaps by reducing time for conventional instruction), just that computers might make a difference. The negative t means, of course, that group 2 (the colleague's students) did better than group 1. Later we'll take up what are called one-tailed tests and be more particular about the sign of t.

Harmony Among the Tests

Note the consistency between the z test, the one-sample t, and the independent t. The numerators are all difference scores, and the denominators all measure data variability (Table 6.1).

Table 6.1   Comparing the z Test, the One-Sample t-Test, and the Independent t-Test

The Test	Type of Ratio	Numerator	Denominator
z test	A difference score to a measure of population variability	$M - \mu_m$	σ_m
One-sample t	A difference score to an estimate of population variability	$M - \mu_m$	SE_m
Independent t	A difference score to a measure of the variability in two samples	$M_1 - M_2$	SE_d

Another Example

Two fifth-grade elementary school teachers who use the same math curriculum wonder whether homework affects student achievement. Accordingly they both teach the same material for 8 weeks, after which their students receive an achievement test. Group A students did 30 minutes of homework a night. Group B students did less than 10 minutes of homework nightly. The data are as follows:

Group A Group B

n 26 26

M 58.627 48.691

s 8.467 7.165

Verify that,

SE_m 1.661 1.405

SE_d 2.176

$t = 4.566$

$t_{.05\ (50)} = 2.009$. The difference is statistically significant.

LOOKING AT SPSS OUTPUT

In Appendix B, there is an "SPSS Primer" for the independent *t*-test. The output below is for the coaching problem.

Group Statistics

	coached	N	Mean	Std. Deviation	Std. Error Mean
Achievement	1	6	52.67	14.137	5.772
	2	6	44.83	13.106	5.350

These are the same as the longhand statistics.

Independent Samples Test

		Levene 's Test for Equality of Variances		*t*-test for Equality of Means						
		F	Sig.	t	df	Sig. (2-tailed)	Mean Difference	Std. Error Difference	95% Confidence Interval of the Difference Lower	Upper
Achievement	Equal variances assumed	.068	.800	.995	10	.343	7.833	7.870	9.702	2.537E1
	Equal variances not assumed			.995	9.943	.343	7.833	7.870	-9.716	2.538E1

Here there are results for three different procedures. Levene's test analyzes whether data variability is reasonably similar in the two groups. Although there's some difference (as comparing the standard deviations reveals) any value in the third column (Sig.) larger than .05 indicates that the difference is probably just random. We can assume equal variances, which means that we follow the values in the top line (equal variances assumed).

The t value and the degrees of freedom match our calculations. Rather than indicating whether t is significant at, say $p = .05$, SPSS indicates whether t could have occurred by chance (the "Sig. (2-tailed)" column). As with the test for equality of variances, a p value of .05 *or less* indicates significance. The result is clearly *not* statistically significant.

The "Mean Difference" column indicates the difference between the means of the two groups (you could have figured that out), and the "Std. Error Difference" value is similar to our SE_d value, with allowance for round-off.

THE CONFIDENCE INTERVAL OF THE DIFFERENCE

■ **The confidence interval of the difference** predicts the interval between the population means suggested by samples.

The last two columns contain the "95% **Confidence Interval of the Difference**." Although the difference between the sample means was 7.833, the confidence interval indicates what the difference between *the means of the corresponding populations* will be a specified proportion of the time.

- A 95% confidence interval ($CI_{.95}$) is the interval within which the difference between the population means will occur 95% of the time.
- A .99 confidence interval indicates the interval within which the difference will occur 99% of the time, and so on.

The confidence interval uses this formula:

$$CI_{.95} = +/-t(SE_d) + (M_1 - M_2) \qquad 6.6$$

Where,

t = the table value for t with specified df

SE_d = estimated standard error of the difference

$M_1 - M_2$ = the difference between sample means

For the coaching problem we have,

$CI_{.95} = +/-t(SE_d) + (M_1 - M_2)$

$CI_{.95} = +/-2.228\ (7.870) + (7.833)$

$CI_{.95} = 25.367, -9.701$

The "+/−" indicates that the related calculation is performed twice, once with *t* as a positive value, and then again as a negative value. On the SPSS output the 25.367 value appears as 2.537E1, which is scientific notation and reflects the fact that the table has to be "scrunched" to fit the value in. The "E1" indicates that one reads the number with the decimal moved one place to the right. The 7 was rounded accordingly. The longhand calculations make it 25.367.

So with 95% confidence, the true difference between the means of the populations represented by the samples is from 25.367 to −9.701. Note that this interval includes a 0 difference. This we might have anticipated. Since the *t* value wasn't statistically significant these two samples may represent populations with the same mean.

Another Example

For the more homework versus less homework problem in the box a little earlier in the chapter, we had the following:

$M_1 = 58.627$

$M_2 = 48.691$

$SE_d = 2.176$

and the table value for $t_{.05\ (50)} = 2.009$

$CI_{.95} = +/-t(SE_d) + (M_1 - M_2)$

$CI_{.95} = +/-2.009\ (2.176) + (9.936)$

$CI_{.95} = 14.308,\ 5.564$

With .95 confidence, the true difference between the population means represented by samples 1 and 2 is somewhere between 14.308 and 5.564. No "0" difference in this interval because *t* is statistically significant.

RESEARCH DESIGN

The point of the coaching example above was to study the impact that coaching teachers have on students' performance. Recall from Chapter 1 that a formal plan for such a study is called a research design.

Part of a research design is specifying the variables involved. The independent variable (*IV*) is the variable manipulated by the researcher. In a *t*-test, the *IV* has two categories, or groups, each of which is presumed to affect the dependent variable (*DV*) differently. Determining whether those differences are statistically significant is the point of the test. Note the independent variables in the designs below:

1. Does job satisfaction change from district to district? If job satisfaction data are gathered from educators in two districts and then compared, the district is the *IV*.

2. If girls' reading performance is compared with boys' in a fourth-grade class, gender is the *IV*.

3. If a language arts program emphasizes two different approaches to teaching writing, and the question is which is better, the type of instruction is the *IV*.

- Random participant selection and random assignment to treatment makes research **experimental**.

- Lacking either, the study is **quasi-experimental**. Lacking both, it's **nonexperimental** or **correlational**.

How the different groups are formed is an important component of experimental design. If individuals are randomly *selected* to groups and the categories of the *IV* are randomly *assigned*, the design is experimental. This could be the case in the third example. In the other two cases, random assignment to groups isn't possible since neither the educator's district nor the student's gender can be manipulated. In those cases, the research designs are descriptive. Sometimes they're called nonexperimental, or correlational designs.

In quasi-experimental designs some independent variables are assigned and some aren't, perhaps because they precede the experiment and can't be manipulated. If there are only two sections of a particular class at a community college and the researchers want to know whether peer tutoring affects student achievement, researchers might randomly select one of the two instructors to use peer tutoring. The instructional technique is randomly assigned, but the students in the two classes weren't randomly selected.

In research of this sort, it's the impact that the different *IV* categories have on the *DV* of that's of interest. In the three examples above, the *DV*s are job satisfaction, reading level, and writing scores, respectively. It's often helpful to lay the problem out this way:

IV	*DV*
1. The school district	→ job satisfaction
2. The student's gender	→ reading level
3. The reading program	→ writing ability

Simplifying the research design like this has a downside. It increases the temptation to assume that the *IV* alone *causes* any differences in the *DV,* that any differences in job satisfaction are because of the district to which the educator belongs, for example. If the treatments that define the independent variable are randomly assigned the case for a causal relationship is easier to make, but often "cause" overstates confidence. If a *t*-test produces a statistically significant result, it is safer (and often more accurate) to say that the *IV* is *associated* with significant differences in the *DV*. Precisely *why* the differences occur is often not clear. Perhaps significant differences in job satisfaction have less to do with differences in the schools than in the communities where educators live. Maybe one is a quiet pastoral setting and the other is in an industrial city where unemployment and crime are high and the city is unattractive. Actual differences in the classroom might be nominal.

Further scrutiny of gender differences in reading might reveal that boys and girls were treated differently, or that they were taught at different times of day, or for different periods of time, making these conditions contributing factors. The point is that the word "cause" is usually too strong. Human subjects and social settings are enormously complex. The independent *t*-test allows the educator to control only one variable, and there may be others at work for which one has not accounted.

Incidentally, the *IV/DV* language is not unique to the independent *t*-test. They're part of all statistical analyses where antecedent variables are used to help explain consequent variables.

The Scale of the Independent and Dependent Variables

In the independent *t*-test the *IV* must be nominal scale, and the *DV* must be interval or ratio scale (Chapter 2). The school district, the student's gender, and the writing program to which the teachers are assigned are all categories that define nominal data. All the *DV*s, job satisfaction (perhaps measured by the number of days absent during the year), reading performance, and writing achievement, are data for which there is at least a consistent interval between data points.

HYPOTHESIS TESTING

Speaking generally, there are two outcomes in an independent *t*-test. Either the two samples are drawn from populations with the same mean, or they aren't. We state those outcomes symbolically this way:

$H_o: \mu_1 = \mu_2$

This is the "null" hypothesis, the hypothesis of no difference. It indicates that the mean of the population represented by sample 1 is equal to the mean of the population represented by sample 2.

$$H_a: \mu_1 \neq \mu_2$$

This is the "alternate" hypothesis. It indicates that the mean of the population represented by sample 1 is *not* equal to the mean of the population represented by sample 2.

If the calculated t is less than the table value, it's possible that μ_1 and μ_2 have the same value. Our statistical decision in that case is to *fail to reject H_o*. One might be inclined to say one "accepts the null hypothesis," but "fails to reject" is actually more accurate. It's one thing to say that we can't reject the possibility that the two populations have equal means, and quite another to say that they do have equal means, something difficult to prove. This doesn't mean there is no difference between the samples. It means that the difference is small enough that something like sampling variability might explain it, and the populations might indeed have the same means.

By convention, statistical decisions are made in terms of the null hypothesis so that if t *is* statistically significant, we *reject H_o* (rather than accepting H_A). We either fail to reject H_o (differences *aren't* statistically significant), or we reject H_o (the differences *are* statistically significant).

The null and alternate *statistical hypotheses* are related to what Kerlinger and Lee (2000) called *substantive hypotheses.* They are where a study often begins. Consider the following:

- A school counselor has been holding test preparation sessions to ready students for a college admissions test. Some students attend the seminars and some don't. The substantive hypothesis: Those who attend will do better than those who don't.
- A community college's administrators want to implement a merit pay program for instructors. Instructors argue that suspicions about the fairness of awarding merit pay will reduce job satisfaction, which is a substantive hypothesis.

THROUGH A WIDER LENS

Although statistical hypotheses state relationships in terms of parameters, substantive hypotheses make predictions about particular variables. Consider these:

- Increasing reinforcement will affect students' response rates.
- Reducing class size will boost student achievement.
- Cooperative learning exercises will impact students' sociability.
- Involving parents in homework influences student's achievement motivation.

Although these seem closer to the alternate than the null hypothesis, it isn't always so. We might have said:

- Increasing reinforcement will have no effect on students' response rates.
- The learning disabled have the same reading tendencies as non-learning disabled slow readers.

TWO-, VERSUS ONE-TAILED TESTS

If the question is whether there's a significant *difference* between two groups, the sign of *t*, indicating the *direction* of the difference ($M_1 > M_2$ or $M_1 < M_2$), doesn't matter. By convention in statistical testing, outcomes occurring $p = .05$ or less often are statistically significant. In a **two-tailed test**, that .05 of the distribution is divided equally into 2½% in the upper and 2½% in the lowest regions of the distribution so that extreme outcomes in *either* direction result in a significant finding. Such tests are two-tailed.

■ For **two-tailed t-tests** significance can occur in either tail. **One-tailed tests** predict the direction.

If there are reasons to predict which group will have higher scores, sometimes researchers use a **one-tailed *t*-test**. The one-tailed test places the entire 5% rejection region in one tail.

- If group 1 is expected to have higher scores, the rejection region is in the positive tail.
- If group 2 is expected to have higher scores, the rejection region is in the negative tail.

Doing this changes the critical values and less extreme values of *t* (half the value as it turns out) will be statistically significant compared to a two-tailed test (Figure 6.2).

If research indicated that computer-aided instruction benefits students, in a design comparing those with computer help to those without it, one might set up a one-tailed test. If Mr. Valero's class is Group 1 (without computers), one may predict a negative value of t because the research says Group 2 will be superior. The alternate hypothesis becomes *Ha:* $\mu_1 < \mu_2$ rather than $\mu_1 \neq \mu_2$ (Figure 6.2).

Figure 6.2 Distributions for Two- Versus One-Tailed Tests

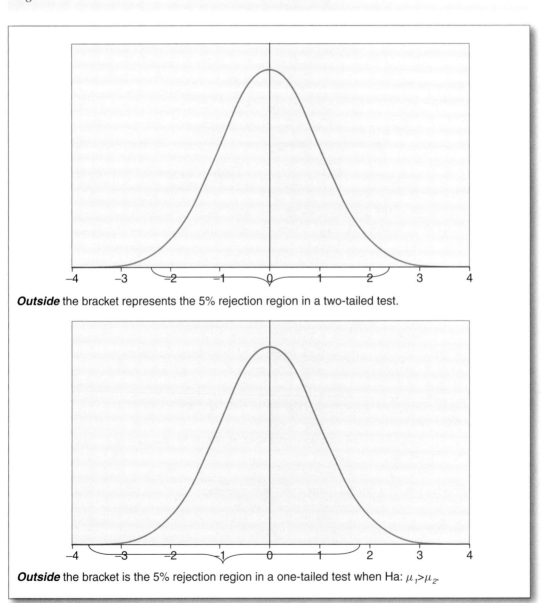

Outside the bracket represents the 5% rejection region in a two-tailed test.

Outside the bracket is the 5% rejection region in a one-tailed test when Ha: $\mu_1 > \mu_2$.

The Risk of Using One-Tailed Tests

The smaller critical value makes it easier to reach statistical significance with a one-tailed *t*-test, *as long as the difference is in the direction predicted*. The drawback is that if something unexpected happens, there's no rejection region in the opposite tail!

Another Example

Perhaps research suggests that computer work boosts test performance. To substantiate this before moving all students into a computer-supplemented curriculum,. a researcher sets up a one-tailed test, collects the data, and does the analysis. Unfortunately, the software is difficult for students to follow. Furthermore, correct solutions yield another problem to solve, but wrong answers produce dazzling graphics. Failing becomes more entertaining than succeeding and learners become conditioned accordingly. Those with computers actually do *less* well on the standardized test than a control group without computers. However interesting such an outcome might be, the result is non-significant no matter how extreme the score since there's no rejection region in the opposite tail. Consequently, many stay clear of one-tailed tests.

Tails Versus Samples

Be careful about the distinction between a one-*tailed* *t*-test and a one-*sample* *t*-test. For one-*tailed* tests, the issue is whether there is a significant difference in the direction predicted. The one-*sample* *t*-test analyzes whether a sample is representative of a population. Likewise, the two-*tailed* test is one where the direction of difference isn't predicted and the two-*sample* test (the independent *t*-test here) just refers to the number of samples involved.

REQUIREMENTS FOR INDEPENDENT *T*-TESTS

Employing the independent *t*-test assumes certain conditions:

1. The samples must be independent. Members of one group cannot also be members of the other.

2. Ideally, the members of each group are randomly selected from the population. (However, this "requirement" is often not met and the test may be appropriate nevertheless.)

3. Samples are homoscedastic—that 50-cent word means that the two groups manifest similar variability (one isn't leptokurtic and the other platykurtic, for example). If there is homoscedasticity, a lack of random selection (requirement 2), becomes less important. This is what the SPSS Levene's test analyzes.

4. The dependent variable is measured on interval or ratio scale. Other tests allow for nominal and ordinal scale *DVs*.

A Reminder About Decision Errors

When accepting or rejecting the null hypothesis, remember that the decision is based on what is probable, rather than what is certain. By definition, occasionally an outcome defies the odds and the most probable statistical decision is erroneous. If one conducts an independent *t*-test, and the calculated value of *t* exceeds the table value, the two samples *probably do not* represent populations with the same mean. But they could.

Although they aren't common (not statistically likely), some of the outcomes that belong to the population *are* extreme because the tails include increasingly improbable results. Even with extreme *t* scores, the two samples may still represent populations with identical means. If they do, rejecting H_o results in an alpha, or type I, error (Chapter 5).

Conversely, perhaps the samples represent populations with significantly different means but because the measuring instrument isn't very sophisticated and important differences aren't detected, *t* is less than the table value and one fails to reject H_o. This is a beta, or type II, error.

Power and Statistical Testing

"Powerful" statistical tests are those which produce relatively few beta errors. That is, they are more likely to detect significant differences. To increase the power of a statistical test, one can:

1. Increase sample size. Other things equal, tests with large samples detect significant differences more readily than those with small samples.

2. Increase the probability at which H_o is rejected. Altering the statistical significance criterion from $p = .01$ to .05 will increase (by a factor of 5), the probability of a significant result. It isn't common, but researchers sometimes raise alpha to .1 (see Taylor, Welch, Kim, & Sherman, 2007, for an example).

3. Improve the measurement instrument. Instruments that detect subtle differences in whatever is measured are more likely to yield significance.

Practical Significance

Suggestion 1 above implies that when samples are large, relatively smaller differences between groups become significant. It's important to note, however, that statistical significance indicates reliability or consistency rather than strength. "Significance" means that repeating the experiment with new data will likely yield the same result. It doesn't mean that the result is necessarily important in practical terms. This is the issue that measures of effect size such as **Cohen's *d*** and ***omega*-squared** address. Because they indicate the importance of the independent variable to the outcome, they are relevant *only when t is found significant.*

Cohen's *d* looks something like the independent *t*-test:

$$d = \frac{(M_1 - M_2)}{s_{dv}}$$ 6.7

Where,

$M_1 - M_2$ are the means of the two samples, and

s_{dv} is the standard deviation of the dependent variable for all subjects (both groups)

In the conventional math instruction versus computer-aided instruction example with uneven sample sizes, we had the following:

$M_1 = 43.30$

$M_2 = 55.545$

We need the standard deviation of all 21 scores:

Mr. Valero's class: 47, 36, 39, 27, 52, 55, 43, 40, 49, 45

The colleague: 41, 45, 59, 61, 59, 58, 49, 55, 63, 57, 64

Verify that *for all 21* scores, $s_{dv} = 9.875$

The Cohen's *d* value becomes:

$$d = \frac{(M_1 - M_2)}{s_{dv}}$$

$$d = \frac{(43.3 - 55.545)}{9.875}$$

$$d = -1.24$$

■ Cohen's *d* and *omega*-squared both indicate the practical importance of a significant *t* value.

Treated as an absolute value, Cohen's *d* has a lower limit of 0, but no upper limit. To help us interpret the value, Cohen suggests that if

d = .4, or lower, the effect of the independent variable is "small"

d = .5 to .7, the effect is "medium"

d = .8, or greater, the effect is "large"

The computer effect is "large."

Omega-squared (ω^2) is another measure of effect size, but unlike Cohen's *d*, omega-squared has an upper limit of 1.0. A zero (the lower limit) means that none of the variance is explained by the independent variable. A value near zero is unlikely except with extremely large samples and values of *t* that just meet the critical (table) value. At the other extreme, $\omega^2 = 1.0$ indicates that the *IV* explains *all* of the variance. This is even more unlikely since *t* controls just one *IV* and with people, at least, there are usually many variables at work.

For an independent *t*-test *omega*-squared is:

$$\omega^2 = \frac{t^2 - 1}{t^2 + n_1 + n_2 - 1}$$

6.8

Where *t* = the calculated value of *t*

n_1 = the size of sample 1

n_2 = the size of sample 2

When we compared Mr. Valero's students with his colleague's, we found that *t* = −3.578 and that it was statistically significant. That value and the sizes of the two groups are all we need to proceed.

$$\omega^2 = \frac{t^2 - 1}{t^2 + n_1 + n_2 - 1} = \frac{-3.578 - 1}{-3.578^2 + 10 + 11 - 1} = .360$$

The value indicates that about 36% of the difference between the two groups of students' math scores can be explained by the type of instruction (whether instruction was supplemented with computer work). The other approximately 64% of the difference is due to other factors. Perhaps:

- The two groups of students didn't have equivalent abilities to begin with.
- One class did more homework than the other.
- The colleague is a better instructor than Mr. Valero.

Performance differences usually have a number of explanations, which is why we want to determine how much of the difference is traceable to the *IV* we've controlled.

Three footnotes to this discussion:

1. Neither Cohen's *d* nor *omega*-squared is calculated unless the difference between groups is statistically significant. If one fails to reject the null hypothesis there's nothing to explain because any difference between the two groups is assumed to be a random outcome.

2. Take care that the value of *t* used in *omega*-squared is the *calculated* value of *t*, not the table value.

3. Unfortunately, neither of these statistics is an option in SPSS. Of the two, Cohen's *d* is probably more common but *omega*-squared may be easier to interpret.

Another Example

Checking the table for critical values of *t* indicates that if we had two samples of 61 people each the critical value is 1.9799 at *p* = .05 and 120 *df*. If a test yielded *t* = 1.98, the result would be statistically significant. How much of the variance is explained in such an outcome?

$$\omega^2 = \frac{t^2 - 1}{t^2 + n_1 + n_2 - 1} = \frac{1.98^2 - 1}{1.98^2 + 61 + 61 - 1} = \frac{2.920}{124.920} = .023$$

With this sample size and this value of *t* the result, although statistically significant, allows one to explain just 2% of the variance! Is it statistically significant? Yes. Is it practically significant? Probably not.

SUMMARY

We began with questions about how to determine a significant difference between the performance of Mr. Valero's students and students statewide. With neither the standard deviation for the population (σ) nor a population standard error of the mean (σ_m) we abandoned *z* for the one-sample *t*.

There's a risk involved in using statistics to estimate the value of parameters. Sometimes statistics are poor equivalents for the parameters they replace. Occasionally an SE_m value is substantially unlike the σ_m value it estimates. The adjustment is a "sliding scale" of critical values indexed to degrees of freedom with larger critical values used for small samples since that's where the risk is greatest that the sample may not represent the population.

With the independent *t*-test, rather than a significant difference between sample and population, the issue is whether the populations from which the samples are drawn have the same mean—Mr. Valero's students versus his colleague's. Like the z test and the one-sample t, we created a ratio of the difference between means compared with the variability within groups. When the ratio is larger than the critical value from the table, the difference is statistically significant.

Both one-sample and independent t-tests can be configured as one- or two-tailed tests. Although two-tailed tests are more common, occasionally prior research will indicate the direction of the difference allowing it to be predicted with some confidence. At such times one can place the entire rejection region in one tail, but the trade-off is no rejection region in the other tail to cover an unexpected outcome.

Remember that statistical significance means only that something isn't likely to have occurred by chance. It doesn't reveal whether the outcome matters in a practical way, but Cohen's d and *omega*-squared address that issue. They indicate the magnitude of the effect that the independent variable has on the dependent variable.

Finally, this is a good time for a progress check. Stay with the concepts in this chapter until you're reasonably comfortable (is that the right word?) with them because they're the foundation for what is coming. Nothing in the next couple of chapters is inherently more complex than what is here, however, so if you understand this chapter you'll do fine with analysis of variance. Stay with it!

EXERCISES

1. A group of eighth-grade students in an Honors English program have the following reading comprehension scores: 67, 55, 88, 74, 69, 81, 72, 70.
   a. What is the value of SE_m?
   b. Is this group representative of the population of all eighth-grade students for whom $\mu = 66.0$?

2. The admissions officer at a university is reviewing admissions scores from a group of applicants. They are 375, 400, 425, 425, 490, 500, 510, 530. Nationally, the mean is 500 points. Are these applicants representative of the national sample?

3. Eighth-grade students have the following reading comprehension scores: 52, 58, 64, 67, 67, 69, 70, 71. Are they significantly different from the honors students in item 1?

4. What is the equivalent in a one-sample t-test of the standard error of the difference in the independent t-test?

5. If a significance test is conducted at $p = .05$ and one rejects the null hypothesis, what is the probability of a type I error? Of a type II error?

6. The question is whether verbal reinforcement affects response rates. Subjects in Group 1 are verbally reinforced every time they respond to the instructor's questions. Subjects in Group 2 are not. After 2 weeks, the two groups are compared by gauging the number of

students who raise their hands when questions are asked. Group 1: 13, 15, 12, 17, 14, 14. Group 2: 10, 12, 12, 11, 13, 9.

a. Does Group 1 perform significantly better than Group 2?
b. What is the alternate hypothesis for "a"?
c. What is the value of Cohen's *d*? What does it mean?
d. How much of response rate can be explained by whether students are reinforced (ω^2)?

7. Someone is interested in comparing the spelling performance of students in two different classrooms.

a. What is the independent variable?
b. What is the dependent variable?
c. What must be the scale of the *IV* in order to use an independent *t*?
d. What will be the scale of the *DV* in order to use an independent *t*?

8. Other things equal, what will be the effect on the power of an independent *t*-test of increasing *n*?

9. A college counselor wonders whether second semester students take fewer units than first semester students. From the population of each group she selects 10 at random. Before she can secure the data, one of the second semester students transfers to another school leaving her with the following:

First semester students: 10, 12, 14, 14, 15, 15, 15, 16, 16, 18
Second semester students: 6, 9, 9, 10, 12, 12, 12, 13, 14

a. Is this a one- or a two-tailed test?
b. What is the alternative hypothesis in this case?
c. Is the difference statistically significant? If so,
d. How would you explain the effect size (*d*)?
e. With .95 confidence, what are the lower and upper bounds of the differences between the means of the related populations?

10. The California Department of Education maintains a site for reporting test results (http://star.cde.ca.gov/star2007/index.asp). *If* (The "if" is there because the standard deviations are estimated. The website provides test means, numbers of students, and a wealth of other information but no standard deviations) seventh-grade students at two schools in a particular district achieved the following on the California Achievement-test (CAT):

School #1: $M = 672.0$, $s = 106.927$, $n = 490$
School #2: $M = 633.9$, $s = 94.285$, $n = 390$

a. Is the difference in scores statistically significant even though both schools come from the same district? (When the table doesn't list the particular degrees of freedom, use the critical value for the next lower *df*.)
b. According to *omega*-squared, how much of the variance in student achievement is attributable to the school?

REFERENCES

Kerlinger, F. N., & Lee, H. B. (2000). *Foundations of behavioral research* (4th ed.). Fort Worth, TX: Harcourt College Publishers.

Taylor, S. E., Welch, W. T., Kim, H. S., & Sherman, D. K. (2007). Cultural differences in the impact of social support on psychological and biological stress responses. *Psychological Science, 18,* 831–837.

Vogt, W.P. (1999). *Dictionary of statistics and methodology* (2nd ed.). Thousand Oaks, CA: Sage.

THE FORMULAE AND THEIR SYMBOLS

Formula 6.1: $SE_m = \dfrac{s}{\sqrt{n}}$

This is the formula for the estimated standard error of the mean.

Formula 6.2: $t = \dfrac{(M - \mu_m)}{SE_m}$

This is the test statistic for the one-sample *t*-test.

Formula 6.3: $= t = \dfrac{(M_1 - M_2)}{SE_d}$

The test statistic for the independent *t*-test.

Formula 6.4: $SE_d = \sqrt{(SEm_1^2 + SEm_2^2)}$

The estimated standard error of the difference, the denominator in the independent *t*-test, when sample sizes are equal.

Formula 6.5: $SE_d = \sqrt{\left[\dfrac{(n_1 - 1)s_1^2 + (n_2 - 1)s_2^2}{(n_1 + n_2 - 2)}\right]\left[\dfrac{1}{n_1} + \dfrac{1}{n_2}\right]}$

This is the formula for the standard error of the difference when sample sizes are unequal. It will work for equal sample sizes as well but it's more work than Formula 6.4.

Formula 6.6: $CI_{.95} = +/-t(SE_d) + (M_1 - M_2)$

This is the formula for a .95 confidence interval for the difference between the means of the two populations represented by the samples in an independent *t*-test.

Formula 6.7: $d = \dfrac{(M_1 - M_2)}{s_{dv}}$

This is Cohen's d, a statistic that indicates the effect size for a significant t in an independent t-test.

Formula 6.8: $\omega^2 = \dfrac{t^2 - 1}{t^2 + n_1 + n_2 - 1}$

This is the formula for *omega*-squared, a statistic that provides an estimate for the amount of variability in the dependent variable that can be attributed to the impact of the independent variable.

STUDENT STUDY SITE

Visit the Student Study Site at **www.sagepub.com/tanner** for additional learning tools.

Chapter 7

ONE-WAY ANALYSIS OF VARIANCE

THE PROBLEM: HOW TO DETECT SIGNIFICANT DIFFERENCES IN MORE THAN TWO GROUPS

In a rural school district, three elementary schools feed the middle school. All the elementary schools serve students who are demographically similar, but the philosophies of the principals are very different. The principal at Roosevelt Elementary is very involved with his teachers. He often monitors their instruction and creates opportunities for them to meet with one another to discuss what works well in their classrooms. The principal at Anthony is supportive and encouraging, but prefers to allow her teachers more latitude regarding how they approach their classroom activities. The principal at MacArthur Elementary is primarily oriented toward managing the school. His priority is to see procedures followed, schedules maintained, and students' behavior managed. Organization is his by-word. The superintendent's question is whether the different leadership styles are reflected in students' performances.

QUESTIONS AND ANSWERS

❑ How can the analyses performed with *t*-test be extended to more than two groups?

This question will bring us to analysis of variance (*ANOVA*).

❑ If results in a comparison of more than two groups indicate significance, which groups are significantly different from which?

This question will bring us to what are called *post-hoc* tests.

❑ With *t*-test an effect size calculation indicated the importance of a significant outcome. Is there an equivalent for *ANOVA*?

There are actually several ways to estimate effect size. We'll use *eta*-squared.

A CONTEXT FOR ANALYSIS OF VARIANCE

■ **Analysis of variance** is a procedure for detecting significant differences among any number of groups with one test.

Analysis of variance (*ANOVA*) allows one to compare any number of groups and with one test, determine whether there are significant differences between any two of the groups. The name deserves some comment. Since they both examine how scores vary between groups, doesn't it seem that z test and the t-tests should also be called analyses of variance? In fact those procedures do analyze variance. Indeed, nearly all statistical procedures analyze variance, but the analysis of variance we're concerned with here is a procedure associated with Ronald Fisher who, in naming it as he did, emphasized the need to analyze variability coming from multiple sources. The test statistic for *ANOVA* is, not coincidentally, labeled *F*.

Fisher believed that one could answer important questions about differences among groups by analyzing the variance from multiple sources in relatively small samples, and do so all in one experiment. For example, and directly relevant to the superintendent's problem in the introduction, Fisher's approach at an agricultural station in the English countryside was to have several small plots of ground each with different levels of whatever independent variables he was studying (fertilizer, pesticide), and then note the different impact on crops. This was in contrast to the approach by his primary professional adversary, Karl Pearson (yes, the *Pearson Correlation* Pearson, if you're familiar with that procedure). Pearson advocated altering just one variable at a time and employing the largest samples possible. Fisher and Pearson became highly critical of each other. Their conflict spilled into the public arena when they attacked one another's conclusions in the published literature.

In an irony of ironies, when Pearson died, Fisher was offered Pearson's endowed chair at University College, London. The story gets even better because a second endowed chair was awarded to Pearson's son, Egon. To pursue what seems too much like a soap opera now, the Fisher/Pearson acrimony continued unabated to the second Pearson generation. Fisher resented the criticism he had received when Pearson was an established scholar and Fisher was just beginning his career, and of course Pearson's son felt the need to defend his father's legacy.

In any event, in the course of his interest in biology and in genetics particularly, Fisher made an enormous contribution to the development of statistical analysis. The *ANOVA*, testing the null hypothesis, and the .05 criterion for statistical significance are all connected to Fisher. He also did a great deal to develop some of the nonparametric statistical procedures that we'll cover in later chapters.

A Look Backward

It's easy to become a little overwhelmed with all that a statistics course involves, but at least there's a consistency to what we've done. To this point, the dependent variable in each procedure has been interval or ratio scale, and the independent variable has been nominal scale. This pattern holds for z test, the t-tests, and now continues with *ANOVA*.

Furthermore, note that the z and the t-tests' test statistics are all based on ratios. They are ratios of the difference *between* groups ($M - \mu_M$, or $M_1 - M_2$), to some measure of the variability *within* the groups (σ_M, SE_M, or SE_d). Although the notation will change as we shift to a new measure of data variability, the pattern of comparing between-groups variability with within-groups variability to determine the value of the test statistic continues with the *ANOVA*. The test statistic is F rather than t or z, but the ratio indicates a comparison similar to those earlier tests. There *is* order in the statistical universe!

The Advantages of Analysis of Variance

Gossett's t-tests (Chapter 6) allow one to determine whether there are statistically significant differences between a sample and a population, or between two groups. Since the superintendent has three groups (three elementary schools), why not just use the t-test to make all possible comparisons between the performance of students at Roosevelt, Anthony, and MacArthur schools and answer the question that way? For example:

t-test #1: compare Roosevelt students to those at Anthony

t-test #2: compare Roosevelt students to those at MacArthur

t-test #3: compare Anthony students to MacArthur students

Extending this to more than three groups will reveal one of the problems with this approach. Calculating all possible comparisons with three schools is one thing, but it becomes unmanageable with large numbers of groups. What if there were six schools? Table 7.1 provides a matrix indicating all possible comparisons for six groups. Completing three independent t-tests probably isn't an inordinate amount of work, but completing 15 tests (the number of groups times the number of groups minus 1, divided by 2) starts to look more than a little tedious, even with computer help!

Table 7.1 How Many Possible Comparisons Are There Among Six Schools?

The Schools		A	B	C	D	E	F
	A		AB	AC	AD	AE	AF
	B			BC	BD	BE	BF
	C				CD	CE	CF
	D					DE	DF
	E						EF
	F						

Assuming that one *were* masochistic enough to compare several groups two at a time, there is a more insidious problem. Recall that whenever one rejects the null hypothesis in a statistical test, there is a risk of committing a type I (alpha) error. The probability of type I error when the result is found to be significant is indicated by the level adopted for the test, typically .05. The .05 probability signifies that for any statistically significant outcome there is a 1 in 20 chance that the result actually *is* characteristic. At 1 in 20 it's unlikely perhaps, but our problem is that if one completes a series of tests using the same data, the potential for type I error *increases with each successive significant finding*. By the time multiple "significant" comparisons are completed, the .05 criterion no longer accurately indicates the probability of a type I error. The risk can become substantially greater than whatever probability level one has selected for the test, as the box just below indicates.

To Underscore the Point: Increasing Alpha Levels

If there *were* six schools, and we decided to conduct the 15 possible *t*-tests, we can calculate the changing level of alpha with the formula below. If we conducted the first *t*-test at $\alpha = .05$, found the result to be significant, and then continued onto the second test and likewise found that significant, and so on until the 15th comparison, what would the risk of type I error be for the final comparison?

$$\alpha_e = 1 - (1-\alpha)^d$$

where α = the established level of type I error

α_e = the estimated level of type I error after successive significant findings.

d = number of decisions to reject.

$$\alpha_e = 1 - (1 - \alpha)^d$$

$$= 1 - (1 - .05)^{15} = .463$$

(note: $1 - .05 = .95$; 95^{15} is keyed with ".95 y^x 15 =")

If each prior decision is a decision to reject, by the time we get to the 15th comparison, a coin flip to decide whether the result is statistically significant provides a decision almost as accurate (Meyers, Gamst, & Guarino, 2006)!

The great advantage of *ANOVA* is that any significant difference between any two of the groups involved can be detected with just one test. Because it's one test, we avoid the problem of mounting type I error that remains at the initial level.

THE ONE-WAY *ANOVA*

The superintendent wants to know whether differences in fifth-grade reading performance are associated with differences in principals' leadership styles. All the students in the district have taken the reading portion of the Iowa Test of Basic Skills (ITBS). If the only difference between the groups is the principal's leadership, a comparison will indicate whether leadership style is significant to understanding students' performance. There are other factors that could influence students' reading performance, of course. They include differences in students' demographic characteristics, students' levels of ability, the support parents offer for school activities, teachers' aptitude, teachers' experience, teachers' instructional approaches, and so on to name just a few.

It would take a very carefully controlled experiment to have confidence that none of these other variables are factors in students' performance differences, but we need to rule them out because this first *ANOVA* procedure is called a **one-way *ANOVA*.** It's a test for analyzing the impact of multiple levels or manifestations of *one* independent variable on a dependent variable. In our case, the multiple manifestations of the *IV* are the principals' different leadership styles and the *DV*, of course, is students' performance on the reading test. Recall that if there were just two levels of the *IV* (if there were

■ One-way *ANOVA* analyzes any number of groups for significant differences, but accommodates just one independent variable.

two schools rather than three), we could also answer the question with an independent *t*-test. This makes sense because the two procedures have important similarities. Besides both producing test statistics that are ratios of between-groups variability to within-groups variability as we mentioned above, note the similarities in the scale of the data involved:

Independent
The <i>IV</i> Variable   Dependent
The <i>DV</i> Variable

Independent *t*-test	nominal scale	interval or ratio scale
One-way *ANOVA*	nominal scale	interval or ratio scale

The Hypotheses

If there are no significant differences associated with the principals' leadership styles, and all other conditions are constant across the three schools, the students from three schools all represent populations with the same mean level of reading achievement. This is the assumption that the null hypothesis makes:

$$H_o: \mu_1 = \mu_2 = \mu_3.$$

If leadership style doesn't affect reading scores, the superintendent will "fail to reject" the hypothesis. Because this test is a test of all possible differences between groups, we're looking for *any* significant differences between *any* of the groups. Any significant difference will prompt the superintendent to reject the null hypothesis. Because there are multiple groups and multiple possible combinations of differences, there are actually several possible alternate hypotheses. Consider the following:

a. $H_A: \mu_1 \neq \mu_2 \neq \mu_3$—the means of the populations from which each group is drawn are all significantly different from each other

b. $H_A: \mu_1 = \mu_2 \neq \mu_3$—the mean of the population from which Group 3 is drawn is significantly different from the means of the populations of each of the other two groups

c. $H_A: \mu_1 \neq \mu_2 = \mu_3$—the mean of the population from which Group 1 was drawn is significantly different from the means of the populations from which the other two groups were drawn

d. $H_A: \mu_1 = \mu_3 \neq \mu_2$—the means of the population from which Groups 1 and 3 were drawn are significantly different from the mean of the populations from which Group 2 was drawn

Perhaps prior research indicates that the students at the laissez-faire principal's school (those at MacArthur School, No. 3) will perform differently than students at the other two schools. If that's the hypothesis being tested, "b" is the alternate hypothesis. Ordinarily, however, the question is just whether there is a significant difference anywhere, so rather than listing all alternatives, something that gets messy with multiple groups, the alternate hypothesis is just a general:

H_A: *not so*

This abbreviated alternate hypothesis just indicates that all groups do *not* represent populations with the same mean; that somewhere there's a difference.

In the event that all groups don't belong to populations with the same means and we reject H_o, there's a problem we didn't have with the *t*-test. The *ANOVA* test won't indicate which group is significantly different from which, or whether all are different from each other, only that somewhere there's a significant difference. We'll tackle that problem later in the chapter with what are called *post-hoc* tests.

The Sources of Variance

Conceptually at least, much of what Fisher did was not entirely novel. We keep noting that in the independent *t*-test, Gosset examined the variability between groups ($M_1 - M_2$, the numerator in the *t* ratio) and within groups (the standard error of the difference SE_d, the denominator in the *t*-ratio) and there are corollaries in *ANOVA*. But rather than using the variance statistics used in the *t*-tests, the estimated standard error of the mean (SE_M) and the standard error of the difference (SE_d), Fisher used the **sum of squares** (SS) to measure data variability. Like any of the other measures of data variability, the sum of squares indicates how much scores tend to vary from a mean, and also like the others, the minimum possible SS value is 0; there's no such thing as negative variance.

■ **Sum of squares** values are the sum of the squared deviations of individual scores from a mean.

The Total Sum of Squares

Analysis of variance involves a number of group means. Besides the means of each group, M_1, M_2, and so on we will need a mean for all of the data. It's the sum of all the scores in all of the groups divided by the total number of all subjects, N. We'll call this mean the grand mean (M_G). Recall from Chapter 2 that part of what we did to calculate variance and standard deviation statistics was to subtract the mean of the group from each individual score, square the differences, and then sum the squared differences.

If one were to follow that same procedure with the M_G, subtracting it from each score in all of the groups, the result is a measure of data variability for all the groups together. Based on the *sum of the squared deviations* of all the individual scores from the grand mean, it's called a sum of squares value. In this case, because it's based on data from all the individuals in all of the groups it's called the sum of squares total, SS_{tot} and it's an important component of analysis of variance. The formula for SS_{tot} is as follows:

$$SS_{tot} = \Sigma(x - M_G)^2 \qquad\qquad 7.1$$

Where,

SS_{tot} = the total sum of squares

x = each individual score

M_G = the mean of all scores, "the grand mean"

$\Sigma(x - M_G)^2$ = the sum of the squared differences between each individual score in each group and the grand mean

To repeat the steps for calculating SS_{tot}:

1. Calculate the mean of all scores from all groups combined (M_G)

2. Subtract M_G from each individual score

3. Square each of the differences

4. Sum the squared differences to get SS_t

There are other ways to calculate SS_{tot}, as well as the other SS values that are coming up, but they all result in the same values. When there are large data sets and a good deal of longhand calculating, some authors recommend the use of what are called "calculation formulae" (see, for example, Sprinthall, 2007). They make the work less tedious, but sometimes the logic isn't very clear. Since using the computer is likely how you'll do most of your *ANOVA* work anyway, we'll take a conceptual approach so that the logic behind these SS statistics makes more intuitive sense.

Remember that the designation "SS_{tot}" indicates that this statistic includes all variability from all sources. The "analysis" in analysis of variance is the business of deriving and comparing the variance between individual groups and the grand mean M_G, and the variability that occurs within the individual groups. The *ANOVA* test statistic, F, is going to be the ratio of the between-groups variability to the within-groups variability.

Study Figure 7.1 for a moment. Although the three groups in 7.1A and the three groups in 7.1B all exhibit about the same amount of difference between the means of the groups, the variability *within* the groups is very different from A to B. The "A" groups overlap each other a good deal in their tails; the "B" groups don't. *Statistical significance in ANOVA occurs when the ratio of between variability to within variability is large.* Which trio of groups is more likely to yield a statistically significant difference?

Figure 7.1   Three Groups: Characteristic of the Same (A), or of Different (B) Populations?

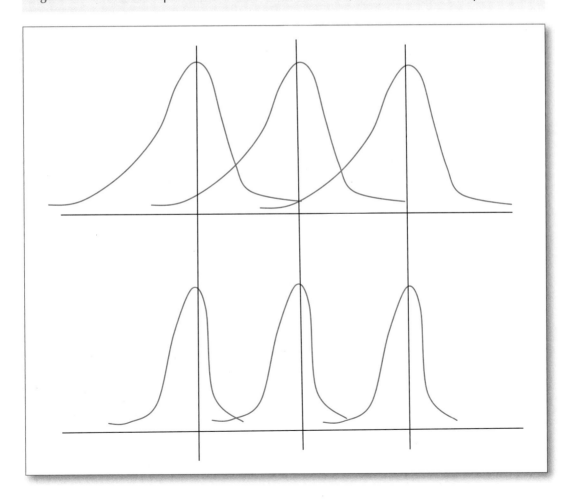

With the same between variability in both, but much more within variability in the "A" groups, can you see that the "B" groups are going to yield a much larger ratio of between-to-within variability? The within variability is likely going to overwhelm the between variability in the "A" groups. Although we're calculating variability differently, it is still the ratio of between groups variability to within groups variability that we're interested in, just as it was with the independent t-test in Chapter 6.

Now back to our problem. In order to pursue her question about significant differences between reading students the superintendent randomly selects six fifth-grade students from each school and checks their reading scores. As percent of items correct, the scores are as follows:

Schools Students	Roosevelt	Anthony	MacArthur
1.	34	48	38
2.	39	54	42
3.	42	65	47
4.	48	79	54
5.	53	85	64
6.	60	92	73

In Table 7.2, the SS_{tot} is determined for these data, a value you will want, or at least ought, to confirm.

Recall that SS_{tot} is the sum of the squared deviations of individual scores (x) from the mean of all the scores (M_g). The result is a measure of the variability from all sources. The $SS_{tot} = 4826.500$.

The Between and Within Sums of Squares

Because the SS_{tot} consists of the variability between the groups (SS_{bet}) as well as the variability within the groups (SS_{with}), we need to "partition" the variance. The SS_{bet} measures how much individual group means (M_1, M_2, M_3) differ from the grand mean (M_G). If we've controlled the other things that could affect students' reading, the SS_{bet} will measure whether the independent variable (the principals' leadership styles) has had a significant impact on the dependent variable (students' reading scores).

Even the most carefully constructed study never controls all other factors completely, so some of the variance between the groups and M_G is going to be "error variance," and is unrelated to the treatment. We'll have to account

Table 7.2 Calculating the Total Sum of Squares (SS_t)

$SS_{tot} = \Sigma(x-M_G)^2$

Grand Mean (M_G) = (276 + 423 + 318)/18 = 56.5

Student	School								
	Roosevelt			Anthony			MacArthur		
	x_a	$x-M_G$	sq'd diff	x_b	$x-M_G$	sq'd diff	x_c	$x-M_G$	sq'd diff
1.	34	−22.5	506.25	48	−8.5	72.25	38	−18.5	342.25
2.	39	−17.5	306.25	54	−2.5	6.25	42	−14.5	210.25
3.	42	−14.5	210.25	65	8.5	72.25	47	−9.5	90.25
4.	48	−8.5	72.25	79	22.5	506.25	54	−2.5	6.25
5.	53	−3.5	12.25	85	28.5	812.25	64	7.5	56.25
6.	60	3.5	12.25	92	35.5	1260.25	73	16.5	272.25
Sum	276		1119.5	423		2729.5	318		977.5

$SS_t = 1119.50 + 2729.50 + 977.50 = \textbf{4826.50}$

for the error variance, but in the meantime, our formula for SS_{bet} when there are three groups is

$$SS_{bet} = (M_a - M_G)^2 n_a + (M_b - M_G)^2 n_b + (M_c - M_G)^2 n_c \qquad 7.2$$

Where M_a = the mean for group A

M_G = the grand mean

n_a = the number in group A

$(M_a - M_G)^2 n_a$ = the square of the difference between the mean of group A and the grand mean, divided by the number in group A

The formula calls for us to

1. Determine the mean of all of the data (M_G) (which we already have from calculating SS_{tot})

2. Determine the mean for each group (M_a . . . M_k)

3. Subtract M_G from each group mean

4. Square the difference

5. Adjust for sample size by multiplying the squared difference by the number in each group

For the students from the three schools, the group means are

- Roosevelt $M_a = 46.0$
- Anthony $M_b = 70.50$
- MacArthur $M_c = 53.0$

For *all* the data together the mean $(M_G) = 56.5$ (Table 7.2). Since $n = 6$ in each group, we calculate SS_{bet} as follows:

$$SS_{bet} = (46 - 56.5)^2 6 + (70.50 - 56.5)^2 6 + (53.0 - 56.50)^2 6 = \mathbf{1911.00}$$

The SS_w, conversely, is a measure of how much data vary *within* the groups. Because they differ individually, even students from the same school don't all respond the same way to a stimulus (the principal's leadership). Unavoidably, some of this variability shows up in SS_{bet}, but in SS_w it's *all* differences within groups. The evidence for it is the differences there are between the scores of individuals in the same group. We'll measure SS_w by comparing scores in each group to their group means. Consider Formula 7.3:

$$SS_{with} = \Sigma (x_a - M_a)^2 + \Sigma (x_b - M_b)^2 + \Sigma (x_c - M_c)^2 \qquad 7.3$$

This formula indicates that there are three groups, a, b, and c (representing the three schools), and we understand the terms as follows:

SS_{with} = the sum of squares within and

Σ = summation, or sum of x_a = for each score in group "a"

M_a = the mean of the scores in group "*a*"

$\Sigma (x_a - M_a)^2$ = the sum of the squared differences between individuals in group a (x_a) and the mean of group a

To calculate SS_w

1. Determine the mean of the scores from group "a" (M_a)

2. Subtract M_a from each score in group "a"

3. Square each difference value

4. Sum the squared differences for the group

5. Repeat Steps 1–4 for each of the other groups

6. Sum the results across the groups

In Table 7.3, the SS_w is determined for the reading scores for students from the three schools; $SS_{with} = \mathbf{2915.500}$.

Technically, since $SS_{tot} = SS_{bet} + SS_{with}$, we might have determined SS_{with} by subtraction because it's going to be whatever is left from the SS_{tot} after SS_{bet} is removed. The various $(x - M)$ calculations are tedious, but they also clarify that it is actually within-groups variability that's being calculated. Besides, it's a good accuracy check. Taking the shorter approach

$$SS_{with} = SS_{tot} - SS_{bet}$$ 7.4

$4826.500 - 1911.000 = 2915.500$

Table 7.3   Calculating the Within Sum of Squares (SS_w) for a One-Way *ANOVA*

$SS_{with} = \Sigma(x_\alpha - M_a)^2 + \Sigma(x_b - M_b)^2 + \Sigma(x_c - M_c)^2$

	$M_a = 46.0$			$M_b = 70.5$			$M_c = 53.0$		
	x_a	$x-M_a$	$(x-M_a)^2$	xb	$x-M_b$	$(x-M_a)^2$	x_c	$x-M_c$	$(x-M_a)^2$
	34	−12	144	48	−22.5	506.25	38	−15	225
	39	−7	49	54	−16.5	272.25	42	−11	121
	42	−4	16	65	−5.5	30.25	47	−6	36
	48	2	4	79	8.5	72.25	54	1	1
	53	7	49	85	14.5	210.25	64	11	121
	60	14	196	92	21.5	462.25	73	20	400
Sum	276		**458**	423		**1553.50**	318		**904**

$SS_w = 458 + 1553.50 + 904 = \mathbf{2915.50}$

Subtraction is certainly the easier approach, but if we derive SS_{with} this way and there is an error with the SS_{bet} calculation, it's just perpetuated with SS_{with}. If the SS_{bet} and SS_{with} are calculated independently, we can always double-check when finished to make sure they sum to SS_{tot}.

Interpreting the Variability Measures

So what do these SS values mean? Although sums of squares are variability measures like standard deviation and variances, a difference is that sums of squares values increase as the number of scores increases. Recall that standard deviation and variance measures values tend to shrink with additional data because scores near the mean of the distribution are more common than scores in the tails. Sums of squares don't shrink. Adding scores means more squared differences to add, which will always result in larger values.

■ The **mean square** in *ANOVA* is the sum of squares divided by its degrees of freedom.

This characteristic can make SS values difficult to interpret. A large SS value may indicate that individual scores tend to vary widely from whatever mean is subtracted from them, or it may just indicate that there are many scores in the group. Consequently, we do something analogous to creating an *average* by dividing SS values by their degrees of freedom. The result is another measure of variability called the **mean square** (*MS*).

Degrees of Freedom and the ANOVA

To continue with the one-way *ANOVA* procedure, we'll need *MS* values for both the SS_{bet} and the SS_{with}. They each have their own degrees of freedom, as does the SS_{tot}, by the way. They are as follows:

df for $SS_{tot} = N - 1$ where $N =$ the number of subjects in all groups

df for $SS_{bet} = k - 1$, where $k =$ the number of groups

df for $SS_{with} = N - K$, the total number of subjects, minus the number of groups

A *MS* value based on SS_{tot} doesn't help us with *ANOVA*. There isn't any need for an average measure of total variability, but we do need the *MS* values for the between and within SS. First, we'll calculate the MS_{bet}. Since there are three groups

$$df_{bet} = k - 1 = 2$$

$$SS_{bet} = 1911.00, \text{ so}$$

$MS_{bet} = 1911.00 \div 2 = \mathbf{955.50}$

For the MS_w, with an $N = 18$ and $k = 3$

$df_{with} = N - k = 18 - 3 = 15$

$SS_{with} = 2915.500$, so

$MS_{with} = 2915.500 \div 15 = \mathbf{194.367}$

The F Ratio

Once we have the mean square values, the next step is to calculate F, the test statistic in *ANOVA*. It's the ratio of the MS_{bet} to the MS_{with}:

$$F = MS_{bet} \div MS_{with} \qquad\qquad 7.5$$

The variability in MS_b reflects the variability in scores related to the independent variable, principals' leadership styles in our case, and some error. As a measure of person-to-person differences within the groups, the MS_w, the variability reflects *only* error. Regarding error, remember that in statistics, error refers to variability that isn't explained in the analysis; it isn't error in the sense of making a mistake. Some error is almost inevitable in a one-way *ANOVA* where, as we noted earlier, one can control just one independent variable. Assurances that other things are equal, notwithstanding, procedures that provide for control of just one variable when explaining human behavior will usually have a substantial error component.

Theoretically, if there were no treatment effect (the principals' leadership style had no impact on students' performance), the F ratio becomes a ratio of the measurement error to measurement error since the only thing left in MS_{bet} would be error and MS_{with} consists of only error. The numerator and the denominator of the F statistic could both have the same value resulting in an F statistic of 1.0.

For this problem, however, there *is* a treatment effect and the value is as follows:

$F = MS_{bet} \div MS_{with}$

$F = 955.50 \div 194.367 = \mathbf{4.916}$

As an aside, although we didn't speak of them as such, you've been calculating the equivalents of sums of squares and mean squares since Chapter 2. Consider Formulae 2.3 and 2.4 for the sample variance and the sample standard deviation, respectively. In either case the numerator is the sum of the squared deviations of individual scores from their mean, $\Sigma(x - M)^2$. That makes those numerators SS values. The denominator was $n - 1$, *the* degrees of freedom value. Dividing the SS value by their df produces what we have here called the mean square!

The Critical Value of F

The F value is interpreted relative to a table value. In the appendix at the back of the book, locate the table for "Critical Values of F in *ANOVA*," Table C. Just like the t table, it is indexed by degrees of freedom and the corresponding critical value identifies the point at which a calculated F value becomes statistically significant. *Un*like the table for critical values of t, F requires *two* df values, one for df between and one for df within. For the problem we just calculated

1. Read across the top of the table for the *between df*, 2 in this case, and down the left side for *within df*, 15 for this problem.

2. The intersection of the column for 2 across the top of the table and 13 down the side provides values for $p = .05$ and for $p = .01$.

3. Using the traditional $p = .05$, the related critical value is 3.68.

Except when presenting the critical value in a table as we will just below, it's a good idea to indicate the test level ($p = .05$ here), as well as the df (2 and 15 in our case) this way:

$$F_{.05\ (2,15)} = 3.68$$

This presentation makes it easy to distinguish the critical value of F from the calculated value.

The ANOVA Table

The results of the several things we did above to complete the *ANOVA* are presented in an *ANOVA* table. The columns will indicate

- The source of the variance
- The sum of squares values for each source
- The degrees of freedom for each
- The mean square values
- The value of f
- The table value with which F is compared

For the problem we've been working, the table looks this way:

Source	SS	df	MS	F	F_{crit} (.05)
Total	4826.50	17			
Between	1911.000	2	955.50	4.916	3.68
Within	2915.50	15	194.367		

Understanding the Calculated Value of F

The critical value indicates the point at which *F* becomes statistically significant and one rejects the null hypothesis. Unlike *t* and *z*, *F* can't be negative. As soon as we squared scores for the *SS* values we did away with that possibility; *F* can only be positive.

Because the calculated *F* (4.916) exceeds the table value (3.68) it's evident that somewhere in the populations represented by these three groups the means are unequal; the $\mu_1=\mu_2=\mu_3$ that was the null hypothesis does not hold; we reject H_o. That's a partial answer for the superintendent. Principals' leadership styles are related to statistically significant reading achievement differences among fifth-grade students, but *F* doesn't tell us which group is significantly different from which. It was easy with *t*. A significant difference meant that Group 1 was significantly different from Group 2. There was no other possibility, but a 3+ group *ANOVA* complicates things.

The *Post-Hoc* Test

The question "where's the difference?" is answered with a ***post-hoc test***. Literally an "after this" test, the *post hoc* is performed when *ANOVA* produces a significant *F*. If the *F* isn't significant, by the way, we're done.

■ *Post-hoc* tests identify which groups are significantly different from which after an *ANOVA.*

There are several *post-hoc* tests to choose from, each with its different strengths. We'll use *Tukey's HSD*. The *HSD* stands for "honestly significant difference." Maybe it's because the name makes us feel reassured, or because it's easy to calculate, but Tukey's HSD is a very popular *post-hoc* test.

The process is simple; we determine a value, and then look for any pair of groups for which the difference between their means is equal to or greater than that value. The formula for computing the *HSD* value is:

$$HSD = x\sqrt{MS_{with} / n} \qquad 7.6$$

Where,

x = a table value indicated by the number of groups (*k*) and the within degrees of freedom (df_{with})

MS_{with} = the *mean square within* value from the *ANOVA* table

n = the number in any group, *assuming equal group sizes*

Steps to computing the *HSD* value:

1. Divide the MS_{with} value by n

2. Take the square root of the result

3. Multiply by the value from the Tukey's table, Table D in Appendix A

The x value in the *HSD* formula comes from Table D:

1. Move across the top of the chart to the value indicating the number of groups in the problem (*not* the $k - 1$ we used for F)

2. Move down the left side of the chart to the appropriate MS_{with} *df*, which for this problem are 13

3. The value at the intersection of 3 across the top and 13 down the side for $p = .05$ is 3.73. Note that this isn't the value of *HSD*; it's a value we use in the formula for *calculating HSD*

If the *ANOVA* is run at $p = .05$, then any *post-hoc* test should likewise be conducted at the same level of probability.

To solve for *HSD*:

$$HSD = x\sqrt{(MS_{with}/n)}$$
$$= 3.73\sqrt{(194.367/6)}$$
$$= 21.230$$

Using the *HSD* value to locate significant differences isn't difficult if a matrix is prepared that indicates the difference between each pair of group means. The matrix for this problem makes up Table 7.4.

Any difference between a pair of means equal to, or larger than, the calculated *HSD* value indicates a statistically significant difference. For our problem, only the difference between the means of Roosevelt and Anthony meets that requirement, with *HSD* = 21.230, and the difference between the mean of Roosevelt and the mean of Anthony = 24.50.

- Students' reading scores at Roosevelt are significantly different from those at Anthony.
- Other differences (Roosevelt versus MacArthur, Anthony versus MacArthur) are not statistically significant.

Table 7.4   Using Tukey's *HSD* to Determine Significantly Different Groups

	Roosevelt M = 46.0	Anthony M = 70.50	MacArthur M = 53.0	
Roosevelt M = 46.0		24.50	7.0	The Differences Between Means
Anthony M = 70.50			17.50	
MacArthur M = 53.0				

The Effect Size

The *ANOVA* and Tukey's *HSD* respond to two important questions:

1. Are there significant differences in reading achievement and, if so,

2. Which group(s) is/are significantly different from which?

There is a third question to ask whenever *F* is significant:

1. From a practical point of view, how important is the difference?

The question is relevant because a significant difference only means (in this case) that the difference between students at Roosevelt and those at Anthony is unlikely to be a chance difference. Not all nonrandom differences are necessarily important. If a significant difference has very little effect, the superintendent will probably react quite differently than if the students at one school are performing very differently than those at another.

With the *t*-test in Chapter 6, we used Cohen's *d* and *omega*-squared (ω^2) to measure the effect size for a significant *t*. Although Cohen's *d* is specific to *t*-test, omega-squared isn't and, with some modifications in the way it's calculated, it could have been used here as well. However, SPSS provides a different statistic called, **partial *eta*-squared** (the Greek letter η is

■ Partial *eta*-squared gauges the proportion of variance in an *ANOVA* explained by the IV.

pronounced like "ate a"), so we'll use that instead. It answers the same question that *omega*-squared answered for *t*-test:

> How *much* of the variability in the *DV* (reading scores) can be attributed to the *IV* (the principal's leadership style)?

The formula for partial *eta*-squared is

$$\eta_p^2 = \frac{SS_{bet}}{SS_{bet} + SS_{with}}$$
7.7

This is an easy calculation since the sums of squares values needed are already available from the *ANOVA* table. For our data the value of partial *eta*-squared is:

$$\eta_p^2 = 1911.00/(1911.00 + 2915.50)$$

$$= .396$$

About 40% (the η_p^2 value multiplied by 100 and rounded) of the group differences in reading scores can be explained by the principal's leadership style. This *eta*-squared value is probably unrealistically high, of course. Learners and learning environments are far too complex to make it likely that one variable will explain so much of the variance in reading achievement. Anyway, it's the calculation and interpretation we're interested in just now, not the validity as such.

Requirements for the One-Way *ANOVA*

1. Because it's a "one-way" *ANOVA*, there can be just one *IV*. That variable may have any number of levels or expressions more than one, but there can be just one variable whether it's the type of instruction, the school with which the group is associated, the level of drug the patient is given, or whatever.

2. The independent variable data either must be in categorical form (nominal scale) to begin with, or reduced to categorical form.

3. The dependent variable data must be at least interval scale.

4. The groups or categories must be independent. Subjects cannot belong to more than one group in this form of *ANOVA*.

"Rather than a play-off to determine the championship, we suggest a *post-hoc* test conducted at $p = .05$."

5. There must be the same homogeneity of variance that t-test requires—all groups must be distributed similarly.

6. Finally, it is assumed that the population from which the subjects are drawn is normally distributed.

Happily, *ANOVA* is pretty forgiving (the statistical lingo is "robust") when homogeneity of variance and normality assumptions are violated, particularly when the groups are relatively large. So unless there is a fairly obvious problem with the way the data are distributed, or with their normality, one needn't worry too much about these particular requirements.

LOOKING AT SPSS OUTPUT

If the problem just completed is done on SPSS, the following output is the result

	Sum of Squares	df	Mean Square	F	Sig.
Between Groups	1911.000	2	955.500	4.916	.023
Within Groups	2915.500	15	194.367		
Total	4826.500	17			

This table provides the same information that is in the table we made, except for the last ("Sig.") column. Note also that SPSS lists total sum or squares last instead of first. Regarding that last column, instead of listing a critical value and determining whether the calculated value of F exceeds that value, SPSS calculates the probability that the F value could have occurred by chance. If the Sig. value is .05, *or less*, the result is statistically significant by the usual standard. As with the t-tests on SPSS *the smaller the significance value, the less likely it is that the calculated value of the statistic could have occurred by chance*.

SUMMARY

In this chapter, we adapted many of the Chapter 6 concepts to accommodate more than two groups (although the *ANOVA* works for two groups as well). The sums of squares measures were new, but *ANOVA* has much in common with the independent t-test. In both cases, the test statistics are ratios of variability between groups, to variability within groups.

With *ANOVA* there can be three questions:

- Are there significant differences between two or more groups? If so,
- Which groups are significantly different from which?
- How important are the differences?

The test statistic is F, which, when significant, is followed by a *post-hoc* test to pinpoint which groups are significantly different from which. In this chapter we used Tukey's *HSD*, but there are other choices. When *ANOVA* is completed on SPSS and *post-hoc* tests are requested, there is a list of several from which to choose.

If F is statistically significant, it's also important to calculate some sort of effect size. These statistics suggest whether a significant difference has practical importance. In this chapter, we used partial *eta*-squared. When the *F* isn't statistically significant, by the way, both the *post-hoc* test and the effect size calculation are irrelevant since any variation between the characteristics of the groups is just random.

The one-way *ANOVA* is an important advance in statistical analysis, but very few of the problems instructors, counselors, or administrators are interested in lend themselves to single-variable explanations. Such approaches leave too much of the variance uncontrolled. The factorial *ANOVA* discussion that is Chapter 8 will allow us to include additional independent variables that are important to the analysis and so limit the variability that otherwise becomes error variance.

This analysis of variance chapter is probably the single most involved chapter in the book, but here you are and you ought to be reassured for having navigated it. Well done! Having triumphed over *ANOVA*, do the end-of-chapter problems while the concepts are fresh and then restudy the chapter to be sure that you can explain what you've done. The next chapter on factorial *ANOVA* builds squarely on this material.

EXERCISES

1. A group of learners is assigned a task that they may discontinue at any time. Using the number of minutes they remain on task as a measure of motive strength, we have the following measures: 1.0, 1.5, 1.5, 2.25. 3.0, 5.0 6.25. What is the sum of squares total for these data?

2. In a one-way *ANOVA*, identify the following:
    a. The measure of all variance from all sources
    b. The measure that indicates the average impact of the *IV*
    c. The average measure of uncontrolled variance

3. We have the following data on number of units for two groups of university students signing up for classes. One group is international students, and the other is from the local area. Treating the problem as an *ANOVA* in spite of the fact that there are just two groups, is there a significant difference in the number of units for which students in each group register?
    a. International Students: 12, 14, 16, 16, 17, 18, 18 18
    b. Domestic Students: 12, 12, 12, 14, 14, 14, 14, 16

4. Complete an independent *t*-test for the data in problem 3. If you square the value of *t* (t^2), what's its relationship to the *F* value in problem 3?

5. Even should the *F* be significant, why is a *post-hoc* test unnecessary in a problem like 3?

6. What's the point of calcuating η_p^2?

7. Three groups of students involved in the same curriculum are obliged to study for 15 minutes, 30 minutes, or 90 minutes a night for 8 weeks before taking a mathematics test. Their scores are as follows:

    15 minutes: 43, 39, 55, 56, 73
    30 minutes: 55, 58, 66, 79, 82
    90 minutes: 61, 66, 85, 86, 91

a. Are the differences statistically significant?
b. If F is significant, which group(s) is(are) significantly different from which?
c. How much of the difference in mathematics performance can be explained by how long students study?

8. In item 7, what is the independent variable?
   a. What is the data scale of the independent variable?
   b. What is the dependent variable?
   c. What is the data scale of the dependent variable?

9. A particular *ANOVA* problem involves four groups with 10 in each.

   $SS_{bet} = 24.0$
   $SS_{with} = 72$
   What's the value of F?
   Is F statistically significant?

10. Fill in the missing values:

Source	SS	df	MS	F	Crit.
Total	94				
Between		2			
Within	63		3		

REFERENCES

Meyers, L. S., Gamst, G., & Guarino, A. J. (2006). *Applied multivariate research: Design and interpretation*. Thousand Oaks, CA: Sage.

Sprinthall, R. C. (2007). *Basic statistical analysis* (8th ed.). Boston, MA: Allyn & Bacon.

THE FORMULAE AND THEIR SYMBOLS

Formula 7.1: $SS_{tot} = \Sigma(x - M_G)^2$ The total sum of squares, the total of all variance from all sources in an *ANOVA* problem.

Formula 7.2: $SS_{bet} = (M_a - M_G)^2 n_a + (M_b - M_G)^2 n_b + (M_c - M_G)^2 n_c$

The sum of squares between, which includes the effect of the *IV*(s) plus error variance, is a measure of how much individual groups differ from the mean of all the data.

Formula 7.3: $SS_{with} = \Sigma\,(x_a - M_a)^2 + \Sigma\,(x_b - M_b)^2 + \Sigma\,(x_c - M_c)^2$

The sum of squares within is a measure of how much individuals within a group differ when exposed to the same level of the *IV*(s). It's a measure of error variance.

Formula 7.4: $SS_{with} = SS_{tot} - SS_{bet}$ An alternate method for determining SS_w, it indicates that if the SS_{bet} is subtracted from SS_t, what is left is SS_w.

Formula 7.5: $F = MS_{bet} \div MS_{with}$. The *F* is the test statistic in analysis of variance. It's a ratio of treatment effect plus error variance, to just error variance.

Formula 7.6: $HSD = x\sqrt{(MS_w/n)}$ Tukey's *HSD* is a *post-hoc* test used to determine which groups in an *ANOVA* are significantly different from which.

Formula 7.7: $\eta_p^2 = SS_{bet}/(SS_{bet} + SS_w)$ Partial *eta*-squared is an estimate of effect size. It suggests the proportion of variance explained by the particular component. In this configuration it's the variability between groups.

STUDENT STUDY SITE

Visit the Student Study Site at **www.sagepub.com/tanner** for additional learning tools.

Chapter 8

THE FACTORIAL *ANOVA*

THE PROBLEM: HOW TO ANALYZE MULTIPLE INDEPENDENT VARIABLES IN AN *ANOVA*

The superintendent referenced in the Chapter 7 introduction is familiar with the research on the impact that parental support may have on students' reading performance. Satisfied that she knows how the principal's leadership style may affect students' achievement, the question now is how to factor differences in parental support into the mix. Is it too an important component to understanding students' performances?

QUESTIONS AND ANSWERS

❑ The one-way *ANOVA* accommodates just one independent variable. Does adding a second *IV* clarify the factors influencing the dependent variable?

The extension of one-way *ANOVA* to include more than one *IV* defines the *factorial ANOVA*.

❑ If multiple independent variables (*IV*s) are used in an analysis, is there a way to measure the impact that each has on the dependent variable (*DV*) so that one can gauge relative importance?

At this point, calculating effect sizes is no longer new. There are several effect size statistics that can be calculated for a factorial *ANOVA*. They each allow one to determine how well a particular *IV* or combination of *IV*s explains the *DV*. In this chapter, we'll use partial *eta*-squared.

LIMITATIONS IN THE INDEPENDENT *t*-TEST AND ONE-WAY *ANOVA*

The prior two chapters represent an important progression for anyone who does data analysis. In Chapter 6 the independent *t*-test allowed us for the first time to deal entirely with sample data—no need for population parameters in any of the calculations. The limitation, however, was that we could look for significant differences between just two independent groups at a time.

One-way *ANOVA* in Chapter 7 expanded our analytical abilities from two groups, to any number of groups for statistically significant differences, as long as all groups are tied to the same independent variable. The *IV* in a one-way *ANOVA* can have any number of categories of something like ethnicity, or religious affiliation, but all of the categories must be rooted in the same *IV*. In that regard the independent *t*-test and the one-way *ANOVA* are similar. They each accommodate just one independent variable. In the problem that provided much of the structure for Chapter 7 that one *IV* was the principal's leadership style. There might have been any number of schools involved in that analysis with as many distinct leadership styles as one might be able to define, but there's no place to include in the one-way *ANOVA* other factors that might be of interest.

When the subjects in a research study are people, being limited to one *IV* is a serious drawback. People are enormously complex, and an attempt to understand something that seems as straight-forward as student achievement is quickly oversimplified when the explanation is tied to just one factor. Achievement is multifaceted. You probably knew bright students who were indifferent achievers. You probably also knew students of relatively modest intellectual talent who consistently found a way to grind out top grades. Academic achievement is a function of multiple independent variables.

This raises questions. If some phenomenon is actually a product of several different influences, what happens when the explanation involves just one influence? What happens to the differences in whatever one is measuring (the *DV*) that are the result of factors other than the one in the analysis?

Remember that in an *ANOVA*, the measure of total variability is sum of squares total (SS_{tot}). In the one-way *ANOVA* that value had two components, the sum of squares between (SS_{bet}) and the sum of squares within (SS_{with}).

- The SS_{bet} value is the variability in the *DV* scores related to the influence of the *IV*, plus some error variance.
- The SS_{with} includes just the variability among subjects in the same groups. It's all error variance.

The limitation in the one-way *ANOVA* is that any scoring variability that isn't connected to the single *IV* has to emerge as error variance. It's uncontrolled variance that, you will remember, is what defines error in statistical analysis. If parental support isn't included in the analysis, any differences in students' reading scores that are related to differences in parental support have to emerge as error variance. They become part of the SS_w term.

THE FACTORIAL *ANOVA*

These are the circumstances that create a context for **factorial analysis of variance**. In the language of *ANOVA*, independent variables are "factors," and a "factorial" model is one in which there are two or more *IV*s in the analysis. There are some practical limitations, but in theory a researcher could introduce as many *IV*s into a factorial *ANOVA* as were thought necessary to explain the *DV*.

So back to the superintendent; if she has reason to believe that the principal's leadership style and parental involvement *both* have a significant impact on students' reading achievement, she can introduce them both into the analysis. But in order to do this, she'll have to figure out a way to measure parental involvement.

Perhaps among the students there are two kinds of parents, those who listen to their children read each week night for 20 minutes and a second group who do not. In this case we can "measure" this variable in terms of whether they did or did not listen. This will make both the principal's leadership style, which by inference is the school the child attended, *and* whether the parents were involved both independent variables. The reading scores remain the dependent variable.

With a second independent variable there are three kinds of data for each of the 18 students. To set up the analysis one must know

- Which school the student attended, which is the first *IV*
- Whether the parents were involved in the reading, which is the second *IV*
- How the student scored on the reading test, the *DV*

Note that for both the *IV*s the data are nominal scale. That's a constant in *ANOVA* problems. The independent variable either must be nominal scale to begin with or reduced to nominal scale along the way.

With factorial ANOVA problems it's helpful to arrange the data in a table where the rows represent the categories of one *IV*, the columns represent the categories of the other *IV*, and the *DV* scores are entered into the cells where the two *IV*s intersect. This is how Table 8.1 is organized. The schools are the rows, parents' involvement is represented in the columns, and the reading scores are entered in the cells.

- Cell "a" contains reading scores for those at Roosevelt (*IV* #1) who had parental support (*IV* #2).
- Cell "b" contains the reading scores for students at Roosevelt who were without parent support.

■ **Factorial analysis of variance** is *ANOVA* with more than one independent variable.

Table 8.1 Arranging the Data in a Factorial *ANOVA*

School	Parental Involvement		
	Yes (1)	No (0)	
Roosevelt	34, 39, 42 M = 38.333 a	48, 53, 60 M = 53.667 b	For a, b, M_{ab} = 46.0
Anthony	79, 85, 92 M = 85.333 c	48, 54, 65 M = 55.667 d	For c, d, M_{cd} = 70.5
MacArthur	54, 64, 73 M = 63.667 e	38, 42, 47 M = 42.333 f	For e, f, M_{ef} = 53.0
	For a, c, e, M_{ace} = 62.444	For b, d, f, M_{bdf} = 50.556	M_G = 56.5

- Cell "c" is reading scores for those at Anthony who had parental support.
- Cell "d" contains the reading scores for students at Anthony who were without parent support in their reading.
- Cell "e" is reading scores for those at MacArthur who had parental support.
- The lower right cell ("f") is the reading scores for students at MacArthur whose parents didn't listen to their reading.

Describing the Factorial *ANOVA*

The various factorial *ANOVA* models are described by the number of categories there are in each independent variable.

- With three categories of one *IV* (the three schools) and two levels of the other (parents listened, or parents didn't), the model is a 3 × 2, or a "3 by 2" *ANOVA*.
- If there were four schools involved and three levels of parental involvement ("high involvement," "some involvement," and "no involvement," for example), it would be a 4 × 3 *ANOVA*.

- Regardless of the number of categories involved, all *ANOVA* procedures that involve two *IV*s are called "two-way *ANOVA*s."
- If the superintendent decides to factor in students' gender with the other *IV*s, we have a three-way, $3 \times 2 \times 2$ *ANOVA*, with the final "2" indicating the two categories of gender.

How Many Variables?

With many independent variables in an *ANOVA*, results become increasingly complex. That complexity makes the results more difficult to interpret. There's another problem. As the number of variables increases so, logically, does the number of categories for which there must be data. But those are practical limitations. There are no theoretical limits to the number of independent variables that can be included in a factorial *ANOVA* research experiment.

If gender were included for what would be a three-way *ANOVA*, the data become more difficult to depict in a table. It requires a drawing with a third dimension for the additional variable (giving it depth as well as height and width). With a fourth *IV* it becomes more difficult still, so we'll stick to two-way *ANOVA*s. Just know that the logic for any additional number of *IV*s is the same as it is for a two-way model.

The Components of SS_{bet}

In the one-way *ANOVA*, we noted that SS_{tot} is SS_{bet} plus SS_{with}, so once we have the other two, SS_{with} can be derived by subtraction. That's true in any *ANOVA*; SS_{with} is what's left after SS_{bet} is removed from SS_{tot}. Or to put it more generally, any one of the three sums of squares can be derived from the other two. We'll rely on this relationship below.

Just as the SS_{tot} is composed of the SS_{bet} and the SS_{with}, in a factorial *ANOVA* the SS_{bet} is likewise a composite measure. In the factorial *ANOVA* the SS_{bet} includes

- Any error variance, of course, as well as
- The variability in the dependent variables that's related to *each* of the independent variables, and
- Any variability in *DV* scores that stems from the combined effect of multiple *IV*s.

■ An **interaction** occurs when multiple *IV*s in an *ANOVA* have a combined effect on the *DV*.

This variance due to the combined effects of the *IV*s is called the **interaction** sum of squares, $SS_{interaction}$. Sometimes the impact of one independent variable is conditioned, or affected, by other independent variables in the same analysis—the combined effect is different than the effect that either variable has independently. When this occurs, we have an interaction.

The opportunity to detect and analyze interactions is part of the advantage of factorial *ANOVA*. Because they are the combined effect of multiple *IV*s, interactions can't emerge when one variable is studied at a time as they are in a one-way *ANOVA*. For example, the research literature suggests that particularly for younger students, smaller class sizes are associated with higher achievement. Actually this could be examined with a one-way *ANOVA*. The performance of similar students who are in the same grade but in classes of different sizes could be compared on some achievement criterion.

But what if some other variable alters the relationship between class size and student achievement? What if sometimes class size has a much greater impact than at others? If we include the ethnicity of the student in the analysis as a second *IV*, we might find that the benefits of smaller classes vary depending upon the student's ethnicity, which is to say that in some instances class size and student ethnicity interact. This is what Finn and Achilles (1990) found. They noted that smaller classes were generally associated with improved performance but that the impact of smaller classes was much greater for minority students. Should their study have been approached with a one-way *ANOVA*, the way ethnicity and class-size interact to affect reading performance can't emerge.

THROUGH A WIDER LENS

You're likely already aware of interactions. The potential for an interactive effect is why some medications aren't to be taken with other medications—their combined effects are different, and sometimes less predictable, than the sum of their individual effects. Possible interactions are why consumers are cautioned against combining alcohol and sedatives, for example.

Calculating the SS_{bet} Components

In addition to the impact of the principal's leadership style, the superintendent wishes to know whether parental involvement is a factor in students' performance. With two independent variables an interaction between them is possible. We'll need to partition SS_{bet} so that these three potential sources of variability in reading scores can be analyzed.

Table 8.1 has three rows corresponding with the principal's leadership style.

- row 1 (cells a and b)
- row 2 (cells c and d)
- row 3 (cells e and f)

Any significant differences in the leadership *IV* are reflected in the fact that the data in one of those three rows significantly different from the data in at least one of the other rows.

The columns in Table 8.1 reflect the two levels of parental support.

- column 1 (cells a + c + e)
- column 2 (cells b + d + f)

Any significant differences in reading scores related to the parental support variable will be reflected in differences between the scores in the two columns.

With more than one potential source of variability all coming from SS_{bet} we'll adapt the notation so as not to confuse them. We'll abbreviate leadership style to "ldr" and parental involvement to "par" and attach those subscripts to the *SS* notations as follows:

SS_{ldr} will include the variability related to the first *IV*

SS_{par} will include the variability related to the second *IV*

In each school we now have a group of students who had parental support and a group who did not. With three leadership styles and two levels of parental support, we have $3 \times 2 = 6$ groups. Treating each of the 6 groups as we did the 3 groups in the one-way model, we have the following to calculate SS_{bet}:

$SS_{bet} =$

$(M_a - M_G)^2 n_a + (M_b - M_G)^2 n_b + (M_c - M_G)^2 n_c + (M_d - M_G)^2 n_d + (M_e - M_G)^2 n_e + (M_f - M_G)^2 n_f$

The formula is the same as it was for SS_{bet} in the one-way model except that here it must accommodate six groups rather than three. Substituting the means of each *cell* into the formula and adjusting the sample size to 3, we have the following for SS_{bet}:

$(38.333 - 56.5)^2(3) + (53.667 - 56.5)^2(3) + (85.333 - 56.5)^2(3) +$

$(55.667 - 56.5)^2(3) + (63.667 - 56.5)^2(3) + (42.333 - 56.5)^2(3) = \mathbf{4266.514}$

The First Factor

Remember that besides the ever-present error in any factorial *ANOVA*, the SS_{bet} is an aggregate of the variance stemming from two *IV*s and any interaction that there might be between them. We need to be able to analyze each source.

We'll deal with the variance due to the leadership style *IV* first. The formula for calculating the measure of the *IV* for leadership style is as follows:

$$SS_{ldr} = (M_{ab} - M_G)^2 n_{ab} + (M_{cd} - M_G)^2 n_{cd} + (M_{ef} - M_G)^2 n_{ef}$$ 8.1

Where,

M_{ab} = the mean of the scores in cells a and b combined

n_{ab} = the number of subjects in cells a and b combined

Cells a and b are combined because between the two of them they contain all the scores of the students from the first school (and that school principal's leadership style). Cells c and d students were exposed to the second leadership style, and so on.

After calculating and inserting the relevant numbers we have:

$$SS_{ldr} = (46.0 - 56.5)^2(6) + (70.5 - 56.5)^2(6) + (53.0 - 56.5)^2(6) = \textbf{1911.00}$$

If you're willing to flip back to Chapter 7 for a minute, we can check something here. In the one-way *ANOVA*, leadership style was the entire SS_{bet}. That means that the value of SS_{ldr} here should be the same as the value of SS_{bet} was in the one-way model. As it turns out it is, and we can continue with some added confidence.

The Second IV

Above we noted in reference to Table 8.1 that the effect of the parental support variable is reflected in differences in the reading scores in the two columns. Following the same thinking that we used to set up the formula for SS_{ldr} we can create a formula for SS_{par}. With just two levels of parental support, there will be just two terms in the equation. Adjusting Formula 8.1 to fit the different cell combinations we have:

$$SS_{par} = (M_{ace} - M_G)^2 n_{ace} + (M_{bdf} - M_G)^2 n_{bdf}$$ 8.2

Where,

M_{ace} = the mean of the scores in cells a, c, and e combined

n_{ace} = the number of subjects in cells a, c, and e combined

and so on

For our data we have

$$SS_{par} = (62.444 - 56.5)^2(9) + (50.556 - 56.5)^2(9) = \mathbf{635.960}$$

The Within Sum of Squares (SS$_{with}$)

Because additional variables that are related to student achievement have been included in the analysis, there ought to be less error variance, less unexplained scoring variability. However, there is still bound to be some error variance because

- of error in the way reading performance is measured, and
- within any particular cell students will have different reading scores even though they have the influence of the same combination of the two variables. This emerges as error variance.
- A second *IV* doesn't mean that there aren't other variables that also explain some of the variance that aren't yet included. The variance due to these not-included variables is reflected in error variance.

All these elements aggregate in SS_{with}, which in a factorial *ANOVA* is sometimes called the *error sum of squares*. We need to determine that value here just as we did for the one-way *ANOVA* in Chapter 7, and it's calculated the same way except that we're working with six groups (cells) rather than with the earlier three. In Chapter 7 the formula for SS_w, which included three groups, was given this way:

$$SS_w = \Sigma(x_a - M_a)^2 + \Sigma(x_b - M_b)^2 + \Sigma(x_c - M_c)^2$$

Adapting the formula to six groups gives us the following:

$$SS_w = \Sigma(x_a - M_a)^2 + \Sigma(x_b - M_b)^2 + \Sigma(x_c - M_c)^2 + \Sigma(x_d - M_d)^2 + \Sigma(x_e - M_e)^2 + \Sigma(x_f - M_f)^2$$

To calculate the SS_{with}:

- Subtract the cell mean from each score in the cell
- Square each of the differences
- Sum the squared differences for each cell
- Sum the totals across the several (6 in this case) cells

The calculations for determining SS_{with} appear in Table 8.2. Verify that

$SS_{with} = \mathbf{560.002}$.

Table 8.2 Calculating the Within Sum of Squares (SS_w) for the Factorial ANOVA

Formula 7.10: $SS_w = \Sigma(x_a - M_a)^2 + \Sigma(x_b - M_b)^2 + \ldots \Sigma(x_f - M_f)^2$

x_a	M_a	$x_a - M_a$	$(x_a - M_a)^2$	x_b	M_b	$x_b - M_b$	$(x_b - M_b)^2$
34	38.333	−4.333	18.775	48	53.667	−5.667	32.115
39	38.333	.667	.445	53	53.667	−.667	.445
42	38.333	3.667	13.447	60	53.667	6.333	40.107
		$\Sigma =$	32.667			$\Sigma =$	72.667
x_c	M_c	$x_c - M_c$	$(x_c - M_c)^2$	x_d	M_d	$x_d - M_d$	$(x_d - M_d)^2$
79	85.333	−6.333	40.107	48	55.667	−7.667	58.783
85	85.333	−.333	.111	54	55.667	−1.667	2.779
92	85.333	6.667	44.449	65	55.667	9.333	87.105
		$\Sigma =$	84.667			$\Sigma =$	148.667
x_e	M_e	$x_e - M_e$	$(x_e - M_e)^2$	x_f	M_f	$x_f - M_f$	$(x_f - M_f)^2$
54	63.667	−9.667	93.451	38	42.333	−4.333	18.775
64	63.667	.333	.111	42	42.333	−.333	.111
73	63.667	9.333	87.105	47	42.333	4.667	21.781
		$\Sigma =$	180.667			$\Sigma =$	40.667

$SS_w = 32.667 + 72.667 + 84.667 + 148.667 + 180.667 + 40.667 = \mathbf{560.002}$

The Interaction

Although there are two IVs in this factorial ANOVA, compared to the one-way ANOVA that we completed in Chapter 7, the total variance hasn't changed. It's apportioned differently between the different components, but the SS_{tot} still = 4826.50, just as it was calculated in Table 7.2. From that total sum of squares value, if we subtract the sums of squares for each of the *IV*s (SS_{ldr}, SS_{par}),and the error sum of squares (SS_{with}), whatever is left is the variability due to the interaction of the independent variables ($SS_{interaction}$). This is what Formula 8.3 does.

$$SS_{interaction} = SS_{tot} - SS_{factor1} - SS_{factor2} - SS_{error} \qquad\qquad 8.3$$

For our data we have

$$SS_{interaction} = 4826.500 - 1911.00 - 635.960 - 560.00 = \mathbf{1719.554}$$

SOURCE: Created by Suzanna Nielson.

"I'm going to have to call Match-em-up.com for a date. Otherwise the probability of a significant interaction is near zero."

The Results

We'll enter what we've done in an *ANOVA* table similar to what we developed for the one-way analysis, but because there are multiple *IVs* this time there are more sources of variability.

Checking Results

The relationships among the different *SS* values provide an opportunity to check the accuracy of our results.

- Since $SS_t = SS_{bet} + SS_w$, we can verify this as follows:

  $4266.514 + 560.002 = 4826.516$ (with some allowance for differences due to round-off).

- *The variability due to the IVs and the interaction are the components of SS_b* and so should sum to that value, which we can check as follows:

  $SS_{ldr} + SS_{par} + SS_{int} = SS_{bet}$,
  $1719.554 + 635.960 + 1911.0 = 4266.514$.

The Degrees of Freedom for a Factorial ANOVA

Just as before, except for SS_{tot}, each *SS* value must be divided by its *df* to determine the *MS* values.

- *df* for SS_{tot} remain $N - 1$, all the individuals in all groups, minus one
  Here that value is $18 - 1 = \mathbf{17}$
- *df* for SS_{bet} remain at $k - 1$ with k the number of cells: $6 - 1 = \mathbf{5}$
- *df* for each *IV* are the number of categories of the *IV*, -1 for SS_{ldr}, $3 - 1 = \mathbf{2}$, and for SS_{par}, $2 - 1 = \mathbf{1}$
- *df* for $SS_{interaction}$ is the product of the *df* for the *IVs*: $2_{ldr} \times 1_{par} = \mathbf{2}$
- *df* for SS_{with} remains $N - K = 18 - 6 = 12$

The F Ratios

Recall that the *F* ratio in the one-way *ANOVA* was the MS_{bet} divided by the MS_w. That same ratio of treatment variance (plus some error variance) to error variance is also central to the factorial *ANOVA* but in this case the MS_{bet} can be further reduced so that we can examine the separate influence of the two *IVs* as well as any variability from their interaction. This is done by calculating *multiple F* ratios. Each one is the result of dividing the particular *MS* value by the MS_{with}. For the problem we're working we have the following:

- $MS_{bet} \div MS_{with}$ produces the *F* for the entire model. This is a measure of the effect of leadership style and parental involvement *together* on fifth-grade students' reading achievement.
- $MS_{ldr} \div MS_{with}$ produces the *F* for the impact of leadership style on reading achievement.
- $MS_{par} \div MS_{with}$ produces the *F* for the connection between parental involvement and reading achievement.
- $MS_{interaction} \div MS_{with}$ is a measure of how the two *IV*s act in concert to influence student reading achievement.

Each of these four sources of variance, and the resulting *F* ratios, must be tested for statistical significance. Just as with the one-way *ANOVA*, the critical value is taken from Table C in the Tables of Critical Values appendix. It's determined by the degrees of freedom for the numerator and the degrees of freedom for the denominator in the particular *F* ratio. It's just that here there are three different *df* combinations. *Each time the degrees of freedom change, so must the related critical value.*

- The *F* value for Between has 5 and 12 *df*
- The *F* for both the Leadership *IV* and the Interaction have 2 and 12 *df*
- The *F* for Parent Involvement has 1 and 12 *df*

The ANOVA *Table*

Source	SS	df	MS	F	F_{crit}
Total	4826.50	17			
Between	4266.514	5	853.303	18.285	3.11
School	1911.00	2	955.50	20.475	3.88
Parent Involve	635.960	1	635.960	13.628	4.75
The Interaction	1719.554	2	859.777	18.424	3.88
Within	560.002	12	46.667		

■ In factorial *ANOVA*,
a **significant main
effect** indicates
that the particular
independent
variable is
statistically
significant.

All four calculated *F* values exceed their associated table values; all *F*s are significant. In the language of statistics we have a statistically **significant main effect** for leadership style (which we already knew from the one-way *ANOVA* in Chapter 7), a significant main effect for parental involvement, and a significant interaction.

The Post-Hoc *Test*

For purposes of the *post-hoc* test, the data in a two-way factorial *ANOVA* are treated like two separate analyses, one for each independent variable. Ordinarily, at this point we would complete a *post-hoc* test for the leadership *IV* because although it's significant, with three types of leadership it isn't apparent which subjects performed significantly different from which. It would involve comparing the combination of cells a and b to c and d, and to e and f, but we did that earlier with the one-way *ANOVA*, and there's no need to repeat it here.

The parental involvement variable (cells a + c + e compared with b + d + f) needs no *post-hoc*. Since there are only two categories—parents assisted or they didn't—there is only one possibility: Students whose parents assisted performed at a significantly different level than those whose parents did not.

As for the interaction, Hopkins and Glass (1978) noted that *post-hoc* tests are "ordinarily not used in interactions—interactions are a generic phenomenon best understood by studying the interaction graph" (p. 384), which is the reason for Figure 8.1 below. Indeed, when a factorial *ANOVA* is completed on SPSS, a request for *Tukey's HSD* will provide only *post-hoc* comparisons within the main effects. There isn't the option to compare across the cells of multiple main effects, so that one can check for a significant difference between cell a and cell d in our model, for example. This position isn't universal. Diekhoff (1992) adapts the *HSD* formula to make such comparisons by making *n* the number in any one cell (3 in our model) rather than the number in the level of the main effect (6 for the levels of school).

Using a Graph to Explain the Interaction

The fact that the *F* for the interaction is significant introduces a bit of a twist to the results, and it should condition the way we understand the main effects. In fact, a significant interaction suggests that it may not be possible to understand either main effect without referring to the other because each apparently affects the other. When an interaction is statistically significant, a graph (Figure 8.1) can help one interpret it. The graph is only necessary when the interaction is significant.

Note how the graph is developed. When there are two *IV*s:

- The vertical (*y*) axis indicates the range of *DV* (reading) scores.
- The categories of one of the *IV*s are indicated on the horizontal (or *x*) axis.
  - If one of the *IV*s has only two categories (parent involvement) it's visually simpler to place that variable on the *x* axis.

- The other *IV* is located *in* the graph by using the cell means to anchor a line that extends between the levels of the variable that is on the *x* axis.

In Figure 8.1, reading scores are on the *y* axis and parent involvement is represented on the *x* axis, with one category at either end of the axis. A pair of means is calculated for the reading scores in each of the three leadership styles, one of reading scores for the students whose parents were involved, the other of the reading scores of students whose parents were not involved. The line for the Roosevelt students, for example, goes from:

38.333 on the *y* axis (the mean for cell a—Roosevelt students whose parents were involved) above the "yes" category for parent involvement, to

53.667 on the *y* axis (the mean for cell b—Roosevelt students, parents not involved) above the "no" category for parent involvement.

The significance tests provide definitive answers about statistical significance which the graph doesn't provide, but the appearance and orientation of the lines can provide a wealth of supplemental information. For our particular analysis:

- The fact that the points at which the lines begin are quite different from one another suggests that there are differences from school to school between students whose parents assist.
- The positions of the line ends on the right-hand side of the graph indicate that reading score differences related to leadership style among the three groups of students whose parents were not involved are less pronounced than among the students whose parents listened to reading nightly.
  - When the lines steeply incline or decline, it indicates differences *within* a leadership style between the reading scores of students whose parents were involved versus those whose parents were not.

Figure 8.1   The Interaction of School and Parental Involvement

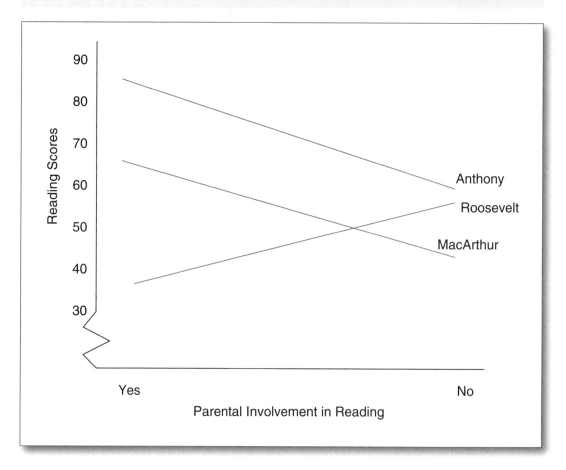

- The fact that the lines are not parallel is evidence of a possible interaction although it's the F value from the table that will indicate whether it's statistically significant.

In this particular graph, the line for Roosevelt has a very different angle from the lines of the other two schools, both of which follow a similar trajectory. This suggests that whether or not parents are involved has a different impact on Roosevelt students than it does for students at Anthony or MacArthur. The graph indicates that when parents are involved with students from Anthony and MacArthur schools, performance increases. For Roosevelt students the opposite occurs; parent involvement is associated with *lower* levels of student performance.

There might be several ways to explain this interaction. Perhaps there is a history of noninvolvement by the parents of Roosevelt students, and perhaps Roosevelt teachers have urged only the parents of the lowest performers to participate in the hope that it will give them a boost (which it obviously hasn't, yet). Or perhaps the Roosevelt parents were mistakenly instructed to help the students with their spelling, which detracted from their reading time. For whatever reason, the two variables together have a different impact on the reading scores of students at Roosevelt than on those at the other schools.

The Effect Sizes

With the one-way *ANOVA*, we were careful to distinguish between statistical and practical significance and noted that because a result is a nonrandom outcome (statistically significant) doesn't necessarily mean that it's important in the everyday world. We used the partial *eta*-squared value as a measure of practical importance. With $\eta_p^2 = .396$ in the one-way *ANOVA* we found that about 40% of the variance in reading scores was related to differences in the principals' leadership styles.

Since we have partitioned variance into multiple components in the factorial model, accompanying the multiple Fs, we need to calculate a corresponding effect size for each significant *F*. We'll use the same formula we used in Chapter 7, adjusting it according to the particular effect size we're calculating. For "between," recall that the formula for partial *eta*-squared was:

$$\eta_P^2 = \frac{SS_{bet}}{SS_{bet} + SS_{with}}$$

Because we have controlled more of the error variance in the factorial *ANOVA* we should expect a larger value for SS_{bet}. With the new value for SS_{bet} the recalculated value for partial *eta*-squared for that source of variance is:

$$\eta_P^2 = \frac{4266.514}{4266.514 + 560.002} = \mathbf{.884}$$

This larger value compared to the one-way *ANOVA* result reflects the fact that by including an additional *IV* and the possible interaction of the *IVs*, more of the variance in scores is explained.

For the first main effect (leadership style) the formula is adjusted to become:

$$\eta_p^2 = \frac{SS_{ldr}}{SS_{ldr} + SS_{with}}$$

When we substitute the appropriate values we have:

$$\eta_p^2 = \frac{1911}{1911 + 560.002} = \textbf{.773}$$

Note that the SS_{with} is constant in the calculations. It's the SS for the particular *IV* or interaction that changes. For the second main effect (parental involvement) the formula is:

$$\eta_p^2 = \frac{SS_{par}}{SS_{par} + SS_{with}}$$

With the proper values substituted we have:

$$\eta_p^2 = \frac{635.96}{(635.96 + 560.002)} = \textbf{.532}$$

For the interaction effect, the formula is:

$$\eta_p^2 = SS_{interaction}/(SS_{interaction} + SS_{with})$$

With the appropriate values we have:

$$\eta_p^2 = \frac{1719.554}{1719.554 + 560.002} = \textbf{.754}$$

A glance indicates that the partial *eta*-squared for the entire model can't be the sum of the partial *eta*-squares for the main effects and the interaction. In this case that would be a value greater than 1.0 (more than 100% of the variance explained?). There is overlap among the main effects and the interaction. Part of what each component explains is also explained by the others. Having noted that, these partial *eta* values still indicate that (were these not contrived data) each component would have practical as well as theoretical importance for why reading scores vary among fifth-grade students.

As a footnote, the *omega*-squared (ω^2) that we calculated for *t* is a more conservative effect size statistic, as we noted earlier. Part of its value is that it can be more safely generalized beyond the particular problem. Partial *eta*-squared, conversely, produces a value specific to the particular data set.

To Underscore the Point: Effect Sizes

Effect sizes, such as partial *eta*-squared, provide a measure of the importance of significant findings in the real world. Most effect sizes range in value from 0 to 1.0 (although there are exceptions such as Cohen's *d* that we calculated for the independent *t*-test in Chapter 6), and they provide an estimate of the proportion of total variance explained by the particular component.

Looking at SPSS Output

The *General Linear Model* (*GLM*) is the procedure under which SPSS completes factorial *ANOVA*. The *GLM* isn't specific to *ANOVA* problems. It's a general procedure for a variety of analyses that involve a linear relationship between *IV*(s) and *DV*(s). As a result, some of the output isn't particular to the *ANOVA* and in fact we won't need some of the information that a solution will generate. To understand the output we'll connect the language SPSS uses to what we did with the factorial *ANOVA*.

The GLM Term	The ANOVA Equivalent
Corrected Total	SS_{tot}
Corrected Model	SS_{bet}
Error	SS_{with}

If the factorial problem that we did longhand was completed under the *GLM*, the result would be the data in Table 8.3.

Take a minute to examine the table, make the label substitutions noted above, and you'll see the same values that we produced longhand, including some others that we didn't calculate. The *SS* values are as they were labeled when the data were entered: "ldr" refers to the *SS* for leadership style

Table 8.3　The Factorial *ANOVA* on SPSS

Source	Type III Sum of Squares	df	Mean Square	F	Sig.
Corrected Model	4266.500[a]	5	853.300	18.285	.000
Intercept	57460.500	1	57460.500	1231.296	.000
Ldr	1911.000	2	955.500	20.475	.000
Par	636.056	1	636.056	13.630	.003
ldr * par	1719.444	2	859.722	18.423	.000
Error	560.000	12	46.667		
Total	62287.000	18			
Corrected Total	4826.500	17			

a. *R* Squared = .884 (Adjusted *R* Squared = .836)

differences, "par" refers to the *SS* for parental involvement, and "ldr * par" is how the *GLM* lists the *SS* for the interaction of the two independent variables. The *R*-squared value given immediately below the table is a measure of the variance in test scores that is explained by the combination of leadership style and parental involvement. It's an alternative to partial *eta*-squared, which the *GLM* will produce if the effect size is requested.

SUMMARY

Relatively little of what one may want to understand about human behavior lends itself to a one-variable explanation. Although the *t*-tests and the one-way *ANOVA* both have important application and are particularly important for the conceptual orientation they provide for analyses of significant differences between groups, they accommodate just one independent variable at a time. The factorial *ANOVA* allows multiple independent variables to be introduced and allows one to analyze the unique impact that each *IV* has on the dependent variable. Perhaps the most important contribution, however, is that it allows one to examine the impact that multiple variables can have when they produce an interaction, when the combined effect is different than the cumulative effect of multiple variables. This combined effect is called an interaction and of course it can never emerge when the independent variables are viewed one-at-a-time.

Now it's time for a slightly different direction. To this point, whether with the *t*-tests or the *ANOVAs* we have assumed independence among the multiple groups involved. In the next chapter we'll lift the independence requirement and extend the Chapter 6 (*t*-test), and Chapter 7 (one-way *ANOVA*) topics to what are called "repeated measures designs."

EXERCISES

1. What effect size statistic does the *GLM* procedure perform for factorial *ANOVA*?

2. A researcher wishes to determine whether ethnicity and marital status are factors in the performance of university students during their senior year. The dependent variable is grade-point average (GPA) on a 4.0 scale.

   Married students in ethnic group 1: 2.9, 3.0, 3.3, 3.5 3.7
   Unmarried students in ethnic group 1: 2.2, 2.6, 2.8, 2.8, 2.9
   Married students in ethnic group 2: 2.8, 2.9, 3.0, 3.1 3.4
   Unmarried students in ethnic group 2: 3.3, 3.4, 3.4, 3.5, 3.7
   Married students in ethnic group 3: 2.8, 3.4, 3.7, 3.7, 3.8
   Unmarried students in ethnic group 3: 2.4, 2.4, 2.6, 2.7, 2.8

   a. Describe the kind of a factorial *ANOVA* this is (2 × 2, etc.).
   b. How many *F* values will be calculated in the course of completing this problem?
   c. Are there significant differences related to ethnicity?
   d. Are there significant differences related to marital status?
   e. Is the interaction of marital status and ethnicity significant?
   f. How much of the variance in grades can be explained by marital status, ethnicity, and the interaction of the two?

3. An *ANOVA* problem involves 3 levels of the first *IV* and 3 levels of the second *IV*.

   a. What will be the degrees of freedom for the first *IV*?
   b. What will be the degrees of freedom for the interaction?

4. For a particular *ANOVA* problem:

   $SS_{tot} = 450$
   $SS_{bet} = 255$
   SS for the first *IV* = 85
   SS for the second *IV* = 110

   What is the SS_{with}?
   What is the $SS_{interaction}$?

5. If there is a statistically significant interaction in a factorial *ANOVA*, what's the argument for interpreting the interaction before tackling the main effects?

6. In an ANOVA with two *IVs*, the data are arranged so that:
   - Cells a and b represent level 1 of main effect 1
   - Cells c and d represent level 2 of that same *IV*
   - The second *IV* has level 1 (cells a and c)
   - Level 2 (cells b and d)
   - If M_a = 12.5, M_b = 6.0, M_c = 7.75, and M_d = 13.0, draw the interaction.

7. In a 2 × 3 *ANOVA*:
   a. How many *IVs* are there?
   b. What will be the degrees of freedom for each *IV*?
   c. How many groups are there?

8. What constitutes "error variance" in statistical analysis?

REFERENCES

Diekhoff, G. (1992). *Statistics for the social and behavioral sciences: Univariate, bivariate, multivariate.* Dubuque, IA: William C. Brown Publishers.

Finn, J. D., & Achilles, C. M. (1990). Answers and questions about class size: A statewide experiment. *American Educational Research Journal, 27,* 557–577.

Hopkins, K. D., & Glass, G. V. (1978). *Basic statistics for the behavioral sciences.* Englewood Cliffs, NJ: Prentice Hall.

Pedhazur, E. J., & Schmelkin, L. P. (1991). *Measurement, design, and analysis: An integrated approach.* Hillsdale, NJ: Lawrence Erlbaum.

THE FORMULAE AND THEIR SYMBOLS

Formula 8.1: $SS_{ldr} = (M_{ab} - M_G)^2 n_{ab} + (M_{cd} + M_G)^2 n_{cd} + (M_{ef} - M_G)^2 n_{ef}$

In a factorial *ANOVA* the variability between groups is partitioned into the *SS* due to each of the *IVs* and the interaction. This formula is for an *IV* labeled "ldr." In a table with rows designating one *IV* and columns another *IV*, the levels of this variable were cells a plus b, cells c plus d, and cells e plus f.

Formula 8.2: $SS_{par} = (M_{ace} - M_G)^2 n_{ace} + (M_{bdf} - M_G)^2 n_{bdf}$

This formula is for an *IV* labeled "par." In a table with rows for one *IV* and columns the other, the cells related to this variable were a, c, and e for one level, and b, d, and f for the other.

Formula 8.3: $SS_{interaction} = SS_{tot} - SS_{ldr} - SS_{par} - SS_{with}$

The interaction variance in the *DV* ($SS_{interaction}$) that is the *IVs* creating a combined effect is the total sum of squares (SS_{tot}) minus each of the *SS* for the main effects (*IVs*), minus the *SS* for error (SS_{with}).

STUDENT STUDY SITE

Visit the Student Study Site at **www.sagepub.com/tanner** for additional learning tools.

Chapter 9

DEPENDENT GROUPS TESTS FOR INTERVAL DATA

THE PROBLEM: DETECTING SIGNIFICANCE IN DEPENDENT GROUPS

Ms. Hindley teaches reading to remedial seventh-grade students. Since no one else has the students and conditions she has, her problem is whom to compare her students with in order to get a sense of their progress.

QUESTIONS AND ANSWERS

❑ When one wishes to test for significant progress in a group without another group with which to compare it, what are the options?

One answer is to compare the group with itself over multiple measures of the *DV*. When there are just two measures of an interval or ratio scale *DV*, this is a before/after *t*-test. A variation using two groups matched on some important characteristic is called the matched pairs *t*-test. They are both "dependent samples" tests.

❑ Since both the "before/after" *t*-test and the matched pairs *t*-test are limited to two measures, how does one analyze a *before, after, after* procedure?

Just as the one-way *ANOVA* was the answer when there were too many groups for *t*-test to handle, there is an equivalent for dependent samples. It's the within-subjects *F* test.

WORKING BACKWARD TO MOVE FORWARD

In Chapter 6, we found that Gosset's *t*-tests allowed us to compare two independent groups and determine whether there was a statistically significant difference between them. Recall that the *t* statistic we calculated (Formula 6.3) had this form:

$$t = \frac{M_1 - M_2}{SE_d}$$

When the number of individuals in each group is equal, the estimated standard error of the difference in the denominator (Formula 6.4) has this form:

$$SE_d = \sqrt{(SE^2_{m1} + SE^2_{m2})}$$

Clearly, the standard error of the difference is directly related to the standard error of the mean, and the standard error of the mean ($SE_M = s/\sqrt{n}$, Formula 6.1) is based on the standard deviation (Formula 2.4) that, to use physics language, is something like an "elementary particle" in t-testing. There is evidence of the impact of the standard deviation throughout the procedures that make up the t-test because of the following:

- A group with heterogeneous scores will produce a relatively large standard deviation (s).
- In turn, large s values produce large standard errors of the mean, particularly if the sample size is small (small sample, small divisor in the formula, besides which small samples tend to be platykurtic anyway).
- If the standard errors of the mean are relatively large, the standard error of the difference will be large, and the difference between means has to be proportionately greater in order for t to be statistically significant.

The reason that these measures of variability are so important, of course, is that the t value is a ratio of the variance between the two groups, represented in $M_1 - M_2$, to the uncontrolled variability represented in those three statistics. Uncontrolled scoring variability, whichever statistic it's represented in, works against the ability to detect statistically significant outcomes. The point of this chapter is to introduce tests that can minimize error variance and, in doing so, provide greater clarity to the impact of the independent variable.

STATISTICAL POWER AND THE STANDARD ERROR OF THE DIFFERENCE

The fact that large amounts of uncontrolled variability in the denominators of z, t, and F statistics diminishes the potential for finding significant results is, by now, old news of course, but it provides an important context for the before/after t-test that comes up here. Besides the variability *within* each group represented by the standard deviations, the standard errors of the mean, and ultimately the standard error of the difference in the calculations, the value of t is also affected by pre-existing differences *between* the groups.

It's convenient to assume that if a counselor is comparing the impact of different levels of a certain treatment on two groups of clients the two groups are identical before the treatment is introduced so that any difference can be attributed to the treatment. But although random selection and large sample sizes can result in quite similar groups, groups are never going to be identical, and any pre-existing differences add to error variance to statistical tests of significant differences.

So, one must contend with scoring differences from sources that have nothing to do with the effect of the independent variable. They include at least

- Differences *within* the groups because individuals respond differently to the same stimulus, as when 20 students all receive the same reading prompt but have different answers to the test items.
- Differences *between* the groups before the treatment is even administered.

Ideally, any before-the-treatment differences between the two groups will be minimal. Indeed, the logic behind random selection is that two groups randomly drawn from the same population will differ only by chance, but that's small comfort if the chance difference happens to be substantial, as it will be occasionally, and if it affects the way subjects respond to the independent variable. Pre-existing differences conspire against a significant *t*.

THE DEPENDENT SAMPLES *t*-TESTS

The dependent samples *t*-test offers two ways to resolve pre-existing differences between groups. The **before/after *t*-test** eliminates initial between-groups differences by using just a single group. The researcher measures subjects on the dependent variable, introduces the independent variable, and then measures them again. There will still be *within*-group differences, but unless something unrelated to the *IV* changes the way the group responds between the first and second measurement, any between-group differences will be minimal.

Perhaps a counselor measures students' self-esteem, implements a program to enhance self-esteem (the *IV*, or "the treatment"), and then measures self-esteem again. The "before" and "after" refer to measuring subjects before and then after the *IV* is introduced. The self-esteem measures are the dependent variable scores.

Ideally, any changes in self-esteem measures occur because of the independent variable, which is the self-esteem program. Even with a

■ The **before/after** *t*-test controls initial between-groups differences by using the same group twice.

before/after approach, however, other influences can creep in and "muddy up" the result, particularly when the time lapse is substantial.

If a classroom teacher measures students' attitudes toward mathematics, institutes a new mathematics program, and then measures students' attitudes about math a second time 4 months later, any difference can be attributed to the new program only if all other variables remain constant. What if, incidental to the new program, the teacher offers treats for homework successes? The effect of the reinforcer can be easy to confuse with the effect of the new program. The longer the interval between measures, the greater the potential for what are called confounding variables, or just "confounds."

However, if the time between measures is minimal, the potential for unrelated factors to confound results is also minimal. Of course a limited time also may minimize the opportunity for the independent variable to have an effect. It's unlikely that a program to boost self-esteem is going to have any lasting effect after a few minutes.

The Matched Pairs Design

■ Matched pairs designs are also dependent samples tests. They control initial between-groups differences by avoiding independent groups.

As an alternative to the before/after *t*-test, there is the **matched pairs design** in which one minimizes initial between-groups differences by matching each individual in Group 1 to a companion with similar characteristics in Group 2 so that those characteristics don't become part of the difference between groups. Having created groups that mirror each other on the relevant characteristics, each group receives a different level of the *IV*, and then their performances are compared for significant differences.

As an example of a matched pairs design, perhaps a reading specialist wants to know which of two instructional techniques has the greater effect on students' reading. To control pre-existing differences in reading achievement, subjects in the two groups are matched so that each group has a similar profile. It makes sense to match subjects on some prior measure of reading ability, for example. Someone whose reading score on a previous test was at the 85th percentile in one group is matched in the second group to someone with a similar score. This is done throughout the two groups so that each individual in one group has a companion in the other group with a similar initial reading score. The treatment (*IV*) is then introduced, and one can have more confidence that any differences stem from the *IV* rather than from something else.

Both matched pairs and before/after designs are called **dependent samples designs** because the scores on which statistical decisions are based *don't* come from independent groups. In the before/after design the same group is measured twice. In the matched pairs design, there are two groups, but individuals in each group are paired to be similar; the groups can't be considered independent. The point of both approaches is to minimize differences that are unrelated to what we're really interested in measuring. The differences between before/after and matched pairs are conceptual and organizational, but not mathematical, as we shall see.

Interpreting Result

As is the case for all statistical tests, the decision in this case about whether the result is significant is made by comparing the t value with a population of possible outcomes. For dependent samples t-tests, it's the same distribution of difference scores used with the independent t-test.

There are several ways to calculate the dependent groups t. One quite common approach is based on the correlation between the two sets of scores, but since we haven't yet taken up correlation (Chapter 10), we'll use an alternative. In the approach used here, it's the differences between each pair of scores from either the repeated measures, or the paired subjects' scores, that's of interest. Specifically, the issue is whether the mean of the difference scores so varies from the mean of the distribution of all possible difference scores (which, in Chapter 6, we determined to be 0) that we can conclude that it is statistically significant outcome.

First, the test statistic:

$$t = M_d/SE_{md}$$ 9.1

Where,

M_d = the mean of the difference scores

SE_{md} = the standard error of the mean for the difference scores

Technically, the numerator of the test statistic is $M_d - \mu_1-\mu_2$, the mean of the sample of difference scores minus the mean of the population of all difference scores. As we keep noting, however, the value of $\mu_1-\mu_2$ is going to be 0, and it's common to delete this component from the test statistic just as we did with the Chapter 6 t-tests.

Calculating the t Statistic

The steps for calculating this type of t-test are the following:

1. Set up the data in columns with the subject's first score and second score (or the matched pairs of scores) on the same line.

2. Calculate the difference between each pair of scores, d.

3. Calculate the mean of the difference scores (M_d).

4. Calculate the standard deviation of the difference scores (s_d)

5. Calculate the standard error of the mean for the difference scores (SE_{md}) by dividing the standard deviation by the square root of the number of pairs.

6. Calculate t by dividing M_d by SE_{md}.

7. Compare the calculated value of t to the critical value from Table B in the Tables of Critical Values in the appendix with the number of *pairs* of scores, *−1* degrees of freedom.

The null hypothesis is that the mean of the first set of scores equals the mean of the second. The alternate hypothesis is that there is a difference.

An Example

Back to the school counselor and self-esteem for the moment, assume that the counselor is working with 10 students and that the Youth Self Esteem Questionnaire (Y-SEC) yields interval scale data (which may be a bit of a stretch since most surveys like this yield ordinal data, but for the sake of the example . . .). The counselor administers the Y-SEC, provides a treatment designed to enhance self-esteem, and then administers the Y-SEC a second time. The data are in Figure 9.1 where we have calculated the mean and the standard deviation of the difference scores. The d_i indicates the difference between the two scores:

With the standard deviation of the difference scores in hand, we can calculate the *standard error of the mean* for the difference scores. The procedure is the same as it was in Chapter 6 except that the numerator in the formula is the standard deviation *of the difference scores* rather than the standard deviation of the original scores:

$$SE_{md} = s_d / \sqrt{n}$$

$$= 1.829 / \sqrt{36} = .578$$

Now the value of t,

$$t = M_d / SE_{md}$$

$$= -1.7 / .578 = \mathbf{-2.941}$$

Figure 9.1   The Mean (A) and Standard Deviation (B) of Differences for the Before/After t

A.	Before	After	d_i	B.	$d_i - M_d$	$(d_i - M_d)^2$
1.	4	7	−3		−1.3	1.69
2.	5	6	−1		.7	.49
3.	3	8	−5		−3.3	10.89
4.	4	4	0		1.7	2.89
5.	7	9	−2		−.3	.09
6.	6	5	1		2.7	7.29
7.	8	8	0		1.7	2.89
8.	5	8	−3		−1.3	1.69
9.	6	9	−3		−1.3	1.69
10.	7	8	−1		.7	.49

$$\Sigma d = -17 \qquad\qquad \Sigma = 30.10$$

$$M_d = \Sigma_d / n = -17/10 = -1.7$$

$$s_d = \sqrt{[\Sigma(d_i - M_d)^2]/n - 1}$$

(8.2)

$$s_d = \sqrt{30.10/9} = 1.829$$

Finally, we compare the calculated value of t with the Table B value for df $= n - 1$ with n representing *the number of pairs of scores*. For this problem,

$$t = -2.941 \text{ and}$$

$$t_{.05\ (9)} = 2.262$$

Interpreting the Result

The critical value comes from the same table (Table B) used for the other t-tests. With a calculated value of $t = -2.941$, and a table value of $t_{.05\ (9)} = 2.262$, we reject the null hypothesis. The difference between the before and after self-esteem scores is statistically significant.

The Give and Take of the Before/After *t*

Besides everything else that we've noted, another important difference between the independent and dependent samples *t*-test is the degrees of freedom. Remember that as degrees of freedom diminish, the critical value required for *t* to be significant increases, and at first blush this seems like a drawback to using tests with dependent measures. Why would anyone opt for the dependent samples approach when it seems that the smaller critical value that comes with an independent *t*-test makes that procedure more sensitive to differences? The answer is that when the two sets of scores are closely related (because we're either using the same group twice or we've matched subjects so that each group initially mirrors the other) we gain more than we lose. What is accomplished by eliminating initial between-group differences more than offsets the loss of degrees of freedom and the accompanying larger critical value from Table B.

So the gamble taken with the dependent-groups approach (assuming that one has a choice) is that the error variance eliminated because the scores are related increases the likelihood of a significant finding more than the loss of degrees of freedom diminishes it.

It might not always be so. If the "matched" pairs aren't closely matched to begin with, the procedure might be *less* powerful than a corresponding independent *t*. Perhaps there aren't enough subjects in the pool to match each person in one group to someone with a similar score in the other so that some of the "pairs" really aren't paired very closely. Perhaps the time between the before and after measures is so great that factors other than the *IV* affect the "after" measures. In such situations, the value of *t* may be diminished, and with it, the probability that the result will be statistically significant.

A Matched Pairs Design

A personnel officer at a community college is interested in whether faculty members who hold a terminal degree in their disciplines tend to have a longer tenure at the college than those who don't. She divides the faculty into two groups, those with doctoral degrees or the equivalents, and those with master-level degrees. She suspects that age and discipline may have an impact on the results, however, so she elects to use a matched pairs design. The faculty members with master's degrees are matched with faculty holding doctoral degrees who are of similar age and who teach in the same discipline. The data for length of tenure at the institution for 10 faculty members are in Figure 9.2.

Figure 9.2   A Matched Pairs *t*-Test

	Master's deg.	Doctoral deg. Difference (*d*)	
1.	6	11	−5
2.	5	4	1
3.	7	4	3
4.	8	5	3
5.	17	6	11
6.	10	8	2
7.	4	2	2
8.	11	5	6
9.	4	6	−2
10.	7	8	−1
			20

Verify:

1. The differences
2. $M_d = \Sigma_d/n = 2.0$
3. $s_d = \sqrt{[\Sigma(d_i - M_d)^2]/n - 1}$

	$d_i - M_d$	$(d_i - M_d)^2$
1.	−7	49
2.	−1	1
3.	1	1
4.	1	1
5.	9	81
6.	0	0
7.	0	0
8.	4	16
9.	−4	16
10.	−3	9
		$\Sigma = 174$

$$s_d = \sqrt{(174/9)} = 4.397$$

4. $SE_{md} = s_d/\sqrt{n} = 1.390$

5. $t = M_d /SE_{md} = 2.0/1.390 = 1.439$

6. $t_{.05\ (9)} = 2.262$

The differences in the length of tenure between those who hold master's and those who hold doctoral degrees are not statistically significant.

Why is the result in the figure not significant? The easy answer, of course, is that the calculated value of t isn't large enough to meet the table value, but why is it not? After all, the average master's degree instructor has been at the college 2 years longer than the average instructor holding a doctoral degree ($M_d = 2.0$). The culprit is the standard error of the mean for difference scores. With difference scores ranging from −5 to 11, there is so much variability that the standard deviation of the difference scores and the standard error of the mean for the difference scores both become quite large. In this problem, those statistics are measures of chance (uncontrolled) variability. When the denominator in a t ratio is relatively large, it has a diminishing effect on value of t.

We know that overall variability tends to shrink as sample sizes get larger. In this case, a sample of $n = 10$ is too small to absorb what may be unusual variability in the length of tenure among these faculty members. The personnel officer should probably repeat this experiment with a new, larger sample of instructors.

The Dependent Samples t-Test Versus the Independent t

The point at the beginning of the chapter was that using the dependent-samples design controls a portion of the extraneous variance that otherwise becomes part of the standard error of the difference. We can illustrate how this might work by comparing results from the two approaches based on the same set of data.

As implausible as it may be to the reader, a researcher with wide-ranging interests wishes to analyze the level of anxiety among graduate nursing students before a statistics test. He measures students' heart rates 40 minutes before they take an exam, administers a placebo explained as a mild, over-the-counter sedative, and then measures heart rate a second time 20 minutes later.

If this were completed as an independent t-test, we could assume that there are *two* groups of 12 students and the heart rates of students in both groups are measured, but in the second group the measurement occurs 20 minutes after a placebo is administered as a "mild sedative." What are the results of each procedure when testing at $p = .05$? The data are in Figure 9.3.

The difference between outcomes is largely the difference between the denominators in the t ratios. Although the numerators are about the same:

- In the independent t-test, the standard error of the difference is the variability in the first sample *plus* the variability in the second—it's the variability in the two groups combined.

Figure 9.3   Comparing the Before/After and the Independent *t*-Tests

	Test 1	Test 2	d_i	$(d_i - M_d)$	$(d_i - M_d)^2$
	The Dependent Samples Results				
1.	6	5	1	−1.5	2.25
2.	5	2	3	.5	25
3.	4	−2	6	3.5	12.25
4.	5	−2	− 4.5	20.25	
5.	8	8	0	−2.5	6.25
6.	11	3	8	5.5	30.25
7.	9	11	−2	−4.5	20.25
8.	7	0	7	4.5	20.25
9.	7	7	0	−2.5	6.25
10.	6	6	0	−2.5	6.25
11.	5	1	4	1.5	2.25
12.	9	4	5	2.5	6.25
			$\Sigma_d = 30.0$		$\Sigma(d_i - M_d)^2 = 133.00$

$$M_d = \Sigma_d/n = 30/12 = 2.50$$

$$s_d = \sqrt{[\Sigma(d_i - M_d)^2]/n-1}$$

$$= \sqrt{133.0/11} = 3.477$$

$$SE_{md} = s_d/\sqrt{n} = 3.477/\sqrt{12}$$

$$= 1.004$$

$$t = M_d/SE_{md} = 2.5/1.004 = 2.490$$

$$t_{.05(11)} = 2.201$$

Differences between scores *are* significant. The placebo appears to have an effect.

The Independent Samples Results

For the sake of the example, we'll use the same data, treating them as though they were from independent groups, the before-the-placebo group as Group 1 and the after-the-placebo group as Group 2.

(Continued)

Figure 9.3 (Continued)

Group 1	Group 2		
6	5		
5	2		
4	−2		
3	5		
8	8	$SE_{m1} = s/\sqrt{n} = 2.309/\sqrt{12} = .667$	(6.1)
11	3		
9	11	$SE_{m2} = s/\sqrt{n} = 3.639/\sqrt{12} = 1.050$	
7	0		
7	7	$SE_d = \sqrt{(SE_{m1}^2 + SE_{m2}^2)} = 1.244$	(6.4)
6	6		
5	1	$t = (M_1 - M_2)/SE_d$	(6.3)
9	4	$= (6.667 - 4.167)/1.244 = 2.010$	
$M = 6.667$	4.167	$t_{.05(22)} = 2.074$	
$s = 2.309$	3.639	The difference is not statistically significant.	

- With the before/after t, the issue is just the variability within the difference scores, which is comparatively minor.
- For the independent t-test, the random variability in the denominator overwhelms the treatment effect (the effect of the placebo) and the results aren't significant.

Figure 9.4 Contains one more example of the before/after t.

Looking at SPSS Output

If we do the Figure 9.4 problem on SPSS, we get the table below. The first two tables, which aren't included here, provide descriptive statistics for the two sets of scores, including a correlation value for the relationship between the two sets of scores. In fact, the way SPSS approaches the before/after t is based on the correlation between scores rather than the difference scores we used, but the concept is the same and the value for t is the same in either case.

Paired Samples Test

	Paired Differences							
		Std. Deviation	Std. Error Mean	95% Confidence Interval of the Difference		t	df	Sig. (2-tailed)
	Mean			Lower	Upper			
Pair 1 Before - After	−4.000	3.899	1.592	−8.091	.091	−2.513	5	.054

Figure 9.4   Another Before/After *t*-Test

An instructor teaching algebra 1 to ninth-grade students wishes to analyze the relationship between student achievement on standardized tests and the availability of an online help resource to which students can go for assistance. For 6 weeks students work with conventional, in-class and homework resources, and then for the next 6 weeks, an online help desk is made available to them. For 6 students scores on a district benchmark test for the first and second 6 weeks periods are as follows:

	1st	2nd	d_i	$(d_i - M_d)$	$(d_i - M_d)^2$
1.	22	28	−6	−2	4
2.	18	21	−3	1	1
3.	33	32	1	5	25
4.	20	25	−5	−1	1
5.	23	33	−10	−6	36
6.	27	28	−1	3	9
					76

1. $M_d = \Sigma_d / n = -24/6 = -4$

2. $s_d = \sqrt{[\Sigma(d_i - M_d)^2]/n - 1}$

   $S_d = \sqrt{(76/5)} = 3.899$

3. $SE_{md} = s_d/\sqrt{n} = 1.592$

4. $t = M_d /SE_{md} = -4/1.592 = -2.513$

5. $t_{.05\,(5)} = 2.571$

- The "Mean" value is the difference between the means of the two sets of scores.
- The "Standard Deviation" value is the same standard deviation of the difference scores that we calculated, as are the "Standard Error of the Mean" and the *t* values.
- The longhand calculation indicated that the calculated value of *t* (*t* = −2.513) was just smaller than the table value ($t_{.05(5)}$ = 2.571).
- In the SPSS output we see how far we "missed" being significant another way. Since SPSS calculates the probability that the value of *t* could have occurred by chance. In this case it is *p* = .054 and our cutoff is *p* = .05. A difference of p = .004 makes the outcome not significant!

The confidence interval values, by the way, indicate that with .95 confidence, the difference between the means of the populations represented by these two sets of scores is somewhere between −8.071 and .091. Here it's a nonissue since the difference between the two sets of measures wasn't significant. That's why one of the possible values for the difference between

SOURCE: Created by Suzanna Nielson.

"And so we thought we'd manage within-group variability by just measuring the same person 78 times."

the means in that range from −8.071 and .091 is 0. Statistically, the two groups of scores still belong to populations with the same means.

The Within-Subjects *F*

Suppose that rather than a before/after design, one wishes a before, an after, and then *another* after test? That is, what if more than two measures are needed? Just as *ANOVA* gives the flexibility to include more than two independent groups, the alternative to the dependent samples *t*-tests for more than two groups is the **within-subjects** *F*. The *F* is (still) for Fisher. This test is an adaptation of the one-way *ANOVA*.

■ The **within-subjects** *F* is the dependent groups equivalent of *ANOVA*.

Just as with the dependent samples *t*-test, there are two approaches. One can either use the same group repeatedly, or match subjects across groups so that unrelated differences are neutralized. As a practical matter, however, matching is increasingly difficult as the number of groups climbs. It's one thing to match two groups on some important characteristic, and quite another to realistically match three, or four, or more groups as we can illustrate.

The Difficulty of Matching Multiple Groups

Consider the administrator who is interested in the relationship between the time mentor teachers spend helping beginning teachers and the improvement in the beginning teachers' effectiveness.

- The first group is tutored for 1 hour per week.
- The second group is tutored for 2 hours per week.
- The third group is tutored for 3 hours per week.
- The fourth group is tutored for 4 hours per week.

At the end of the month, principals complete an observation instrument regarding the new teachers' effectiveness. One group examined under the 4 different conditions would take 4 months to complete. But if subjects in 4 different groups are matched, the entire study could be completed in 1 month because all four groups can run simultaneously. To have some confidence that any differences stemmed from the amount of time spent mentoring new teachers, however, one would need to control, at a minimum:

- Initial differences in the new teachers' experience
- Initial differences in the new teachers' effectiveness
- Any differences in the mentor teachers' counsel/direction unrelated to time

Matching is increasingly difficult as the number of groups increases. For these reasons, with more than two groups it's much more common to see one group used repeatedly than it is to see multiple groups matched in spite of the increased time required to complete the study.

Examining Sources of Variability

An educator wishes to analyze the progress of second language speakers in an adult remedial reading program offered after hours at the local elementary school. Perhaps reading comprehension is gauged at 30-day intervals for four subjects so that the issue is whether there is a relationship between how much time individuals spend in the program and how well they do. The data are as follows:

	Month		
Subject	Sept.	Oct.	Nov.
Imelda	27	32	38
Toua	34	43	55
Mai	19	18	26
Lorenzo	22	24	29

The column-to-column differences (September, October, November) represent changes in reading comprehension related to time, which is the independent variable. In the one-way *ANOVA* this measure-to-measure variability was the variability that became the sum of squares between (SS_{bet}). Once divided by its degrees of freedom, it became the mean square between (MS_{bet}) and the numerator in the *F* ratio.

The differences from row-to-row are the person-to-person differences among subjects in the study. Although they are a source of error variance, just as they were in the one-way *ANOVA*, by using the same people repeatedly (or by matching the subjects) the subject-to-subject differences are similar for each group of measures. Below, we'll measure this within-subjects variation, and then, because it's common to all conditions, eliminate it from the analysis. There will still be error (uncontrolled) variance to contend with, but the *F* ratio won't include initial between-groups differences or person-to-person differences. In the one-way *ANOVA*, because the groups weren't identical, the within-groups variability was different for each group and had to be factored in.

Calculating the Within-Subjects F

The within-subjects F procedure is to

- First calculate all variability from all sources, the same SS_{tot} value we calculated when we did one-way and factorial $ANOVA$ in Chapter 7:
- $SS_{tot} = \Sigma(x-M_G)^2$, the sum of the squared differences between each individual (x) and the mean of all scores (M_G)

  For those in the remedial reading program, $M_G = 30.583$

  Working along the rows we have the following $for\ SS_{tot}$:

  $(27 - 30.583)^2 + (34 - 30.583)^2 + (19 - 30.583)^2 + (22 - 30.583)^2 +$
  $(32 - 30.583)^2 + (43 - 30.583)^2 + (18 - 30.583)^2 + (24 - 30.583)^2 +$
  $(38 - 30.583)^2 + (55 - 30.583)^2 + (26 - 30.583)^2 + (29 - 30.583)^2 = \mathbf{1264.912}$

- The calculations are tedious but at least it's easy to see why this is a "sum of squares" value. It's also easy to see why this is considered a "conceptual" formula; it makes the process of summing the squared values very clear. Other formulae will provide the same answer without the tedium of all the subtracting and squaring, but the logic, as we noted in Chapter 7, is also less clear.
- Next, calculate the variability for the treatment effect, SS_{treat}. This variability is reflected in the column-to-column differences.
  - o The subscript $_1$ indicates the scores in the first column
  - o $_2$ indicates scores in the second column, and so on
  - o To the last column ("i")

    For the variability *due to the treatment* we have:

    $SS_{treat} = (M_1 - M_G)^2 n_1 + (M_2 - M_G)^2 n_2 + \ldots (M_i - M_G)^2 n_i$
    $= (25.50 - 30.583)^2(4) + (29.25 - 30.583)^2(4) + (37.0 - 30.583)^2(4) =$
    $\mathbf{275.168}$

- Then, the variability between subjects, SS_{subj}. is calculated so that it can be removed from the analysis. The notation:
  - o $_{r1}$ indicates the scores for the subject in row 1, $_{r2}$ for the subjects in the second row, and so on.

For the variability due to the subjects we have:

$$SS_{subj} = (M_{r1} - M_G)^2 n_{r1} + (M_{r2} - M_G)^2 n_{r2} + \ldots (M_{rk} - M_G)^2 n_k$$
$$= (32.333 - 30.583)^2(3) + (44.0 - 30.583)^2(3) + (21.0 - 30.583)^2(3) +$$
$$(25.0 - 30.583)^2(3) = \mathbf{918.247}$$

- In the one-way *ANOVA*, SS_{tot} minus SS_{bet} leaves SS_{with}, which was the error variability. Here, we calculate the subject-to-subject difference and remove it from further analysis since the subjects are the same for each measure. What will remain is error variability *not* related to differences between subjects; it's residual variance.

The "residual" sum of squares, SS_{res}.

$$SS_{res} = SS_{tot} - SS_{treat} - SS_{subj}$$
$$= 1264.912 - 275.168 - 918.247 = \mathbf{71.497}$$

The issue was whether the increasing lengths of time that adults spend in the reading program is associated with changes in reading scores. Like the Chapter 7 *ANOVAs*, the test statistic is an *F* ratio created from mean square (*MS*) values. The *F* value will be the MS_{treat} divided by the MS_{res}. As before, *MS* values are *SS* ÷ their *df*.

First the *df* values:

- df_{treat} = number of treatments −1 (3 − 1 here)
- df_{subj} = number of subjects −1 (4 − 1)
- $df_{res} = df_{treat} \times df_{subj}$ (2 × 3)

Then the *MS* values:

- $MS_{treat} = SS_{treat} \div df_{treat}$
- $MS_{res} = SS_{res} \div df_{res}$

Summarizing the Results

The within-subjects *F* results are presented in the familiar *ANOVA* table. The line for "total" remains, but rather than lines for "between" and "within" variability, "Treatment," "Subjects," and "Residual" variability are listed. With *SS* and *df* values, *F* can be calculated.

Source	SS	df	MS	F	F_{crit}
Total	1264.912	11			
Treatment	275.168	2	137.584	11.546	$F_{.05\ (2,6)} = 5.14$
Subjects	918.247	3			
Residual	71.497	6	11.916		

The SS_{tot} and SS_{subj} values provide access to SS_{res}, but once that value is determined, the SS_{tot} and SS_{subj} play no further part in the analysis except as accuracy checks. For example, note that:

- The SS values for treatment + subjects + residual sum = SS_{tot}.
- The df values for treatment + subjects + residual sum = df_{tot}.

Interpreting the F Value

Does more time result in significantly different scores? Comparing the calculated value of F to F for 2 and 6 degrees of freedom indicates that it does. At $p = .05$, there is a significant difference between at least two of the sets of measures.

This was an analysis based on repeated measures of one group, an approach taken to keep initial group differences at bay. We also determined the amount of person-to-person variance there is and, because it's likely to be very much the same for each measure, could eliminate it from further analysis. Both initial group differences and differences within groups can obscure results in a conventional *ANOVA*. Eliminating them in this test allows one to reduce the amount of error one must contend with. The SS_{res} indicates that there is still error, but it isn't related to differences between groups (there was only one) or to person-to-person differences.

A significant F in the repeated measures *ANOVA* gives rise to the same problem that occurs in the independent groups *ANOVA*s. Which set of measures is significantly different from which? Once again, a *post-hoc* test will answer that question.

Another Within-Subjects *F* Example

The question among a group of university tutors is whether study time among students increases as the quarter progresses and final exams loom. The tutors select four students who fill out time sheets at the end of each week indicating the number of hours spent in personal or group study for their classes. The data are as follows:

Student	Mean Hours Studied Per Week				
	1st month	2nd month	3rd month	row totals	row means
1	8	11	16	35	11.667
2	6	6	15	27	9.0
3	12	12	20	44	14.667
4	11	11	23	45	15.0
Column Totals	37	40	74	151	
Column Means	9.250	10.0	18.50		

$SS_{tot} = \Sigma(x - M_G)^2$ working down the columns,

$= (8 - 12.583)^2 + (6 - 12.583)^2 + (12 - 12.583)^2 + (11 - 12.583)^2 +$

$(11 - 12.583)^2 + (6 - 12.583)^2 + (12 - 12.583)^2 + (11 - 12.583)^2 +$

$(16 - 12.583)^2 + (15 - 12.583)^2 + (20 - 12.583)^2 + (23 - 12.583)^2 = \mathbf{296.917}$

$SS_{treat} = (M_1 - M_G)^2 n_1 + (M_2 - M_G)^2 n_2 + (M_3 - M_G)^2 n_i$

$= (9.25 - 12.583)^2(4) + (10.0 - 12.583)^2(4) + (18.50 - 12.583)^2(4) = \mathbf{211.167}$

$SS_{subj} = (M_{r1} - M_G)^2 n_{r1} + (M_{r2} - M_G)^2 n_{r2} + (M_{r3} - M_G)^2 nr_3 + (M_{r4} - M_G)^2 nr_4$

$= (11.667 - 12.583)^2(3) + (9.0 - 12.583)^2(3) +$

$(14.667 - 12.583)^2(3) + (15.0 - 12.583)^2(3) = \mathbf{71.586}$

With measures of all variability (SS_{tot}), the treatment effect (SS_{treat}), and the subject- to -subject-to-subject differences, the residual error (SS_{res}) is determined by subtracting treatment and subjects SS values from SS_{tot}.

$SS_{res} = SS_{tot} - SS_{treat} - SS_{subj} = 296.917 - 211.167 - 71.586 = \mathbf{14.164}$

Now, the *ANOVA* table:

Source	SS	df	MS	F	F_{crit}
Total	296.917	11			
Treatment	211.167	2	105.584	44.720	$F_{.05\,(2,6)} = 5.14$
Subjects	71.586	3			
Residual	14.164	6	2.361		

Is there a significant relationship between how much time students spend studying, and the immediacy of end of term? The calculated *F* exceeds the critical value of *F* from Table C so the answer is "yes." Actually, we could see from the means of the column scores that students reported more time spent as the semester progressed. But the test results indicate that it isn't likely a random difference. A *post-hoc* test will determine the pairs of months for which the amount of study time is significantly different.

Locating Significant Differences

As with any type of *ANOVA* involving more than two groups or sets of measures, a statistically significant *F* only tells us that, in this case at least, one set of measures is significantly different from at least one other set. For our problem there are four possibilities:

- The first month results are significantly different from the second month results.
- The first month results are significantly different from the third month results.
- The second month results are significantly different from the third month results.
- All groups are significantly different from all.

Again we'll use Tukey's *HSD*. Recall that Formula 7.6 is:

$$HSD = x_{.05} \sqrt{(MS_w/n)}$$

Recall that MS_{with} was the error term in *ANOVA*. The equivalent in the within-subjects *F* is MS_{res}, which we'll substitute into the formula. Note that we always conduct the *post-hoc* test at the same probability level as the original test was conducted, $p = .05$ in our case.

1. The value of x must come from Table D in the Tables of Critical Values appendix.

   a. The value is a function of the number of groups in the problem. In our case, it's the number of sets of scores, 3, across the top of the table, and

   b. Down the left side of the table for the df for MS_{res} (rather than the MS_{with}) for the problem.

2. Divide the MS_{res} value from the ANOVA table (C) by the number of measures in any one set of scores. In our case that's 4.

   $2.361 \div 4 = \textbf{.590}$

   a. Determine the square root of the result

   $\sqrt{590} = \textbf{.768}$

   b. Multiply by the value from the Tukey table (D), which for our 3 sets of measures and MS_{res} df of 6 was **4.34** (Step 1).

   $4.34 \times .768 = \textbf{3.334}$

   $$HSD = \times_{.05} \sqrt{(MS_w / n)}$$
   $$HSD = 4.34 \sqrt{(2.361 \div 4)}$$
   $$HSD = \textbf{3.334}$$

Any difference between the means of hours studies for any 2 months that is equal to or greater than 3.334 will be statistically significant.

The differences between means are as follows:

- The mean of the first month minus the mean of the second month $(9.25 - 10) = \textbf{.75}$ —this difference is *not* statistically significant
- From the first month to the third $(9.25 - 18.5) = \textbf{9.25}$ *is* significant
- From the second month to the third $(10 - 18.25) = \textbf{8.25}$ *is* significant

Is the imminence of final exams associated with more time spent studying? It seems so.

How Much of the Variance Is Explained?

Besides determining which groups of measures are significantly different from which, a significant F calls for a measure of effect size. Recall that partial *eta*-square, η_p^2, estimates the proportion of the variance a particular variable explains. For the current problem, the independent variable is the month in which students studied.

$$\text{Formula 7.7 was } \eta_p^2 = \frac{SS_b}{SS_b + SS_w}$$

By substituting SS_{treat} for SS_{bet}, and SS_{res} for SS_w, we have:

$$\eta_p^2 = \frac{SS_{treat}}{SS_{treat} + SS_{res}}$$

Substituting the values from the *ANOVA* table we have:

$$\eta_p^2 = \frac{211.167}{211.167 + 14.164} = .94$$

About 94% of the variance in study time can be explained by the month of the quarter. This value is unrealistically high, which can happen when the data are contrived. Study habits are probably explained by a combination of several variables rather than being predominantly explained by just one.

Comparing the Within-Subjects *F* With the One-Way *ANOVA*

The rationale for using dependent samples tests, whether *t* or *F*, was that with much of the difference between groups excluded by either repeatedly measuring the same group, or by matching subjects, there is less error variance. This makes the test more powerful. We demonstrated this earlier by comparing how an independent *t*-test and a before/after *t*-test would prompt different conclusions for the same data. We can make a similar comparison between a one-way *ANOVA* and the repeated measures (within subjects) *F*.

If the 3 months' measures treated as measures from independent groups, the subject-to-subject differences remain as a component of the error variability, and the results below are the result:

Source	SS	df	MS	F	F_{crit}
Total	296.917	11			
Between	211.167	2	105.584	11.082	$F_{.05\,(2,9)} = 4.26$
Within	85.750	9	9.528		

Since the critical value of F at $p = .05$ for 2 and 9 degrees of freedom is 4.26, the result is still statistically significant, so is anything really gained by completing the problem as a within-subjects F? First of all, note how different the two measures of error variance are for the two procedures:

$SS_{res} = 14.164$ for the within-subjects test

$SS_{with} = 85.750$ for the one-way ANOVA

Clearly, there was much more uncontrolled variance in the one-way test, something that in other circumstances might well be the difference between a random outcome and statistically significant results. But a related issue is the amount of variance explained, *eta*-squared. Since the denominator in that effect size statistic includes the error term from whichever ANOVA is used, note the difference. For the one-way ANOVA we have:

$$\eta_p^2 = \frac{SS_b}{SS_b + SS_w} = \frac{211.167}{211.167 + 85.750} = \mathbf{.711}$$

For the within-subjects F we had:

$$\eta_p^2 = .940$$

Using the within-subjects test, we explained about 23% more of the variance than with the one-way procedure. The measures of total and between/treatment variance are the same in either case. It's the change in error variance from SS_{with} to the SS_{res} that makes the difference. Figure 9.5 contains another within-subjects F problem.

In truth, of course, groups are either independent or they aren't. There won't be situations where, once the data are collected, one can decide which procedure to use. The nature of the relationship between groups pre-determines this. The two approaches were used here to contrast the difference between the error terms and so illustrate the potential there is for greater statistical power with a repeated measures design. The comparative *eta*-square values indicate that the difference is also manifested in the effect sizes that are calculated for significant results.

A Comment on the Within-Subjects *F* and SPSS

It's been our practice to follow longhand calculations with the SPSS equivalent for the procedure. In keeping with that there's a computer example of a repeated measures ANOVA in the SPSS Primer at the end of the book, but one should note that commands and the output for these procedures are a little more involved than they are for an independent groups ANOVA.

Figure 9.5   Another Example of a Within-Subjects F

A principal in a private secondary school wonders whether different incentive levels for teachers translate into higher test scores among students on quarterly tests. She offers a $25 gift certificate for teachers whose students improve by 5 percentile points on the first-quarter test, $50.00 for a 5 percentile improvement in the second-quarter and $100.00 for the same improvement in the third-quarter. For 5 teachers, the data are as follows:

teacher	Q_1	Q_2	Q_3	M_{row}
		Percentile Improvement		
1	2	2	3	2.333
2	1	2	4	2.333
3	4	3	3	3.333
4	3	5	6	4.667
5	2	4	5	3.667
	$M_{col} = 2.40$	3.20	4.20	
	$M_G = 3.267$			

1. $SS_{tot} = \Sigma(x - M_G)^2 = \mathbf{26.933}$ (the sum of squared differences between scores and M_G).

2. $SS_{quarter} = (M_{Q1} - M_G)^2 n_1 + (M_{Q2} - M_G)^2 n_2 + (M_{Q3} - M_G)^2 n_3$

   $= (2.40 - 3.267)^2 5 + (3.20 - 3.267)^2 5 + (4.20 - 3.267)^2 5 = \mathbf{8.133}$

3. $SS_{subj} = (M_{r1} - M_G)^2 n_{r1} + (M_{r2} - M_G)^2 n_{r2} + (M_{r3} - M_G)^2 n_{r3} + (M_{r4} - M_G)^2 n_{r4} + (M_{r5} - M_G)^2 n_{r5}$

   $= (2.333 - 3.267)^2 3 + (2.333 - 3.267)^2 3 + (3.333 - 3.267)^2 3 +$

   $(4.667 - 3.267)^2 3 + (3.667 - 3.267)^2 3 = \mathbf{11.607}$

4. $SS_{res} = SS_{tot} - SS_{quarter} - SS_{subj} = 26.933 - 8.133 - 11.607 = \mathbf{7.20}$

Source	SS	df	MS	F	
Total	26.933	14			
Quarter	8.133	2	4.067	**4.519**	$F_{.05\,(2,10)} = \mathbf{4.10}$. F is sig.
Subjects	11.60	4			
Residual	7.20	8	.90		

The *post-hoc* test: $HSD = x_{.05}\sqrt{(MS_w/n)} = 4.04\sqrt{(.9/5)} = 1.714$; first- versus third-quarter scores.

	M1 = 2.4	M2 = 3.2	M3 = 4.2
M1 = 2.4		.8	1.8
M2 = 3.2			1.0
M3 = 4.2			

$\eta_p^2 = \dfrac{SS_{quarter}}{SS_{quarter} + SS_{resid}} = \dfrac{8.133}{8.133 + 7.20} = .53$; 53% of score variance is related to incentives.

Computer packages tend to have procedures specifically designed for some of the more common procedures, like *t*-test and *ANOVA*, that are quite straightforward because they're used so frequently. Other procedures that may not be used quite so commonly are often accessed as subcomponents of other tests, rather than being available as "stand-alones." This is the case for the within-subjects *ANOVA*, which is accessed under a more general set of procedures called the General Linear Model, or *GLM*, in SPSS.

The GLM provides for a variety of analyses involving situations where there is a linear relationship—situations where the relationship is direct and constant—between *IV*(s) and *DV*(s). Several analytical approaches fit this description, including the within-subjects *F*. Everything we calculated longhand can be found in the computer output, but it also includes a good deal more than just our analysis because it was designed to answer a variety of related questions as well.

SUMMARY

Ms. Hindley's problem at the beginning of the chapter was the lack of another group with which to compare her remedial students. Both the before/after *t*-test and the within-subjects *F* accommodate this by using one group multiple times. These tests have much in common with the independent *t*-test and the one-way *ANOVA*. In either case, the independent variable must have nominal scale form, and the dependent variable must be interval or ratio scale and, of course, all of these tests analyze groups' scores for significant differences. The groups in this chapter aren't independent, however. The practice of either using one group repeatedly or matching groups on extraneous variables that might otherwise differ for independent groups, and contribute error variance, allows one to diminish the error term in the denominators of both the *t* and *F* ratios. With less error variance, more modest effects from the independent variable can provide a statistically significant result. So other things equal, the dependent samples tests will detect a significant difference more readily than the independent groups tests.

There are drawbacks, of course. When one group is used repeatedly, these "repeated measures" designs take more time to execute than a design that allows a researcher to measure all groups concurrently. Furthermore, the matching used to establish group equivalence and so provide a way around the time problem can be difficult to accomplish, particularly with more than two groups. Matching, particularly if there are many subjects in each group, often requires a very large pool of subjects from which to draw. On balance, however, the before/after *t* and the within-subjects *F* have substantial appeal.

Implicit in the concept of dependent samples tests is the idea that since the multiple sets of scores all come from the same subjects, even as scores change because of the independent variable, the scores are likely to co-vary. Subjects who score relatively high on the first set of measures tend to do likewise on the second set. Because this co-variation is consistent from set to set of scores, it's variance we can control, something not possible with independent groups tests.

In fact, the power of both of these tests—their ability to detect significant differences when they are present—has much to do with the strength of the correlation between sets of scores. But whether measured with difference scores or correlation values, there is a connection between the repeated measures, which brings us to the next topic.

To date, our tests have been focused on detecting significant *differences*. In Chapter 9 we will chart new territory and investigate the companion to tests of differences, tests of the strength of *associations*. The language and procedures may be new, but the underlying concepts are going to sound very familiar and you'll find you pick them up quite readily, so on to associations!

EXERCISES

1. There are data available for the number of absences by grade in an elementary school during the week before and the week after state-required standardized testing. Since school officials make a concerted effort to have students represented for testing purposes, the educators wish to know whether there are significant differences in the number of absences. For 6 randomly selected classrooms, the before-and-after data are as follows:

	Before	After
1.	2	5
2.	3	4
3.	4	7
4.	9	5
5.	5	8
6.	7	8

a) What is the standard deviation of the difference scores?
b) What is the standard error of the mean for the difference scores?
c) What is the calculated value of t?
d) Are the differences statistically significant?
e) If instead of the above the question were, "Do students miss significantly more school the week after testing than the week before?"

   i. What sort of test would it become?
   ii. What would be the critical value of t in this case?

2. A group of counselors set up a hotline for parents calling the school after hours with questions about schedules and assignments. They track the number of inquiries from parents of 10 randomly selected students before and after an information session explaining the service.

   a) Are there significant differences in the number of inquiries?

	Before	After
1.	0	1
2.	2	2
3.	0	4
4.	3	7
5.	1	3
6.	2	4
7.	5	6
8.	0	0
9.	1	2
10.	2	5

   b) What is the value of t if this is done as an independent t-test?
   c) Explain the difference between before/after and independent t-tests.

3. A group of 8 second-grade students receive 3 different kinds of reinforcement for responding to teacher questioning, no reinforcement, verbal reinforcement, and a tangible reinforcer (a sticker) for responding. The dependent variable is the number of responses.

	Non	Verb	Token
1.	2	4	5
2.	3	5	6
3.	3	4	7
4.	4	6	7
5.	6	6	8
6.	2	4	5
7.	1	3	4
8.	2	5	7

   a) What's the independent variable?
   b) What's the scale of the dependent variable?
   c) Are the differences related to type of reinforcer statistically significant?

d) Where are the significant differences?

e) How much of the variance in response rate can be explained by the type of reinforcer?

4. How are subject-to-subject differences eliminated from the analysis in a within-subjects F test?

5. Why are subject-to-subject differences not similarly eliminated in a one-way *ANOVA*?

6. In an effort to understand test anxiety better, an educational researcher attempts to opera-tionalize anxiety by informing subjects that completing a task in the time limit is required if the subject is to receive a reward. Each subject receives four sets of 10 simple calculation problems. Each set imposes a more stringent time requirement than the one preceding after which anxiety is gauged. Anxiety scores for 8 subjects are as follows:

	time1	time2	time3	time4
1.	8	8	9	9
2.	7	7	8	10
3.	4	4	4	5
4.	2	3	5	5
5.	5	6	6	8
6.	5	5	7	9
7.	4	4	5	4
8.	2	3	6	7

a) Does anxiety appear to be related to time limits?

b) How much of anxiety is a function of increasing time limits?

c) At what point is the difference in the level of anxiety statistically significant?

7. A biology instructor wishes to know whether students' participation in lab activities is related to their performance on the end of semester exam. She randomly selects 8 students from a section of introductory biology requiring a lab and matches those 8 students by grade average to 8 students to another section of the same class which requires no lab. The final exam scores of the 8 pairs of students are as follows:

	No Lab	Lab
1.	56	63
2.	73	74
3.	61	73
4.	85	81
5.	43	57
6.	60	68
7.	45	39
8.	86	93

a) What is the dependent variable?
b) What is the value of the standard error of the mean for difference scores?
c) Are the differences between groups statistically significant?
d) What conclusion should the instructor draw?

8. A researcher is interested in the amount of time per week instructors at a college devote to research and writing before and after they receive tenure. Twelve instructors selected at random from among the ranks of nontenured faculty are asked to indicate how many hours they devote weekly to writing and research. Five years later, after 7 of them have been tenured, these 7 are asked a second time. The results are as follows:

	Before tenure	After tenure
1.	10	4
2.	8	6
3.	12	13
4.	6	5
5.	7	4
6.	10	7
7.	9	6

a) Are the differences statistically significant?
b) What would the value of t have been if these had been independent groups?
c) What element makes the standard error of the difference for the independent t larger than for the paired t?

9. The guidance counselor at a high school believes that truancy is most prevalent late in the semester when struggling students begin to give up hope of passing their classes. He gathers a list of the 7 students who have the lowest grades in an 11th-grade language arts class at the end of September, and tracks their attendance for the first 2 weeks of each of October, November, and December. He finds the following number of absences:

	Oct	Nov	Dec
1.	2	1	4
2.	0	0	1
3.	3	5	7
4.	2	2	3
5.	4	4	7
6.	3	3	8
7.	2	0	3

a) Are there significant differences related to the month?
b) What is the independent variable in this analysis?
c) How much of the variance in days missed is related to the month?

10. If the data in item 9 are treated as though the groups were independent and the analysis completed as for a one-way *ANOVA*:

   a) What is the value of *F*?
   b) How can you explain the difference between the one-way *ANOVA* and the within-subjects *F* outcomes?

THE FORMULAE AND THEIR SYMBOLS

Formula 9.1: $t = \dfrac{M_d}{SE_{md}}$

The formula for calculating the dependent samples *t*-test.

Formula 9.2: $S_d = \sqrt{[\Sigma(d_i - M_d)^2]/n - 1}$.

The formula for calculating the standard deviation of the difference scores in the dependent samples *t*-test.

There are certainly other formulae used in this chapter, but they are close variations to procedures raised in earlier chapters so the thought was not to clutter things up any more than necessary and perhaps curb the number of 3×5 cards filling your backpacks and briefcases.

STUDENT STUDY SITE

Visit the Student Study Site at **www.sagepub.com/tanner** for additional learning tools.

PART IV

Association and Prediction

Chapter 10

CORRELATION

THE PROBLEM: MEASURING THE STRENGTH OF RELATIONSHIPS

A guidance counselor and an assistant principal are responsible for administering an after-school program designed to help students who wish to raise their academic standing either to improve their opportunity for college admission or to ensure high school graduation. Particularly for students in danger of not graduating, the problem is to help students recognize the relationship between their homework and their academic progress. One of the complications is that some students are involved in other after-school activities such as athletics, band, the biology club, and so on. Those administering the tutoring program reason that because these other activities compete in some of the same time slots as the tutoring program, perhaps they are having a negative effect on overall academic performance.

QUESTIONS AND ANSWERS

❑ Is there a significant relationship between homework and grades?

A Pearson Correlation will answer this question. It quantifies the strength of the relationship between two interval scale variables.

❑ It's still a correlation issue, but if one were interested in whether involvement in extracurricular activities was connected to student achievement, the issue is the correlation between a nominal scale item with two categories (are/are not involved) and an interval or ratio scale item (grade average, or a test score). A point-biserial correlation will answer this question.

A CONTEXT FOR CORRELATION

Before now, the discussions of statistical significance have centered on differences. There were differences between samples and populations, differences between two groups, and differences

■ Tests such as *t*-test, *ANOVA*, Mann-Whitney, and many other tests of significant differences are based on the assumption of significant *differences* between groups. Collectively, these tests fall under the umbrella of the **hypothesis of difference**.

■ Procedures such as Pearson's *r*, Spearman's *rho*, and *phi* coefficient which detect significant *associations* between groups fall under the **hypothesis of association**.

among more than two groups. Whether we dealt with independent groups or related groups, the issue was always about difference. All of these procedures fall under a conceptual umbrella called the **hypothesis of difference**. With correlation, the focus shifts to the **hypothesis of association**. We're still interested in statistical significance, but now the point of focus is whether *the associations* are statistically significant or just random.

When variables are correlated, they vary in concert with each other—they co-vary. That term is important because one of the pitfalls in studying correlation is that it's very tempting to make the leap from correlation to causation. If nurses in some nursing programs have a degree program that includes more classes than those in other programs, and if they perform better on their board licensing exams, it seems not to take very long for someone to argue that if others adopted the lengthier program, their graduates too would pass the test at a higher level. For the first of many times, be warned against making such assumptions. Causal relationships are very difficult to validate in research with people. In spite of the fact that two variables change together, one can generally think of some other variable that might explain the connection. Might the alignment of the nursing curriculum with the test have an impact on test performance? Is the quality of the instruction an issue? Is the fact that the nursing students in the more successful program tend to be a highly homogeneous group compared with those in other programs a factor? If more classes and higher test scores are correlated does it necessarily indicate that taking more classes *causes* higher scores? There are many reasons why this might not be so. Although there are statistical procedures designed to deal with it specifically (Chapter 16), imputing cause is usually very difficult to definitively establish.

Even without knowing the causal factors, a significant correlation gives an educational decision-maker powerful information. If two measures co-vary in a nonrandom fashion, it becomes possible to predict the value of one from the value of the other, an outcome of great importance to what we will do in Chapter 11.

A Little History

The name "Pearson" is almost synonymous with correlation, and with good reason. Karl Pearson did more to develop correlation concepts, and perhaps more to develop quantitative analysis generally, than anyone else. It was his desire to establish statistics as an independent field of applied mathematics, and by almost any measure, he succeeded. Besides developing the correlation procedure that bears his name, he developed the regression procedures that are the subject of Chapters 11 and 12, the *chi*-square tests we will learn how to use in Chapter 13, and much more. He is the person who coined the term "standard deviation," and with two others he founded what is perhaps the preeminent journal in statistical analysis, *Biometrika*.

It would have been easy to predict some other career for him. Always a gifted student, Pearson's studies at Cambridge covered areas well afield of mathematical statistics. He was interested in religion and philosophy, and in postgraduate studies in Germany demonstrated unusual scholarship in German literature. His interest in religion deserves an additional mention. When he was at Cambridge, attendance at chapel was compulsory for all students. He challenged compulsory attendance, and with the assistance of his father (who was a prominent lawyer), managed to have the requirement lifted. Having prompted a change in regulations Pearson attended chapel, but because he chose to, rather than because it was required.

Pearson's independence probably helped him develop many of the analytical procedures we still use. His multiple interests prompted him to wonder whether there was not some grand explanation that would unite all mathematical theories. Although the discipline is a little different, the pursuit of a general field theory also preoccupied a far more famous contemporary of his, Albert Einstein. But our focus here is on the statistical procedure most closely associated with Pearson, the correlation coefficient.

WHAT CORRELATION OFFERS

A correlation between variables means that as one changes, the other tends to change accordingly. When the correlation is statistically significant, it means that every time we collect new data on the two variables and perform the analysis, the relationship emerges. Even without knowing the cause of the relationship, statistically significant correlations can be very helpful. If college admission test scores are significantly correlated with students' future performance in college, the admissions committee has a better-than-chance way of knowing who are most likely to succeed, which is why colleges and universities often require that students submit admissions tests scores. If the number of times a student is involved in disciplinary procedures is correlated with dropping out of school, counselors and administrators have an indicator of whether the student will leave school prematurely and perhaps an opportunity to intervene.

Another advantage to correlation is its flexibility. It lets one determine the relationship between different *kinds* of variables. In the after-school program at the beginning of the chapter, correlation allows educators to determine the relationship between the number of hours students study and their grades. Although those variables are both at least interval scale, they are entirely different characteristics. Whether they have something in common is the reason for doing correlation analysis.

Quantifying the relationship between different kinds of variables is a point of departure for us. To now we've been interested in whether groups that are otherwise comparable respond differently to some stimulus or characteristic. With correlation the variables are often very different to begin with. Indeed, that's the point of the analysis, to see whether different characteristics vary in concert. Often, the more different they are, the more intriguing the relationship is for the analyst. We don't think it odd that there might be a correlation between a learner's participation in the ecology club and the level of parents' education, two very different kinds of variables. The correlation coefficient will indicate the strength of the relationship between them and, to the degree that they co-vary, a measure of one will even suggest the magnitude of the other.

THE SCATTER PLOT

■ With two scores for each individual, **scatter plots** represent two data distributions in one graph.

When two variables are correlated it is because they each contain some of the same information. The correlation coefficient quantifies what is common between variables. Perhaps the easiest way to visualize correlation is with a **scatter plot,** which allows one to plot two data distributions in one figure. The amount of scatter in the points that are plotted suggests the strength of the relationship between variables. Assume that educators want to know how closely the time students spend doing homework is related to their grades. They gather data from a sample of eight of those participating in the after-school program, which produces the data set below. Homework is indicated in the number of hours completed per night. Grades are tabulated on a 4-point scale.

	homework	grades
1.	.25	2.00
2.	.50	1.75
3.	.75	2.00
4.	1.00	2.50
5.	1.00	2.00
6.	1.25	2.25
7.	1.50	2.00
8.	2.00	3.60

Take a minute to orient yourself to the data set. The lines represent scores for eight people, two scores for each. These data can be represented in a graph as follows:

- Prepare a graph with homework hours represented on the vertical (y) axis with score ranging from 0 to 2.25.
- Represent grade averages from, say, 0 to 4.0 along the horizontal (x) axis.
- The data point for the first person is located by identifying .25 on the x axis and then moving vertically to a horizontal line from 2.0 on the y axis.

It's important to remember that each data point represents two scores for the individual. When the data in the list above are plotted, the result is Figure 10.1.

Perhaps at first glance the points in the graph look random, but study it a moment and a trend emerges. Generally, the points are from lower left to upper right in the graph. This is the case when the relationship (the correlation) between variables is positive. As the measure of one increases the measures of the other tend to likewise. The relationship isn't universally positive for these eight people, however. The second person reports more homework than the first, but has lower grades.

Figure 10.1   The Relationship Between Homework and Grades

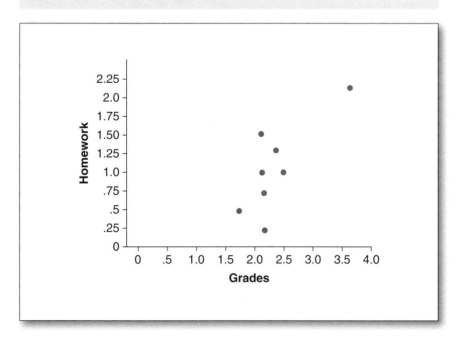

Should the relationship be negative, the points would scatter from the upper left corner to the lower right. In that case, as the measure of one variable increases, the measures of the other decrease. Perhaps the relationship between academic performance and the hour at which the third-grade student goes to bed at night is negative—the later the hour, the lower the performance.

The correlation procedures we'll use in this chapter assume that the measured relationship is linear, but not all are. Consider the relationship between anxiety and performance on a homework assignment (Figure 10.2). If there is no anxiety at all about completing the task, perhaps the student ignores it. Initially, the relationship is probably positive—more anxiety is associated with an increase in the motivation to perform. Note that if these first few data points were all we had, the relationship would *look* positive (want better performance, then increase the anxiety level). This is one of the problems that stems from what is called **attenuated**, or restricted, **range**. Including the rest of the data reveals that there is a point where if anxiety gets too high, performance begins to decline, and then does so rapidly. Apparently, learners reach a point at which more anxiety makes it increasingly difficult to perform. In any event, recognizing a curvilinear relationship often requires data that are *un*attenuated, data that occur across the entire range of possible scores rather than just a portion.

■ **Attenuated range** exists when data don't occur over their entire range. It can distort the relationship between variables.

Figure 10.2 The Relationship Between Test Performance and Anxiety

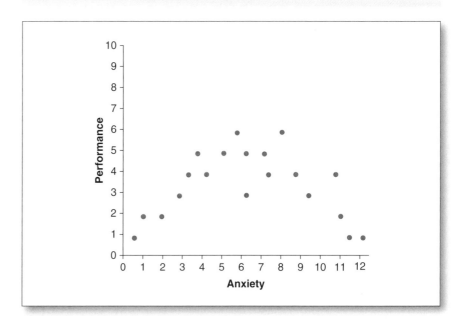

When the relationship between two variables is linear, stronger relationships are indicated by less scatter along the line formed by the data points. If there is a *perfect* linear relationship, the points form a straight line. Clearly, this isn't the case here. Even without a graph, it's evident that the relationship isn't perfect; some values of x have more than one corresponding value of y. Two students with 1.0 hour of homework each day had different grade averages. Several students have the same 2.0 grade averages, but different amounts of homework each day—there are multiple x values for the same y.

If the variables entered in the plot are both normally distributed, and if they are completely unrelated, what pattern would there be in the resulting points? Now think about this for a minute. If the data are normally distributed, where will most of the data occur? How will that be manifested in a scatter plot? If you answered that the points would make up a circular pattern in the plot, you're correct. Most of the points will fall in the middle of both the horizontal and vertical scales because of the central tendency of data in normal distributions.

Correlation values range anywhere from +1 to −1. Correlations of either +1 or −1 are *perfect* correlations. The difference between +1 and −1 is only whether as the value of one variable goes up, the other does also (a positive correlation) or whether the other declines (a negative correlation). The sign of the correlation has nothing do with its strength.

As we noted, perfect correlations are exceedingly rare in education or any of the social sciences, but they do occur in mathematics, for example. The area of a circle can be found by $A = \pi r^2$. The formula always works because there is a perfect relationship between the radius of the circle and its area. In the world of people and social institutions, however, such relationships are rare, if they exist at all.

VARIATIONS ON THE CORRELATION THEME

The way we speak of correlation usually presumes a relationship between two variables, and certainly such **bivariate correlations** are the most common, but there are other kinds. There can be correlations between one variable and an aggregate of others. Perhaps one is interested in how well mathematics achievement motivation correlates with a combination of mathematics aptitude and past mathematics grades.

■ **Bivariate correlation** refers to the correlation between two variables.

one variable	with a combination of variables
math achievement motivation	$\left\{ \begin{array}{l} \text{math aptitude} \\ \text{past math grades} \end{array} \right.$

There can also be correlations between groups of variables. Perhaps one is interested in how a combination of attitude variables, such as clerical staff members' sense of independence and their willingness to accept responsibility for outcomes, is related to a set of behavioral variables such as their absentee rate and their working relationships with others.

a combination of variables

$\left\{\begin{array}{l}\text{independence}\\\text{responsibility}\end{array}\right.$

with a combination of variables

$\left\{\begin{array}{l}\text{absenteeism}\\\text{relationships with others}\end{array}\right.$

Even bivariate correlations aren't all of a sort. There can be:

- Correlations between nominal variables,
- Correlations between ordinal variables,
- Correlations between interval/ratio variables, and
- Correlations between variables of different data scales.

We might be interested in the correlation between gender, a nominal variable, and the amount of homework the students complete, a ratio variable. Here and in Chapters 12 and 14, we'll refer to several different kinds of correlations, but for now we're interested in correlations between just two variables that are either interval or ratio scale.

As we proceed we'll use x to indicate the first variable in the pair, and y to indicate the second. The assignment of x and y is usually arbitrary in correlation analysis.

THROUGH A WIDER LENS

When people speak of correlations they usually mean bivariate correlations, which involve the association between two variables. Economists speak of consumer confidence and the stock market, implying that those two variables are related. The idea of correlation has been around a very long time. Anciently, people associated solar eclipses with impending disasters. It is a correlation without scientific merit perhaps, but as far as they were concerned, a correlation nevertheless. Farmers' almanacs once correlated the harshness of coming winters with the thickness of animals' coats in the preceding autumn.

THE PEARSON CORRELATION

Probably the most commonly used correlation value is the Pearson Correlation, formally the Pearson Product Moment Correlation. It has the following characteristics:

- The correlation is bivariate—there are just two variables involved.
- Both variables are measured on at least an interval scale.
- The variables have a linear relationship.
- The populations from which the data are drawn are normally distributed.

There are many formulae for the Pearson Correlation, and as long as they are adjusted for whether the formula is for sample or for population data, they all provide the same answer. Formula 10.1 is perhaps the most visually simple:

$$r_{xy} = \frac{\Sigma[(z_x)(z_y)]}{n-1} \qquad\qquad 10.1$$

Where,

z_x = the z score for each measure of the x variable

z_y = the z score for each measure of the y variable

n = the number of pairs of scores

The z values for x and y indicate that the correlation coefficient is based on the z score equivalents of the x and y variables rather than on the original "raw" scores. Remember from Chapter 4 that the z transformation is $z = (x - M)/s$ (Formula 4.1). The steps for calculating the Pearson Correlation with Formula 10.1 are as follows:

1. Calculate the mean and standard deviation for both sets of data.

2. Determine the equivalent z value for each measure of the x variable (z_x).

3. Determine the equivalent z value for each measure of the y variable (z_y).

4. For each individual, find the product of z_x times z_y.

5. Sum the products of z_x times z_y.

6. Divide the sum of the z_x times z_y products by the number of pairs of scores, minus 1.

It's common, by the way, to see Formula 10.1 with N rather than $n - 1$ in the denominator. The difference is whether the coefficient is based on population or sample data. Pearson was a staunch advocate of always using population data. Our more common reality, however, is that we're much more likely not to have access to population data than to have it, and $n - 1$ is the adjustment we make for sample data. Recall that there was a similar adjustment with standard deviations. The Pearson Correlation using z scores for the hours of homework and grades data is in Table 10.1A.

Table 10.1 Calculating the Pearson Correlation

A: Formula 10.1

Hmwrk (x)	Grades (y)	Hmwrk z_x	Grades z_y	z products
.25	2.00	−1.400	−.450	.630
.50	1.75	−.952	−.878	.836
.75	2.00	−.504	−.450	.227
1.00	2.50	−.056	.407	−.023
1.00	2.00	−.056	−.450	.025
1.25	2.25	.392	−.021	−.008
1.50	2.00	.840	−.450	−.378
2.00	3.60	1.736	2.292	3.979
$M_x = 1.031$	$M_y = 2.263$	$(z_x - M_x)/s_x$	$(z_y - M_y)/s_y$	$\Sigma = 5.288$
$s_x = .558$	$S_y = .584$			

$$r_{xy} = \frac{\Sigma[(z_x)(z_y)]}{n-1} = \frac{5.288}{7} = .755$$

B: Formula 10.2

Hmwrk (x)	Hmwrk sq'd	Grades (y)	Grades sq'd	xy
.25	.063	2.00	4.0	.50
.50	.250	1.75	3.063	.875
.75	.563	2.00	4.0	1.50
1.00	1.0	2.50	6.250	2.50
1.00	1.0	2.00	4.0	2.0
1.25	1.563	2.25	5.063	2.813
1.50	2.250	2.00	4.0	3.0
2.00	4.0	3.60	12.960	7.20
$\Sigma x = 8.25$	$\Sigma x^2 = 10.688$	$\Sigma y = 18.10$	$\Sigma y^2 = 43.335$	$\Sigma xy = 20.388$
$n = 8$				

$$r_{xy} = \frac{n\Sigma xy-(\Sigma x)(\Sigma y)}{\sqrt{[n\Sigma x^2-(\Sigma x)^2]}\sqrt{[n\Sigma y^2-(\Sigma y)^2]}} = \frac{8(20.833)-(8.25)(18.10)}{\sqrt{[8(10.688)-8.25^2]}\sqrt{[8(43.335)-18.10^2]}}$$

$$= \frac{163.104 \quad 149.325}{\sqrt{(85.504-68.063)}\sqrt{(346.68-327.61)}} = \frac{13.779}{\sqrt{17.441}\sqrt{19.07}}$$

$$= \frac{13.779}{(4.176)(4.367)}$$

$$= \textbf{.756}$$

The correlation between the amount of homework the students do and their grades is $r_{xy} = .755$. If a perfect correlation is $r_{xy} = 1.0$, then $r_{xy} = .755$ seem at least "substantial," but we can't even know whether it's statistically significant until we have something to compare it with. Once again the index is a table value. If the calculated value meets or exceeds the table value, the correlation probably isn't chance—it's statistically significant.

Table E is the "Critical Values for the Pearson Correlation" and *degrees of freedom for the Pearson Correlation are the number of pairs of data, minus 2.* Note that it's the number of *pairs*, rather than the number of scores. By reading down the left side of the table for the appropriate degrees of freedom (6 in this case), we find that the value for $p = .05$ is .707. We distinguish the calculated value ($r_{xy} = .755$) from the table value ($r_{.05(6)} = .707$) by their subscripts. The r_{xy} indicates the calculated value, and $r_{.05(6)}$ indicates the table value. The calculated value is larger so the correlation is statistically significant.

Formula 10.1 may make the process for calculating correlation coefficients easier to understand, but it's also impractical. With more than just a few pairs of data, the need to first transform all of the raw scores into z scores, find the sum of the their products, and so on, is quite tedious. Several "raw-score" formulae have been developed that don't require first transforming the data into z scores. Formula 10.2 is one of them. Because correlation coefficients *are* occasionally completed longhand, and because we'll need to do some in the next chapter on regression, we'll work with Formula 10.2. It has this form:

$$r_{xy} = \frac{n\Sigma xy - (\Sigma x)(\Sigma y)}{\sqrt{[n\Sigma x^2 - (\Sigma x)^2]}\sqrt{[n\Sigma y^2 - (\Sigma y)^2]}} \qquad 10.2$$

Where,

x = the first score in each pair

y = the second score in each pair

n = the number of *pairs* of scores

Σxy = the sum of the products of each x,y pair

Σx^2 = the sum of the squared individual scores for x

$(\Sigma x)^2$ = one sums the x scores and then squares the total

Σy^2 = the sum of the squared individual scores for y

$(\Sigma y)^2$ = one sums the y scores and then squares the total

This raw-score formula looks intimidating, but it really isn't difficult. If your calculator has a standard deviation function, it will give you the values for Σx and Σx^2. Just treat each set of data like a standard deviation problem. In fact, many hand-held calculators will complete the entire correlation problem. If your calculator has symbols on the keypad or in a read-out that include Σxy, Σx, Σy, Σx^2, and Σy^2, it will do correlation, but if you need to complete the steps one-at-a-time the sequence is,

1. Multiply each x value by its y value and sum the products (Σxy).

2. Multiply Σxy by n, the number of pairs of scores ($n\Sigma xy$).

3. Multiply the sum of the x values (Σx) and the sum of the y values (Σy).

4. Subtract from $n\Sigma xy$ the product of ($\Sigma x \cdot \Sigma y$). This is the numerator.

5. Square each x value and sum the squares (Σx^2).

6. Multiply Σx^2 by n.

7. Subtract from $n\Sigma x^2$ the square of the total of the x values ($\Sigma x)^2$.

8. Take a square root of the result.

9. Complete Steps 5–8 for the y values.

10. Multiply the result of Step 8 by the result of Step 9. This is the denominator.

11. Divide the numerator (Step 4) by the denominator (Step 10).

The correlation coefficient using the *calculation* formula for hours of homework and grades is part B in Table 10.1. The difference of .001 between the two different formulae is due to rounding and unimportant.

The Correlation Hypotheses

Although the focus is association rather than difference, we're still interested in null and alternate hypotheses.

- The null hypothesis states that there is no significant correlation between the variables. In the unique language and symbols of statistics, the null hypothesis is written:

  H_o: $\rho = 0$

- The alternate hypothesis is that there *is* a significant correlation:

  H_A: $\rho \neq 0$

What looks like a lowercase p is the Greek letter *rho* (pronounced "row" as in "row your boat") and it's often a symbol for correlation. "*Rho* = zero" is the statistical way to say that there is no significant correlation. Speaking in a more theoretical vein, accepting the null hypothesis is tantamount to saying that there is no corresponding correlation in the population as a whole. For our data, it would mean that if there were no significant correlation between hours of homework and grade among these 8 students, neither is there likely to be such a correlation in the population of all such students. It means that "another go at it" with new data would yield similar results.

The alternate hypothesis is that the relationship isn't zero, that there *is* a statistically significant correlation. As before, the statistical decisions are made in terms of only the null hypothesis. One rejects, or fails to reject H_o. In Figure 10.3, there's another example of a Pearson Correlation using Formula 10.2.

Looking at SPSS Output

The table below is the result if we complete the problem in Figure 10.3 on SPSS. It indicates that we named our variables just "*x*" and "*y*" as they were in the figure. The table is what is called a "correlation matrix." It indicates the correlation of each variable included in the analysis with each other variable.

Figure 10.3 Another Example of a Pearson Correlation

For ninth-grade students, we have both reading comprehension (x) and analytical ability (y) scores for 6 students. The scores are as follows:

x:14, 11, 12, 7, 8, 10

y: 7, 5, 5, 3, 4, 6

Verify that:

$n = 6$

$\Sigma x = 62$

$\Sigma x^2 = 674$

$\Sigma y = 30$

$\Sigma y^2 = 160$

$\Sigma xy = 326$

$$r_{xy} = \frac{n\Sigma xy - (\Sigma x)(\Sigma y)}{\sqrt{[n\Sigma x^2 - (\Sigma x)^2]}\sqrt{[n\Sigma y^2 - (\Sigma y)^2]}}$$

$$= \frac{6(326) - (62)(30)}{\sqrt{[6(674) - (62)^2]}\sqrt{[6(160) - (30)^2]}}$$

$$= \frac{96}{\sqrt{200}\sqrt{60}} = \frac{96}{(14.142)(7.746)}$$

$$= .876$$

The correlation between reading comprehension and analytical ability among these 9th grade students is $r_{xy} = .876$. Since the critical (table) value is $r_{.05(4)} = .811$, we reject the null hypothesis, the correlation *is* statistically significant.

That's why there is a 1.000 correlation—it's the correlation of the particular variable with itself—x with x in the top half of the table, and y with y in the bottom half. But what we're interested in is the correlation of x with y which is $r_{xy} = .876$ (the same result we had with our raw-score formula).

As with the other tests we've done on SPSS, the output tells us the probability that a correlation of this size and with these degrees of freedom could have occurred by chance. In this case, it's $p = .022$. Since that probability is less than $p = .05$, we conclude that the correlation is statistically significant. To make sure we don't miss it, that statement occurs just below the table. The "N" value indicates that there are 6 pairs of scores.

Correlations

		x	y
X	Pearson Correlation	1.000	.876*
	Sig. (two-tailed)		.022
	N	6.000	6
Y	Pearson Correlation	.876*	1.000
	Sig. (two-tailed)	.022	
	N	6	6.000

*. Correlation is significant at the 0.05 level (two-tailed).

Assumptions and Attenuated Range

Like any statistical procedure, there are certain conditions or assumptions associated with calculating and interpreting a Pearson Correlation. The data (the measures of the x and y variables) are:

- Measured on either an interval or a ratio scale
- Randomly selected
- Normally distributed
- Related in a linear fashion

When data are normally distributed, large samples will include scores along the entire range of data. If the range of scores in a correlation problem is attenuated, or truncated for whatever reason, the resulting coefficient will be inaccurate. In Figure 10.3, if the first person's scores had been 10 and 5 (rather than 14 and 7), the range of scores would have been slightly restricted, and it affects the correlation. If we make that substitution and recalculate the coefficient, it drops.

Instead of the $r_{xy} = .876$ that we determined earlier,

changing the scores from 14 and 7 to 10 and 5 results in $r_{xy} = .763$,

and the coefficient becomes nonsignificant in the bargain!

You can verify this easily enough. Calculate the x and y means for the data and compare the 14 and 7 with the 10 and 5. It would be excellent practice to also recalculate the correlation coefficient with the new data and verify that the coefficient that results from using 10 and 5 becomes $r_{xy} = .763$.

As data within either variable become more similar, correlation values decline. Statistically significant coefficients require some scoring variability.

Interpreting the Correlation Coefficient: Direction and Strength

Interpreting the coefficient involves two issues, one related to the sign of the correlation, the other regarding the coefficient's strength. When we first discussed correlations, we noted that they can be negative. We also noted that the visual evidence for a negative correlation in a scatter plot is data points that drift from the upper left to the lower right of the graph. They indicate that as the measures of one variable increase, the measures of the other decline. Unemployment and consumer confidence are negatively correlated. Increases in one are associated with decreases in the other. The symbol for a negative correlation is simply a minus sign preceding the correlation value such as, $r_{xy} = -.472$.

But remember that the *sign* of the relationship has nothing to do with its strength. A correlation of $r_{xy} = -.472$ is just as strong as $r_{xy} = .472$. People sometimes have difficulty interpreting negative correlations. There's an example in Figure 10.4.

Because the sign of the correlation isn't related to its strength, neither is it relevant to whether the coefficient is significant. The exception to this is when one predicts the direction of the relationship (positive or negative) and makes of the correlation analysis a one-tailed test, as we can with the *t*-test. This is uncommon enough that many statistics texts publish tables only for two-tailed tests. There may be times when we have a hypothesis about the direction of the correlation—the people doing the analysis in Figure 10.4 certainly had one—but it's generally the absolute value of the coefficient we're interested in and it's all we'll deal with here.

Our data indicate that $r_{xy} = -.798$ is unlikely to be a random relationship. As the number of hours per week the students work increases, their test scores tend to decline. Those who conducted the analysis suspected this and now they have some evidence.

Regarding the Strength of the Correlation

Setting the sign of the correlation aside, what constitutes a "strong" correlation? The answer is that it depends upon how complex the circumstances are and what is at issue. The "it depends" answer can be

Figure 10.4   A Negative Pearson Correlation

Perhaps those administering the after-school program are trying to convince several students who work after school to cut back their hours and come in instead for some help before they take their college admissions test. To make their argument more convincing, they gather data from last year's juniors and analyze the relationship between the number of hours per week students are employed and their scores on the test. Here's what they find for 7 students randomly selected from among those employed in last year's junior class:

No. hours worked: 5, 10, 15, 12, 10, 16, 20

Test score: 84, 47, 62, 51, 78, 39, 35

Verify that:

$n = 7$, $\Sigma xy = 4536$, $\Sigma x = 88$, $\Sigma x^2 = 1250$, $\Sigma y = 396$, $\Sigma y^2 = 24540$

Therefore,

$$r_{xy} = \frac{n\Sigma xy - (\Sigma x)(\Sigma y)}{\sqrt{[n\Sigma x^2 - (\Sigma x)^2]}\sqrt{[n\Sigma y^2 - (\Sigma y)^2]}}$$

$$r_{xy} = \frac{7(4536) - (88)(396)}{\sqrt{[7(1250) - (88)^2]}\sqrt{[7(24540) - (396)^2]}}$$

$$r_{xy} = \frac{-3096}{\sqrt{1006}\sqrt{14964}} = -.798 \; ; \; r_{xy.05(5)} = .754.$$ The correlation is significant.

tiresome, but the strength of a correlation really is context-specific. Be patient; help is one the way with the coefficient of determination just below.

A correlation of $r_{xy} = .3$ between breathing secondhand tobacco smoke (x) and later developing respiratory problems or lung cancer (y) would probably be considered a strong relationship. Conversely, such a correlation between intelligence and school achievement among elementary school children would probably not be thought particularly compelling. As a rough rule of thumb, correlations of:

- 0 to .3 are considered "weak" correlations
- .3 to .7 are considered "moderate" correlations, which leaves one wondering how to interpret a correlation of .3, weak, or moderate, and whether a correlation of .7 can be either "moderate" or "strong."
- 7 up, are considered "high" correlations (Visual Statistics, 2009).

The Coefficient of Determination

■ The **coefficient of determination** is a Pearson Correlation squared. It's the proportion of either variable explained by the other.

Significant correlations indicate that the correlated variables contain some information in common. That's the logic not only for correlation coefficients, but also for the **coefficient of determination**. Interpreted much like effect sizes for t-test and *ANOVA* but far simpler to calculate, the coefficient of determination is simply the square of the Pearson Correlation, r^2_{xy}. When a correlation coefficient is statistically significant, its square indicates the proportion of the variance in y that can be explained by manipulating x, or vice versa. When the coefficient isn't significant, of course, any relationship is assumed to be random and the issue is moot; r^2_{xy} isn't calculated for nonsignificant correlations.

In the case of hours of homework (x) and grades (y), $r_{xy} = .755$. Therefore, $r^2_{xy} = .570$ ($.755^2 = .57$), which indicates that 57% of the variance in grades can be explained by changes in the amount of homework students complete. Since we're making no judgment about cause, we can turn the explanation around. It's possible that high grades are a stimulus for doing more homework, in which case one could argue that 57% of the variance in amount of homework can be explained by differences in their grades.

Referring back to the discussion of what constitutes a strong correlation, if $r_{xy} = .3$ for the correlation between intelligence and achievement for fourth-grade students (although, a correlation of .5 for elementary school children is closer according to Neisser [1995]) that would suggest that just 9% of the variance in student achievement stems from intelligence differences ($.3^2 = .09$). That probably wouldn't be considered very important.

Conversely, if exposure to secondhand smoke correlated with the development of lung cancer at $r_{xy} = .3$, someone would quickly seize the argument that for every 100 children exposed to secondhand smoke who never smoke themselves, 9 will probably develop lung cancer. This undoubtedly *would* be considered an important finding.

The point is that the importance of a significant correlation value depends in large measure on its implications. If the relationship between intelligence and academic achievement were weak, it indicates that other factors also explain why students do well. A finding that 9 in 100 of those who are exposed to secondhand smoke will develop lung cancer also indicates that there are other factors involved, but the implications of this one finding are so devastating to the 9% that those reporting the results would probably react very differently than they would to the intelligence/school achievement result.

*The Correlation Coefficient Versus
the Coefficient of Determination*

Besides the proportion of variance explained, calculating the coefficient of determination accomplishes something else. Although they're based on equal-interval data, correlation coefficients *do not reflect equal intervals*. That is, the increase in the strength of the relationship from $r_{xy} = .3$ to $r_{xy} = .4$ isn't the same incremental increase as from .8 to .9. The number line below is intended to suggest that increasing correlations by a tenth involves a much stronger relationship as the coefficients approach 1.0:

$r_{xy} = .1 \quad .2 \quad .3 \quad .4 \quad .5 \quad .6 \quad .7 \quad .8 \quad .9$

Part of the beauty of the coefficient of determination (r^2) is that it standardizes the amount of variance explained. Once squared, the correlation values provide a consistent gauge along the range of possible values. The difference in the amount of variance explained is the same from $r_{xy}^2 = .3$ to $r_{xy}^2 = .6$ as it is from $r_{xy}^2 = .4$ to $r_x^2 = .7$, which makes it a little easier to interpret them.

$r_{xy}^2 = \quad .1 \quad .2 \quad .3 \quad .4 \quad .5 \quad .6 \quad .7 \quad .8 \quad .9$

Significance and Sample Size

In earlier chapters we noted that there is a relationship between statistical significance and sample size. The connection is particularly clear with correlation. As samples sizes increase, the magnitude of the coefficient required for significance declines. When data sets are small, it's comparatively easy for "relationships" to emerge, which are actually just random. To counter this, the critical value from the table (E) is relatively large when *df* (the number of pairs of scores, − 2) are small. As *df* (and so sample sizes) increase, the risk of "finding" a relationship that is actually just random diminishes as the true relationships between variables have a chance to stabilize. The critical values shrink accordingly.

This is particularly evident in Table E. Note how large the correlation must be in order to be statistically significant when there are 3 pairs of scores (for $n = 3$, $df = 1$). Now note what the value must be for a sample size of 1002 pairs of scores ($df = 1000$). For $df = 1$, r_{xy} must be .997 or larger to be significant. For $df = 1000$, if $r_{xy} = .062$ it's significant. Clearly sample size has a huge impact on what is considered statistically significant.

The contrast between these very different correlation values, although both may be statistically significant, suggests another reason for calculating the coefficient of determination. A correlation of .997 suggests that 99% of the variance in y can be explained by manipulating x (whatever x and y are). But a correlation of .062 indicates that only about .004, or 4/10ths of 1% of y can be explained by x. Is such a relationship likely to have occurred by chance? No. Is it important for how much it explains? Also, probably no. Calculating the coefficient of determination helps keep us grounded. It makes it less likely that we might confuse statistical significance with practical importance.

THE POINT-BISERIAL CORRELATION

Sometimes the relationship we wish to understand is that between a variable with only two values and another that is of interval/ratio scale. One of the questions at the beginning of the chapter was of the connection between participation in extracurricular activities and overall academic achievement. This is an important consideration since in difficult budget times it's often the extracurricular programs, treated as nonessential "extras," that feel the bite of the budget axe first.

Perhaps the Dean of Student Life at a college wants information on the relationship between extracurricular involvement and students' grades. If extracurricular involvement is a dichotomous variable (that is, it has just two levels) and the measure of grades is interval scale (we'll come back to the discussion of grades and scale later, but assume for the moment that they are interval scale), we can calculate the relationship with a point-biserial correlation. The only adjustment we need to make is to code the dichotomous variable (extracurricular involvement) as a "0" (not involved) or a "1" (involved). We then proceed as we did with the Pearson Correlation.

The Director of Institutional Research finds 12 students, 6 of whom were involved in extracurricular, college-sponsored activities. He checks their grades and finds the following:

Extracurr.	Grades
0	2.7
0	2.4
0	3.0
0	3.1

0	2.9
0	2.8
1	2.9
1	2.5
1	3.3
1	3.6
1	3.7
	3.6

Verify that,

$n = 12$, $\Sigma xy = 19.6$, $\Sigma x = 6$, $\Sigma x^2 = 6$, $\Sigma y = 36.5$, $\Sigma y^2 = 113.07$

$$r_{xy} = \frac{n\,\Sigma xy - (\Sigma x)(\Sigma y)}{\sqrt{[n\Sigma x^2 - (\Sigma x)^2\,]}\,\sqrt{[n\Sigma y^2 - (\Sigma y)^2]}}$$

$$r_{xy} = \frac{12(19.6) - (6)(36.5)}{\sqrt{[12(6) - (6)^2\,]}\sqrt{[12(113.07) - (36.5)^2\,]}}$$

$r_{xy} = 16.2/(\sqrt{36} \cdot \sqrt{24.59}) = .544$; $r_{xy.05(10)} = .576$. Fail to reject H$_\text{o}$.

The correlation isn't significant at $p = .05$. Whether students are involved in extracurricular activities appears to be unrelated to their grades, which, if the data weren't contrived, would be bad news for those who wish to argue that extracurricular activities provide a grade advantage to those who are involved.

The point-biserial correlation coefficient is interpreted the same way any Pearson Correlation value is interpreted. The issue is still the strength of the relationship between two variables. We still base our decision about significance on whether the calculated value meets or exceeds the table value, and the value comes from the same Pearson Correlation table (Table E) we used earlier. It's just that in this instance one variable has two levels and the other is an interval scale variable.

The two levels must be coded 0,1, by the way (the formula depends on those two integers). Reversing the coding of the dichotomous variable will change the sign of the resulting correlation coefficient, but not its numerical value.

ANOTHER THOUGHT ON INTERPRETING CORRELATION VALUES

If the grades/extracurricular involvement data just above were from your master's thesis, might you be able to report that the correlation value "approached" significance? After all, the calculated value falls only a little short of the table value. By convention an outcome is either significant or it isn't. Be strong! Avoid the temptation to ameliorate what may be an unhappy or unexpected nonsignificant outcome by speaking in terms of a result that is "almost significant."

NONPARAMETRIC CORRELATIONS

One of the questions we might have raised at the beginning of the chapter was about how to gauge the relationship between students' attendance at the after-school program and their *attitudes* about the program. Attendance is easy enough to quantify and the scale is ratio, which fits the requirement for calculating a Pearson Correlation, but attitudes are different. Certainly one could quantify attitude in terms of how many assignments students submit, data of ratio scale, but those probably involve other factors, like perhaps parental pressure.

Often attitudes are gauged using something like a Likert-type scale where respondents read a series of statements ("I believe that my time in the after-school program is time well-spent.") and then indicate their level of agreement ("strongly agree," "agree," and so on to "strongly disagree"). Such responses constitute ordinal data because they are really rankings. We know that "strongly agree," for example, represents a more positive opinion than "agree," but from such responses there isn't any way to know *how much* more positive. We can rank the responses, the hallmark of ordinal data, but the different possible responses probably don't reflect equidistant intervals.

Likert-type data aren't interval scale and so don't meet the requirements for a Pearson Correlation. When we wish to analyze data that aren't normally distributed, or aren't measured on an interval or ratio scale, we enter the realm of procedures called **nonparametric statistics.** There are several correlation procedures designed for nonparametric data. One of the more common is **Spearman's *rho* (r_s).** Besides accommodating ordinal data, Spearman's *rho* can also be used for interval/ratio, if those data are reduced from interval scale to the rankings that constitute ordinal data. With that

■ **Nonparametric** procedures like **Spearman's *rho*** let one analyze data that aren't normally distributed, or aren't interval/ratio scale.

reduction, by the way, any information about the magnitude of the difference between scores is lost. Rather than "give away" the additional information that interval/ratio data provide, investigators retain the interval scale data and use the Pearson Correlation when both sets of data meet the relevant assumptions. Based only on rankings (and less information about what is measured) Spearman's *rho* is ordinarily less powerful than the Pearson; it's less likely to detect a statistically significant relationship. There will be a more thorough examination of Spearman's *rho* in Chapter 14, along with several other statistical tests for ordinal scale data.

A PARTIAL LIST OF BIVARIATE CORRELATIONS

There are other bivariate correlation procedures besides the Pearson and Spearman tests. Without the details of how they're calculated, we'll just make a partial list of some of the more common.

Beside the after-school tutoring program, some other extracurricular activities, such as the science club, academic competitions, and perhaps the debate club, may have a positive impact on students' development. If that is so, and if there is concern that students of different ethnic backgrounds do not participate equally in such activities, perhaps one may wish to investigate this by correlating students' participation in extracurricular activities with their ethnicity. *Phi* coefficient and Pearson's **coefficient of contingency** both address this issue. If there is no significant correlation between ethnicity and participation, student involvement is not along ethnic lines.

Rank-biserial correlation coefficient determines the relationship between a dichotomous ("yes/no" or "married/single") nominal variable and an ordinal variable. Perhaps having read some of the professional literature on gender differences in achievement, one is interested in whether there is a statistically significant relationship between gender and class rank among high school seniors. In gender we have a dichotomous (female/male), nominal scale variable and class rank is ordinal. A statistically significant result will indicate that class ranking and gender are related.

Recall that one of the questions implied at the beginning of the chapter was whether participation in extracurricular activities detracts enough from students' studies that their academic achievement suffers. We measured extracurricular participation in terms of "did not" (0) and "did" (1) and determined the relationship with grade-point average, which is often treated as an interval variable (although since the letter grades from which grade

■ The *phi* **coefficient** is a correlation procedure for two nominal scale variables based on the *chi*-square value. An alternative is Pearson's **coefficient of contingency** which has the disadvantage of never being able reach a value of 1.0.

■ The **rank-biserial correlation** is a correlation procedure when one variable has two levels, male/female, for example, and the other variable is ordinal scale.

averages are often computed are more like rankings than interval scores, they may be thought of as ordinal data). This was the point-biserial correlation that we worked with above.

Spearman's *rho* allows one to determine the correlation between two ordinal variables, between an ordinal and an interval variable, or even between two interval variables, but the procedure requires that anything measured on interval or ratio scale be reduced to ordinal scale.

■ **Pearson's** *r* is a correlation procedure for two variables which can be either interval or ratio scale.

And finally, the domain of **Pearson's** *r* is the correlation of interval or ratio scale variables that are normally distributed and have a linear relationship. Not only is the Pearson Correlation widely used, but it's the foundation for the least squares regression procedures that are the subject of Chapter 11.

We've limited the summary above to just the more common bivariate correlations and provided a list of them in Figure 10.5

SOURCE: Created by Suzanna Nielson.

"Watkins is worried. He says that with .95 confidence, his 401(k) has become a 101(k)."

Figure 10.5 A Summary of Some of the More Common Bivariate Correlations

The Measurement Scale of the Variables to Be Correlated	The Correlation Procedure
Two nominal scale variables	*Phi* coefficient, or Pearson's coefficient of contingency
A dichotomous nominal scale variable with an ordinal scale variable	Rank-biserial correlation
A dichotomous nominal scale variable with an interval scale variable	Point-biserial correlation
Two ordinal scale variables	Spearman's *rho*
An ordinal scale variable with an interval scale variable	Spearman's *rho*
Two interval or ratio scale (or one of each) variables	Pearson's *r*

SUMMARY

Chapter 10 represents a turning point in the book because the questions addressed are about significant relationships. Everything in the preceding chapters dealt with analyses of differences. Correlation coefficients quantify associations, and one of their characteristics is that they will quantify relationships between variables that measure entirely different qualities; therein lies much of their value in statistical procedure.

In spite of what can be important qualitative differences, correlated variables share information. Some of what is contained in one variable also occurs in the other. The amount of that shared information is reflected in the magnitude of the coefficient. Once we know that two variables are correlated we can make better-than-chance predictions of the value of one from a measure of the other. This is the point of regression in Chapter 11.

Correlation procedures must fit the scale of the data. The Pearson Correlation measures the relationship between two interval or ratio scale variables. We used it to answer the question about the correlation between homework and grades. The point-biserial correlation, on the other hand, is designed for interval and nominal data correlations, and it provided a coefficient for the relationship between students' participation in extracurricular activities and their grades.

The square of the Pearson Correlation (r^2_{xy}) is the coefficient of determination. It's interpreted like the effect size for *ANOVA*, which was partial *eta*-squared, η_p^2 was interpreted in Chapter 7. The r^2_{xy} value indicates the proportion of variance in either the x or y measures that is explained by the other variable.

The Pearson Correlation assumes that the relationship between the variables is linear. Should there be evidence that the relationship isn't linear, and the best evidence might be the data in a scatter plot, the Pearson Correlation isn't an appropriate test for the relationship.

There are other correlation procedures besides Pearson and point-biserial. Without pursuing them, we made a partial list. Some of them will come up when we discuss nonparametric procedures in later chapters.

Correlations are fundamentally descriptive statistics. When variables are related, correlation offers some of the same descriptive advantages that other descriptive statistics provide. Perhaps this is why correlation is so widely used and why analysis and decision making often bring one to testing the hypothesis of association.

As a measure of progress, this chapter often marks the end of the road for first-semester statistics classes. If you've reached this point, and it's still semester one, well done! If you're working beyond this chapter, so much the better; clearly you're absorbing the concepts well and you're ready for more. In the process of working with regression and the nonparametric statistics that follow, don't forget to go back and review the earlier materials on descriptive statistics, standard scores, and so on. It's unsettling how quickly even the best students forget.

EXERCISES

1. What is the range of values possible in a Pearson's r?

2. When we calculated a significant F in *ANOVA* (Chapter 8), we also calculated η_p^2 as a measure of effect size. What is the equivalent statistic for a significant Pearson Correlation?

3. What's the relationship between data variability and correlation values?

4. What is "attenuation of range"?

5. The learning director at a high school is concerned that students' academic progress is limited by how much sleep they get. He gathers data on the hour at which students typically retire and their grade-point averages. The data are as follows with the hour of retirement reported as a decimal (9:45 = 9.75)

	Retire	GPA
1.	9.0	3.0
2.	9.5	2.8
3.	11.0	2.5
4.	11.5	2.0
5.	10.0	3.5
6.	9.75	2.6
7.	10.0	3.1
8.	10.25	2.9

a. What is the relationship between time of retirement and grades?
b. Are the learning director's fears justified?
c. How much of the variance in grades can be explained by hour of retirement?

6. Seventh-grade students have just taken a test battery that includes both math and spelling measures. The data for 12, randomly selected students are as follows:

Student	Math	Spelling
1.	15	10
2.	5	4
3.	16	11
4.	10	8
5.	11	13
6.	3	4
7.	12	10
8.	11	8
9.	10	7
10.	14	9
11.	8	6
12.	9	9

a. What is the null hypothesis for this problem?
b. At $p = .05$, should one reject H_o?
c. What proportion of the variability in spelling can be explained by differences in math ability?

7. In an extension of the example in the chapter dealing with study time and grades, educators are curious about the relationship between whether teaching students study strategies results in higher grades. They develop a series of seminars at the beginning of the year and provide students the option of attending. In three 1-hour seminars, they note the number of minutes students attend and then, at the end of the semester, note their scores on a measure of verbal aptitude. Assuming that the data are randomly selected from normal populations, they are as follows:

Student	Minutes	Score
1.	15	57
2.	120	84
3.	0	74
4.	75	92
5.	30	65
6.	150	60
7.	22	85
8.	15	88

a. Is the relationship statistically significant?

b. How much of the variance in test scores can be explained by differences in the amount of time spent in the seminars?

8. A school counselor has just received students' scores on a particular admissions test required by a local college. She also has their performance on a recent measure of reading comprehension.

Student	Adm.	Comp.
1.	110	92
2.	76	74
3.	55	82
4.	80	85
5.	45	67
6.	62	65
7.	73	83
8.	95	88
9.	65	83
10.	40	51

a. What is the correlation between the two?

b. At $p = .05$, is it likely that this relationship occurred by chance?

9. A district psychologist is working with developmentally disabled students in a special education setting and is curious about the relationship between students' persistence on puzzle tasks (measured in the number of minutes they remain on task) and their number of absences from class.

Student	Persist	Absent
1.	12	3
2.	4	3
3.	15	5
4.	18	7
5.	12	1
6.	5	4
7.	8	3
8.	9	4

Is the relationship between persistence and attendance statistically significant at $p = .05$?

10. The director of institutional research at a regional university has SAT-verbal scores and GPA data for Liberal Studies majors. (If the large numbers are unmanageable in your calculator, divide all the aptitude values by 10. It won't change the relationship between aptitude and GPA, and it does make the numbers easier to deal with. You can do the same with GPA since they all end in 0s. You're welcome!):

Students	Aptitude	GPA
1.	430	2.00
2.	500	2.50
3.	550	3.00
4.	625	3.50
5.	400	2.00
6.	550	2.50
7.	750	3.80
8.	440	2.50
9.	510	2.10
10.	610	3.80

a. At $p = .05$, is the relationship statistically significant?
b. How much of GPA can be explained by differences in verbal aptitude?

11. A district superintendent is curious about the relationship between stress and job performance indicators among educators. He finds a way to quantify job performance in terms of multiple, interval scale variables and then asks each educator to indicate whether he/she feels stressed by the job. Responses are "yes" and "no."

a. What is the appropriate correlation procedure?
b. What is the relationship?
c. Is it statistically significant?

	Stress	Perform
1.	no	11
2.	no	8
3.	yes	4
4.	no	11
5.	yes	16
6.	no	11
7.	yes	4
8.	yes	8
9.	yes	6
10.	no	12

12. Curious about the relationship between age and educators' willingness to embrace new curricular initiatives, researchers administer Rokeach's Dogmatism Scale adapted from political to curriculum issues, and correlate results with age. Assume that the conservatism scores are interval scale.

	Age	Conserv.
1.	64	3
2.	31	6
3.	40	4
4.	40	3
5.	27	8
6.	32	5
7.	38	1
8.	22	9

a. What is the relationship between age and conservatism?
b. Is the correlation statistically significant?

REFERENCES

Neisser, U. (1995). *Stalking the wild taboo*. Report of a task force established by the Board of Scientific Affairs of the American Psychological Association.

Visual Statistics. (2009). *Correlation: Interpretations*. Retrieved from http://www.visualstatistics.net/Visual%20Statistics%20Multimedia/correlation_interpretation.htm

THE FORMULAE AND THEIR SYMBOLS

Formula 10.1: $r_{xy} = \dfrac{\Sigma[(z_x)(z_y)]}{n-1}$

is a z score formula for the Pearson Correlation. It indicates the strength of the relationship between two sets of interval or ratio scale data. The raw scores first must be transformed into z scores.

Formula 10.2: $r_{xy} = \dfrac{n\Sigma xy - (\Sigma x)(\Sigma y)}{\sqrt{[n\Sigma x^2 - (\Sigma x)^2]}\sqrt{[n\Sigma y^2 - (\Sigma y)^2]}}$

is the raw score formula for Pearson Correlation. It is also used for the point-biserial correlation.

STUDENT STUDY SITE

Visit the Student Study Site at **www.sagepub.com/tanner** for additional learning tools.

Chapter 11

REGRESSION WITH ONE PREDICTOR

THE PROBLEM: PREDICTING THE VALUE OF ONE VARIABLE FROM ANOTHER

A psychologist employed by the local college has worked with a variety of students ranging from those with disabilities to those with unusual academic gifts. Familiar with the research on intelligence, she suspects that with all students both reading comprehension and spatial ability are related to a common underlying cognitive ability. Because the college regularly gathers reading comprehension data for entering students, she wonders whether those data could be used to determine students' levels of spatial ability, data that are less accessible. If comprehension data *can* be used to predict spatial ability scores, is there a way to determine how accurate the prediction is?

QUESTIONS AND ANSWERS

❑ If reading comprehension and students' level of achievement motivation are correlated, will the value of one indicate the value of the other?

The answer is yes, and the analytical procedure is what is called *simple*, or *bivariate*, regression. The stronger the correlation, the more accurate the prediction.

❑ Can the accuracy of the prediction be determined?

We'll answer with an estimate of the error in the predicted value called the standard error of the estimate. We'll use that value to establish a range of values within which the true measure of the variable is likely to occur.

If people are attracted to what they find most useful, perhaps this will be one of the chapters that readers most value. It's about prediction, and since everyone makes predictions of one sort or another, your author predicts that figuring out how to use relationships to predict outcomes will appeal to the reader's sense of utility.

REGRESSION ANALYSIS

There is something of a dichotomy in statistics classes between what students must understand in detail, and so pursue with longhand calculations, and the material for which a conceptual grasp is probably adequate and so is consigned to something like SPSS. Although regression calculations are actually quite straightforward, those using them rarely do any of the calculations longhand, so why bother with them here? The answer is that the logic of regression is connected somehow to virtually every higher statistical procedure that shows up in educational research. Working the calculations makes the logic more transparent than it is when one just stares at computer output, no matter how "user-friendly" it is. The discussion here is more detailed than it is difficult. The keys are patience and persistence.

This chapter is largely an extension of the topics we took up in Chapter 10. As important as correlation discussions are for their own sake, here we are interested in exploiting correlation for the utility it has as a prediction tool. When there is a nonrandom (which is to say, a statistically significant) relationship between the number of words a child uses in her speech and the speed with which she learns to read, regression procedures allow one to predict how quickly the child will read based on the breadth of her vocabulary. When the amount of time administrators spend with parent groups correlates with the job performance ratings the public assigns to them, one can predict that a certain number of hours with parents will likely result in a particular performance rating. Although none of these predictions will be perfectly precise each time, they will consistently be more accurate than random guesses.

Prediction is common to all sciences. Because economists know that changes in orders for manufactured goods correlate with growth in the national product, they rely on changes in those orders to predict the rate of growth. Meteorologists know that air pressure fluctuations correlate with changing weather patterns so they can use evidence of developing low pressure to predict a coming storm. Astronomers use the presence of solar flares to predict communications problems on earth, and so on. Prediction fuels decision making.

Prediction is particularly important in education. If the scores from assessments that classroom teachers create for their students correlate with students' scores on a state-required standardized test, maybe December reading assessment results will predict May scores on the upcoming high-stakes test. If children's primary school grades correlate with their tendency to remain in school, one can use achievement data to predict the probability that a particular student will drop out of school prematurely. The accuracy of the prediction, as we shall see, depends upon the strength of the relationship between the predictor and the variable predicted.

We will call the variable which we're trying to predict the **criterion variable** and the variable used in the prediction (logically), the **predictor variable**. In SPSS, by the way, the predictor is called the independent variable and the criterion variable is termed the dependent variable.

■ In regression, a **predictor variable** predicts the value of a **criterion variable**.

In Chapter 10 we warned that correlation alone doesn't establish a causal relationship. The number of hours students study may correlate with their academic achievement, but that fact makes it unclear which causes which, or even whether some third variable is responsible for both study time and achievement. The stimulus value of maintaining one's scholarship might be the causal factor for both study time and academic achievement, or the approval of one's family members, or maybe it's just the pressure to avoid a career in fast food that prompts both more hours studied *and* higher grades. Those earlier warnings are still important. The fact that one may predict the value of one variable from the value of another doesn't presume that the predictor causes the criterion variable.

Either variable in a statistically significant correlation can predict the other. Because the correlation between study time and the students' achievement level is obviously the same as that between an achievement score and study time, either can predict the other.

Which variable is used to predict which may not be an arbitrary decision, however. Sometimes the accessibility of the data is a factor. If we know that reading comprehension and intelligence are significantly correlated, we would probably use reading comprehension scores to predict intelligence scores. Reading scores can be gathered much more economically than intelligence scores, which usually require time-consuming individual (and, therefore, expensive) testing, and parental permission if the students are minors.

Economy aside, sometimes only one approach makes sense. If someone develops a mathematics placement test to guide the assignment of students to algebra or prealgebra it's (hopefully) because there is a correlation between the students' scores on the placement test and their achievement scores in the subsequent class. Either of the test score and the scores in the subsequent class could be used to predict the other with equal accuracy, but it makes little sense to work chronologically backward using algebra scores to predict ("post-dict?") placement test scores.

Recall that variables correlate because each contains information that the other also contains. Higher correlations indicate more information in common. As the amount of shared information (the strength of the correlation) increases, the magnitude of the error in the prediction correspondingly shrinks, something we can depict in a scatter plot.

Back to Scatter Plots

We used scatter plots to illustrate correlation in Chapter 10. When they are used for regression problems the vertical axis represents the criterion variable, "y," the one we're trying to predict. The horizontal axis represents a predictor variable, "x." Once the xy data points are entered just as they were for correlation, a straight line positioned so that it's as close as possible to all the data points in the plot is called the **regression line**. Figure 11.1 is a scatter plot of the relationship between verbal aptitude and achievement on a language arts test, with a regression line through the data points.

If the correlation between predictor and criterion is perfect ($r = 1.0$), the dots are all aligned and the regression line is simply a straight line that connects the dots. But with less than perfect correlations, there will be some scatter in the plot. Scatter indicates that multiple x values have the same y, or vice versa. The consequence is that when we predict the value of y from that of x there will be some error; the predictor is going to be "off" some. Later in the chapter we'll estimate the amount of error.

We're actually pretty familiar with error in prediction, and we're reasonably tolerant of it.

Figure 11.1   A Scatter Plot and Regression Line for the Relationship

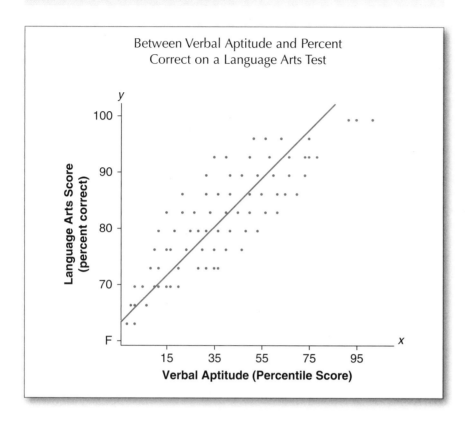

Between Verbal Aptitude and Percent
Correct on a Language Arts Test

- The weatherman predicts that the high for the day will be 76 degrees, but we check the thermometer anyway because we know there can be some variance.
- Superintendents try to predict what their budget will be for next year based on tax revenue and state funding from last year. They try to be reasonably precise, but no one expects perfect precision and they make adjustments along the way accordingly.
- Principals look at the number of new houses being built within school boundaries and try to predict how many new students are likely to register for school in the new year.

Perhaps in none of these examples will these people run a mathematical regression to predict the outcome but as long as there are statistically significant correlations between the variables involved, they could.

The Least Squares Criterion

■ **Least squares regression** satisfies the **least squares criterion**: squaring **residual scores**, the difference between predicted and actual scores, has the lowest possible value.

To keep the notation straight, y indicates the *actual* value of the criterion variable. The *predicted* value of y is called y', ("y prime"). The difference between the two ($y - y'$) is a **residual score** that is the evidence of prediction error. With less than perfect correlations, prediction errors are inevitable, but reliable regression procedures minimize them. Our solutions must meet what is called the **least squares criterion,** which means that the sum of the squared differences between the actual and predicted values must have their lowest possible value. Prediction procedures which satisfy this least squares criterion give rise to what is called **least squares regression**.

If there were a data set available for which all the values of x and y were known (we knew, for example, what the student's verbal aptitude scores and subsequent grades in school were), we could set up a regression problem and use verbal aptitude (x) to predict grades (y') even though we already know the grades. The advantage of doing this is that we could then compare the predicted values with the actual values from the original data set. It will indicate how much error there is in the prediction. Unless $r_{xy} = 1.0$, $y - y'$ will always result in a value other than 0. Least squares regression is designed to minimize the sum of the squared differences between y and y'.

Once the regression line is positioned, one could select a value of x on the horizontal axis of the scatter plot, move vertically to the regression line, and then go left to the y axis to determine the corresponding (predicted) value of y. Using Figure 11.1, we can see that someone with a verbal aptitude score of 35 will probably score a little below 80 on the language arts test. Theoretically, we could make all our predictions from such a chart, but it wouldn't be precise enough for a criterion variable with many scores and relatively small intervals between them. Rather than relying on the graph for something of a "guesstimate," we'll use mathematics to make the prediction.

The Regression Equation With One Predictor

■ **Bivariate,** or **simple, regression** predicts values based on where the regression line **intercepts** the y axis, and how steeply it **slopes**.

When one variable is used to predict the criterion variable those two variables constitute a **bivariate,** or simple regression, procedure. Consider Figure 11.1 for a moment. To position the regression line we need to know two things. We need to know where the line intercepts the y axis, something that we'll refer to as the *a* value, and we need to know just how steeply the line **slopes** up or down, a *b* value. There is a simple equation for each of *a* and *b* and then they both become components in the regression equation. We'll start with that equation:

$$y' = a + bx \qquad\qquad 11.1$$

Where y' = the predicted value of the criterion variable

a = the intercept

b = the slope of the regression line

x = the value of the predictor variable

Calculating the Intercept and the Slope

The regression equation is simple enough. It tells us that y' (the predicted value of y) is a function of a value for the intercept a, a value for the slope b, and a value for the predictor variable. So we must have values for the intercept and the slope first. They involve statistics you're already familiar with.

$$a = M_y - bM_x \qquad\qquad 11.2$$

Where a = the intercept

b = the slope of the regression line

M_y = the mean of the criterion variable

M_x = the mean of the predictor variable

So a, the intercept, is calculated by

1. Taking the mean of the criterion variable (the one we're trying to predict)

2. Minus b times the mean of the predictor variable (the one we're using to make the prediction)

Because the slope value (b) is part of what we need to calculate the intercept (a) we'll need to begin with the value of the slope.

$$b = r_{xy}\ (s_y/s_x) \qquad\qquad 11.3$$

Where b = the slope of the regression line

r_{xy} = the correlation coefficient for the two variables

■ The **regression coefficient** is another name for the b value (slope) calculated in regression.

s_y = the standard deviation of the criterion variable

s_x = the standard deviation of the predictor variable

The b value is also called the **regression coefficient**.

Interpreting the Slope

Note that if r_{xy} = 1.0, the slope of the regression line is exactly the ratio of the standard deviation of the y variable to that of x. When the correlation is less than perfect, b is a smaller proportion of the s_y/s_x ratio.

If the value for the slope (b) is positive, it indicates how much y *increases* for every 1.0 increase in x. If b is negative, it indicates how much y *decreases* for every unit (1.0) change in the predictor.

Negative correlations, and therefore negative regression slopes, are not unusual. The level of parental involvement in the schools is negatively correlated with student absenteeism. With negative correlations the regression line moves from upper left to lower right in the scatter plot. If the number of absences is used to predict a student's test grade, the b value indicates how much the grade *declines* for every absence.

Interpreting the Intercept

The intercept value, a, is the value of y when x = 0. If the number of absences is used to predict a student's test grade, a indicates what the student's score will be if the student misses 0 days.

Calculating bivariate regression isn't complicated. It involves these five steps:

1. Calculate the mean and standard deviation for both the predictor (x) and the criterion (y) variables.

2. Calculate the correlation (r_{xy}) between the two variables.

3. Calculate the regression coefficient, b (Formula 11.3).

4. Calculate the **regression intercept**, a (Formula 11.2).

5. Calculate y'. It is the value of the regression constant, plus the product of b times the value of the predictor, x.

In Figure 11.2 we have an example of calculating the regression equation and predicting y. It responds to the counselor's question at the beginning of the chapter about whether one can use reading scores to predict spatial ability.

Figure 11.2   A Regression Problem: Using Reading Comprehension to Predict Spatial Ability

Suppose that the literature indicates a correlation between reading comprehension (measured on a 15-point scale) and spatial ability (the ability to manipulate an object in mental space without having to do it physically). Therefore, one wishes to use data from eight children to predict spatial ability from reading comprehension scores. Specifically, for a reading comprehension score of 8, what is the corresponding level of spatial ability?

	Reading Comp. (x)	x^2	Spatial Ability (y)	y^2	xy
1.	12	144	10	100	120
2.	2	4	3	9	6
3.	5	25	7	49	35
4.	9	81	5	25	45
5.	11	121	9	81	99
6.	10	100	8	64	80
7.	4	16	6	36	24
8.	$\dfrac{1}{54}$	$\dfrac{1}{492}$	$\dfrac{3}{51}$	$\dfrac{9}{373}$	$\dfrac{3}{412}$

$$(\Sigma x)^2 = 2916 \qquad M_x = 6.75; \quad S_x = 4.268$$
$$\Sigma x^2 = 492 \qquad M_y = 6.375; \quad S_y = 2.615$$
$$(\Sigma y)^2 = 2601$$
$$\Sigma y^2 = 373$$

$$r_{xy} = \frac{n\Sigma xy - (\Sigma x)(\Sigma y)}{\sqrt{[n\Sigma x^2 - (\Sigma x)^2]}\sqrt{[n\Sigma y^2 - (\Sigma y)^2]}}$$

$$r_{xy} = \frac{8(412) - (54)(51)}{\sqrt{[8(492) - (2916)]}\sqrt{[8(373) - (2601)]}}$$

$$= \frac{542}{(31.937)(19.570)} = \mathbf{.867}$$

$y' = a + bx$

$\quad a = M_x - b\,M_y$
$\quad b = r\,(s_y/s_x)$

$\quad b = .867\,(2.615/4.268) = .531$
$\quad a = 6.375 - .531(6.75) = 2.791$

$y' = 2.791 + .531(8) = 7.039$

The researchers are able to predict that for someone with a reading comprehension score of 8, the spatial ability score will be 7.039.

"I've decided to rush *Sigma Chi*. I understand they have a smaller rejection region."

If reading comprehension is 0, it means that the best prediction for spatial ability is 2.791. Don't get too carried away with interpreting this value in isolation. (Suggesting that someone's reading comprehension is zero??) Just remember that this value represents a, the intercept, or in the language of SPSS, the regression constant.

Regarding the slope, b, if reading comprehension increases by 1.0, spatial ability will increase by .531. The a and b values are the basis for plotting the regression line in Figure 11.3.

Regress Which Variable on Which?

In the language of regression, we regressed spatial ability on reading comprehension in Figure 11.2. If the data were equally accessible, and accessibility is often the issue as we noted earlier, we might just as easily have regressed reading comprehension on spatial ability. Mathematically it certainly makes no difference. Having used the correlation coefficient to establish that there is a statistically significant relationship between the variables, one needs only means and standard deviations in order to predict the value of one from the other.

Figure 11.3   Using the Regression Constant and the Regression Coefficient to Plot the Regression Line

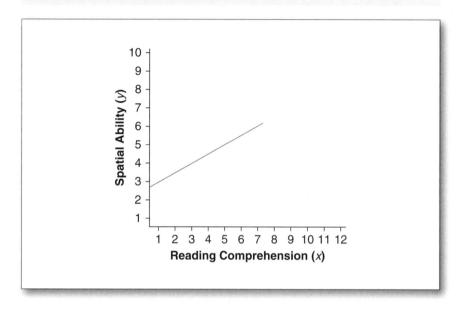

Accessibility aside, there are instances where only one alternative makes logical sense. We noted that it makes little sense to use college performance to estimate the admissions test scores which would have preceded them. By the same token, if there is a significant relationship between teacher candidates' practice teaching and their subsequent performance in their own classrooms, it is logical to quantify student teaching performance and use those measures to predict who the best teachers will be. One might then strengthen the components that improve candidates' potential to be effective teachers. It wouldn't be as valuable to use classroom performance after graduation to indicate what sort of student teachers they were, but the math certainly doesn't care which way we go.

PREDICTION ERRORS

If the correlation between the predictor and criterion variables used in a regression procedure is < 1.0, prediction error will be a constant companion. If one were to make a large number of predictions with data from a large data set, some of those y' estimates will be too low and some will be too high, but

■ By definition, the **standard error of the estimate** is the standard deviation of all possible differences between the actual and predicted values of y. In practice, a simple formula estimates it.

taken as an aggregate, they will all balance out because the under-predictions will be countered by the over-predictions, and so on. Symbolically [$\Sigma(y - y')$ = 0]. However the fact that all the prediction errors sum to zero is small consolation when there is just one prediction to be made. Since perfect correlations in the social world are rare as hen's teeth, we're always going to have some prediction error so we want at least to be able to estimate their magnitude. This is what the **standard error of the estimate** (SE_{est}) does.

Remember that any standard error-of-the-whatever statistics are measures of data variability just as the standard error of the mean and the standard error of difference were. Like those other standard error measures, the standard error of the estimate is related to the standard deviation. In fact the SE_{est} is the standard deviation of all the error scores, the *prediction* error scores to be more specific. Recall that the difference between the actual value of the criterion variable (y) and its predicted value (y') is called a residual score. If we were to calculate all possible residual scores from all possible predictions and then calculate the standard deviation of those scores that value would be the SE_{est}.

Calculating the Standard Error of the Estimate

A standard deviation of all residual scores seems like one of those "thanks, but that's not particularly helpful" statistics. If we had all the actual values of y to compare with y' so that we could derive all of the residual scores and calculate their standard deviation, we wouldn't need the standard error of the estimate. Since we would have all the actual values of y we wouldn't need regression either. The idea is theoretical. It helps us understand what the standard error of the estimate represents. In practice we'll estimate SE_{est} just as we estimated the standard error of the difference SE_d and the standard error of the mean, SE_m, but it's important to remember what it represents.

$$SE_{est} = S_y = \sqrt{1 - r_{xy}^2}$$

11.4

Where,

SE_{est} = the standard error of estimate

S_y = the standard deviation of the criterion (y) variable

r_{xy}^2 = the square of the correlation coefficient

For the sake of example, perhaps the counselor at the beginning of the chapter has reading comprehension and spatial ability data for a number of freshman applicants. He has used the reading scores for each applicant to predict the applicants' spatial ability scores. He has those data for only some.

- The reading comprehension/spatial ability correlation is $r_{xy} = .658$
- The standard deviation of spatial ability scores is $s_y = 3.771$
- What is the standard error of the estimate for his predicted values?

$$SE_{est} = S_y = \sqrt{1 - r_{xy}^2}$$

$$SE_{est} = 3.771 \ S_y = \sqrt{(1 - .658^2)}$$

SE_{est} (The estimate of the standard deviation of all error scores) = **2.840**

Understanding the SE_{est}

The r_{xy}^2 statistic came up in Chapter 10. Recall that it's the proportion of y explained by x (or vice versa). As a component in the error estimate, $1 - r_{xy}^2$ makes particular sense since it must represent the proportion of the variability in y that x does *not* explain. Look closely at Formula 11.4 for a moment. If the correlation between x and $y = 1.0$, the $SE_{est} = 0$ (the square root of $1 - 1^2 = 0$). Zero times the standard deviation of the y variable = 0. If there's a perfect correlation, there's no prediction error. In the other extreme, if the correlation is zero, SE_{est} equals the standard deviation of the criterion variable. These two circumstances establish the minimum and maximum possible values of the SE_{est}. It ranges from 0 to the standard deviation of the variable we're predicting. This can be helpful when you're doing the calculations. If your answer is outside of the 0 to s_y range, there's an error somewhere.

Another Example of Calculating SE_{est}

Presume that one is interested in using the educator's level of formal schooling as a predictor of instructional quality. Ignoring the difficulty in defining instructional quality (!), if the correlation between that measure (y) and the educator's number of credits beyond a baccalaureate degree (x) is $r_{xy} = .17$, and the standard deviation of instructional quality is 4.296, using Formula 11.4 we have the following:

$$SE_{est} = S_y = \sqrt{1 - r_{xy}^2}$$

$$= 4.296\sqrt{1 - .17^2}$$

$$= \mathbf{4.233}$$

Why is the standard error of the estimate so nearly the same value as the standard deviation for instructional quality? It's because the correlation is so low. With very large samples, recall that even very modest correlations can be statistically significant. By the time .17 is squared, the value subtracted from one is very small indeed, leaving the multiplier for the standard deviation quite near to 1.0.

A Confidence Interval for the Estimate of y

■ A regression **confidence interval** is a range for the true value of the criterion variable with a stated probability.

Since y' is the best estimate we can make of the value we're trying to predict given the data we have, and SE_{est} is an estimate of the error in the prediction, we can use them together. In fact we'll use them together to determine boundaries within which the true value of y will occur, with a specified level of probability. As you may have recognized, we're going to calculate a **confidence interval** for the estimate, something like we calculated confidence intervals for t-test solutions in Chapter 6.

Using values from Table B (Appendix A) one can determine an interval for any level of probability, but the usual practice is to rely on probabilities of .95 or .99. A .95 confidence interval is interpreted to mean that the probability is $p = .95$ that the true value of y will fall within the range the confidence interval (CI) defines. For the .95 CI, the procedure is the following:

$$CI = +/- t \ (SE_{est}) + y' \qquad\qquad 11.5$$

Where,

CI = the confidence interval

t = the value from Table B with df = the no. of pairs of data, -2

SE_{est} = the standard error of the estimate for the data

y' = the predicted value for the criterion variable

For the problem on reading comprehension and spatial ability, we predicted a spatial ability score of 7.039 for someone with a reading comprehension score of 8.0. A .95 confidence interval is determined by calculating the SE_{est}, and then the CI.

$$SE_{est} = S_y \ \sqrt{(1 - r^2_{xy})} = 2.615\sqrt{(1 - 1.867^2)} = 1.303$$

$$CI = +/- t_{n-2} \ (SE_{est}) + y' = +/- 2.447 \ (1.303) + 7.039 = \mathbf{10.227, \ 3.851}$$

With .95 confidence, the level of spatial ability for someone with reading comprehension of 8.0 is between 10.227 and 3.851. Or, 95% of the time the spatial ability measure for someone with reading comprehension of 8.0 will be between 3.851 and 10.227.

The range from 3.851 to 10.227 is quite a sizeable interval. The calculations reveal why.

- With small groups, there are inherent risks to normality. The critical value from the t table has to reflect the risk involved in using a sample of 8; smaller samples mean fewer degrees of freedom and a larger t value.
- Although fairly robust here, the strength of the correlation is inversely related to the size of the CI; smaller r_{xy}, larger SE_{est} and CI.
- Finally, the confidence interval is affected by the variability in y. A large s_y value prompts a larger SE_{est} and a larger CI.

To put all the foregoing in perspective, remember that everything in regression analysis hinges on the relationship between predictor and criterion. The stronger the relationship, the more precise the prediction and the smaller any error component will be. If there is no relationship between predictor and criterion ($r_{xy} = 0$), what's the best prediction for the value of y? Because of the nature of normal distributions and central tendency, it will be the mean of the criterion variable, M_y, but that isn't terribly helpful when much depends on the outcome of the analysis. With $r_{xy} = 0$ the corresponding SE_{est} value is going to be very large.

The earlier example of predicting teaching quality by using a rather weak but statistically significant correlation with the teachers' level of education demonstrates how some of these issues impact regression confidence intervals. We determined that given a correlation of $r_{xy} = .17$, a standard deviation of instructional quality of 4.296, and Formula 11.4 that $SE_{est} = 4.233$.

If $y' = 27.519$ (predicted teaching quality for a particular teacher), and $N = 30$ teachers in the analysis, using Formula 11.5 we have the following .95 confidence interval:

$$CI = +/- t \ (SE_{est}) + y' = +/- 2.048(4.233) + 27.519 = \mathbf{38.188, \ 18.850}$$

The weak correlation and substantial amount of variability translated into a comparatively large SE_{est}, and consequently, a large confidence interval.

Small samples reduce the math burden, but when we can avoid them, small samples are a poor research practice, particularly for regression procedures. Small samples (and their fewer df values) result in larger critical values of t. They also tend to be reflected in larger standard deviations (s_y) and lower correlations (r_{xy}). Small samples conspire against precise regression solutions.

By way of a summary, if there is a correlation between students' vocabulary scores at the end of the year and their spelling test results mid-term, a regression solution can be completed in which vocabulary scores are predicted with spelling scores. The prediction for one student is a value represented as y'. That predicted value represents the best prediction, given the data that are available, of what the student's true vocabulary score (y) actually is. The y' value is called a point estimate; it is *one* possible value of the student's vocabulary score. Absent a perfect correlation between spelling and vocabulary, there is going to be some error in the prediction. The standard error of the estimate suggests the likely magnitude of the error. The confidence interval uses SE_{est} to determine the boundaries within which the *actual* value of y is likely to occur with the specified level of probability. As the level of certainty that the actual vocabulary score occurs in a particular interval rises, so must the width of the confidence interval.

From the Top

Having worked through confidence intervals, we'll now complete a regression problem from the beginning. Suppose that a researcher has the following data on task persistence (*ta-pe*) and problem-solving ability (*probsa*) for eight subjects:

ta-pe	probsa
3	1
5	6
6	6
4	5
5	7
3	4
5	4
7	8

The researcher has one more person for whom the task persistence score is 2, with no accompanying *probsa* score. He wishes to determine a .95 confidence interval for someone with that score of 2. He'll need to do the following:

1. Calculate the means, standard deviations for each set of scores

2. Calculate the correlation of the two sets of scores

3. Determine the regression coefficient, *b*

4. Determine the intercept value, *a*

5. Solve for *y'*

6. Calculate the standard error of the estimate

7. Calculate the confidence interval

1. Verify that the means and standard deviations are as follows:

ta-pe (*x*)   probsa (*y*)

M 4.750   5.125

s 1.389   2.167

2. Now the correlation.

$$r_{xy} = \frac{N\Sigma xy - (\Sigma x)(\Sigma y)}{\sqrt{N\Sigma x^2 - (\Sigma x)^2}\ \sqrt{N\Sigma y^2 - (\Sigma y)^2}}$$ 10.2

$$= \frac{8 \cdot 212 - 38 \cdot 41}{\sqrt{(8 \cdot 194 \cdot 38^2)}\sqrt{(8 \cdot 243 \cdot 41^2)}} = .819$$

3. The regression coefficient is as follows:

$b = r_{xy}\ (s_y/s_x) = .819\ (2.167/1.389) = \mathbf{1.278}$

4. The intercept value:

$a = M_y - bM_x = 5.125 - (1.278 \cdot 4.750) = \mathbf{-.946}$

5. The regression equation lets the researcher solve for y':

$y' = a + bx = -.946 + (1.278 \cdot 2) = \mathbf{1.611}$

6. The standard error of the estimate is as follows:

$SE_{est} = s_y\ \sqrt{(1 - r_{xy}^2)} = 2.167\sqrt{(1 - 819^2)}\ \ = \mathbf{1.243}$

7. And finally, the .95 confidence interval:

Note that the *t* value for *df* = 6 is 2.447

$CI = +/- t\ (SE_{est}) + y' = +/-\ 2.447*(1.243) + 1.611$

$= \mathbf{-1.431,\ 4.653}$

The data indicate that the best prediction of a *probsa* score on the problem-solving ability measure for someone who as a task persistence score of 2 on the *ta-pe* is 1.611, which is the *y'* value the researcher calculated. As far as a .95 confidence interval, with a standard error of the estimate of 1.243, the lower and upper bounds for the confidence interval are −1.431 and 4.653.

It's a rather wide interval, but not surprising given the small sample size and the relatively substantial variability in the criterion variable where the standard deviation is nearly half the value of the mean. The researcher won't be distracted by the fact that the lower bound of the confidence interval is a negative value, by the way. He's predicting a score for the criterion variable from a very low score on the predictor variable and although a negative score on the *probsa* probably isn't possible, the confidence interval formula makes no allowance for that contingency.

Looking at SPSS Output

Completing the regression problem represented in Figure 11.2 on SPSS produces the three tables below. They cover the range of procedures involved when one uses the computer to complete a regression analysis. This first one lists the descriptive data regarding r, r^2, and an r^2 value "adjusted" for the size of the sample involved and the number of variables. Although SPSS uses the symbol R, when there's just one predictor, the statistic calculated is a Pearson correlation, r. The standard error of the estimate value won't match ours because it's based on the adjusted r^2 value.

Model Summary

Model	R	RSquare	Adjusted R Square	Std. Error of the Estimate
1	.867[a]	.752	.711	1.407

a
Predictors: (Constant), readcomp

ANOVA

Model		Sum of Squares	df	Mean Square	F	Sig.
1	Regression	36.000	1	36.000	18.190	.005
	Residual	11.875	6	1.979		
	Total	47.875	7			

Coefficients

Model		Unstandardized Coefficients		Standardized Coefficients		
		B	Std. Error	Beta	t	Sig.
1	(Constant)	2.788	.977		2.854	.029
	Readcomp	.531	.125	.867	4.265	.005

The null hypothesis for the *ANOVA* test is that there is no relationship between reading comprehension and spatial ability, so it's a significance test for the correlation. For the regression output to be helpful of course we need to be able to reject H_o. We can. The *F* value is statistically significant.

The third table contains the regression output. The "constant" value is what we termed the intercept. The table value is close to the *a* value that we calculated. The "readcomp" score is the regression coefficient, *b* and identical to our value. As usual, SPSS provides more than what we requested, but note in the last column the results of a *t*-test of the regression coefficient. The "Sig. = .005" indicates that reading comprehension is a statistically significant predictor of spatial ability, the criterion variable, *y*.

Because there is just one predictor, the significance values for the *t*-test and the *ANOVA* will match. Both are .005. This reflects the relationship between *t* and *F* values. Recall from the end of Chapter 7 exercises that $t^2 = F$ when we're testing two groups for significant differences. Here, the *t* value squared (4.265^2) equals the *F* value, 18.190.

SUMMARY

Although correlations alone don't establish causal relationships, correlated variables do have information in common and that connection offers the potential to predict one variable from the value of another. This is the regression domain.

When the correlations between predictor and criterion variable are less than 1.0, there will be some error in the prediction. This is clear from a scatter plot, particularly one with many data points. The "scatter" in the scatter plots illustrates that more than one measure of *y* can be associated with the same value of *x*, and correspondingly, more than one measure of *x* can correspond to the same *y*. Although the error in a prediction solution is suggested by the degree of scatter in the plot, we actually calculated it with the standard error of the estimate (SE_{est}) statistic. Besides providing an estimate of prediction error, the standard error of the estimate can be used to calculate the confidence interval, and range of values within which the true value of the criterion variable will occur, with the specified level of probability.

In any regression procedure, the quality of the prediction is a function of multiple conditions. In simple regression the factors are the correlation between the predictor and criterion variable, the size of the sample, and the variability in the criterion variable, *y*. When the correlation is weak, the sample sizes are relatively small, or there tends to be a good deal of variability in the criterion variable, prediction error increases. There's something of a connection here to what we did with *ANOVA*. Our rationale for moving from one-way models to factorial *ANOVA* was to control more of the extraneous variance, and so reduce the error term. We'll do a similar thing in Chapter 12 when we try to improve the quality of our predictions by including more than one predictor in the problem.

EXERCISES

Correlation* Matrix

	SATV	SATM	GREV	GREQ	Rdg	Math
SATV	1.0	.726	.833	.598	.919	.714
SATM	.726	1.0	.767	.857	.734	.894
GREV	.833	.767	1.0	.686	.736	.740
GREQ	.598	.857	.686	1.0	.534	.852
Rdg	.919	.734	.736	.534	1.0	.675
Math	.714	.894	.740	.852	.675	1.0

*All correlations are statistically significant.

Descriptive Statistics

Test	Mean	Std.Dev.
SATV	438.000	98.441
SATM	468.500	109.317
GREV	465.500	108.893
GREQ	485.000	116.144
Reading	52.750	12.502
Math	54.850	15.250

1. Noting the correlation between SAT-V and the reading score, what reading score can we predict for a student whose SAT-V score is 490?

   a. How much will reading increase for every 1.0 increase in the SAT-V?
   b. What value will reading have if SAT-V is 0?
   c. In terms of regression solutions, why is the value of reading when SAT-V is 0 relevant?

2. What is the standard error of the estimate for the item 1 solution?

3. Calculate a .99 confidence interval for the item 1 solution. Assume $n = 52$.

   a. What is the confidence interval expected to contain?
   b. On average, how often will the assumption referred to in a) be wrong?
   c. What could a researcher do to "shrink" the confidence interval?

4. If two sets of data are uncorrelated, what is the best prediction for the value of y?

5. What impact does a negative correlation between x and y have on the slope of the regression line?

6. What are the factors that determine error in a regression prediction?

7. Referring to the matrix at the beginning of the exercise, what variable will provide the best prediction of GRE-V scores? Explain.

8. From the matrix at the beginning of the exercise, what math score is predicted for someone who has an SAT-M score of 575?

9. What GRE-V score is predicted for someone who has a reading score of 60?

10. You have the following data for the number of times students are reinforced and for their response rates per class period.

Reinforcement	No. of Responses
2	3
5	6
4	5
1	3
3	4
5	5
4	4
6	8

   a. What's the correlation between reinforcement and response rates?
   b. What's the best prediction for number of responses for someone who has been reinforced 5 times?
   c. Assume $n = 52$ and determine a .95 confidence interval for the b) solution.

THE FORMULAE AND THEIR SYMBOLS

Formula 11.1: $y' = a + bx$ This is the bivariate regression equation.

Formula 11.2: $a = M_y - bM_x$ This is the formula for determining the value of the intercept, the a value in Formula 11.1.

Formula 11.3: $b = r_{xy} (s_y/s_x)$ This is the formula for determining the slope of the regression line, b in Formula 11.1.

Formula 11.4: $SE_{est} = S_y = \sqrt{(1-r^2_{xy})}$ This is the formula for the standard error of the estimate in simple regression. It estimates the amount of error in the prediction.

Formula 11.5: $CI = +/- t (SE_{est}) + y'$ This formula allows one to calculate what is called a confidence interval, a band around the predicted value of a criterion variable (y') within which the true value of the criterion will occur with a specified probability. The procedure acknowledges that although we can make better than chance predictions of one variable from another when they're significantly correlated, the prediction isn't without error unless the correlation is perfect.

STUDENT STUDY SITE

Visit the Student Study Site at **www.sagepub.com/tanner** for additional learning tools.

Chapter 12

REGRESSION WITH MORE THAN ONE PREDICTOR

THE PROBLEM: HOW TO EMPLOY MORE THAN ONE PREDICTOR

In the course of his work, an admissions officer at a college has noted the relationship between measures of verbal ability such as the SAT-verbal, which students are required to take as a condition for admission, the GRE-verbal, which they take when they decide to pursue graduate school, and a variety of other verbal ability tests, such as reading measures. Since when two measures are correlated one can predict the value of the other, when two are related to a third, together can they predict the third even better?

QUESTIONS AND ANSWERS

❏ Can more than one predictor improve the prediction?

Often it can, although it depends upon whether the additional predictors provide new information about the variable predicted. When more than one predictor is involved, the process is *multiple* regression.

MULTIPLE REGRESSION

Using *more* than one predictor in a regression problem brings us to **multiple regression**. A school counselor has a hypothesis that age (predictor A) and achievement motivation (predictor B) will predict reading comprehension (the criterion variable, C). Including a second predictor variable to regression introduces two problems:

- The Pearson Correlation, which is the heart of simple regression, accommodates just two variables. To measure the relationship between multiple predictors and a criterion variable we need a new statistic.
- Related to the first problem, besides being correlated with the criterion variable, multiple predictors are usually correlated

■ **Multiple regression** allows the value of a criterion variable to be predicted by two or more predictor variables as a result of a correlation between the criterion variable and each of the predictors.

with each other. If two predictors provide some of the same information about the criterion variable, how can we measure the unique contribution of each?

> ■ Multiple correlation (R) measures the relationship between multiple predictor variables and one criterion variable.

Both of the problems noted above are related to procedures completed in Chapters 10 and 11, but they each introduce a bit of a "twist." The first which is called **multiple correlation**, or sometimes called just **multiple R**, is an extension of the Pearson Correlation and allows one to correlate multiple predictor variables with a criterion variable. The problem of how to determine the unique contribution of each variable when there are more than two involved we'll tackle two ways, first with yet another correlation procedure that addresses this question directly, and then with a new way to calculate the regression coefficient so that when there are multiple predictors the contribution of each is distinct.

Multiple R, or Multiple Correlation

Multiple R is the correlation between a criterion variable and multiple predictor variables which, recognizing that they have something to do with the value of the criterion variable, are also called independent variables. Formula 12.1 is the formula for R with two independent variables. Before you panic, look closely. The whole formula is based on three Pearson Correlations (which by now you can probably do in your sleep).

$$R_{y,x1x2} = \sqrt{\frac{r_{yx_1}^2 + r_{yx_2}^2 - 2r_{yx_1}r_{yx_2}r_{x_1x_2}}{1 - r_{x1x2}^2}}$$

12.1

Where,

$R_{y,x1x2}$ = the correlation between a criterion variable, y, and a combination of two predictors, $x1$ and $x2$

r_{yx1} = the correlation of the criterion variable and predictor x_1

r_{yx2} = the correlation of the criterion variable and predictor x_2

r_{x1x2} = the correlation of the two predictor variables, x_1 and x_2

Calculating Multiple R

Figure 12.1 contains an example of a multiple correlation problem. Although the discussion here is restricted to just two predictor variables

$(x_1$ and $x_2)$, in theory at least, R can be used to determine the correlation between any number of predictor variables and a criterion variable.

Note that the multiple correlation of reading speed and recall ability with reading comprehension is greater than the Pearson Correlation of either predictor variable with the criterion variable. This shouldn't be surprising. The multiple correlation procedure allows one to include more information about the y variable than either the particular x_1 or x_2 can contribute independently.

Recall that if the Pearson Correlation is squared (r^2) we have the coefficient of determination, which indicates the proportion of variance in y that can be explained by changes in x. The square of the multiple correlation (R^2) can be interpreted the same way. It indicates how much of the variance in y the combination of the x variables, x_1 and x_2 in our examples, explains.

The second complication we noted with multiple predictors is that they tend to be correlated with each other as well as with the criterion variable. This will virtually always be the case when working with human subjects. The Venn diagram in Figure 12.2 illustrates these overlapping relationships (Diekhoff, 1992).

Figure 12.1 Calculating Multiple R

Data indicate that there is a statistically significant relationship between reading comprehension, reading speed, and recall ability. We wish to know how well reading comprehension correlates with a combination of reading speed and recall ability.

The correlation matrix:

	Comp. (y)	Speed (1)	Recall (2)
Comp. (y)		.75	.70
Speed (1)	.75		.30
Recall (2)	.70	.30	

$$R_{y,12} = \sqrt{((r_{y1}^2 + r_{y2}^2 - 2r_{y1}r_{y2}r_{12})/1 - r_{12}^2)}$$

$$= \sqrt{((.75^2 + .70^2 - 2 \cdot .75 \cdot .70 \cdot .30)/(1 - .30^2))}$$

$$= .900$$

Figure 12.2 Three Related Variables

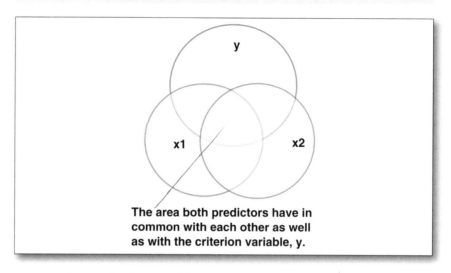

The area both predictors have in
common with each other as well
as with the criterion variable, y.

Another Multiple R Problem

Suppose a school principal is interested in the multiple correlation of
student performance on a nationally standardized reading test (y) with a
combination of the number of hours spent in differentiated instruction (x_1),
where students are grouped according to reading level, and the number of
hours students spend in peer tutoring situations (x_2) during a semester. The
Pearson Correlations are as follows:

$r_{y1} = .625$

$r_{y2} = .413$

$r_{12} = .373$

Using Formula 10.6 we have:

$$R_{y,x1x2} = \sqrt{\frac{r_{yx1}^2 + r_{yx2}^2 - 2r_{yx1}r_{yx2}r_{x1x2}}{1 - r_{x1x2}^2}}$$

$$= \sqrt{\frac{625^2 + .413^2 - 2(.625)(.413)(.373)}{1 - .373^2}}$$

$$= \sqrt{.428}$$

$$= .654$$

The correlation of the students' test performance with a combination of the number of hours they spend in differentiated instruction and the number of hours they are involved in peer tutoring is $R_{y.12} = .654$.

The correlation of both the x variables with the y variable is greater than the correlation of either x with y independently. However, why is the value of $R_{y.12}$ only modestly greater than r_{y1}? It seems that the correlation of time in peer tutoring with student test performance adds little that the correlation of differentiated instruction with test performance has not already provided.

The Second Problem

At the beginning of the chapter we noted that two related problems emerge when there are multiple predictors in a regression problem. The first was the problem of how to correlate more than two variables, a problem that is central to multiple regression since everything in regression is based on correlation. This is the problem that R solves.

The other problem was how to determine the unique contribution of each of multiple predictor variables, a problem that emerges because multiple predictors tend to be correlated with each other besides being related to the criterion variable. When this happens it's likely that the x variables provide redundant information about the y variable. Areas 1 and 2 in Figure 12.2 suggest the correlation between x_1 (age) and reading comprehension (y). Note that part of the area that the predictor variables have in common is also shared with the criterion variable. This area of shared variance must be part of any accurate prediction, but as soon as the first predictor variable is introduced (r_{yx1}), it's already been "counted." How can we also use the r_{yx2} correlation without increasing the error in the prediction?

To determine how much of a problem this can be, we need a correlation procedure that will separate what each multiple predictor variable independently contributes to the correlation value. This is what **partial correlation** does.

■ **Partial correlation** is the correlation between two variables, controlling the influence of others in both.

Partial Correlation

A partial correlation indicates the correlation between two variables exclusive of the correlation some third variable may have with both. For the sake of illustration, perhaps review of the published literature indicates the following correlations:

1. Problem-solving ability (x_1) with critical thinking (x_2), $r = .825$

2. Problem-solving ability (x_1) with reasoning ability (y), $r = .764$

3. Critical thinking (x_2) with reasoning ability (y), $r = .703$

A researcher wishes to know of the correlation between problem-solving ability (x_1) and reasoning ability (y), exclusive of whatever critical thinking has in common with both. The answer is to calculate a partial correlation of problem-solving ability (x_1) with reasoning ability (y), ruling critical thinking (x_2) out of both variables. The formula for partial correlation is the following:

$$r_{y,x1\cdot x2} = \frac{r_{y,x1} - (r_{y,x2})(r_{x1,x2})}{\sqrt{(1-r_{y,x2}^2)(1-r_{x1,x2}^2)}}$$

12.2

The notation indicates that it's the "2" variable, the variable indicated after the dot, that's being controlled. It's the y and x_1 correlation that we're interested in, exclusive of whatever the x_2 variable has in common with both x_1 and y. So, substituting the correlation values into the formula results in:

$$r_{y,x1.2} = .764 - (.703)(.825)$$

$$\sqrt{(1-.703^2)(1-.825^2)}$$

$$r_{y,x1\cdot2} = \frac{.184}{\sqrt{(.506)(.319)}}$$

$$= .458$$

The Pearson Correlation of problem-solving ability (x_1) with reasoning ability (y) is $r = .764$. If we use partial correlation to control what both of those variables have in common with critical thinking, the result of removing that component is a more modest $r_{y1.2} = .458$. This is what problem-solving and reasoning ability have in common after whatever critical thinking has in common with both variables has been removed. If we do what we did in Chapter 10 and square that value, it will tell us the proportion of the variance in reasoning ability that can be explained by changes in problem-solving ability, $r_{y1.2}^2 = .210$; about 21% of the variance in reasoning ability can be explained by problem-solving ability.

Note that we could turn this formula around now and determine the partial correlation between critical thinking (y) and reasoning ability (x_2), holding problem-solving ability (x_1) constant in both. In that case we adjust the x_1 and x_2 values as follows:

$$r_{y,x2.x1} = \frac{r_{y,x2} - (r_{y,x1})(r_{x1,x2})}{\sqrt{(1-r_{y,x1}^2)(1-r_{x1,x2}^2)}}$$

If the appropriate values are inserted, the partial correlation of critical thinking and reasoning ability, holding problem-solving ability constant in both, is:

$$r_{y,x2 \cdot x1} = \frac{703 - .(764)(.825)}{\sqrt{(1 - .764^2)(1 - .825^2)}}$$

$$= .199$$

Making the Application to Regression

The control exercised over that third variable in the partial correlation problems above is similar to what must occur in multiple regression. When there are multiple predictor variables, there is a separate regression coefficient, a separate slope, for each. Recall that the regression coefficient indicates the change in the y value that corresponds to each increase of 1.0 in the predictor. In order for that measure of change to be accurate for each predictor variable, each regression coefficient must include only information that isn't also present in some other regression coefficient(s). The process is to control the effect of other variables just as we did in partial correlation.

The regression coefficients in multiple regression problems, therefore, are actually **partial regression coefficients.** The data shared with other predictors are "partialed out" before the coefficient is calculated.

■ **Partial regression coefficients** indicate the change in y' for each predictor with the other predictors constant.

The Multiple Regression Equation

We can visualize simple regression problems in two dimensions as we did in Figures 11.1 and 11.3. The regression line moves from left to right, inclining or declining depending upon whether it's positive or negative. A second predictor introduces a third dimension to the problem (and with each additional predictor, another dimension).

Imagine standing in the middle of a room facing a corner. Think of the vertical line where two walls meet as the y axis in a graph. The line along the floor to your left where the wall meets the floor is like the axis for x_1 and the line to your right where the floor meets the wall on your right is the axis for x_2. If regression lines are created for each of those two predictors and then are joined all along their lengths to each other, the result would be *a regression plane,* something like that represented in Figure 12.3 (Diekhoff, 1992).

Line drawings fail us with more than two predictors because there isn't any way to represent four dimensions in a drawing, but Figure 12.3 indicates how the regression plane might look with two predictors that and positive regression coefficients. You'll have to use a little imagination here, but the plane increases in elevation as it moves toward the viewer.

To arrive at a solution using the regression plane one identifies the point on the "floor" of the illustration where the values of x_1 and x_2 intersect, point A in Figure 12.3, and then travels vertically to where that point intersects the plane, point B, then horizontally back to the value of the criterion variable, point C. Like the regression line, the plane is fixed according to the least squares criterion. Prediction errors are as small as the correlations among the variables permit. In spite of the difficulty we have picturing the result when there are more than two predictors, multiple regression can be adapted to any number of predictors, as Formula 12.3 suggests:

$$y' = a + b_1 x_1 + b_2 x_2 + \cdots + b_k x_k \qquad\qquad 12.3$$

Figure 12.3   A Multiple Regression "Plane"

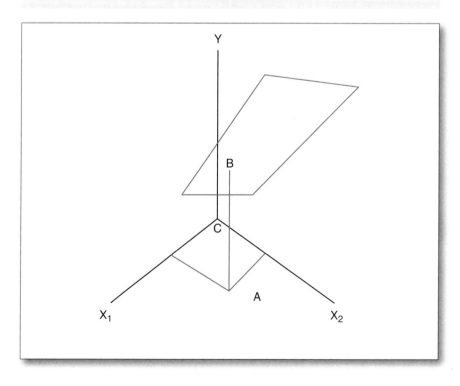

Where,

y' = the predicted value of the criterion, or dependent variable

a = the regression constant; the value of y when all x values are 0

$b_1 \ldots b_k$ = the regression coefficients, or weights for independent variables 1 through k; collectively they determine the slope of the plane

$x_1 \ldots x_k$ = the several predictor variables, from the 1st to the "kth"

As we noted, the regression coefficients ($b_1 \ldots b_k$) are actually partial regression coefficients. Each b value is adjusted for any correlations the particular predictor has with the other predictors so that what each predictor contributes is unique.

- Conceptually, b_1 explains how much y will change for every increase of 1.0 in the first predictor variable (x_1) *when the effects of the other predictors ($x_2, x_3, \ldots x_k$) are held constant.*
- The second regression coefficient, b_2, explains how much y will change for a 1.0 increase in x_2 when the effects of the other predictors ($x_1, x_3, \ldots x_k$) are held constant, and so on.

With two predictors, the multiple regression equation has its simplest form:

$$y' = a + b_1 x_1 + b_2 x_2 \qquad 12.4$$

Before we can complete the prediction we must have values for a (the intercept), for the first regression coefficient (b_1), and for the second regression coefficient (b_2), and just as before, we need b (in this case, *both b* values) before we can solve for a. The formulae we need are these:

$$a = M_y - b_1 M_{x1} - b_2 M_{x2} \qquad 12.5$$

$$b_1 = \frac{r_{y,x1} - r_{y,x2} \cdot r_{x1,x2}}{1 - r_{x1,x2}^2} (s_y / s_{x1}) \qquad 12.6$$

$$b_2 = \frac{r_{y,x2} - r_{y,x1} \cdot r_{x1,x2}}{1 - r_{x1,x2}^2} (s_y / s_{x2}) \qquad 12.7$$

Examine the b_1 and b_2 equations for a moment. If the x_1 and x_2 variables (the predictors) were uncorrelated, that is:

- if $r_{x1x2} = 0$, then
- $b_1 = r_{yx1}\ (s_y/s_{x1})$, and
- $b_2 = r_{yx2}\ (s_y/s_{x2})$

These last two regression coefficients ought to look familiar. Except for the 1 or 2 subscripts to b, they're exactly what we used for the slope in simple regression. In an ideal research world, the predictor variables wouldn't be correlated with each other, which means that there would be no redundancy between predictors to worry about. If the predictors were uncorrelated, each regression coefficient would be calculated with the same version of the formula used in simple regression where there was just one predictor.

SOURCE: Created by Suzanna Nielson.

"Spring break was great and I'm not ready to go back to studying. I think a partial regression is the wiser course."

Using Multiple Regression

However, the fact that predictor variables are nearly always correlated is what makes social science research, including educational research, so interesting, as well as so complex. In the case of multiple regression at least, accommodating the multiple associations doesn't make the regression coefficients particularly difficult, just longer. The only terms involved are the standard deviations for each variable and the correlations of each of the variable with all others. In Figure 12.4 we have a solution to a multiple regression problem raised at the beginning of the chapter. Based on the relationships between two admissions tests (SAT-V and GRE-V) that students often take, the solution predicts a score on a subsequent test of reading ability.

Because data from the SAT-V and the reading test both correlate with GRE-V scores, values for the predictors allow one to make a better-than-chance prediction of what the score will be on the criterion variable. In this problem, the researcher determined that the best GRE-V prediction for someone with an SAT-V score of 375 and a Reading score of 38 is about 420.

That predicted value (y') is based on a regression coefficient (slope) for each of the independent variables, the b_1 and b_2 values in this case, and an intercept value, a. Those values and the raw scores for the predictors are all the regression formula requires.

If we have significant correlations as well as the means and standard deviations of the variables involved, we can use what's accessible to predict what isn't. Here, SAT, GRE, and reading scores were all available from students' records. Because all those measures are correlated with each other, one can predict the value of one, from either or both of the other two. Someone recruiting students to a graduate program can predict what their GRE scores are likely to be. Or SAT and GRE data (from students anticipating graduate study) can be used to predict the reading test scores that might be required for some sort of certification, or a licensure exam.

If mechanical aptitude and the tendency to be reflective thinkers are correlated with success in athletics coaching, one can gather data on aptitude and the tendency to be reflective (versus impulsive) and use those data in hiring decisions. Aptitude and reflectivity lend themselves to more ready assessment than does coaching success, a criterion that may emerge only after a good deal of time, perhaps years. Figure 12.5 contains another multiple regression problem and solution.

In this problem the specialist used the student's age and level of spatial ability to predict an algebra score. This problem is interesting because the student is well younger than the mean age for all students, about a standard

Figure 12.4   A Multiple Regression Problem

Problem: A researcher has scores for 30 graduate students from their undergraduate admissions packet (SAT verbal) and a reading placement test taken at the university during undergraduate study (Rd). The data indicate that verbal portion of the Graduate Record Exam (GRE verbal) is correlated with SAT-V and Rd. The researcher has decided to predict GRE scores from the others. What GRE-V score can the researcher predict for someone with SAT-V = 375, and Rd = 38?

In the correlation matrix we will treat SAT-V as x_1, Rd as x_2, and GRE-V as y:

	x_1	x_2	y
x_1		.919	.833
x_2	.919		.736
y	.833	.736	

Descriptive Statistics:

	Mean	Standard Deviation
SAT-V	438.0	98.441
Rd	52.75	12.502
GRE-V	465.5	108.893

$$y' = a + b_1 x_1 + b_2 x_2$$

$$a = M_y - b_1 M_{x1} - b_2 M_{x2}$$

$$b_1 = \frac{r_{y,x1} - r_{y,x2} \cdot r_{x1,x2}}{1 - r_{x1,x2}^2}(s_y/s_{x1})$$

$$= \frac{.833 - (.736)(.919)}{1 - .919^2} \cdot \frac{108.893}{98.441} = \mathbf{1.115}$$

$$b_2 = \frac{r_{y,x2} - r_{y,x1} \cdot r_{x1,x2}}{1 - r_{x1,x2}^2}(s_y/s_{x2})$$

$$= \frac{.736 - (.833)(.919)}{1 - .919^2} \cdot \frac{108.893}{12.502} = \mathbf{-1.655}$$

$$a = 465.5 - (1.115)(438) - (-1.655)(52.75) = \mathbf{64.431}$$

$$y' = a + b_1 x_1 + b_2 x_2$$

$$= 64.431 + 1.115(375) + -1.655(38) = \mathbf{419.666}$$

For one with an SAT-V score of 375 and a Reading score of 38, the predicted GRE-V score is 419.666.

Figure 12.5 Another Multiple Regression Solution

A specialist wishes to predict pre-algebra students' ability to cope with the subject with measures of students' ages and their spatial ability. Specifically, what algebra score can she predict for a 12-year-old with a spatial ability of 36?

	Mean	Std. Dev.
Algebra scores (y)	74.931	8.367
Age (x_1)	14.355	2.334
Spatial ability (x_2)	30.638	4.520

The Correlations are as follows:

	Algebra (y)	Age (x₁)	Spat Ab. (x₂)
Algebra (y)	1.0	.538	.724
Age (x_1)	.538	1.0	.337
Spat Ab (x_2)	.724	.337	1.0

The correlations are in a "correlation matrix." It's a compact way to see the correlation of all with all. Of course each variable is perfectly correlated with itself ($r = 1.0$). Note that each possible correlation appears twice. The formulae are:

$$y' = a + b_1 x_1 + b_2 x_2$$

$$a = M_y - b_1 M_{x1} - b_2 M_{x2}$$

$$b_1 = \frac{r_{y,x1} - r_{y,x2} \cdot r_{x1,x2}}{1 - r_{x1,x2}^2}(s_y / s_{x1})$$

$$b_2 = \frac{r_{y,x2} - r_{y,x1} \cdot r_{x1,x2}}{1 - r_{x1,x2}^2}(s_y / s_{x2})$$

Solving for y' we will calculate the regression coefficients first.

$$b_1 = \frac{.538 - .724 \cdot .337}{1 - .337^2} \cdot \frac{8.367}{2.334} = \mathbf{1.189}$$

$$b_2 = \frac{.724 - .538 \cdot .337}{1 - .337^2} \cdot \frac{8.367}{4.520} = \mathbf{1.133}$$

Then the intercept (regression constant):

$$a = 74.931 - (1.189)(14.355) - (1.133)(30.638) = \mathbf{23.150}$$

and finally the predicted value of y:

$$y' = 23.150 + 1.189(12) + 1.133(36) = \mathbf{78.206}$$

In spite of a young age relative to the other students, the relatively high level of spatial ability that this student possesses makes it likely that he or she will do better than the average student in algebra.

deviation younger as it turns out, but had spatial ability well above the mean for the group. Because age is less well correlated with algebra scores than spatial ability and the student's measure of spatial ability is quite high, the resulting algebra score predicted is higher than the mean for all students.

A Comment About SPSS Output

In the SPSS appendix, there are directions for completing a multiple regression problem using the software. The output for a multiple regression problem provides unstandardized coefficients, symbolized by B or b, as well as standardized coefficients indicated by "beta," or its symbol, β. The unstandardized values are what we calculated. They are based on raw scores. As perhaps you guessed, the standardized regression coefficients are based on the z score equivalents of the raw scores.

The reason for providing both coefficients is that although they're less work to compute, comparing unstandardized regression coefficients can be deceptive because they are affected by the magnitude and variability of the raw scores. The reading test scores in Figure 12.4 have a potential range of 20 to 80 points (although that isn't evident from the example), and a standard deviation of about 12.5. The SAT scores, conversely, range from 200 to 800, with a standard deviation of nearly 100. These differences impact the related b values and can result in unstandardized regression coefficients which, when compared directly with each other to determine which might be the most important, are misleading. But with all score magnitudes and variability statistics based on a common scale, the β coefficients can be compared directly with each other. (Recall that z scores always have a mean of 0 and a standard deviation of 1.0 regardless of the range of the original raw scores.)

The Standard Error of the Multiple Estimate

Although we introduced multiple correlation (R) as the statistic we need in order to gauge the relationship between multiple predictors and a criterion variable, it isn't needed in order to calculate a regression solution. It's notably absent from everything we've done to now, except for actually calculating multiple correlations. But it does have another use. Multiple correlation is an integral part of estimating the error in a multiple regression prediction.

With simple regression, we used the standard error of measurement. Here, we'll use the **standard error of multiple estimate**, SE_{mest}. The only difference between the two is the use of R instead of the Pearson Correlation, r.

$$SE_{mest} = s_y \sqrt{(1 - R^2_{y,x1x2})}$$

12.8

■ The **standard error of multiple estimate** estimates error in a multiple regression solution.

Where,

s_y = the standard deviation of the criterion variable

$R^2_{y,x1x2}$ = the multiple correlation of the criterion variable with the two predictors

The first task is to determine the value of R. Using Formula 12.1:

$$R_{y,x1x2} = \sqrt{\frac{r^2_{yx1} + r^2_{yx2} - 2r_{yx1}r_{yx2}r_{x1x2}}{1 - r^2_{x1x2}}}$$

Table 12.1   Correlations, Means, and Standard Deviations

Correlation Matrix						
	SAT-V	SAT-M	GRE-V	GRE-Q	Rdg	Math
SAT-V	1.0	.726	.833	.598	.919	.714
SAT-M	.726	1.0	.767	.857	.734	.894
GRE-V	.833	.767	1.0	.686	.736	.740
GRE-Q	.598	.857	.686	1.0	.534	.852
Rdg	.919	.734	.736	.534	1.0	.675
Math	.714	.894	.740	.852	.675	1.0

Descriptive Statistics		
Test	Mean	Std.Dev.
SAT-V	438.000	98.441
SAT-M	468.500	109.317
GRE-V	465.500	108.893
GRE-Q	485.000	116.144
Reading	52.750	12.502
Math	54.850	15.250

Substituting the values from the correlation matrix in Table 12.1 we have,

$$R_{y,x1x2} = \sqrt{\frac{.833^2 + .736^2 - 2(.833)(.736)(.919)}{1 - .919^2}} = .836$$

As an aside to calculating R, if the square root is omitted, the result is R^2, which is what we need for the standard error of multiple estimate.

Now the standard error of multiple estimate:

$$SE_{mest} = S_y \sqrt{(1 - R^2_{y,x1x2})}$$

$$= 108.893\sqrt{(1 - 836^2} = \mathbf{59.753}$$

The Confidence Interval for y'

The SE_{mest} suggests the size of the error in a multiple regression solution just as the SE_{est} did for simple regression, and the value is often used the same way, in a confidence interval. It answers this question: Within what range of values is there a specified probability (usually .95) of finding the *true* value of y which corresponds with these predictor scores? Just as before, the strength of the correlation (R) the variability in y, and the size of the sample dictate the magnitude of the confidence interval.

Substituting SE_{mest} for the SE_{est} in Formula 11.5, for a .95 CI we have:

$$CI = +/- t \ (SE_{mest}) + y'$$

For $n = 30$, the degrees of freedom for t are 28, and the critical value from Table B is $t = 2.048$. For the problem in Figure 12.4 the confidence interval then is:

$$CI = +/- 2.048 \ (59.753) + 419.666$$

$$= 297.292, 542.040$$

With $p = .95$, the GRE-V score for someone with a SAT-V score of 375 and a reading score of 38 (Figure 12.4) is somewhere between the rounded values of 297 and 542. One can see from the way the formula is set up that the predicted value will always be in the middle of the confidence interval. In this case, because the sample is relatively small ($n = 30$) and there is a good deal of variability in the data (the large standard deviation of y), the answer isn't particularly precise, but it's better than a guess.

Another Confidence Interval Example

Using the predicting algebra performance data from Figure 12.5 the specialist can now calculate a confidence interval for the predicted algebra score. For a .95 CI,

First the specialist must determine the multiple correlation, $R_{y.12}$.

$$R_{y.12} = \sqrt{\frac{r_{y1}^2 + r_{y2}^2 - 2r_{y1}r_{y2}r_{12}}{1 - r_{12}^2}}$$

$$\sqrt{\frac{538^2 + .724^2 - 2(.538)(.724)(.337)}{1 - .337^2}} = .788$$

Then the SE_{mest}

$$SE_{mest} = S_y\sqrt{1 - R_{y.12}^2}$$

$$= 8.367\sqrt{1 - .788^2} = 5.151$$

If the specialist has data for 47 students, then the t value for $df = 45$ is 2.014, and the confidence interval can be completed as follows:

$$CI = +/-t\ (SE_{mest}) + y'$$

$$CI = +/- 2.014\ (5.151) + 78.206 = 88.580,\ 67.832$$

Incidentally, what happens to the confidence interval if the specialist needs more certainty of capturing the true value of y in the interval? Remember that the level of probability and the need for precision in the estimate pull the confidence interval in opposite directions. As the probability increases (as one must be more certain of including the actual value of y), the interval must increase and precision is reduced. An interval for the algebra student's score at $p = .99$ rather than .95 results in the following:

$$CI = +/-t\ (SE_{mest}) + y'$$

$$CI = +/- 2.690\ (5.151) + 78.206 = 92.062,\ 64.350$$

What changed was the critical value of t, which at $p = .01$ and $df = 45$ is 2.690 rather than the earlier 2.014. That substitution into the calculation results, inevitably, in the wider interval.

The standard error of the multiple estimate and the confidence interval provide a way to gauge the precision of a multiple regression solution. Such estimates are important because the value of y', because it is a discrete value, sometimes creates the impression of a higher level of precision than the data allow one to deliver. The y' value is a better-than-chance estimate, but the SE_{mest} and confidence intervals keep us grounded by reminding us that a prediction may or may not be particularly precise.

Overfitting the Data and Shrinkage

■ In regression a solution is **overfitted** when the solution doesn't generalize well from the sample upon which it was based, to the general population.

■ **Shrinkage** is the degree to which a regression solution loses predictive accuracy when it is applied to new data.

In a problem related to prediction error, regression solutions usually fit the particular sample for which they are calculated data better than they fit the population; the solution may be **overfitted** to the sample. The risk of overfitting is greatest when:

• The ratio of number of predictors to number of cases is large
• Sample sizes are relatively small
• The sample isn't randomly selected

If a solution is overfitted, the decline in predictive accuracy for other samples is called **shrinkage**. Although analyzing shrinkage is beyond the scope of this book, Pedhazur and Schmelkin (1991) have a very readable discussion.

Significance Tests

When we looked at SPSS in Chapter 11, we noted that the software automatically calculates an *ANOVA* test for the significance of the correlation between predictor(s) and criterion and t-tests for each of the regression coefficients. The *ANOVA* can be viewed as a significance test of the entire model—all predictors. The t-tests are tests of the individual predictors.

In the case of the *ANOVA*, a significance value of .05 or less means that collectively the predictors (the x variables) are significantly correlated with the criterion variable, y, and so can provide a statistically significant prediction of the value of that variable. In the case of the t-test, a statistically significant result means that each individual x is a better-than-chance predictor of the value of the criterion variable, y.

In multiple regression analysis, the whole is sometimes greater than the sum of its parts. It is possible to have a significant model even though none of the partial regression coefficients is significant. That may prompt the temptation to revise the model because one or more of the predictors fails to reach significance. The risk is that removing a predictor may alter the relationship between the other predictor(s) and the criterion variable. In some instances removing what appears to be a nonsignificant predictor may weaken the model as a whole. The gain in economy may come at the risk of a model that predicts the value of the criterion variable less well.

SUMMARY

Multiple regression provides the advantage of using multiple independent variables in order to make a more accurate prediction of the dependent, or criterion, variable than just one predictor can provide. The ability to do this, however, depends on having a correlation procedure that allows multiple x variables to be correlated with one y. This was the niche that multiple correlation, R, fills. The R procedure responds to one of the questions raised at the beginning of the chapter.

The problem related to using multiple predictors is that variables correlated with the value to be predicted are also often correlated with each other. This introduces redundancy in the information available in the prediction. Specifically, the issue was how to use multiple predictors and extract only the information from each that was unique to that variable. We illustrated the task with partial application where two variables can be correlated while holding a third, with which they are both correlated, out of both. We applied that to regression when we calculated partial regression coefficients.

Even with multiple predictors there will be error in the prediction. With simple, or bivariate, regression the amount of error was gauged with the standard error of the estimate (SE_{est}). For multiple regression the equivalent statistic is the standard error of the multiple estimate (SE_{mest}). That statistic can then be used to calculate a confidence interval, which will indicate by determining the size of the interval within which y' is likely to occur, the precision of the estimate.

In any regression procedure, the quality of the result is partly a function of the size of the sample and the number of predictors. When sample sizes are relatively small, the number of predictors, relatively large, the researcher runs the risk of a good deal of "shrinkage" in the solution. It occurs when the solution is tailored too closely to the sample to be of equal value for other data drawn from the related population.

Multiple regression comes up again in Chapter 16 where some different approaches to using multiple predictors are mentioned, but let us not get ahead of ourselves. Having weathered regression, this is a good time to take the academic equivalent of the seventh inning stretch. Well done! You have navigated some very important material and emerged, if not masters of your universes, at least captains of your statistical fates. Nearly every more advance statistical test or technique that the reader is likely to encounter will bear some sort of family resemblance to multiple regression. It represents a very important analytical tool. An ad campaign used to ask "Where do you want to go from here?" It's a good question for someone with a working knowledge of multiple regression because the analytical possibilities are nearly limitless.

EXERCISES

1. Using the data in Table 12.1, determine the multiple correlation (R) of GRE-Q (y), with SAT-M (x_1) and the math test (x_2).

2. What is the correlation between GRE-Q and the math test, if SAT-M is controlled in both of the other two?

   If a college applicant has SAT-V = 490 and reading = 46:

   a. What GRE-V score is predicted?
   b. Why is it risky to try to determine which of those two predictors is best, based on the comparative values of the regression coefficients?

3. What term in a multiple regression solution indicates the value of the criterion variable, when both the predictor variables have values of 0?

4. What does it mean to "overfit" a sample in regression?

5. If $R = .749$ and $s_y = 4.683$, $SE_{mest} = ?$

6. If $y' = 16.745$ and $n = 52$, calculate a .99 confidence interval using the data from item 6.

7. If $R = 0$, what will be the value of the SE_{mest}?

8. From the data in Table 12.1:

   a. What GREQ score is the best prediction for someone for whom Rdg. = 60 and Math = 62?
   b. How is it that a reading measure can predict a quantitative ability (GREQ) value?
   c. What will a .95 confidence interval be for the problem in (a) if the sample has $n = 32$?

9. If one moves from a .95 to a .99 confidence interval for a regression solution, what happens to the width of the interval? Why?

10. What are the factors that explain the magnitude of the standard error of the estimate?

11. What do standardized regression coefficients allow that unstandardized coefficients make problematic?

REFERENCES

Diekhoff, G. (1992). *Statistics for the social and behavior sciences: Univariate, bivariate, and multivariate.* Dubuque, IA: William C. Brown Publishers.

Pedhazur, E. J., & Schmelkin, L. P. (1991). *Measurement, design, and analysis: An integrated approach.* Hillsdale, NJ: Lawrence Erlbaum.

THE FORMULAE AND THEIR SYMBOLS

Formula 12.1: $R_{y,12} = \sqrt{((r_{y1}^2 + r_{y2}^2 - 2r_{y1}r_{y2}r_{12})/1 - r_{y12}^2)}$

This is the formula for multiple correlation. It is used when the question is of the relationship between two or more x variables, and a y variable.

Formula 12.2: $r_{y1.2} = r_{y,1} - r_{y,2}r_{1,2}$

This is the formula for partial correlation. It indicates the $\sqrt{(1-r_{y,2}^2)(1-r_{1,2}^2)}$ correlation between the "y" and the "x_1" when the influence of the "x_2" variable is ruled out.

Formula 12.3: $y' = a + b_1x_1 + b_2x_2 + \ldots + b_kx_k$

This is the formula for multiple regression when there are any number of predictors from 2 to k.

Formula 12.4: $y' = a + b_1x_1 + b_2x_2$

This is the formula for multiple regression when there are two predictor variables (x_1 and x_2).

Formula 12.5: $a = M_y - b_1M_{x1} - b_2M_{x2}$

This is the formula for the intercept, or the constant value in multiple regression.

Formula 12.6: $b_1 = \dfrac{\left(r_{y,x1} - r_{y,x2}r_{x1,x2}\right)s_y}{(1-r_{x1,x2}^2)\,s_{x1}}$

This is the formula for the first regression coefficient in a multiple regression analysis with two predictors.

Formula 12.7: $b_2 = \dfrac{(r_{y2} - r_{y1}r_{x1,x2})s_y}{(1-r_{x1,x2}^2)\,s_{x2}}$

This is the formula for the second regression coefficient in a multiple regression analysis with two predictors.

Formula 12.8: $SE_{mest} = S_y\sqrt{(1-R_{y,x1x2}^2)}$

The standard error of multiple estimate is the estimate of prediction error in a multiple regression problem.

STUDENT STUDY SITE

Visit the Student Study Site at **www.sagepub.com/tanner** for additional learning tools.

PART V

Tests for Nominal and Ordinal Data

Chapter 13

SOME OF THE
CHI-SQUARE TESTS

THE PROBLEM: HOW TO ANALYZE NOMINAL DATA

Although a state university serves students from throughout the nation and from several foreign nations, the enrollment is drawn primarily from a five-county area. A dean of admissions wonders whether enrollments are consistent with populations in those counties.

The university sponsors a writing lab for students who must meet a senior writing requirement before graduation. University officials responsible for administering the program are interested in whether the students' majors have something to do with who comes to the lab for help.

There is another question related to students' majors. With many international students, and even some domestic students who speak English as a second language, researchers have asked whether such students pick majors in fields where language may be less of an obstacle than it might be in the humanities or the social sciences.

QUESTIONS AND ANSWERS

❏ Questions about county-by-county differences in the proportions of students who enroll call for the goodness-of-fit *chi*-square test. It's a test for significant differences in nominal data when there is just one variable.
❏ Add a second nominal scale variable for individuals from the same sample (the number of students who seek help versus those who don't, *and* their majors) and the *chi*-square test of independence is the relevant procedure.
❏ Although the issues above appeal to the hypothesis of difference, the relationship between major and language status relates to the hypothesis of association. *Phi* coefficient and Cramer's *V* both quantify the relationship between nominal variables.

✦ – ✦ – ✦

T
he 19th-century British statesman Disraeli observed that what we anticipate seldom occurs and what we least expect generally happens (The Oxford Dictionary, 1980). Some of the analytical tools reviewed in this chapter seem designed precisely for someone who wishes to check the veracity of Disraeli's statement; they let one analyze the differences between what is expected and what actually occurs. (Just so you have a context for him, this is the same Disraeli who noted that there are three kinds of lies: lies, damned lies, and statistics!)

In Chapter 2 we distinguished among descriptive statistics in part according to the scale of the data the statistics describe. For nominal data, for example, only the mode (M_o) makes sense as a measure of central tendency. The discussion we've followed since that point is that it isn't only descriptive statistics that are specific to the scale of the data. The more involved analytical procedures are also often data scale dependent. Recall that the dependent variable in a t-test, a z test, and in the *ANOVA* must be at least interval scale. These distinctions are very important and in fact the scale of the data, along with the nature of the hypothesis (difference or association), and the relationships between the groups involved are guide posts to what is the appropriate statistical test.

The analytical tools in this chapter are quite different from most of what we've done previously. All the analytical procedures to this point are based on assumptions that certain conditions prevail, conditions related to the normality of the data, the equality of groups' variances, the linearity of the data, and so on. But what happens if samples are so small that one can't be confident of their representativeness? What if the data lack the required measurement scale, or they are badly skewed? When we can't satisfy important assumptions about the quality of the data the answer is to move to tests with more relaxed requirements. The *chi*-square tests are "distribution-free," which means we need make no assumptions about how the data are distributed, and there are no requirements regarding their scale. The consequence is a good deal of flexibility in statistical analysis. There are some things we give up, certainly, and we'll discuss drawbacks as we go, but *chi*-square procedures are very common in educational decision making.

THE *CHI*-SQUARE TESTS

Formally the Pearson *chi*-square (yes, the "Pearson Correlation" Pearson, and no, you won't ever be free of him), this is actually one of several tests based on *chi*-square statistics. The particular tests of interest here were suggested by the questions from the beginning of the chapter.

The Goodness-of-Fit *Chi*-Square

If the question is whether the students entering the university represent the counties in the service area in equal proportions, we might proceed as follows. Select a group of enrollees from the service area, determine the county where they resided prior to college, and evaluate the totals from each county for significant differences. In fact, this is what the *chi*-square **goodness-of-fit** test does.

Also called the $1 \times k$ *chi*-square ("one by kay kie square"), in this procedure there is just one variable, thus the "1," divided into any number of categories (k). In our example, the one variable is the student's county. Don't confuse the number of counties (5) with the number of variables (1). It's like treating gender as a variable. Although it has two manifestations (male and female), gender is just one variable.

The measurement part of this process is a matter of sorting the subjects into the county they originally called home and then counting the number in each (which is why nominal data are often called "count" data). What's really at issue is frequency, the frequency with which subjects occur in certain categories. The *chi*-square tests are frequency tests. There aren't degrees of anything related to the county—no one is trying to gauge feelings about whose county provides the highest standard of living, or the best air quality, or the lowest unemployment. The only issue is whether the frequency of students representing each county is different.

The goodness-of-fit name is quite revealing, as it turns out. With this test we determine how well what is observed fits with what we expected to see; the issue is how "good" the results fit. We compare what was observed in the study with what one could have expected to see based on some theory or presupposition. The analysis is the comparison of the two. It's a measure of the "goodness" with which the sample conforms to the expectation. When the gap between observation and expectation becomes large enough, the result is statistically significant, a decision we'll reach by referring to (yet) another table of critical values, this one for the *chi*-square distribution, Table F at the back of the book.

To determine whether students represent the five counties in roughly equal proportions, the university official randomly selects a group of 95 university students and finds that 60 of them come from the five-county service area. She then examines the admissions applications for those 60 students to determine the county in which each student attended high school. The data set below is the result:

Card County.................15

Mountain View County.........8

■ The **goodness-of-fit** *chi*-square, analyzes differences between what is expected and what is observed.

Stirling County.................12

Garden County.................10

Welling County................15

With the counts ranging from 8 to 15, it's easy to see that there are county-to-county differences. The issue is whether the divergence from the expected equality is sufficient to be statistically significant, or could any differences be just the random variations that can occur any time one draws a sample.

Calculating the Test Statistic

The *chi*-square test statistic takes the following form:

$$\chi^2 = \frac{\Sigma (f_o - f_e)^2}{f_e}$$ 13.1

Where,

χ^2 = *chi*-square

f_o = the frequency observed

f_e = the frequency expected

An easy way to calculate the *1 × k* is to create a table like Table 13.1. Each of the rows in the table represents a step in calculating the χ^2 value. The first row, designated f_o, is for the "frequency observed" data. These are the county-by-county values from the list above. Once counted, just plug them in on the first row (how easy was that?). This is always the case with 1 × k problems; the f_o values will be the frequency, or the count, of those actually occurring in the particular category of the variable.

The f_e values are based on what one expects to see, given certain considerations. One consideration in this particular problem is whether the counties have similar populations to begin with, or whether economic conditions are similar in both counties. If Card County is twice as populous as Garden County, or Garden County is made up of blue-collar communities where the tradition of higher education is weaker, it's probably untenable to expect equal numbers of enrollees from the two. For this example, however, we'll assume that for whatever reason, it's expected that there will be equivalent numbers of students from each county.

If there are factors other than population differences that would make it logical to assume that more students would come from one county than from another, an adjustment needs to be made in the f_e values. Perhaps the proximities to the university differ. If Stirling county is 50 miles closer to the university than Welling (and gasoline prices continue to rise), this might affect enrollment. We'll assume that these other conditions are equal across counties and then come back to this issue later in the chapter. If there is no reason to expect differences from category to category,

$f_e = N/k$

Where,

N = the total of all subjects in all categories

k = the number of categories

So, for the problem in Table 13.1 where $N = 60$ and $k = 5$

$f_e = 60 \div 5 = \mathbf{12}$ in each category

Solving the *chi*-square formula is done by just following the order of mathematical operations, ("<u>P</u>lease <u>e</u>xcuse my <u>d</u>ear <u>a</u>unt . . ."). In case you want them, the steps are:

1. Line 1, the f_o values based on observed frequencies.

2. Line 2, the f_e values. When categories are equivalent, $f_e = N/k$.

3. Line 3, for each category, subtract from the f_o value the corresponding f_e.

4. Line 4, square the $f_o - f_e$ difference in each category.

5. Line 5, for each category, divide the squared difference by f_e.

6. Line 6, sum the Step 5 results across the categories. This is the χ^2 value.

7. Compare χ^2 with the Table F value for the appropriate probability and $k - 1$ (the number of categories, minus one) degrees of freedom.

The Chi-*Square Hypotheses*

Like all statistical hypotheses, the null and alternate hypotheses in *chi*-square problems refer to unobserved populations. The null hypothesis is that

Table 13.1 The $1 \times k$ Chi-Square

The data are as follows:

Card County.........................15
Mountain View County..........8
Stirling County.....................12
Garden County....................10
Welling County...................15

Following the steps outlined above:

statistic	Card	Mountain	Stirling	Garden	Welling
f_o	15	8	12	10	15
f_e	12	12	12	12	12
$f_o - f_e$	3	−4	0	−2	3
$(f_o - f_e)^2$	9	16	0	4	9
$(f_o - f_e)^2/f_e$	.75	1.33	0	.33	.75
χ^2	= .75 + 1.33 + 0 + .33 + .75 = 3.16				

the frequency observed equals the frequency expected, which means that in the population there will be no difference between what is counted and what one can be expected to see.

The alternate hypothesis is that what occurs in the population is different from what was expected. Symbolically, the hypotheses can be written this way:

$$H_o: f_o = f_e$$

$$H_A: f_o \neq f_e$$

Interpreting the Test Statistic

Recall that the value of t in an independent t-test was a function of the difference between the means of Group 1 and Group 2. The F statistic in *ANOVA* measured the differences between individual groups' means and what we called the grand mean, the mean of all. The magnitude of the *chi*-square statistic indicates the size of the difference between what was observed in the sample (f_o) and what was expected (f_e). For the problem in Table 13.1, we found that $\chi^2 = 3.16$. The table value for $p = .05$ and 4 degrees of freedom (5 counties, -1) = 9.49. So to finish out the Table 13.1 problem, we enter the following:

$$\chi^2 = 3.16$$

$$\chi^2_{.05(4)} = 9.49. \text{ Fail to reject } H_o.$$

The county-to-county differences aren't statistically significant.

Incidentally, like Table A, most *chi*-square tables round to two decimals. It's a convention we'll follow here as well.

A 1 × k (Goodness-of-Fit) *Chi*-Square Problem With Unequal f_e Values

In the "which county do the students come from" problem we assumed that students would represent the five counties equally, but sometimes f_e values aren't equal. Perhaps the Dean of Admissions has been tracking international admissions among students from two nations in the same region of the world. Some research reveals that the government from nation B subsidizes the students' education costs so that they contribute only half as much of their own funds as students from nation A. Based on this, the admissions officer assumes that there will be twice as many students from nation B as from nation A. This requires a change in the way the f_e values are calculated.

Perhaps a sample of 150 students is taken and 27 of those students come from the two nations in question. The data for the other 123 students are discarded since they're not from the two nations. Of the 27 that remain, 11 are from nation A and the other 16 are from nation B.

Just as with the first problem, the 11 and 16 numbers represent the f_o values. That's the easy part. Because nation B is expected to produce twice as many students as nation A the f_e values can't be equal.

Calculating f_e Values for Unequal Categories

First of all, note that both the frequencies *observed* across the categories, and the frequencies *expected* across the categories, must each sum to the total number of individuals involved in the analysis:

$$\Sigma f_o = N, \text{ and}$$

$$\Sigma f_e = N$$

We can determine the f_e values with a little algebra.

1. Let x be the f_e for nation A.

2. Since we expect twice as many from nation B, let $2x$ be the f_e for nation B.

Because the f_e values must total N, we have

$x + 2x = 27$.

It follows then that $3x = 27$,

and $x = 27/3 = 9$.

Back to the first step,

for nation A, $f_e = 9$,

and for nation B, $f_e = 18$ ($2 \times 9 = 18$).

Now we can proceed to solve for the *chi*-square value (Table 13.2).

Table 13.2   A Second *1 × k* Chi-Square

Statistic	Nation A	Nation B
f_o	11	16
f_e	9	18
$f_o - f_e$	2	−2
$(f_o - f_e)^2$	4	4
$(f_o - f_e)^2/f_e$	.44	.22
χ^2	= .44 + .22 = .66	

$\chi^2 = .66$
$\chi^2_{.05(1)} = 3.84$. Fail to reject H_o.

Interpreting the Results

The result is not statistically significant and so we fail to reject. What does it mean to not reject the null hypothesis in this case when the f_e categories aren't equal? Because the null hypothesis is that the sample data will agree with the expectation ($f_o = f_e$), and the expectation was that there will be twice as many students from nation B as from A, that's our conclusion. Results don't differ enough from that expectation that we can reject that possibility. Although there aren't quite twice as many nation B as nation A students in the sample, the variation from that "1:2" ratio isn't extreme enough to prompt rejecting the null hypothesis.

To pursue this for a minute, some informal data gathering might suggest that nursing students prefer a written exam 4:1 over an oral exam. If one were to test that hypothesis in a *chi*-square problem, the f_e value for written would need to have value 4 times greater than that for oral exams. In that case, *rejecting* the null hypothesis means that the data oblige one to conclude that students *don't* prefer written exams to oral exams by a factor of 4, but by some other ratio.

Another 1 × k Problem With Equal Categories

In the first problem where we examined county-to-county differences, the expectation was that there would be no differences among the counties, a position we couldn't reject. Here, conversely, the null hypothesis was an expectation of a difference between the numbers of students from the different countries. We adjusted the f_e values accordingly and ended up again failing to reject the null hypothesis, but note that the null hypotheses provided for quite different outcomes in those two problems.

Figure 13.1 presents another goodness-of-fit problem with equal categories.

Don't be distracted by the fact that this problem has f_e values that aren't whole numbers ("How can one expect to see 10.6 people in a category?"). Remember that what's at issue here is how much what *is* observed differs from the expectation. In this case, the divergence is statistically significant. The number of students reporting to the writing lab for help is significantly different from the expectation that students with different academic majors will come to the lab with equal frequency.

The *Chi*-Square and Statistical Power

Chi-square procedures are distribution-free (no normality assumptions), and they can be used with small samples. Consequently, they provide tremendous

Figure 13.1   Another *1 × k Chi*-Square Problem

At the beginning of the chapter there was another question about whether university students of various majors seek help at the writing lab at significantly different levels. In a particular week, 53 people come to the lab for help:

7 from English,

13 from math,

10 from history,

18 from biology, and

5 from music.

	English	Math	History	Biology	Music
f_o	7	13	10	18	5
f_e	10.6	10.6	10.6	10.6	10.6
$f_o - f_e$	−3.6	2.4	−.6	7.4	−5.6
$(f_o - f_e)^2$	12.96	5.76	.36	54.76	31.36
$(f_o - f_e)^2/f_e$	1.22	.54	.03	5.16	2.96
Σ	1.22 + .54 + .03 + 5.16 + 2.96 = 9.91, χ^2 = 9.91				

$\chi^2_{.05(4)}$ = 9.49, reject Ho. $f_o \neq f_e$

The fact that the f_e values are all equal indicates an important assumption in the analysis. It suggests that we expect that the number of students who declare the different majors is roughly equivalent to begin with. We would not have equal f_e values if we knew that there were 10 times as many biology majors as music majors, for example.

flexibility, but in the statistical equivalent of the "there's no such thing as a free lunch," there's a downside. The cost an analyst pays for the *chi*-square's flexibility is reduced power. The first two problems we completed indicated that departures from the $f_o = f_e$ position must be rather extreme before the differences become statistically significant.

In the first problem, the expectation was that there would be equal numbers of students from all counties. The differences ranged from a low of

8 to a high of 15 around a mean of 12. Even that much variability produced a value of *chi*-square that wasn't close to significant. In the second problem, the prediction was that of 27 students, nation A should have about 9 and nation B about 18, a 1:2 ratio. For the sample data with 11 (A) and 16 (B) the *chi*-square value was .66 compared with a table (F) value of 3.84. These results have much to do with the fact that the data involved are nominal scale. Such data provide relatively little information about what is measured— less than ordinal, interval, or ratio data provide. Less information in this situation translates into less power in the related statistical testing.

When dealing with the hypothesis of difference, the more sensitive the test is to differences, the greater its power. *Chi*-square is very flexible, but not particularly powerful when compared with parametric alternatives, but then that's really not an issue since the other tests aren't appropriate alternatives when their assumptions regarding normality, equality of variance, and so on can't be satisfied.

Conversely, remember that type I and type II errors are related. As the potential for one is reduced, the probability that the other will occur rises. Although the *chi*-square tests sometimes lack power, they do offer control of type I error. One is less likely than with some other statistical tests to erroneously detect a significant difference.

Looking at SPSS Output

If we let SPSS do the Figure 13.1 problem, we get the following output:

Help

	Observed *N*	Expected *N*	Residual
1	7	10.6	−3.6
2	13	10.6	2.4
3	10	10.6	−.6
4	18	10.6	7.4
5	5	10.6	−5.6
Total	53		

Test Statistics

	help
Chi-Square	9.925
Df	4
Asymp. Sig.	.042

What we called f_o, SPSS calls "Observed N," and its "Expected N" is our f_e. The "Residual" is the difference between the two, our $f_o - f_e$. The value of the *chi*-square statistic in the second table differs from ours slightly because of rounding. The "Asymp. Sig." indicates that there are 42/1000 chances that this value of *chi*-square could have occurred by chance. By the usual standard ($p = .05$), it's statistically significant, just as we concluded in the longhand calculations.

SOURCE: Created by Suzanna Nielson.

"The difference between what my grades are and what you expected isn't statistically significant!"

THE *CHI*-SQUARE TEST OF INDEPENDENCE

In the problems so far, there has been just one variable at a time in the analysis because the goodness-of-fit *chi*-square is limited to just one variable, although it can be divided into any number of categories. If the data had been interval scale and the normality assumptions were satisfied, the alternative could have been a one-way *ANOVA*, but the data were nominal.

Sometimes the information that one variable provides isn't enough to answer the question. One of the examples above involved a hypothesis that nursing students prefer written to oral exams. Maybe the nursing students' ages are also a factor, with older students more confident in their ability to deal with oral exams than the younger students. The multiple variables problems have come up before and are the reason, for example, for the transition from one-way *ANOVA* to the factorial *ANOVA* in Chapter 12. In the *chi*-square tests there's a rough equivalent of the factorial *ANOVA*, but for nominal data. It's the ***chi*-square test of independence**.

Remember that when we added additional variables to the *ANOVA*, *one* of the justifications for just not doing separate one-way *ANOVAs* was that sometimes multiple variables act in concert, an effect which we'd miss if the variables were analyzed independently. This can also occur with nominal data. When there are two variables at work, we have a chance to look at whether they operate independently, or whether one affects the other. This is the thinking behind the *chi*-square test of independence, also called the *r* × *k chi*-square.

■ The *chi*-square test of independence tests whether two variables in a **contingency table's** rows and columns operate independently.

AN EXAMPLE PROBLEM

As the school year begins, a school nurse is trying to make up her mind about recommending that students receive flu shots. She is skeptical because she thinks whether or not students receive them is related to their economic circumstances. To examine that assumption systematically, she gathers a sample of 15 students who are eligible for free lunch, and a second sample of 15 students who are not. She then interviews them to determine whether they received flu shots during the prior year. Among those who are eligible for free lunch, she discovers that 2 of 15 received flu shots the prior year. In the other group, 7 received flu shots.

The two variables, whether students received flu shots, and their economic circumstances, changes the way the f_e values are calculated. In fact the way the data are organized in a problem like this makes it look a little like a two-way *ANOVA*.

The Contingency Table

To accommodate the way the f_e values are determined, a **contingency table** helps us organize the data. In the alternate name for this procedure, the "*r*" in "*r* × *k chi*-square" refers to rows, and the *k* still refers to categories, so the contingency table is a "rows by categories" table (Table 13.3A). With the rows representing the different economic levels of the students, and the columns representing their flu shot history, there is a cell for each possible combination of the two variables.

Table 13.3 The $r \times k$ Chi-Square

A. The Contingency Table

	Flu Shot	No Flu Shot	Row Totals
Qualified for free lunch	a 2	b 13	15
Did not qualify	c 7	d 8	15
Column totals	9	21	N = 30

B. The f_e Values

The cell	Row Total	Column Total	Row × Col	÷ N
a	15	9	135	4.5
b	15	21	315	10.5
c	15	9	135	4.5
d	15	21	315	10.5

C. The Analysis

Statistic	a	b	c	d
f_o	2	13	7	8
f_e	4.5	10.5	4.5	10.5
$f_o - f_e$	−2.5	2.5	2.5	−2.5
$(f_o - f_e)^2$	6.25	6.25	6.25	6.25
$(f_o - f_e)^2/f_e$	1.39	.60	1.39	.60
χ^2	= 1.39 + .60 + 1.39 + .60 = 3.98			

Since there are 15 in each of the economic groups, the rows each total 15. The individual column totals *don't* equal 15 since the number of students who received flu shots differs from the number who didn't, but the sum of the column totals must still equal the value of N, since the sum of those who did and those who did receive flu shots must equal 30.

The f_o and f_e Values in the *Chi*-Square Test of Independence

For the analysis, the four cells in the contingency table are something like the categories in the *1 × k*. The count of the number of individuals that belong to each cell is the f_o value for each combination of economic circumstance and flu shot status. All that is lacking for the calculation of the x^2 is the f_e values, and the contingency table will help us get them.

Remember that what's at issue with this test is whether the two variables operate independently of each other. Pearson tested their independence by comparing what is observed in the particular cell with what is most probable under the circumstances when the variables are unrelated, which is why the null hypothesis is that there is no relationship between the variables. If the variables are not statistically independent (i.e., they're correlated), the best prediction will diverge from the observed value. In that case, $f_o \neq f_e$.

For each cell in Table 13.3B:

- f_e = the total of the row in which *that cell* occurs, times the total of the column in which *that cell* occurs, divided by the total in all cells, N.
- For cell "a", $f_e = (15 \times 9) \div 30 = 4.5$.
- This is repeated for each cell.

Once we have the f_e values for each cell, we proceed with the same table (Table 13.3C) we used for the one-variable *chi*-square.

1. Subtract f_e from f_o
2. Square the difference
3. Divide the squared difference by f_e, and so on

Degrees of Freedom for the Chi-*Square Test of Independence*

The degrees of freedom for this test are the number of rows, minus 1, times the number of columns, minus 1. Using Table 11.3C, we find that:

- $x^2 = 3.98$.
- The degrees of freedom for the test of independence are

- The number of categories of the first variable, minus one, times the number of categories of the second variable, minus one.
- For the problem in Table 13.3 that will be $df = (2 - 1) \times (2 - 1) = 1$.
- $\chi^2_{.05\,(1)} = 3.84$.

The Yates Correction

In 2×2 *chi*-square problems there is a tendency to incorrectly find significance (commit a type I error) when f_e values are low. Note that in cells "a" and "c" of the problem, both have f_e values of 4.5. An English statistician named Yates suggested subtracting .5 from each $f_o - f_e$ cell difference in 2×2 contingency table when *any one* f_e value in the table is 5 (some statisticians argue 10) or less.

The counterargument is that this "Yates correction" may in fact overcorrect making the test of independence unnecessarily conservative. The decision made for this book was not to use it, but Howell (1992) is a good source if the reader wishes to pursue the discussion.

Interpreting the *Chi*-Square Test of Independence

When the calculated value of *chi* square is larger than the table value (F) as it is here, the results are statistically significant. Recall that the null hypothesis that goodness-of-fit and *chi*-square tests of independence share is that the observation, what actually occurred, doesn't differ significantly from what one could have been expected to see, based on the information available. The null hypothesis is the symbolic way of saying that observed frequencies are in basic harmony with the most likely mathematical outcome.

In the case of this test, that mathematical outcome is based on the independence of the two variables. Accepting the null hypothesis means that cell values are not significantly different from what one would expect to see when students' economic status is unrelated to whether they get flu shots. But in this instance the value of *chi*-square *was* significant. Without knowing why (it's the causal versus correlational thing again), economic status and receiving flu shots are *not* independent of each other, which raises a question: since they are apparently related, how strong *is* the relationship between the two variables?

Phi Coefficient and Cramer's *V*

The question about the relationship between the variables changes our focus. Now, instead of questions based on the hypothesis of difference (do students of different economic means receive flu shots in different proportions?) the question is based on the hypothesis of association (what is the correlation between economic circumstances and receiving a flu shot?). The second question is only relevant because we rejected the null hypothesis related to the first question. Had we failed to reject, the conclusion would have been that there is no relationship—the variables operate independently.

To answer the second question, we need a correlation procedure that will gauge the strength of the relationship between nominal variables. There are several. Pearson developed a statistic called the coefficient of contingency, *C*, but it tends to be a very conservative estimate of the relationship and we'll introduce two others, *phi* coefficient, ϕ, and Cramer's V. The *phi* coefficient is based directly on the *chi*-square value, so by the time the independence question has been resolved, ϕ is an easy calculation.

Phi *Coefficient*

The formula for *phi* coefficient is the following:

$$\phi = \sqrt{(\chi^2 / N)} \qquad\qquad 13.2$$

Where,

χ^2 = the resulting χ^2 value from the $r \times k$ procedure

N = remains the total number of subjects

In the economic status and flu shot problem, the calculated value of $\chi^2 = 3.98$, and N = 30. Solving for ϕ we have,

$$\phi = \sqrt{\chi^2 / N} = \sqrt{(3.98 / 30)} = \sqrt{.133}$$

$$\phi = .36$$

The correlation between economic status and receiving flu shots is $\phi = .36$. The ϕ value is interpreted like any other correlation statistic. Values nearer 0 indicate a weak correlation. There is no additional set of table values for ϕ. Because it's based directly on the test of independence result, if the χ^2 value is statistically significant, so is ϕ.

Cramer's V

If either variable in a *chi*-square test of independence has more than two levels, and the χ^2 value is significant, one calculates Cramer's V. It's based on *phi* coefficient so ϕ must be calculated first. When the *chi*-square test has two levels of both variables as our example just above, $V = \phi$. The formula is as follows:

$$V = \sqrt{[\phi^2 / (\text{smaller of rows or columns}) - 1]}$$ 13.3

The problem we just did had a 2×2 contingency table so the ϕ coefficient we already calculated is the appropriate measure of association, but we can demonstrate the equivalence of the two procedures for 2×2 problems by also calculating V.

$$V = \sqrt{[\phi^2 / (\text{smaller of rows or columns}) - 1]}$$

$$V = \sqrt{[.36^2 / (2) - 1]}$$

$$V = .36$$

Another Example of the Test of Independence

Recall that another of the problems from the beginning of the chapter asked whether students' majors are related to their language status. In particular, do students who speak English as a second language tend to avoid majors that are language intensive? For the sake of the illustration, we'll say that chemistry, mathematics, and music employ symbols that are understood across language differences more readily than the language employed in such disciplines as English, history, and journalism. Among a sample of 200 students leaving the university library, we find 87 from the six majors who are willing to indicate their primary language. The data are as follows:

	total	number for whom is English 1st language
Chemistry	9	6
English	26	22
History	16	11
Journalism	8	7
Mathematics	13	7
Music	15	9

There are two variables at work here: the primary language of the student (English/not English), and the discipline the student chooses (symbolic/nonsymbolic). Now we can represent the data as follows:

Group	Total	No. Who speak English first
symbolic group	37	22
nonsymbolic group	50	40

The corresponding contingency table looks this way:

Major	Language Status		Row totals
	English is 1st	English is not 1st	
Symbolic	22 a	15 b	37
Nonsymbolic	40 c	10 d	50
Column totals	62	25	N = 87

Remember, this "test of independence" poses two questions, the second contingent on the first: (a) do major and language status operate independently, and (b) if they are not independent (if $f_o \neq f_e$), what is the strength of the relationship. Remember that we fail to reject the null hypothesis if the variables are independent and there is no statistically significant relationship. The solution for this problem is in Table 13.4.

For the major by first language problem, degrees of freedom are $(2 - 1) \times (2 - 1) = 1$. The Table F (critical) value of χ^2 with 1 degree of freedom is 3.84. With the calculated value we have the following:

$$\chi^2 = 4.39$$

$$\chi^2_{.05(1)} = 3.84.$$

Reject H_o; there is a significant difference between what was expected and what was observed. Rejecting the null hypothesis is tantamount to saying that the students' choice of major is related to whether their first language is English. *Phi* coefficient will indicate the strength of the relationship.

$$\phi = \sqrt{(\chi^2 / N)} = \sqrt{(4.39 / 87)} = .22$$

The statistically significant value for *chi*-square indicates that the two variables, primary language and major, are related, but the relationship is quite modest.

Table 13.4 A Second $r \times k$ Chi-Square

Statistic	a	b	c	d
f_o	22	15	40	10
f_e	26.37	10.63	35.63	14.37
$f_o - f_e$	−4.37	4.37	4.37	−4.37
$(f_o - f_e)^2$	19.10	19.10	19.10	19.10
$(f_o - f_e)^2/f_e$	.72	1.80	.54	1.33
χ^2	= .72 + 1.80 + .54 + 1.33 = 4.39.			

Looking at SPSS Output

If we do the Table 13.4 problem on SPSS, we get the following output:

Symb * Engl Cross-Tabulation

Count

		Engl		
		1	2	Total
Symb	1	22	15	37
	2	40	10	50
	Total	62	25	87

***Chi*-Square Tests**

	Value	df	Asymp. Sig. (2-sided)	Exact Sig. (2-sided)	Exact Sig. (1-sided)
Pearson *Chi*-Square	4.381[a]	1	.036		
Continuity Correction[b]	3.435	1	.064		
Likelihood Ratio	4.359	1	.037		
Fisher's Exact Test				.055	.032
Linear-by-Linear Association	4.331	1	.037		
N of Valid Cases	87				

Symmetric Measures

		Value	Approx. Sig.
Nominal by Nominal	*Phi*	−.224	.036
	Cramer's *V*	.224	.036
N of Valid Cases		87	

The cross-tabulation table is first and looks like the contingency table we created for the problem. In the second table, we're interested in the Pearson *chi*-square data. The value $(\chi^2 = 4.381)$ is the same as what we calculated longhand. The degrees of freedom agree with ours $(2 - 1)*(2 - 1)$, and the significance value indicates that the value of *chi*-square isn't likely to occur by chance, it's lower than $p = .05$. We can ignore the other values provided in the table.

In the last table we have the values for ϕ and for V; SPSS produces both. Because there were two levels of each variable, the two coefficients match except for the sign, which is a function of the way the values were coded in SPSS. Note that because they're both calculated based on the χ^2 value, the significance numbers for ϕ and for V are the same as they were for the χ^2 value, $p = .036$. The SPSS appendix has directions for completing *chi*-square problems on the computer.

SUMMARY

At least from the point of view offered by the *chi*-square tests, perhaps Disraeli's suspicion that what we expect usually isn't what occurs is unduly skeptical. Indeed, what these tests measure is the coherence between expectation and reality. Like the *z* tests, *t*-tests, and *ANOVA* procedures of earlier chapters, they check for significant differences, but unlike those procedures, we need to meet no assumptions about how the data are distributed. Neither do we require particularly sophisticated data. The *chi*-square tests are based on nominal data. The only measurement involved with this scale of data is counting their frequency in a particular category. The facts that the *chi*-square tests accommodate nominal data and are distribution-free makes them very flexible, but they aren't particularly powerful tests. Ordinarily, differences must be substantial before concluding that what one observed was significantly different from what one expected to see. That's less a drawback than an observation. It's not like we usually have a choice between using *chi*-square and something like *ANOVA*. When the data are nominal scale to begin with, *ANOVA* and the *t*-tests simply don't fit. Besides, the *chi*-square tests protect against higher levels of type I error.

There are also several tests for determining the strength of the relationship—the correlation—between two nominal scale variables. Two were introduced here, *phi* coefficient and Cramer's *V*. In the case of *phi* coefficient, the variables are binary—each has two levels. Cramer's *V* will accommodate more than two levels.

These are the first of several difference tests for nonparametric data we'll examine, but they are the only tests we'll cover for nominal data. In the next chapter we'll look at some hypothesis of difference tests and one test of association for ordinal data.

EXERCISES

1. A guidance counselor at a high school wants to be best informed about the universities and colleges that students prefer most frequently. He glances at the institutions attended by last years' graduates and notes that the three closest colleges appear to have about equal appeal. To test this assumption he begins asking students who are planning on postsecondary schooling where they will apply. His data are as follows:

   The technical institute: 22
   The community college: 18
   The comprehensive university: 12

   Are there significant differences in their preferences?

2. Existing research indicates that among seventh-grade history students, a tangible reward is associated with response levels twice as frequent as nontangible rewards. You decide to test this. For 3 weeks you provide verbal praise every time students ask a content-relevant question in class. During the fourth week, you count the number of questions they ask. For the next 3 weeks, you provide a small piece of candy every time someone asks a content-relevant question and then in the fourth week, you count the number of questions asked. The data are as follows: verbal praise—17 questions; tangible reward—27 questions. Do your results support the earlier research?

3. A higher education study indicates that full-time students who are not employed tend to take twice as many units as students who work full-time and 1.5 times more units than students who work part-time. If the f_e for the student who does not work is 16 units, what are the corresponding values for the part-time and full-time employees?

4. If a full-time student takes 16 units, a half-time employee takes 14 units, and a student who works full-time takes 12 units, is the hypothesis in item 3 supported?

5. A study conducted at a major university indicates that the tendency among undergraduates to seek the assistance of tutors differs by ethnic group. You select 25 subjects each from two different ethnic groups of business majors and count the number who sought help. In ethnic group A, 11 sought out tutors at some point. In ethnic group B, 17.
   a. What are the frequency expected values for each group?
   b. Do results support the earlier study?
   c. What does the alternate hypothesis suggest about the relationship between ethnicity and help-seeking?

6. Some rural, suburban, and urban students at a comprehensive university opt for graduate school. If the numbers going to graduate school are 5 of 30 urban students, 10 of 30 suburban

students, and 10 of 20 rural students, are there significant differences in those proportions? (Note that your contingency table will be a 3 × 2, or a 2 × 3)

7. What is the relationship between the location of the students' homes and their inclination to attend graduate school?

8. As a reading instructor, you supervise cross-age tutoring where older students help younger students who are struggling. In an effort to understand why some students volunteer, you notice that many are involved in charitable service outside of school. You select 8 students who tutor and 8 students from the same grade of similar academic aptitude who do not. Of the 8 tutors, 6 are involved in other charitable service. Of the 8 nontutors, 3 are involved in other charitable service. Is the relationship between willingness to tutor and other charitable service significant?

9. As a high school principal with a sociology background, you are interested in a possible relationship between the level of substance abuse among students and the families' tendency to share cultural/religious traditions. You randomly select 30 students and, with parents' permission, administer a questionnaire where students note the number of times a week family members all participate in a shared cultural or religious event. You also ask whether they have abused drugs in the last week. Group one report no religious/cultural observance. Group two report at least one religious/cultural observance per week. Group three are those who reported more than one religious/cultural observance per week. The data are as follows:

Group 1......of 12, 9 reported some substance abuse in the last week
Group 2......of 9, 6 reported some abuse
Group 3......of 9, 2 reported some abuse

   a. What does the null hypothesis predict about the relationship between family observance and substance abuse?
   b. Do you accept the null hypothesis here?
   c. What is the value of χ^2?

10. For the item 9 data, what is the relationship between family observance and substance abuse?

11. An $r \times k$ problem is set up to determine whether the type of reading curriculum students receive is related to whether they meet reading standards for their grade. Of 15 students in curriculum A, 8 met the state standard. Of 18 students receiving curriculum B, 5 met the state standard, and of 16 students receiving curriculum C, 3 met the state standard.

   a. Is there a relationship between whether students met the standard and which reading program they were involved in?
   b. Given the value of χ^2, what can be said about the relationship between type of curriculum and whether students meet state standards?

REFERENCES

Howell, D. C. (1992). *Statistical methods for psychology* (3rd ed.). Boston, MA: The Duxbury Press.

The Oxford Dictionary of Quotations (3rd ed.). (1980). Oxford, England: The Oxford University Press.

THE FORMULAE AND THEIR SYMBOLS

Formula 13.1: $\chi^2 = \dfrac{\Sigma(f_o - f_e)^2}{f_e}$ is the formula for the *chi*-square test statistic. The same formula is used for both "goodness of fit" tests and for the $r \times k$, *chi*-square test of independence.

Formula 13.2: $\phi = \sqrt{(\chi^2/N)}$. *Phi* coefficient is the measure of the correlation of the two variables involved when a **2 × 2** *chi*-square test of independence is statistically significant.

Formula 13.3: $V = \sqrt{[\phi^2/(\text{smaller of rows or columns}) - 1]}$. Cramer's V is the measure of correlation for two variables in a statistically significant *chi*-square test of independence when there are more than two levels of either variable.

STUDENT STUDY SITE

Visit the Student Study Site at **www.sagepub.com/tanner** for additional learning tools.

Chapter 14

WORKING WITH ORDINAL, MORE-, OR LESS-THAN DATA

THE PROBLEM: HOW TO WORK WITH ORDINAL SCALE DATA

Ms. Riddle is the assistant principal at a high school that serves students from a very well-established part of the city. There the tradition is to rank students within their classes. As she reviews students' data, she notes that increasingly both statewide and national testing organizations report scores as percentiles. She has some uncertainty about how class rankings and percentile scores can be used in the various data analysis tasks for which she is responsible.

QUESTIONS AND ANSWERS

❏ How does one analyze data that are ordinal scale?

  ○ If there are two independent groups and the issue is significant differences, the answer is the Mann-Whitney test. It does for ordinal scale data what the independent *t*-test did for interval or ratio scale data.

  ○ If the groups are not independent, the ordinal equivalent of the before/after *t*-test is the Wilcoxon *T*.

  ○ If there are more than two groups and the dependent variable is ordinal scale, the equivalents of the one-way *ANOVA* and the within-subjects F are Kruskal-Wallis and the Friedman's ANOVA, respectively.

  ○ If the issue is of the relationship between two sets of ordinal scale data, Spearman's *rho* is an ordinal equivalent of Pearson's *r*.

✦ – ✦ – ✦

The data scale discussion came up initially in Chapter 2. Differences in scale are differences in the kind of information the data yield. Recall that:

- Nominal scale data indicate what category an individual belongs to.
- Ordinal data allow us to rank the individual on the thing measured but don't reveal the amount of difference between individuals.
- Interval data have consistent differences between consecutive data points.
- With ratio data, a "0" means the quality measured is absent. We can also make ratio comparisons with ratio data, as when one student studies twice as much as another.

The *t*-tests and the *ANOVAs* had this in common—the independent variables were all nominal scale, and the dependent variables were interval or ratio scale. Except for the point-biserial correlation in Chapter 10, the work we did with correlation and regression consistently involved variables of at least interval scale.

Things changed in Chapter 13 when we shifted our attention to the *chi*-square tests. For nominal data, the *chi*-square tests are something like a nonparametric equivalent of *t*-test or *ANOVA*. We'll continue studying nonparametric procedures, but here the focus is on ordinal data.

A Little History

One will read very little of the early research on human intelligence before encountering Charles Spearman's name. First an officer in the British army, Spearman became intrigued by psychology, a discipline in its formative stages at the time. His interest was such that he resigned his commission to study in Germany in the late 1890s with Wilhelm Wundt. Although Spearman was recalled to the army for a time during Britain's conflict with the Boers in South Africa, psychology and human intelligence remained his passion. Like so many prominent English psychologists and statisticians of the age, once he finished his degree at Leipzig, Spearman gravitated to University College, London. Once there he, like R. A. Fisher (*ANOVA*), began feuding with Karl Pearson and also like Fisher, the conflict did not pass quickly. There's a subtle irony in the fact that Pearson and Spearman, who apparently disagreed about so much, are both associated with correlation, procedures that are designed to measure the strength of relationships.

■ Spearman's *rho* correlates ordinal scale variables, or interval scale variables reduced to ordinal scale.

Spearman was curious at the fact that the measures mental characteristics often correlate with each other, which prompted his uni-trait theory of intelligence. Intelligence is one generalized intellectual capacity. In time this line of research lead him to develop a procedure to analyze these multiple correlations called factor analysis that we'll describe briefly in Chapter 16, but here we're interested in a particular correlation coefficient he developed called Spearman's *rho*, or more formally, Spearman's rank order correlation coefficient.

The Hypothesis of Association for Ordinal Data: Spearman's *rho*

With the Pearson correlation in Chapter 10, we measured the relationship between two interval or ratio scale variables. One of the great advantages of correlation is the ability to determine the relationship between qualitatively different variables. With r we can gauge the relationship between the amount of time spent on homework and students' grades, or the number of questions they ask in class and their scores on a standardized test.

The Pearson Correlation imposes some restrictions, however. Most importantly, the data must be at least interval scale, and they must be reasonably close to normal. What if we wish to correlate educators' salaries with their ages? Although salary and age are both ratio variables and so meet the scale requirement, salaries generally have positive skew, so that's a problem. What if the data are class rankings and grade-point averages (GPA)? The GPA data may meet Pearson scale requirement, but by definition, class ranking data are ordinal scale.

With Spearman's *rho* the normality requirements aren't as rigid as they are for Pearson's *r*. Spearman's is a nonparametric procedure. Spearman's *rho* (like "row your boat") is the appropriate measure of association in the following situations:

- Both variables are in interval form, but the populations aren't normal
- The distributions aren't homoscedastic
- One variable is interval scale, the other ordinal
- Both data sets are ordinal

The Formula

The formula for Spearman's rho is the following:

$$r_s = 1 - \frac{(6\Sigma d^2)}{n(n^2 - 1)} \qquad\qquad 14.1$$

Where, r_s is Spearman's *rho,* d indicates a difference score explained below, and n indicates the number of pairs of data.

The rest of the formula (the 1s and the 6) are constant values; they're always used when *rho* is calculated. Note that the initial "1–" *isn't* part of the numerator in this formula; it's 1 minus everything else.

The procedure with *rho* is to independently rank both sets of data starting with a ranking of "1," even if the data are already ordinal scale. The d value in the formula is the difference between the two ranked scores for each individual. Think about this for a moment. If two sets of data are both ranked and the rankings of each pair of scores are quite similar, chances are that the relationship between them isn't random. This is the logic behind Spearman's *rho.*

Calculating *rho*

Here are the calculation steps:

1. Arrange the two sets of scores in columns, and rank each column separately, with a 1 assigned to the highest value in each column, and so on down. Actually, it doesn't affect the value of the statistic if one ranks from bottom up as long as both columns of data are ranked the same way, but for the sake of consistency, we'll start with the number indicating the highest value (not necessarily the largest number, as we will note in the example to follow), assign it a 1, and work down.

2. When scores have the same value, assign them the same ranking. For percentile scores of 98, 76, 55, 55, 43, for example, the ranking for the 98 would be 1, for the 76 it would be 2, and the two 55s, are both 3.5.
   - The two 55s must have the same rank. Since the two of them are the 3rd *and* 4th largest numbers, we average those rankings to determine the rank for both: 3 + 4 = 7, 7/2 = a ranking of 3.5 for both the 55s.
   - This pattern is followed for any number of ties—average the ranks involved and assign the same rank to each of the repeated numbers.
   - Because the two 55s are the 3rd and 4th highest numbers, the 43 is then ranked **5**.

3. Once the scores in each column are ranked, for each pair of scores, subtract the rank of the second score from the rank of the first to get *d*.

4. Square each of the *d* values.

5. Σd^2 is the sum of the squared differences.

6. Enter Σd^2 into the formula.

7. Make *n* the number of pairs of rankings.

8. Solve for r_s.

One of Ms. Riddle's questions is whether students' class standings correlate with their attitudes about school. She developed the School Attitude Survey (SAS) so that she has attitude scores to correlate with students' class rankings. Data for 8 students, of the 150 in the junior class, are as follows.

Student	Class Standing	SAS Score
1	45	21
2	56	19
3	14	24
4	22	24
5	114	15
6	3	28
7	38	22
8	17	23

If we add columns for:

- Converting each score to a ranking,
- A column for the differences between the rankings (d), and
- A column for the square of the differences (d^2) between the rankings, then
- There are four more columns added to the three above.

The "Class Rank" and "SAS Scores" must be ranked (or in the case of "class rank," re-ranked) from "1" down. The person who is 3rd in the class has the highest ranking *in this group* and so is ranked "1." If we turn it around and rank the largest value, 114, "1," the 56, "2," and so on, positive relationships will appear to be negative, and negative relationships will appear positive. In fact this is just what happens when this problem is done on SPSS. Since the computer doesn't know that a class standing of "3" is the highest in this group, it gives the highest ranking (1) to the largest value (114), which makes the relationship appear negative.

Once we've:

1. Subtracted the second ranking from the first for each student,

2. Squared the difference, and

3. Summed the squared differences we have, the following:

Student	Class Rank	SAS Score	Class rank	SAS rank	d	d²
1	45	21	6	6	0	0
2	56	19	7	7	0	0
3	14	24	2	2.5	−.5	.25
4	22	24	4	2.5	1.5	2.25
5	114	15	8	8	0	0
6	3	28	1	1	0	0
7	38	22	5	5	0	0
8	17	23	3	4	−1	1
						$\Sigma d^2 = 3.50$

Now we can solve for r_s.

$$r_s = 1 - \frac{(6\Sigma d^2)}{n\left(n^2 - 1\right)}$$

$$= 1 - \frac{(6)(3.50)}{8(64-1)}$$

$$= 1 - .042$$

$$= \textbf{.958}$$

Interpreting Spearman's rho

Spearman correlations are interpreted as Pearson Correlations were—larger is stronger and values range from –1.0 to 1.0. The statistical significance of the correlation value is determined by comparing it with a critical value for Spearman's *rho* in Table E at the back of the book. There are no degrees of freedom for interpreting this value. Critical values are indexed to the number of pairs of data (n). Note that for 8 pairs of data, the critical value at $p = .05$ is .738; $r_{s.05\,(8)} = .738$. The correlation of class rank and SAS score is significant.

Recall that with the Pearson Correlation we could calculate r^2, the proportion of variance in either variable that is explained by the other. There is no equivalent of r^2 for Spearman's *rho*. Ordinal scale data provide less information than the interval/ratio scale data upon which the Pearson Correlations are based.

Still, Spearman's *rho* is a very helpful correlation statistic and is widely used. Less rigorous assumptions allow Spearman's *rho* to be used where a Pearson's *r* isn't appropriate. In addition, because all scores are reduced to rankings, extreme scores (outliers) distort the resulting coefficient less than in a Pearson Correlation. Recall from the way we calculated r that each score is squared. Squaring makes outliers disproportionately affect results, particularly in small samples. Consider an example. If we were to correlate the values for two variables, and if the scores for one variable were as follows,

15, 13, 11, 9, 8, 8, 7, 5. Turned into rankings those values become 1, 2, 3, 4, 5.5, 5.5, 7, 8.

Now, if instead of 15, that first number had been 30, the ranks aren't affected. Whether the first number is 15, or 30, or any other number larger than 13, it's still the highest number. However, the square of the number that one would calculate in the course of completing a Pearson Correlation changes from 225 (15^2) to 900 (30^2)! The sum of the squared values would change dramatically.

There's another example of Spearman's *rho* in Figure 14.1.

Looking at SPSS Output

If we complete the problem in Figure 14.1 on SPSS, we get the following output:

Correlations

			Tutoringatt	collegeatt
Spearman's *rho*	tutoringatt	Correlation Coefficient	1.000	.650
		Sig. (2-tailed)	.	.081
		N	8	8
	collegeatt	Correlation Coefficient	.650	1.000
		Sig. (2-tailed)	.081	.
		N	8	8

As with a Pearson Correlation, the matrix indicates how each variable correlates with each of the others. Here there are only two variables, and each variable correlates perfectly with itself of course—that's the 1.000. It's the other correlation we're interested in, $r_s = .650$ in this case. As with the other procedures we've completed on SPSS, the "Sig." line indicates the

Figure 14.1   Another Example of Spearman's *rho*

An administrator at a community college is researching the relationship between students' attitudes about a tutoring service the college provides, and students' attitudes about the college generally. Data for both variables come from Likert-type surveys where students indicate whether they strongly agree (5), agree (4), neither agree nor disagree (3), disagree (2), strongly disagree (1) with a series of statements. Higher scores indicate more positive feelings. For eight students, the data are as follows:

	tutoring	college
1.	53	23
2.	31	16
3.	40	14
4.	40	19
5.	27	14
6.	32	14
7.	38	12
8.	26	7

$$r_s = 1 - \frac{6(\Sigma d^2)}{n(n^2 - 1)}$$

Although both sets are already ordinal scale data they must still be ranked.

	tutoring	rank	college	rank.	d	d²
1.	53	1	23	1	0	0
2.	31	6	16	3	3	9
3.	40	2.5	14	5	−2.5	6.25
4.	40	2.5	19	2	.5	.25
5.	27	7	14	5	2	4
6.	32	5	14	5	0	0
7.	38	4	12	7	−3	9
8.	26	8	7	8	0	0
					$\Sigma d^2 = 28.5$	

$$r_s = 1 - \frac{6(28.5)}{8(8^2 - 1)} = 1 - .339 = \mathbf{.661}$$

$r_{s\,.05\,(8)} = \mathbf{.715}$; fail to reject H_o.

Any relationship between students' attitudes about tutoring services and their attitudes about the college generally is random.

probability that a correlation of r_s = .650 could have occurred by chance. At .081 it's not statistically significant. At more than 10 times in 100 that this result could occur by chance, it's too likely that this correlation is just a random outcome.

In this particular case, the SPSS correlation coefficient differs a little from the longhand calculation. It reflects the fact that SPSS handles tied rankings a little differently than we have. When there are no ties, the results will agree.

THE HYPOTHESIS OF DIFFERENCE FOR ORDINAL DATA

As Spearman's *rho* provides an ordinal data equivalent to the Pearson Correlation, there are ordinal data equivalents for the differences tests as well.

SOURCE: Created by Suzanna Nielson.

"I appreciate your enthusiasm for correlation, Jill, but are you sure you want to argue that since overweight people eat low-fat food, that it makes people overweight?"

■ Mann-Whitney *U* is a two independent groups test for an ordinal scale dependent variable.

Two Independent Groups: Mann-Whitney *U*

Both Mann-Whitney *U* and the independent *t*-test analyze two independent groups for significant differences. The difference is the scale of the dependent variable (*DV*), ordinal for Mann-Whitney, interval/ratio for *t*.

Mann-Whitney is based on this question: Do two sets of ranked scores represent identical populations? If the differences are great enough, one concludes that the two groups represent unique populations. Like Spearman's *rho*, Mann-Whitney *U* is appropriate when:

- Both sets of scores are in ordinal form to begin with.
- One set of scores is ordinal scale but the other is interval.
- Both sets of scores are interval, but there are concerns either about the normality of the data or whether the two groups have equivalent variability (homogeneity of variance).

The way we're going to calculate Mann-Whitney here, there must be at least 9 subjects in each group. Smaller group sizes require a different approach not covered in this book. There are two test statistics to calculate, a value of *U* and a value of z_u.

$$U = n_1 n_2 + \frac{n_1(n_1 + 1)}{2} - \Sigma R_1 \qquad 14.2$$

Where, n_1 and n_2 are the number of subjects in each sample

ΣR_1 = the total of the rankings in group 1

The value of *U* is then used to solve for z_u,

$$z_u = \frac{(U - n_1 n_2 / 2)}{\sqrt{[n_1 n_2 (n_1 + n_2 + 1) / 12]}} \qquad 14.3$$

These two formulae look messy, but the only trick is to be careful with order of operations.

Calculating the Mann-Whitney U

1. Rank both sets of data together. Note that this is different from Spearman's rho where we ranked the two sets of scores separately.

2. Sum the rankings *in the first* group, ΣR_1.

3. Solve for U.

4. Solve for z_u and compare with the critical value of z.

The formula for U requires the sum of the rankings for just the first group, but since the two groups are ranked together, by inference the rankings in the first group reflect those in the second group as well.

An Example

A math teacher is familiar with the research indicating gender differences in mathematics performance but suspects that the differences do not extend to problems that primarily emphasize calculation. The teacher constructs a test of this hypothesis by comparing girls and boys in a seventh-grade math class on a timed test of basic arithmetic calculation for which scores have been reported as percentiles. Selecting 10 students of each gender group from the seventh-grade class yields the following data:

Girls	Boys
39	63
86	55
63	72
33	45
40	50
87	58
29	62
42	48
60	68
49	82

If the two sets of scores are converted to rankings and the two columns treated together for purposes of the ranking (R_g = rankings for the girls, R_b = rankings for the boys), the results appear as follows:

R_g	R_b
18	6.5
2	11
6.5	4
19	15
17	12
1	10
20	8
16	14
9	5
$\Sigma Rg = \dfrac{13}{121.5}$	3

Note that any tied scores, the two 63s in this case, are handled just as tied scores were in Spearman's *rho*—their places are averaged and both assigned the same ranking. The ranks for the two 63s were 6 and 7 so both received a 6.5 (6 + 7 = 13 ÷ 2 = 6.5) and the ranking for the next highest percentile score (62 in the boys column) became 8.

1. $U = n_1 n_2 + [n_1 (n_1 + 1)] - \Sigma R_1$

$$= (10)(10) + \frac{[10(11)]}{2} - 121.5 = \mathbf{33.5}$$

2. $z_u = \dfrac{(U - n_1 n_2 / 2)}{\sqrt{[n_1 n_2 (n_1 + n_2 + 1) / 12]}}$

$$= \dfrac{(33.5 - (10)(10) / 2)}{\sqrt{[(10)(10)(10 + 10 + 1)/12]}}$$

$$\dfrac{(33.5 - 50)}{\sqrt{(100)(21) / 12}} = \dfrac{-16.5}{\sqrt{175}} = \mathbf{-1.247}$$

We interpret the value of z_u just as we interpreted z for the z test in Chapter 5. When it exceeds the Table A value for the prescribed level of probability, the result is significant. For $p = .05$ the value was $z = 1.96$, and for $p = .01$ the value was $z = 2.58$.

The value of z in this case indicates that there is a difference, but it isn't statistically significant. It's less than the Table A value, 1.96. Any difference in calculation ability between girls and boys is likely just a random difference.

The Mann-Whitney and Power

Because of the dependent variables scores are ordinal rather than interval, Mann-Whitney U will usually be less sensitive to differences between groups than the independent t-test. *The power handicap isn't absolute, however*. Perhaps there are independent groups measured on some interval scale variable, spelling ability for example. Assume further that it's a very advanced test with some difficult words that one student happens to do very well with. Even if individuals are randomly selected and so on, and we meet the requirements for an independent t-test, if the means are very similar an independent t-test can't yield a significant result (remember that the numerator in the independent t-test is $M_1 - M_2$). But Mann-Whitney is based on the difference in ranks rather than means and so similar measures of central tendency don't necessarily translate into a nonsignificant result.

If Group 1 spelling scores are 14, 10, 10, 12, 14, 10, 11, 15, 11

$m = 11.889$ and $s = 1.965$

If Group 2 spelling scores are 58, 9, 8, 3, 7, 1, 2, 4, 5

$m = 10.778$ and s = 17.913

In this case, $t = .185$, which isn't significant. But $z_u = 2.781$ and *is* significant. (Do the math. Make my day.) So although nonparametric tests are generally less powerful than their parametric counterparts, there are exceptions.

Looking at SPSS Output for Mann-Whitney

If we do the problem in the box just above on SPSS the output produces two tables, but it's the second we're interested in. For this problem, it's as follows:

Test Statistics

	Spelling
Mann-Whitney U	9.000
Wilcoxon W	54.000
Z	−2.797
Asymp. Sig. (2-tailed)	.005
Exact Sig. [2*(1-tailed Sig.)]	.004[a]

The SPSS result is slightly different from what we did longhand where z was 2.781 (notice that SPSS doesn't correct for ties), but the difference will rarely affect the decision about statistical significance. At $p = .004$, we reject the probability that the two sets of rankings came from the same population.

Two or More Independent Groups: Kruskal-Wallis H

■ Kruskal-Wallis H tests for significant differences among two-plus independent groups when the dependent variable is ordinal scale.

When data are ordinal scale, or sufficiently skewed that they don't meet standards for normality, the equivalent to the one-way *ANOVA* is the **Kruskal-Wallis H**. Like *ANOVA* the test can be completed for two groups, but also like *ANOVA* it's usually less work to use the test designed specifically for two independent groups, Mann-Whitney. The Kruskal-Wallis test statistic looks this way:

$$\chi^2_H = \frac{12}{N(N+1)}(\Sigma R^2_1/n_1 + \Sigma R^2_2/n_2 + \cdots + \Sigma R^2_i/n_i) - 3(N+1) \quad 14.4$$

This formula too has constant values. The other terms are as follows:

χ^2_H indicates that the formula produces a *chi*-square value

$N =$ the total number of subjects

$R_1 =$ the rankings in Group 1

$n_1 =$ the number of subjects in Group 1

The value determined for χ^2_H is compared with the critical values on the *chi*-square table for the number of groups, minus 1, degrees of freedom.

Calculating the Kruskal-Wallis H

1. Arrange the data in columns, one for each group, and rank the data in the columns *together* just as with Mann-Whitney.

2. Assign all tied values the same ranking as before by averaging the rankings involved.

3. Sum the rankings in each column.

4. Substitute the summed rankings into the formula.

5. Solve for χ^2_H.

An Example

The graduate coordinator at a university wishes to analyze changes in graduate students' sense of competence as they progress through their doctoral programs. A survey with a series of questions related to the students' sense of their own competence yields the scores below. Higher scores reflect a higher sense of competence.

1st Year	2nd Year	3rd Year
11	12	12
6	12	12
4	9	11
4	9	10
2	8	10
2	7	10
2	6	9
2	6	8
1	5	7
1	4	7

With additional columns for rankings and all scores ranked together we have:

1st	R_1	2nd	R_2	3rd	R_3
11	5.5	12	2.5	12	2.5
6	19	12	2.5	12	2.5
4	23	9	11	11	5.5
4	23	9	11	10	8
2	26.5	8	13.5	10	8
2	26.5	7	16	10	8
2	26.5	6	19	9	11
2	26.5	6	19	8	13.5
1	29.5	5	21	7	16
1	29.5	4	23	7	16
	$\Sigma R = 235.5$		138.5		91.0

$$\chi^2_H = \frac{12}{N(N+1)} (\Sigma R_1^2/n_1 + \Sigma R_2^2/n_2 + \ldots + \Sigma R_i^2/n_i) - 3(N+1)$$

$$= \frac{12}{30(30+1)} (235.5^2/10 + 138.5^2/10 + 91^2/10) - 3(30+1) = \mathbf{14.00}$$

The $\chi^2_H = \mathbf{14.00}$ is compared with *chi*-square with degrees of freedom equal to the number of groups (the number of levels of the independent variable), − 1. That value is $\chi^2_{.05\,(2)} = 5.99$.

At $p = .05$, differences among first-, second-, and third-year doctoral students' sense of competence are statistically significant. The raw data indicate that the third-year students have the highest level of competence and the first-year students the lowest, so sense of competence grows by year. Figure 14.2 is another Kruskal-Wallis example.

Figure 14.2 Another Kruskal-Wallis *H* Example

A sports psychologist has a theory that risk aversion is the key to understanding springboard diving success. Her theory is that more risk aversion translates into more tentative behavior and less success. She tests the theory by collecting risk aversion data on divers from three different teams. Team A had a losing season. Team B was moderately successful, and Team C won their league. The rankings are in color. Higher scores indicate more risk aversion.

Team A	R_A	Team B	R_B	Team C	R_C
20	2	21	1	18	3
15	5	17	4	14	6
11	9	8	13	9	11.5
12	8	7	14	6	15
13	7	10	10	9	11.5
	31		42		47

$$\chi^2_H = \frac{12}{N(N+1)} (\Sigma R_1^2/n_1 + \Sigma R_2^2/n_2 + \ldots + \Sigma R_i^2/n_i) - 3(N+1)$$

$$= \frac{12}{15(15+1)} (31^2/5 + 42^2/5 + 47^2/5) - 3(15+1) = \mathbf{1.34}$$

$\chi^2_{.05\,(2)} = 5.99$. Fail to reject. Risk aversion differences aren't significant.

Looking at SPSS Output for Kruskal-Wallis

If we complete the problem in Figure 14.2 on SPSS, the second output table reports the *chi*-square value and the level of significance. The value is the same as our calculation. The probability that such a value could have occurred by chance ($p = .511$) reinforces our decision not to reject the null hypothesis. Differences in risk aversion among members of these three samples are probably just an artifact of sampling variability.

TestStatistics [a,b]

	aversion
Chi-Square	1.342
Df	2
Asymp. Sig.	.511

a. Kruskal-Wallis Test

b. Grouping Variable: team

Two Related Groups: Wilcoxon *T*

Both of the preceding tests, Mann-Whitney and Kruskal-Wallis, are tests for independent groups. Members of one group cannot also be members of the other. The dependent groups equivalents are the **Wilcoxon *T*** also called the Wilcoxon signed-ranks test, and the **Friedman's *ANOVA*,** that we'll take up below. These two tests do for ordinal data what the before/after *t* and the within-subjects *F* did for interval data, in Chapter 9. They're repeated measures tests.

A ninth-grade English teacher wishes to test whether an intensive reading program is associated with a significant improvement in students' verbal ability scores. Before beginning, a group of students is administered the district's Verbal Aptitude Test (VAT). Scores are in percentile form. At the end of the quarter, the VAT is administered a second time. These conditions are tailored to the Wilcoxon *T*. The test statistic is as follows:

$$Z_T = \frac{T - [N(N+1)]/4}{\sqrt{\{[N(N+1)(2N+1)]/24\}}} \qquad 14.5$$

■ The Wilcoxon *T* is for two dependent groups with ordinal scale data.

■ Friedman's *ANOVA* is a test for two-plus ordinal scale measures from the same group.

Where,

T = the smaller sum of either the positive or negative signed ranks

N = the number of nonzero difference scores

Calculating the Wilcoxon T

The procedure is as follows:

Calculate the difference between the first and second score for each individual. Call it a "d" value.

1. Ignoring whether scores are positive or negative, rank them *from the smallest difference (1) to the largest.*
   a. Any zero differences are ignored for the balance of the analysis.
   b. Differences of the same absolute value (that is, the signs are ignored) receive the same rank just like ties in the earlier tests.

2. The sign of the difference score is transferred to the ranked difference (signed rank).

3. The value of T is the sum of the positive ranks or the negative ranks, whichever is *smaller.*

4. Solve for Z_T

The VAT data for students before the reading augmentation and after are in the "pre" and "post" columns below.

- The "d" column is the difference between the pre and post scores.
- The "rank" column is the ranking of the absolute value of the d values, from the smallest.
- The "signed rank" column applies the sign from the d column to the rank.

	pre	post	d rank	signed	rank
1.	73	78	−5	7	−7
2.	59	66	−7	9	−9
3.	84	82	2	2	2
4.	76	79	−3	4.5	−4.5
5.	52	50	2	2	2

	pre	post	d rank	signed	rank
6.	38	43	−57	−7	
7.	44	44	0		
8.	35	49	−14	10.5	−10.5
9.	17	20	−3	4.5	−4.5
10.	83	85	−2	2	−2
11.	49	54	−5	7	−7
12.	39	53	−14	10.5	−10.5

Sum of positive ranks (2 + 2) = 4.0
Sum of negative ranks (7 + 9 +· · · + 10.5) = 62.0
T (the *lesser* of the two totals) = 4

Because there are 11 nonzero differences (the 7th person had the same pre and post scores), $N = 11$.

$$Z_T = \frac{T - [N(N+1)]/4}{\sqrt{\{[N(N+1)(2N+1)/24\}}} = \frac{4 - [11(11+1)]/4}{\sqrt{\{[11(11+1)(2 \cdot 11+1)]/24\}}} = \frac{4 - 132/4}{\sqrt{[(11 \cdot 12 \cdot 23/24}} = \frac{-29}{\sqrt{11.247}}$$

$$= -2.578$$

Interpreting the Test Statistic, T

As the notation hints, the Z_T value, −2.578 in this case, is compared with values from Table A and our standard, you will remember, is the z value for a test at $p = .05$, which is $z = 1.96$. The difference between pre- and posttest VAT scores is statistically significant.

The T value in the formula was the lesser of the sums of either the positive or the negative ranks. If instead of the smaller you use the larger of the two ranking totals, it won't change the value of the statistic but it does change the *sign*. The answer becomes $z_T = 2.578$, making it appear that the pretest scores were significantly higher than the posttest scores. Figure 14.2 contains another example of Wilcoxon *T*.

Two or More Related Groups: Friedman's *ANOVA*

If one group is measured more than twice and the *DV* is ordinal, the test is **Friedman's *ANOVA* by Ranks**. The "Friedman" involved is Nobel Prize-winning

■ **Friedman's *ANOVA* by Ranks** is a test for significant differences in two or more correlated groups when the data are ordinal.

Figure 14.3 Another Wilcoxon *T* Example

A researcher wonders whether providing students with an algorithm for problem solving affects the ability to solve reasoning problems. Thirteen students are measured, taught an algorithm, and then measured a second time. The subjects represent a small convenience sample. Wilcoxon *T* is used. Is the algorithm associated with improved problem-solving ability?

	pre	post	d	rank	signed rank
1.	23	27	-4	6	-6
2.	19	20	-1	1.5	-1.5
3.	20	20	0		
4.	27	22	5	7.5	7.5
5.	11	18	-7	10.5	-10.5
6.	30	31	-1	1.5	-1.5
7.	26	28	-2	3	-3
8.	22	29	-7	10.5	-10.5
9.	17	20	-3	4.5	-4.5
10.	20	26	-6	9	-9
11.	23	20	3	4.5	4.5
12.	14	19	-5	7.5	-7.5
13.	50	50	0		

sum of positive ranks = 12
sum of negative ranks = 54

With two zero differences, $N = 11$, and the calculated value of $T = 12$.

$$Z_T = \frac{T - [N(N+1)]/4}{\sqrt{[N(N+1)(2N+1)]/24\}}} = \frac{12 - [11(11+1)]/4}{\sqrt{\{[11(11+1)(2\cdot11+1)]/24\}}}$$

$$= \frac{12 - 33}{[(11\cdot12\cdot23)/24]} = \mathbf{-1.867}$$ The calculated value is less than 1.96. It isn't significant; fail to reject.

economist Milton Friedman whose extraordinary talents at the University of Chicago extended also to statistical analysis. The formula looks much like the Kruskal-Wallis test that we used earlier, and like that-test, the product is a *chi-square* value. The formula is:

$$\chi^2_F = (12/(Nk)(k+1)) \; (\Sigma R_1^2 + \Sigma R_2^2 + \ldots \Sigma R_k^2) - 3N(k + 1) \qquad 14.6$$

Besides the constant values the other terms are:

N = the no. of rows of data

k = the no. of column ranks (no. of times the *DV* is measured)

R_1 = the rankings in column 1

Like the other tests for ordinal data, one ranks the scores to start. The difference is that the rankings are within the multiple measures for each individual, independent of the other subjects. With the data set up as usual so that subjects are listed in the rows and their multiple scores are reflected in the columns, the steps are as follows:

1. Rank the scores along each row (among the repetitions).

2. Sum the rankings for each column (sum all the rankings from the first measure, then the second, etc.).

3. Solve for χ^2.

4. Compare χ^2 with the critical value of $\chi^2_{p(k-1)}$.

Note that there is a minimum number of subjects required to run Friedman's *ANOVA*. If each subject has at least 3 scores, there must be at least 10 subjects. If there are 4 measures taken for each individual, 5 subjects are enough.

A Friedman's ANOVA *Example*

The Director of Personnel at a community college suspects that as length of tenure among the faculty increases, so does job satisfaction. Over several years he has administered a job satisfaction survey to the same group of instructors. Higher scores indicate more satisfaction. For 5 instructors the data are as follows:

Number of Years				
	<2	2–3	4–5	>5
1.	17	18	21	22
2.	13	15	16	17
3.	19	19	21	20
4.	18	17	18	20
5.	16	18	20	20

We'll first add columns headings $R_1, R_2, \ldots$, one for each of the multiple measures, and then note the ranks of each subjects' multiple scores from highest to lowest. Note that the fourth measurement for the first subject is 22, that subject's highest score, and is ranked "1," accordingly. Ties are handled the same as with the other procedures for ordinal data.

	<2	2–3	4–5	>5	R_1	R_2	R_3	R_4	
1.	17	18	21	22	4	3	2	1	
2.	13	15	16	17	4	3	2	1	
3.	19	19	21	20	3.5	3.5	1	2	
4.	18	17	18	20	2.5	4	2.5	1	
5.	16	18	20	20	4	3	1.5	1.5	

Having ranked 4 scores for each of the 5 instructors, we sum the rankings by column. Verify that:

$$\Sigma R_1 = 18 \ (4 + 4 + 3.5 + 2.5 + 4)$$

$$\Sigma R_2 = 16.5 \ (3 + 3 + 3.5 + 4 + 3)$$

$$\Sigma R_3 = 9 \ (2 + 2 + 1 + 2.5 + 1.5), \text{ and}$$

$$\Sigma R_4 = 6.5 \ (1 + 1 + 2 + 1 + 1.5)$$

The next step is to solve for *chi*-square.

$$\chi_H^2 = (12/ \ (Nk)(k + 1)) \ (\Sigma R_1^2 + \Sigma R_2^2 + \ldots \Sigma R_k^2) \ - 3N(k + 1)$$

Where,

The number of row/subjects (N) = 5,

The number of measures (k) for each subject = 4

So, $\chi^2 = (12/(5 \cdot 4)(4 + 1)) \ (18^2 + 16.5^2 + 9^2 + 6.5^2) - 3*5(4 + 1)$

$= .12(719.5) - 75$

$= \mathbf{11.34}$

Interpreting the Test Value

For the Friedman's *ANOVA*:

- df = the number of measures for each individual, minus 1
- The relevant value for χ^2 with $df = \mathbf{3}$, $\chi^2_{.05\ (3)} = 7.82$

Because the test value is greater than the table value when testing at $p =$ .05 with $df = 3$, the decision is to reject H_o. Job satisfaction changes significantly over time.

Examining the summed rankings reveals the direction of change. Because the highest job satisfaction scores receive the lowest numerical ranking (1), the column with the lowest summed ranking value indicates the highest level of job satisfaction. The longer these five instructors teach, the higher their job satisfaction rating. There's another Friedman's *ANOVA* problem in Figure 14.4.

KEEPING IT ALL STRAIGHT

With all the new procedures for ordinal data—correlation tests, tests for independent groups, and tests for dependent groups there has been much to absorb. It helps to arrange the tests in a table. The categories in Table 14.1 are:

- The hypothesis to which the procedure responds (difference versus association)
- The scale of the variables
- The number of groups involved
- The relationship between the groups

Figure 14.4   Another Example of Friedman's *ANOVA*

Because the students in a continuation high school are assigned because of trouble of one sort or another, the principal is concerned about their feelings of alienation and well-being. Over a calendar year she uses the Well Being Questionnaire (the WeBeQ for short) to measure students' well-being four times. Data are as follows:

3 Mo.	6 Mo.	9 Mo.	12 Mo.
12	17	18	18
15	15	17	16
11	13	14	15
10	16	17	18
12	12	12	13
11	16	15	15
11	15	18	18
12	11	15	16

Does the WeBeQ indicate significant differences in students' well-being over time?

3 Mo.	6 Mo.	9 Mo.	12 Mo.	R_1	R_2	R_3	R_4
12	17	18	18	4	3	1.5	1.5
15	15	17	16	3.5	3.5	1	2
11	13	14	15	4	3	2	1
10	16	17	18	4	3	2	1
12	12	12	13	3	3	3	1
11	16	15	15	4	1	2.5	2.5
11	15	18	18	4	3	1.5	1.5
12	11	15	16	3	4	2	1
			ΣR	29.5	23.5	15.5	11.5

$\chi_H^2 = (12/(Nk)(k+1))\,(\Sigma R_1^2 + \Sigma R_2^2 + \ldots \Sigma R_k^2) - 3N(k+1)$
  $= (12/(8 \cdot 4)(4+1))\,(29.5^2 + 23.5^2 + 15.5^2 + 11.5^2) - 3 \cdot 8(4+1)$
  $= .075\,(1795) - (120)$
  $= 134.625 - 120 = \mathbf{14.625}.\ \chi_{.05\,(3)}^2 = 7.82$, reject H_o.

Students' sense of well-being changes significantly with time, with the later rankings (lowest numerical values) higher than those taken earlier (the highest numerical values).

Table 14.1 Identifying the Appropriate Statistical Procedure

Scale of the Dependent Variable	The Nature of the Hypothesis						
	Difference					Association	
	No. of Groups						
	1	2		3+		Variable Scale	
		Indep Grps	Dep Grps	Indep Grps	Dep Grps		
Nominal	$1 \times k\ \chi^2$	$R \times k\ \chi^2$				Nominal	C (coefficient of contingency)
Ordinal		Mann-Whitney	Wilcoxon	Kruskal-Wallis	Friedman's ANOVA	Ordinal	ρ (Spearman's *rho*)
						Ordinal/Nominal	
Interval/Ratio	z, or 1 sample t	Indep t	Before/After t	ANOVA	Within-Subj F	Ordinal/Interval	
						Interval	r_{xy} (Pearson's), R (multiple cor), $r_{y(2.1)}$ (semi-partial cor)
						Interval/Nominal	Point biserial

If we're asking questions about differences—between samples and populations or just between samples, the tests on the left side of the table are the tools we need. Then we must determine the scale of the dependent variable, the number of groups, and whether the groups are independent. For example:

- If we had a question about the difference between two, related (dependent) groups with an interval scale dependent variable, the table guides us to "Before/After t."
- If we're asking about the hypothesis of association and the data are a combination of interval and nominal, the table guides us to the point-biserial correlation.

There are some empty categories in the table. It's not for wont of a procedure, but rather because we won't get to it in this book. The number of different statistical tests available is positively dizzying, and even for the few we cover in this book, a table isn't a bad way to keep things straight. Note that there are several procedures that will be introduced very briefly in Chapter 16 that aren't represented in the table.

SUMMARY

Perhaps the most persistent question asked by those facing a quantitative analysis task is, "Which test should I use?" The answer revolves around two other questions:

1. What do you need to know? and

2. What sort of data are you working with?

In this chapter we added tests that allow one to answer questions about association and difference when the data are interval/ratio scale, but don't meet the other requirements imposed by t-test, $ANOVA$, or a Pearson's r; or when the data are ordinal scale to begin with. Five procedures in one chapter are a lot to contend with, but the several tests have much in common with each other and also with several of the other tests examined earlier in the book.

- Spearman's *rho* is interpreted just the way a Pearson Correlation coefficient is interpreted (Chapter 10), but it's applied to data that are ordinal.
- The other four tests are also the ordinal equivalents of procedures we initially dealt with for interval/ratio data. If we compare the tests covered here with those earlier procedures, we have the following:

For Interval Data	The Ordinal Data Equivalent
Pearson Correlation (Ch. 10)	Spearman's *rho*
Independent *t*-test (Ch. 6)	Mann-Whitney *U*
One-Way *ANOVA* (Ch. 7)	Kruskal-Wallis
Before/After *t* (Ch. 9)	Wilcoxon *T*
Within-Subjects *F* (Ch. 9)	Friedman's *ANOVA*

Although the Chapter 14 tests are probably less familiar than those studied earlier (most university students have at least *heard* of a *t*-test or of analysis of variance), they are very important because so much of the data educators gather are actually ordinal scale data. This raises one final issue for the chapter. One need not look far to find someone using a test designed for interval and normal data with scores that are neither. It's an error the reader need not make.

In the next chapter, we will depart some from the topics usually covered in a statistics book. Traditionally, testing issues have been the domain of the educational measurement specialist. However, many of the concepts with which the reader is now familiar can help us understand tests better and answer questions educators have about-test and data quality. Implicitly the chapter suggests that it's time for educators and counselors in the schools to take a greater measure of control.

EXERCISES

1. What is the appropriate test when:
   a. The issue is of significant differences, there are four independent groups involved, and the dependent variable is of ordinal scale?
   b. The issue is of significant differences, the data are of ordinal scale, and there are two groups of subjects paired on some relevant variable?
   c. What is the ordinal data equivalent of the Pearson Correlation?

2. You have 10 subjects' verbal aptitude scores, recorded as percentile scores. After introducing them to a strategy in retrieving vocabulary words, you assess their aptitudes a second time to check for significant differences.
   a. What's the appropriate statistical test?
   b. Is the strategy related to significantly higher levels of verbal aptitude?

	Aptitude A	Aptitude B
1.	53rd	55th
2.	65th	63rd

	Aptitude A	Aptitude B
3.	71st	79th
4.	37th	46th
5.	45th	54th
6.	65th	81st
7.	74th	68th
8.	81st	82nd
9.	47th	53rd
10.	23rd	38th

3. A researcher is interested in the relationship between age and dogmatic behavior in educators. He randomly selects 10 educators who are 25 and younger and a second group who are 40 and older. Higher scores indicate more dogmatic behavior. Dogmatism is measured on an ordinal scale.

   a. What's the appropriate test?
   b. Is dogmatism significantly related to age?

	Age 25 <	Age 40 >
1.	14	19
2.	15	16
3.	19	18
4.	20	24
5.	14	17
6.	16	19
7.	11	12
8.	15	15
9.	12	17
10.	14	15

4. An administrator at a community college is studying the relationship between students' attitudes about a tutoring service the college provides and about the college generally. Data for both variables come from separate Likert-type surveys. On each, students indicated whether they strongly agree (5), agree (4), neither agree nor disagree (3), disagree (2), strongly disagree (1) with a series of statements. For eight students, the data are as follows:

	tutoring	*college*
1.	53	23
2.	31	16
3.	40	14
4.	40	19
5.	27	14
6.	32	14
7.	38	12
8.	26	7

a. What's the appropriate test?

b. Are the two variables significantly correlated?

5. Data are gathered from students involved in a dropout prevention program for at-risk high school students. The data represent the students' optimism about completing high school and are gathered 3, 6, 9, and 12 months after the students enter the program. The data are ordinal scale. Does optimism about graduating change significantly over time?

a. Which is the appropriate test for this problem?

b. What is the scale of the independent variable?

c. What is the scale of the dependent variable?

d. Are the differences statistically significant?

	months			
	3	*6*	*9*	*12*
1.	23	25	37	41
2.	26	25	30	33
3.	43	51	49	55
4.	51	46	48	43
5.	18	16	28	30
6.	64	68	66	73

6. Students in the biology club, the debate club, and the marching band are arguing about whether any of the three organizations' students enjoy higher class rankings than the others. For 8 students from each club, the class rankings are the following:

biology	*debate*	*band*
23	14	35
74	55	39

biology	debate	band
12	6	43
27	31	85
33	19	52
66	38	48
8	2	20
15	11	98

a. What is the appropriate test?
b. What is the equivalent of this test for interval and normal data?
c. Are the differences statistically significant?

7. For a Wilcoxon T problem we have the following data:

Meas1	Meas2
10	9
8	8
10	10
14	12
12	10
9	7
12	14

a. What is the sum of the rankings for Group 1?
b. Are the differences between the measures statistically significant?

8. What is power in statistical testing? Under what circumstances will an independent t-test with interval data be less powerful than Mann-Whitney U applied to the same data?

9. Describe the hypothesis, the number of groups, the relationship between the groups, and the scale of the dependent variable that make the Wilcoxon T the appropriate test.

10. Describe the number of groups, the relationship between the groups, and the scale of the dependent variable that make the Friedman's *ANOVA* the appropriate test.

11. A reading specialist wonders whether children's reading ability correlates with their level of introversion. He identifies 11 students in the primary grades who are reading substantially beyond grade level and to each administers a reading scale and an introversion measure (which is ordinal scale). Is there a statistically significant relationship between the two measures?

	reading	introv
1.	100	11
2.	50	16
3.	90	19
4.	65	20
5.	87	22
6.	75	15
7.	80	13
8.	95	12
9.	80	24
10.	75	25
11.	60	28

12. Teachers at three different schools have different approaches to teaching mathematics. School A relies heavily on parent participation in homework activities. School B uses cooperative learning. School C emphasizes computer-aided instruction. On a standardized math test, national percentile scores for 10 students from each school are the following:

A	B	C
47	87	34
67	63	55
93	45	68
85	79	50
70	73	54
48	53	67
77	86	23
90	71	39
59	53	56
89	78	51

a. Which is the appropriate test?
b. Are differences statistically significant?

THE FORMULAE AND THEIR SYMBOLS

Formula 14.1: $r_s = 1 - \dfrac{(6\Sigma d^2)}{N\,(N^2 - 1)}$

This is the formula for Spearman's *rho*, or Spearman's rank order correlation coefficient. It allows one to correlate two sets of ordinal scale data.

Formula 14.2: $U = n_1 n_2 + [n_1\,(n_1 + 1)]/2 - \Sigma R_1$

This is the formula for U that is the first part of the Mann-Whitney U procedure. It is a test of significant differences between sets of ordinal scale data from two independent groups. The value of U is then used in z_U to complete the Mann-Whitney test.

Formula 14.3: $z_u = \dfrac{\left(U - n_1 n_2 / 2\right)}{\sqrt{[n_1 n_2 (n_1 + n_2 + 1)/12]}}$

This is the second formula used in the Mann-Whitney U test. It produces a value of z_u that can then be compared with values of z from Table A to determine statistical significance.

Formula 14.4: $\chi_H^2 = \dfrac{12}{N(N+1)}(\Sigma R_1^2/n_1 + \Sigma R_2^2/n_2 + \cdots + \Sigma R_i^2/n_i) - 3(N+1)$

This is the formula for Kruskal-Wallis H, a test for significant differences among two or more independent groups when the dependent variable is ordinal scale. It produces a *chi*-square value.

Formula 14.5: $Z_T = \dfrac{T - [N(N+1)]/4}{\sqrt{\{[N(N+1)(2N+1)]/24\}}}$

This is the formula for the Wilcoxon signed ranks test, a test for significant differences in the before/after measures or the measures of matched pairs with two groups, with an ordinal scale DV. The value of Z_T is compared with the values of z in Table A to determine significance.

Formula 14.6: $\chi_F^2 = (12/(Nk)(k+1))\,(\Sigma R_1^2 + \Sigma R_2^2 + \ldots \Sigma R_k^2) - 3N(k + 1)$

This is the formula for Friedman's *ANOVA* by ranks, a test for significant differences among 2 or more dependent groups when the dependent variable is ordinal scale. This repeated measures procedure produces a *chi*-square value.

STUDENT STUDY SITE

Visit the Student Study Site at **www.sagepub.com/tanner** for additional learning tools.

PART VI

Tests, Measurement Issues, and Selected Advanced Topics

Chapter 15

TESTING ISSUES

THE PROBLEM: DETERMINING SCORE ACCURACY

A school district has created a Progress Assessment (PA) test for language arts and mathematics during the year so that educators can use results to make needed adjustments before the all-important state tests at the end of the year. Among the parents and some of the educators, however, the PA has prompted a resurgent discussion about fairness. People wonder whether testing procedures will place some students at a disadvantage for reasons that have little to do with their command of the subjects.

QUESTIONS AND ANSWERS

❏ Characteristics like comprehension and problem-solving ability are abstractions that can't be measured directly. Using an inferential approach involves the constant difficulty of measurement error. Are there indicators of the magnitude of the error?

The standard error of measurement is an estimate of measurement error.

❏ "High-stakes" tests have the name because of the importance of the decisions for which they're used. Important decisions underscore the need to have scores in which one can have confidence. What indicate test scores' technical quality?

This will bring us to data reliability and validity.

❏ Perhaps no criticism of testing is more easily leveled and less understood among laypeople than bias. How is it detected?

Some of the procedures we've already explored will provide at least an introduction.

Throughout the earlier chapters of this book the point has been that studying statistics helps one make, in our case at least, better educational decisions. Correct analyses are based on issues such as the scale of the data, the nature of the hypothesis, the number and nature of the groups, and so on. But actually there is a more fundamental question that precedes even those discussions: Can one have confidence in the data? A reader might fairly ask, why wait until *now* to raise such a question? There really is a method in our madness. To this point we just assumed that the data were solid because we lacked the tools we needed to evaluate them. Now we're ready.

Classical Test Theory

■ Classical test theory says every score consists of the true measure, plus some error.

Gauging characteristics such as analytical ability or one's grasp of the Pythagorean Theorem requires a more nuanced approach than measuring whether one can spell or name the capital city of France. The potential for error is higher when measuring abstractions. For many years **classical test theory** structured the way test construction and test score analysis were approached. That theory maintains that measuring anything that can't be measured directly will include some error. The evidence is fluctuating scores when the measurement is repeated when the other relevant conditions (the learner's knowledge, the testing conditions) remain unchanged. The inference is that if testing procedures can be refined so that a measure administered under constant conditions yields a constant score, the score is more likely to be an accurate measure of the characteristic.

As a theoretical approach to test construction and score analysis, classical test theory has been largely supplanted but it remains very helpful to one trying to understand testing issues. Because the current generation of learners seems likely to be also the most tested generation of learners, we'll begin there.

The substance of classical test theory, also called true score theory, is represented in the equation:

$$x = t + e \qquad\qquad 15.1$$

Where,

x = the test-taker's score.

t = the respondent's true level of whatever is being measured

e = measurement error

Some characteristics are a great deal simpler to measure than others. Determining the mean age for a group of educators or the standard deviation of the height of a basketball team are relatively straightforward tasks. The same isn't true for determining the mean level of reading comprehension for a group of sixth-grade students, however. Reading comprehension must be measured by gauging performance on some task thought to manifest reading comprehension. The measured performance is represented by the x in Formula 15.1.

However, if the selected task doesn't actually represent reading comprehension very well, x can be "off" indicating error in the measurement, the "e" in Formula 15.1.

SCORE RELIABILITY

What indicates whether there is measurement error? The answer is related to score **reliability**. Test data are reliable to the degree that repeated measures of the same trait remain stable as long as the relevant conditions are also stable. This actually defines test-retest reliability. There are other approaches, but test-retest is a good way to think about reliability.

As an illustration, perhaps a special educator in a large school district is licensed to administer intelligence tests. The scores are reliable for a group of referred students if scores remain the same from a first to a second administration.

We use this example because intelligence is thought to be relatively stable over time and multiple measures ought to yield the same scores. But besides the trait measured, *all* the other relevant conditions must also remain static. The testing environment, the time allowed, the instructions given, the test-takers' physical conditions, and so on, all must be as similar as possible across the multiple measures for test-retest measures to work.

■ Reliability can be established by testing and then retesting, or by administering alternate forms of the test to the same people.

The Relationship Between Reliability and Measurement Error

Classical test theory holds that as score reliability increases, measurement error diminishes, and as error declines the test score approaches the true measure of the particular trait. If reliability is perfect, technically $e = 0$, and then $x = t$.

So what statistical tool will gauge the consistency between two sets of scores? Of course the answer is correlation. If one administers a test, waits, and then administers the test a second time to the same group, a correlation coefficient provides a measure of score reliability. If the test yields interval or ratio scale data, the Pearson Correlation (Chapter 10) is the appropriate tool.

Calculating Reliability: An Example

Using the intelligence test example, perhaps the special educator administers the test twice to eight students, waits a month, and then tests a second time. The eight students' scores on the first and second test are as follows:

	First	Second
1.	95	95
2.	90	85
3.	85	85
4.	100	95
5.	100	100
6.	105	100
7.	85	90
8.	95	95

Assuming that intelligence scores are interval scale (there is some debate about this), recall that the formula for a Pearson Correlation (Formula 10.2) has this form:

$$r_{xy} = \frac{n\Sigma xy - (\Sigma x)\,(\Sigma y)}{\sqrt{[n\Sigma x^2 - (\Sigma x)^2}\,\sqrt{n\Sigma y^2 - (\Sigma y)^2]}}$$

Treating the first set of scores as the "x" variable and the second set of scores as "y," verify that:

$n = 8$

$\Sigma xy = 70575$

$\Sigma x = 755$

$\Sigma y = 745$

$\Sigma x^2 = 71625$

$\Sigma y^2 = 69625$; therefore,

$$r_{xy} = \frac{8(70575) - (755)(745)}{\sqrt{[8(71625) - (755)^2]} \sqrt{[8(69625) - (745)^2]}} = \mathbf{.877}$$

The correlation between the first and second set of scores is $r_{xy} = .877$. In the case of test-retest reliability, the correlation value is also a reliability coefficient. In fact, reliability coefficients are also sometimes symbolically represented with a lowercase r. With a value of $r = .877$ (recall that the upper limit for correlation values is 1.0), this reliability coefficient is quite respectable.

If the data are ordinal scale, Spearman's *rho* (Chapter 14) will establish test-retest reliability. The "Another Example" box below describes a situation using ordinal scale data.

Another Example

Perhaps a representative to the district's bargaining team has collected data about how teachers feel about a proposal to institute merit pay. She has designed a survey that contains a rating scale for how teachers feel (ordinal data) about the proposal. Once the responses are coded and a score is totaled for each respondent, she uses Spearman's *rho* (Formula 14.1) to determine reliability:

	First	Second	difference	diff. sq'd
1.	5	6	−1	1
2	3	5	−2	4
3.	6	6	0	0
4.	4	5	−1	1
5.	2	4	−2	4
6.	9	7	2	4
7.	4	7	−3	9
8.	3	2	1	1
9.	3	5	−2	4
10.	1	3	−2	4

$\Sigma d^2 = 32$

$$r_s = 1 - \frac{(6 \Sigma d^2)}{N(N^2 - 1)} = \frac{1 - (6)(32)}{10(100 - 1)} = .806$$

Alternate Forms Reliability

■ **Alternate forms reliability** is a procedure for determining the stability of some measured characteristic by using alternate forms of the same test over time. It's reflected in a situation where those who struggle on form A of a test of problem-solving ability also struggle on form B of the same test, and those who do well on A do well on B. The difficulty in alternate forms reliability is ensuring that both forms measure the same characteristics to the same degree.

A variation on test-retest reliability involves different forms of the same test and is called, logically, **alternate forms reliability**. This approach presumes, of course, that a Form A and a Form B of the same test both measure the same characteristic. The issue is still the correlation between the two sets of scores so the math is the same as for test-retest reliability, but alternate forms reliability offers the advantage that the test-taker's initial exposure to the test doesn't so easily confound the second testing. The obvious drawback is that one must develop multiple forms of the same test, and then be able to demonstrate their equivalence. This is called test equating, and for test development organizations it can be a very technical and expensive process. Although they may occasionally prepare another form of an existing test, most educators aren't able to commit the time and resources that test equating requires.

What's a High Reliability Coefficient?

Just as we asked, "What value indicates a high correlation," in Chapter 10, here we're prompted to ask when a reliability coefficient is high enough to indicate "good" reliability. What constitutes acceptable reliability depends to some degree on the decisions involved. When they have a great impact on people the standard is higher than it is for less important decisions. By most accounts whether an applicant will be admitted to university is important enough that scores from admissions tests are held to a high reliability standard. The SAT published by the College Board and administered by the Educational Testing Service has been used for college admissions for many years. It typically has test-retest reliability in excess of $r = .90$. Data from a survey about which soft drink students at a particular high school prefer are less important and perhaps $r = .65$ is sufficient.

Even when reliability coefficients are high, the National Council on Measurement in Education, the American Educational Research Association, and the American Psychological Association all warn against basing important decisions on just one test score. There are several reasons for the position, but one of the more important is the recognition that even the most reliable scores contain some error.

Expanding Reliability

We keep saying that test-retest and for that matter alternate forms reliability approaches only work if the trait measured is stable. That's a problem when it comes to measuring something like student achievement that, for the good of both students and teachers, better *not* remain unchanged. Internal consistency reliability is the better approach to many classroom situations.

Instead of testing and retesting, the idea with internal consistency reliability is to derive multiple measures from one administration of the test. Does this sound like statistical sleight-of-hand? It makes sense if one considers what is called **split-half reliability**. If we compare test-takers' scores on the even-numbered items with their scores on the odd-numbered items, we can still calculate the agreement between two measures. The two groups of items become the equivalent of the testing and retesting, or the alternate forms reliability approaches for reliability purposes. The reliability coefficient is the correlation of the two sets of scores for each individual just like the correlation of the first set of scores with the second in test-retest. There are some prerequisites to this approach:

■ **Internal consistency** approaches, including **split-half reliability**, derive multiple measures from one test administration.

- So that it's reasonable to compare scores on one half with those on the other half, the entire test must measure the same trait or characteristic.
- Item quality must be consistent over the entire test.
- Item difficulty must be comparable. For this reason it is common to use odd-numbered items versus evens rather than the first half of the test compared to the last half of the test. Often earlier items are less difficult than later items.

THE SPEARMAN-BROWN PROPHECY FORMULA

As it happens, the split-half approach to determining reliability has a drawback. By treating one test as two, each half of the test is, of course, only half the length of the original test. For a test of 28 items, one ends up comparing the scores on the 14 odd-numbered items with the score on the 14 even-numbered items. The problem is that test length is related to reliability. Other things equal, the longer the test, the higher the reliability. Instead of reliability for one test of 28 items we end up with a coefficient for two tests of 14 items each, and the resulting reliability value is artificially low as a measure for the entire instrument.

A rescue of sorts comes in the form of the **Spearman-Brown Prophecy Formula**. The "Spearman" is the same Charles Spearman that studied intelligence and developed Spearman's *rho*—Chapter 14. Rather than crystal balls or tarot cards, the "prophecy" part refers to a technique for predicting reliability for tests of varying lengths. In the case of split-half, we want to

■ The **Spearman-Brown Prophecy Formula** predicts the impact on data reliability of altering test length.

predict the impact on reliability of doubling the number of items (to put the test back to its original length). The formula is as follows:

$$r_{sp/br} = \frac{(nr)}{1+(n-1)r}$$

15.2

Where,

$r_{sp/br}$ = the Spearman-Brown predicted reliability

n = the factor by which test length will change; $n = 2$ indicates

that the test is to be returned to its original length

r = the correlation between the halves

Using the 28-item test as an example, if there was a correlation between the odd-(x) and even-numbered (y) items of r_{xy} = .62, Spearman-Brown will predict reliability for a 28-item instrument. In that case, $n = 2$, since we're doubling the length from 14 to 28 items, and $r = .62$, the correlation between the two halves.

$$r_{sp/br} = \frac{(nr)}{1+(n-1)r} = \frac{(2)(.62)}{1+(2-1).62} = \frac{1.24}{1+.62} = .765$$

Based on just half the actual test length, the split-half reliability coefficient was originally a middling $r = .62$, but that value is artificially low. A better estimate of reliability for the entire test is $r = .765$.

Other Applications for Spearman-Brown

Here we used $r_{sp/br}$ to check what reliability would be for a full-length test that had been halved to accommodate split-half reliability, but the formula can be used to predict the impact on reliability for *any* change in test length. If we discovered that testing and then retesting a 16-item test yielded a reliability coefficient of $r = .57$, we could predict whether it would be worthwhile to add another 8 items. In the Spearman-Brown formula we insert the coefficient value, $r = .57$ and the change in number of items, $n = 1.5$ (we're suggesting an increase from 16 to 24 items, a factor of 1.5), and have the following:

$$r_{sp/br} = \frac{(nr)}{1+(n-1)r} = \frac{(1.5)(.57)}{1+(1.5-1).57} = \frac{.855}{1.285} = .665$$

SOURCE: Created by Suzanna Nielson.

"I think they may have missed something here. They're trying to use the prophecy formula to predict the point-spread in tomorrow's game.

If item quality remains constant, an additional 8 test items will probably boost test reliability from $r = .57$ to about $r = .665$.

Note that there are diminishing returns to adding items. In the first example, doubling the length of the test brought an increase of .145 in the reliability coefficient. Increasing the length of the test by a factor of two doesn't provide anything approaching double the reliability (indeed can't, since $r = 1.0$ is the ceiling). Although the relationship between the length of the instrument and score reliability is positive, as test length increases the effect of adding additional items diminishes. In our second example, 8 more items provided a substantial jump from $r = .57$ to $r = .665$ but another increment as large would take more than an additional 8 items.

Lee Cronbach

Lee Cronbach was something of a prodigy. The story is told that as a 4-year-old with his mother grocery shopping, Lee volunteered that the price per pound for potatoes was lower at another store he had visited earlier with the baby-sitter. A local school psychologist overheard the exchange and offered to administer the Stanford-Binet intelligence test to young Lee. That test was developed by Lewis Terman who was conducting his "Longitudinal Study of the Gifted" at the time. By his own account, Cronbach became "one of Terman's brats." He graduated from Fresno (California) High at 14 and from Fresno State College at 18. After a doctoral degree at the University of Chicago, he made his way to Terman's institution, Stanford University. Cronbach had tremendous influence on the way we approach a variety of measurement problems.

Cronbach's Alpha

■ Coefficient alpha, r_{KR20} and r_{KR21}, estimates internal consistency. The r_{KR} formulae are for dichotomously scored items.

Rather than dividing the test into odd and even item halves to calculate internal consistency reliability, Cronbach devised something more sophisticated. His is perhaps the most commonly used statistic for analyzing reliability when the test is administered just once. It's called "**coefficient alpha**," or in his honor, "Cronbach's alpha."

Rather than dividing the test into halves, Cronbach's approach was to base reliability on the score for each item compared with the score for all of the other items on the test. This approach can be used for items that have weighted scores, scores that may have values other than just 1 or 0. When items are dichotomously scored, such as pass/fail, competent, not competent, there is a separate procedure that we'll come to below. The formula for Cronbach's alpha is:

$$\alpha = \frac{k}{K-1}\left[\frac{1-\Sigma s_i^2}{s^2}\right]$$

15.3

Where,

k = the number of items

s_i^2 = the score variance for item i

Σs_i^2 = the sum of all the individual item variances

s^2 = the total test variance

Calculating Coefficient Alpha

We haven't had much call for the variance statistic except in Chapter 6 for an uneven sample sizes independent t. Recall that it's just the square of the standard deviation value. Steps for calculating coefficient alpha are as follows:

1. Note the number of items on the test, k

2. Calculate the variance in individual item scores, s_i^2—the variance in item 1 scores, the variance in item 2 scores, and so on

3. Sum the individual item score variances, Σs_i^2

4. Total the scores for each test-taker

5. Calculate the variance in test-takers' scores, s^2

6. Solve for α

Table 15.1 includes an example of calculating alpha for an 8-item test with 10 test-takers.

Table 15.1   Score Reliability Using Cronbach's Alpha

The mathematics curriculum specialist for a school district designed an algebra I test to gauge whether students grasp certain basic principles. Each of the items is scored 1–4.

1 indicates the student's response was completely incorrect.

2 indicates that the student demonstrates some understanding of the problem.

3 indicates that with minor errors, the solution was essentially correct.

4 indicates that the solution was completely correct.

(Continued)

Table 15.1 (Continued)

The scores on each of the 8 items for the 10 people who took the test are indicated in the table below.

The Test-Takers												
		1	2	3	4	5	6	7	8	9	10	Item Variances
The Items	1	1	2	2	3	2	3	2	1	2	3	.544
	2	2	3	2	2	3	3	3	1	4	3	.711
	3	3	3	4	3	3	4	3	2	2	3	.444
	4	1	2	3	4	3	4	3	2	3	4	.989
	5	2	3	4	3	2	2	2	3	4	3	.622
	6	1	1	4	2	2	2	2	3	2	3	.844
	7	2	3	4	3	3	4	4	3	3	4	.456
	8	3	2	3	2	3	2	2	2	3	3	.278
Score Totals		15	19	26	22	21	24	21	17	23	26	$\Sigma s^2_i = 4.889$
Total Score Variance = 13.156												

3

Note the number of items on the test, $k = 8$.

Verify the score variance for each item, s_i^2.

Sum the individual item variances and verify that, $\Sigma s_i^2 = 4.889$.

Total the scores for each test-taker.

Calculate the total score variance and verify that $s^2 = 13.156$.

Solve for α.

$$\alpha = \frac{k}{k-1}\left[1 - \frac{\Sigma s_i^2}{s^2}\right]$$

$$= \frac{8}{7}\left[1 - \frac{4.889}{13.156}\right]$$

$$= (1.143)(1 - .372)$$

$$= .718$$

Internal consistency reliability for the math test is $\alpha = .718$.

The data in Table 15.1 produced a reliability coefficient of $\alpha = .718$, which is quite good, given the length of the test. The key is the ratio of the sum of individual item variances to the variance in the total scores. Here it's quite low. As that ratio increases alpha declines.

Looking at SPSS Output

Coefficient alpha can also be computed on SPSS. For the problem that's in Table 15.1, the output is as follows:

Reliability Statistics

Cronbach's Alpha	N of Items
.719	10

The alpha value is about the same as we calculated longhand. The one, one-thousandth difference we can attribute to round-off.

Cronbach's alpha is based on test items that are scored according to the *degree* that whatever is measured is present/absent, or the degree to which answer is correct/incorrect. In an attitude survey, the issue may be *how strongly* the respondent feels. On an achievement test, it's how many points the response was awarded.

The Kuder and Richardson Formulae

The **Kuder and Richardson Formula 20** is an equivalent to the alpha coefficient, but for yes/no, or right/wrong items. The notation is r_{KR20} and the formula has this form:

$$r_{KR20} = \frac{k}{k-1}\left[1 - \frac{\Sigma pq}{s^2}\right]$$

15.4

Where,

k = number of items

p = proportion of test-takers scoring a particular item correctly. If 10 people attempt the item and 7 scored it correctly, $p = .7$

q = proportion scoring a particular item incorrectly. If 10 people attempt the item and 3 scored it incorrectly, $q = .3$

Σpq = the product of the proportion who scored the item correctly and the proportion who scored the item incorrectly summed across all items

s^2 = variance of total scores

Table 15.2 contains an example of calculating r_{KR20} reliability.

One of the limitations to both Cronbach's alpha and r_{KR20} is that one must know how every individual responded to every item in order to complete the calculations. Sometimes only total scores are available. When that's the case, **r_{KR21}** is an option. It is less precise than r_{KR20} but provides a reasonably good estimate of reliability. The formula is the following:

$$r_{KR21} = 1 - \frac{(.8)(M)(k-M)}{(k)(s^2)}$$ 15.5

Where,

M = the test mean

k = no. of items

s^2 = variance in the test score totals

For the data in Table 15.2, if all we had were score totals and the number of items, we could calculate the mean and the variance and then proceed with r_{KR21}. First, $M = 4.8$, $s^2 = 2.400$, and of course, $k = 8$.

$$r_{KR21} = 1 - \frac{(.8)(5.0)(8-5.0)}{(8)(3.778)} = 1 - \frac{12.0}{30.224} s = \textbf{.603}$$

This value is a little low but not surprising since there are only 8 items. The r_{KR20} value was .514. When one has responses to individual items, r_{KR20} will be more accurate. The r_{KR21} calculation is typically more conservative and can be thought of as a "lower bound" for reliability.

SCORE VERSUS TEST RELIABILITY

Although people speak of *test* reliability, reliability is a function of the scores so *score* reliability is more accurate language. A grammar test might yield

Table 15.2 Score Reliability Using Kuder and Richardson's Formula 20

The English department faculty members have decided to refine a published reading comprehension test by modifying the test items. There are questions about technical quality of the scores. Ten 10th-grade students are administered the test and their data are as follows:

The Test-takers

		1	2	3	4	5	6	7	8	9	10	p	q	pq
	1	1	1	1	0	0	1	1	0	1	1	.7	.3	.21
	2	1	0	0	1	0	0	0	0	1	0	.3	.7	.21
The Items	3	1	1	1	0	1	1	1	0	1	1	.8	.2	.16
	4	1	0	1	1	1	1	1	1	1	1	.9	.1	.09
	5	0	0	1	0	0	0	0	0	0	0	.1	.9	.09
	6	1	1	0	1	1	1	1	0	1	1	.8	.2	.16
	7	1	0	1	0	1	1	1	1	1	1	.8	.2	.16
	8	1	0	0	1	0	1	1	0	0	0	.4	.6	.24
Score Totals		7	3	5	4	4	6	6	2	6	5			$\Sigma = 1.32$

Score Variance = 2.400

$$r_{KR20} = (k/k - 1)(1 - (\Sigma pq/s^2)) \qquad 15.4$$

Steps:

Determine the number of test items *(k)*.

Determine the score totals for each test-taker.

Calculate the variance for score totals *(s²)*.

Determine for each item, the proportion who scored the item correctly *(p)*.

Determine for each item the proportion who scored the item incorrectly *(q)*.

Find the product of *pq* for each item.

Sum the pq values *(Σpq)*.

Solve for r_{KR20}

$$r_{KR20} = (8/7)(1 - (1.32 /2.400))$$
$$= (1.143)(1 - .55)$$
$$= \textbf{.514}$$

A reliability value of $r_{KR20} = .514$ is not very good, which isn't surprising given the length of the instrument.

reliable scores for students' grasp of grammar, but unreliable scores as a gauge reading comprehension, something for which it was not intended. To say in the latter case that the test is unreliable misses the point. The fault is with the application rather than the instrument.

Strengthening Reliability

Early in the chapter we noted that as reliability increases, measurement error decreases. So, how does one boost reliability? The answers relate to test length, item scoring, and item clarity.
    Test length.

As long as item quality is consistent, and respondents neither become fatigued nor run out of time, more items mean higher reliability.

    Item scoring.

Although they get a bad press, objectively scored items such as multiple choice items help reliability. Their strength is that they are, well, objectively scored. Even with a carefully prepared rubric, it's difficult to maintain scoring reliability for items where respondents construct, or create, the response. There are certainly reasons to use such items, but they make it more difficult to achieve high reliability.

    Item clarity.

Items that are ambiguous or confusing to those who should understand the material are a problem because if knowledgeable test-takers misunderstand the task, they may respond differently for reasons unrelated to their level of skill or ability.

Classification Consistency

Many situations call for classification. Supervisors need to determine whether a candidate has a required skill. Instructors need to judge whether students have a particular competency. Special educators must determine whether a student manifests a disability. Classification errors can have important implications for the people involved so it's a good idea to have a way to determine the reliability of the judgments involved in classification.

One simple approach is to use results from two judgments of the same competency to calculate an *index* of consistency, C_i (Chase, 1999). The formula is as follows:

$$C_i = \frac{(P + F)}{T}$$
15.6

Where,

C_i = the index of classification consistency

P = the no. who met the standard according to two judges

F = the no. who didn't meet the standard according to either judge

T = the number of individuals for whom judgments are made

Perhaps 50 aspiring teachers have completed a competency test required for certification. Two judges classify the candidates independently.

- Judge 1 determines that 42 of the 50 have demonstrated competence.
- The remaining 8 are judged not competent by Judge 1.
- Of the 42 judged competent by judge 1, Judge 2 determines that 37 are competent. Therefore, $P = 37$.
- Of the 8 judged not competent by Judge 1, 6 were also judged not competent by Judge 2; $F = 6$.

Solving for C_i we have:

$$C_i = \frac{P + F}{T} = \frac{37 + 6}{50} = \textbf{.86}$$

If there is perfect agreement between the judges, $C_i = 1.0$. This means more than that there must be the same P and F numbers from the first to the second administration. The same *people* must be judged to have passed or failed both times.

What is variously called inter-rater reliability, judgment reliability, or consistency are conceptually simple enough, but they can be difficult to pursue unless the criteria are very clear and there is training available for those making the judgments. The disagreements at international ice-skating competitions are a case in point.

THE STANDARD ERROR OF MEASUREMENT

Earlier the expression $x = t + e$ was used, among other things, to introduce the concept of error in measurement. The abstract nature of comprehension, problem-solving ability, and other characteristics to be gauged, increases the likelihood of error in measurement. But can we actually measure error and so gain a sense of the test-taker's true score?

Theoretically, the average score when an instrument is administered many times with conditions held constant would be the true score. By that approach it would take a rare set of circumstances to know the true measure of someone's achievement motivation, for example. It may be a useable definition, but it's an impractical way to proceed.

■ The **standard error of measurement** estimates the error in a mental measurement.

The alternative is to *estimate* the error, and this is where the **standard error of measurement** (*SEM*) comes in. By now you know that rather than interpreting the various standard error statistics as some sort of mistake, in statistical terms "error" indicates variability. By extension, then, the standard error of measurement indicates how much variability there is in measurement. Specifically, if an individual was tested multiple times under the same conditions, unless there is no error in the measurements, the scores will likely change a little each time. The *SEM* indicates the standard deviation of those multiple scores and so suggests the magnitude of the measurement error. Large standard deviations indicate larger amounts of error, since it's error that makes the scores change with each retesting. The formula for calculating the *SEM* is the following:

$$SEM = s\sqrt{1-r}$$

15.7

Where,

SEM = the standard error of measurement

s = the standard deviation of the test scores

r = the reliability coefficient for the set of scores

Formula 15.7 clarifies the relationship between score reliability and error. It indicates that error is affected by the standard deviation of the test scores (*s*), and the reliability of the scores (*r*). A combination of highly variable scores (large *s*) and low reliability results in the largest amount of error.

The problem at the beginning of the chapter referenced the performance assessment or PA designed to predict how students will perform on the state-required test at the end of the year. Perhaps some analysis indicates that seventh-grade students who score 65 on the PA will pass the state mathematics standard. A student who scores 60 points won't meet the state standard and perhaps begin some intensive remediation before the state test. But that judgment assumes that one can have confidence in the predictive ability of the PA scores; it assumes little error. For that to be accurate the observed score on the test (x) better be very nearly equal to the true measure (t) of the student's math ability.

Suppose PA data for seventh-grade math students yield the following:

- Cronbach's α is determined to = .85. This is a reliability value and is inserted in the place of r below
- The standard deviation of the scores is s = 15.0
- Since $SEM = \sqrt{1-r}$, $= 15\sqrt{1-.85}$ = **5.809**

Interpreting SEM

Remember from Chapter 3 that the area under the curve from +1 to −1 standard deviation includes approximately 68% of the population. That extends to the population of measurement errors as well. In our example, SEM = 5.809. That being the case, the individual's true score will fall +/− 5.809 from the observed score 68% of the time. It's +/− because for some students the error inflates the observed scores and for others it diminishes it. For any one student it might have been either.

So back to that one student who scored 60 points on the PA. The alpha coefficient indicates that there is error in the score. That means that p = .68 that the true measure of math ability is *somewhere between*:

$$60 - 5.809 = \mathbf{54.191} \text{ and}$$

$$60 + 5.809 = \mathbf{65.809}$$

Since the cut-off score for meeting the state standard is 65, the student's score may meet the state standard after all. Deciding that the student didn't meet the standard may result in a type II error, a false negative. With a score near the lower bound of the interval, certainly the odds are against the student, but the standard error of measurement should remind us to be careful with any score near a decision point. There's a .68 probability that the true measure of the student's score is somewhere between 54.191 and 65.809.

Just as +/– 1 *SEM* indicates the range within which a true score will occur 68% of the time, +/– 2 *SEM* is the range within which the true score occurs 95% of the time. If a particular intelligence test has $s = 15$ and a test-retest reliability coefficient of $r = .90$, what is the range within which an individual's true measure of intelligence will fall 95% of the time if the individual scores 110 on the test? First the standard error of measurement:

$$SEM = s\sqrt{1-r} = 15\sqrt{1-.90} = \textbf{4.743}$$

To accommodate $p = .95$ we need the +/– 2 *SEM* interval around x. With

- x = 110 and
- *SEM* = 4.743,

the interval for *t*, the true score, is from

- **100.513** (110 – 2 × 4.743) to **119.487** (110 + 2 × 4.743)

In our two examples, reliability is quite high, which translates into relatively small *SEM* values. But the error term grows quickly when scores are highly variable and/or reliability is poor.

Reliability for the Group Versus the Individual

Whether high or low, a reliability coefficient is a generalization. In test-retest examples, reliability reflects how well scores from an initial testing agreed with scores from a second administration *for the group who took the test*. As long as the group is representative, their results should translate well for other, similar groups. However, scores which are highly reliable for a *group* of test-takers, and for which error is therefore minimal on average, may still contain a significant amount of error for *one person* within the group. In the group as a whole, positive and negative measurement errors tend to cancel each other out, but this can't be so for one individual. This is one of the reasons for the earlier caution about making decisions based on just one test score.

SCORE VALIDITY

This chapter has been about the topics related most closely to score reliability. Because of the connection between reliability and validity, before moving on we need to make some mention of score validity.

Perhaps the most common and general definition of score validity is that scores are valid to the degree that they measure what they purport to measure. Although this actually best fits what is called **construct validity**, it's a good place to begin. If it's valid, a score's magnitude indicates the quantity of whatever is measured. If two students take a spelling test and one receives a higher score than the other, the higher score must indicate the better speller, or the scores aren't valid.

> ■ When a measure indicates the amount of the construct measured, a score has **construct validity**.

The connection between reliability and validity is this: Reliability is necessary, but not sufficient for validity. Scores which are valid are also reliable, but reliability doesn't assure validity. The story is told of a principal who gauged his teachers' classroom management skills based on how tidy the Venetian blinds were in the classroom windows. However stable that indicator might be (the same teachers probably tend to have tidy or untidy blinds in their windows day after day), it's hard to think of anything in the research literature suggesting a connection between blind neatness and classroom management. The principal has an indicator with good reliability and at best, unproven validity.

THE MOST TESTED GENERATION

For all the criticism that's leveled at them, standardized test results remain perhaps the most widely publicized indicator of educational progress. Inevitably, performance differences have also been widely reported, particularly when they relate to students' gender, their ethnic group membership, their social class, or to some other characteristic.

Ironically, when the differences are person-to-person we aren't surprised. In any normal distribution (Chapter 3) we expect that whatever is measured will be distributed along an approximately 6 standard deviation range. But scoring differences which appear to follow gender, ethnic group, or social class lines attract attention. The accompanying charge is often that the test is biased against whichever group performs least well. Documenting cases of scoring bias can involve a variety of statistical analyses, including some of the procedures covered earlier in this book.

Bias in Admissions Testing

Reasoned discussions about why gender group, ethnic group, or income groups perform differently on standardized tests can quickly deteriorate into an emotionally charged argument (see Kincheloe & Steinberg, 2007; Sandoval, Frisby, Geisinger, Sheuneman, & Grenier. 1999; Skelton, Francis, & Smulyan,

■ **Test bias** occurs when scores systematically vary for reasons unrelated to actual differences in the quality measured.

2006 as cases in point). Although experts recognize that a variety of factors can explain why one group consistently does better than another, **test bias** is at least one of the explanations. To support a charge of bias, analysis must indicate that scores systematically favor (or diminish the performance of) one group over another *for reasons unrelated to associated differences in the quality measured*.

By that description, *random variability* doesn't give rise to bias. Random variability is reflected in things like inconsistent instructions to test-takers, distractions during the testing period, and other factors that diminish score reliability. They are problems certainly, but they don't constitute bias unless the problems affect only one group, if only one group is exposed to a distraction, for example. Controlling those sources of variance is one of the reasons that those who administer the tests make such an effort to standardize the testing conditions.

Scores may vary systematically and be unbiased as long as the quality measured also varies. If students in one gender group consistently read better than those in the other gender group we have systematic variability, but as long as the scoring differences are an accurate indicator of how well the two groups read, any difference doesn't reflect a bias problem stemming from the test. Perhaps the teaching was better in the higher performing group.

If the two groups read equally well but scores indicate a difference, however, the situation changes. How can we know if an instrument produces biased scores? A university admissions test provides a way to analyze one dimension of the problem.

An Example

For the sake of illustration assume that a consortium of universities all require that entering freshman students take the University Admissions Test, the "U-at" (as in "What university are you at?" . . . sorry), and then base admissions decisions partly on the score. Their support for the test is based in their understanding that it predicts how well students will perform in their first year of university study.

After some years of using the test critics begin to argue that the scores have a gender-bias. A researcher decides to investigate the claim and selects a random sample of 10 females and 10 males who have taken the "U-at." Their test scores are listed in Table 15.3.

How should one pursue the bias question? The logical first step would be to look at descriptive statistics according to gender. Verify that means and standard deviations for the test scores (ignore the GPA data for now) in Table 15.3 are as follows:

Table 15.3   Examining Admissions Test Scores to Detect Bias

Female Students		Male Students	
Test Score	Fresh. GPA	Test Score	Fresh. GPA
35	2.20	33	2.00
43	2.20	51	2.20
49	2.30	56	2.40
53	3.00	71	2.85
55	3.20	77	2.70
59	3.00	78	2.75
64	3.00	82	2.50
67	3.30	85	2.95
75	3.20	89	3.20
81	3.00	90	2.90

	M	s
Females	58.10	14.161
Males	71.20	18.725

Clearly there's a difference. These 10 male students performed better on the test than the females. Their scores are also a little more variable. But putting on the statistician's hat, the analyst asks, "Ah, but is the difference statistically significant?"

Because there are two independent groups and the dependent variable is (presumably) interval scale, the question lends itself to the independent t-test (Chapter 6). Recall that the independent t-test requires the means and standard deviations for each group, the standard error of the mean for each group, and the standard error of the difference for both groups together. With those in hand we can calculate the t value and compare it to the critical value from the table (Table B in this case).

$$SE_m = s/\sqrt{n} \qquad\qquad 6.1$$

For Females: $14.161/\sqrt{10} = \mathbf{4.478}$

For Males: $18.725/\sqrt{10} = \mathbf{5.921}$

$$SE_d = \sqrt{(SE_{m1}^2 + SE_{m2}^2)} \qquad\qquad 6.4$$

$$= \sqrt{(4.478^2 + 5.921^2)} = \mathbf{7.424} \qquad\qquad 6.3$$

$$t = (M_1 - M_2)/SE_d$$

$$= (58.10 - 71.20)/7.424 = \mathbf{-1.765}$$

Dutifully checking Table B for critical values of t reveals that for $df = 18$ and $p = .05$ the value is 2.101, the significance value for a two-tailed. The absolute value of the test statistic is lower than the table value, so yes, there's a difference, but it isn't statistically significant. Someone defending the use of the "U-at" is off the hook, right?

Actually this independent t-test approach is a little risky. Besides the fact that statistical significance is partly a function of sample size (although $t = 1.765$ is never going to be statistically significant regardless of sample size), if this test were run as a one-tailed test, there would have been a different outcome. If the researcher had reason to believe to begin with that females would score less well, the analyst might have predicted that and done a one-tailed test. In that case, the result would have been statistically significant ($t_{.05\ (18)} = 1.734$).

What would it mean if the difference between the two groups *were* significant? Perhaps one gender group takes different classes in high school than the other and those differences in the students' experiences and learning are what give rise to the different "U-at," scores. In that case the test is a messenger of the differences but not their cause. If we used one of the procedures that will be discussed in Chapter 16 to control those other possible sources of variability, and the difference is still significant, there may be a problem.

Another Point of View

The differential course-taking and one-versus two-tailed issues aside, there are other issues involved in a problem like this one. The rationale for using the test was its prediction of the student's potential for success in university study, once admitted. From the standpoint of its value as a predictor maybe whether males and females score differently is less an issue than whether the scores suggest how well things will go during that first year of university study.

In other words, the argument for using the test is that there is a correspondence between scores and freshman year performance. If the correspondence is high, maybe the scores are worthwhile tools for culling through admissions applications. How might we gauge that correspondence? Correlation seems like a logical answer. If we correlate the test scores with students' freshman year grade averages, the results will at least indicate whether there is a statistically significant relationship between the two variables.

Recall that the formula for a Pearson Correlation (we'll assume that both variables are measured on at least an interval scale) is

$$r_{xy} = \frac{n\Sigma xy - (\Sigma x)(\Sigma y)}{\sqrt{[n\Sigma x^2 - (\Sigma x)^2]}\sqrt{[n\Sigma y^2 - (\Sigma y)^2]}} \qquad 10.2$$

Treating the test scores as the x variable and the grade averages as the y variable, verify that:

$\Sigma x = 1293$

$\Sigma x^2 = 89411$

$\Sigma y = 54.85$

$\Sigma y^2 = 153.518$

$\Sigma xy = 3631.3$, and of course that

$N = 20$

$$r_{xy} = \frac{20(3631.3) - (1293)(54.85)}{\sqrt{[20(89411) - (1293)^2]}\sqrt{[20(153.518) - (54.85)^2]}} = .636$$

The critical value for r (Table E), with $df = 18$ (the number of pairs, minus 2) is

$r_{xy.05(18)} = .444$. It's a significant correlation.

So, we at least have the assurance that the relationship between the two variables is not random. Although that's helpful, it doesn't address the issue directly. A bias problem will be reflected in the fact that the correlation between test score and performance is different for males than it is for females. Dividing the two sets of scores according to gender and redoing the calculations we have:

$$r_{xymales} = \textbf{.898}$$

$$r_{xyfemales} = \textbf{.768}$$

Checking the table indicates that both correlation coefficients are statistically significant. But do the differences between the correlation values matter? The "U-at" scores for males have more in common with freshman year GPA than they have for females. Because of the higher correlation for males, a prediction based on the test score is going to be more accurate for males than it is for females.

This difference is made more apparent in the square of the Pearson Correlation, which you will remember from Chapter 10 is the *coefficient of determination* (r^2). Recall that r^2 values will indicate how much of the variance in y can be explained by manipulating x (or vice versa). For us the issue is how much of freshman grade average can be explained by whatever the "U-at" measures.

$$r^2_{xymales} = .806$$

$$r^2_{xyfemales} = .590$$

■ **Predictive validity** indicates how well a measure predicts some future, related behavior or measure.

The difference between the two, about 22% of the variance, is substantial. If these were real data from a real test, it would probably be enough of an issue to raise concerns about the value of the test as a predictor of college performance for female students. The test significantly correlates with their freshman year grades, but it does so at different levels for female than for males. The issue here is what is called **predictive validity**, and in this example, it's stronger for males than for females. Although it's difficult to identify the point at which the difference in what is actually predictive validity becomes a bias problem, certainly the "U-at" needs some work.

Teaching the Test

There are other situations for which the evidence of some sort of difficulty is statistical, and in some cases, it's quite easy to detect. When bodies of influential educators and leaders decided that educational quality in the United States was mediocre and that the nation was "at-risk," states responded with an accountability movement. One after another, states in the early 1980s imposed standardized tests on elementary and secondary school students. Those tests had norms, of course—standards of typical performance. After a year or two of testing, states began reporting surprising results; *most* of their students were scoring beyond the national norms for the test (Cannell, 1988). Now that should give one pause. Under what circumstances could most of those in any normal distribution score above the mean?

What Cannell (1988) reported was what Phillips and Finn (1988) termed the "Lake Wobegon effect," a reference to that mythical place in the National Public Radio program of years ago where all the children were "above average." The explanation was that once states adopted standardized tests as measures of student progress, educators began to align their curricula with the tests. As one would expect, students scored better each year as what was measured increasingly dictated what was taught.

But that shouldn't have been a problem. The scores still probably represented a normal distribution, but it was a normal distribution with a higher mean than that of the year before, and that was at the root of the difficulty. School districts and state departments of education reported current year performances but compared them with prior year national means (Phillips & Finn, 1988). As students in the states and districts continued to improve (as one would hope they would), more and more of them exceeded the outdated norms.

Those doing the reporting probably had qualms about using current data and outdated norms but the pressure to demonstrate progress, particularly at the elementary and secondary school level, can sometimes be almost overwhelming. Perhaps the justification they used had something to do with the difficulty of securing updated national norms. Without pursuing the problem further, the point is that what you learned in the early chapters of this book allows you recognize that an "everyone is above the mean" conclusion is more than implausible. It's impossible, unless the performance and the means are mismatched. Had someone tried to make such an argument within your hearing, you would have known straight away that there was a problem and (your author feels sure) felt driven to investigate.

SUMMARY

Not all test data are created equal. The point of this chapter is to bring earlier topics like correlation and standard deviation to bear on the problem of analyzing the technical quality of test data. In our discussion

- Classical test theory reminded us that mental measurements will nearly always include some element of error.

- We noted that error is diminished when data are reliable.
- The way reliability is determined depends upon whether the characteristic is stable over time, and whether it is manifested by its presence/absence or by degree.
- The standard error of measurement is an estimate of score error and is a function of score reliability and score variability.
- Measurement error can be diminished by a number of adjustments, including improving weak items, increasing the number of items, and minimizing distractions during the testing period.
- Data reliability imposes a ceiling to data validity. Although validity can be lower than reliability, it can be no higher.

Whatever their virtues or shortcomings, standardized test data have become the most closely watched gauge of educational progress. Without trying to be exhaustive, the issues raised in this chapter were an effort to provide a sense of how quantitative analysis can help one understand testing issues and improve decision-making.

EXERCISES

1. A school counselor develops a measure of achievement motivation. The test is administered twice with a 1-month interval to 8 randomly selected students. Scores are as follows:

	first admin	second admin
1.	54	58
2.	43	44
3.	87	85
4.	39	43
5.	55	56
6.	41	55
7.	72	66
8.	65	69

a. What is the test-retest reliability for the instrument?
b. If the test were doubled in length and the quality of the items remained constant, what should one expect the reliability coefficient to become?

2. A particular set of scores has reliability $\alpha = .73$ and a standard deviation of $s = 6.839$.

   a. What is the standard error of measurement?
   b. About 68% of the time, what is the range within which someone's true measure of ability will occur if that person has a score of $x = 64$?

3. A school district has prepared a comprehensive exam to determine how well students are prepared to take a state-mandated test at the end of the year. They have Form A and Form B with scores as follows for 10 students:

	Form A	Form B
1.	23	28
2.	26	33
3.	35	38
4.	43	42
5.	46	51
6.	49	44
7.	51	52
8.	62	52
9.	71	82
10.	78	61

   a. What is the alternate forms reliability for the instrument?
   b. If the test has 30 items, what impact will an additional 15 items of similar quality have on reliability?

4. Test-retest reliability for a particular measure of problem-solving ability is $r = .648$. If the current instrument contains 30 items, what will be the impact on reliability of adding another 30 items?

5. A certain achievement test with 35 right/wrong items yields the following scores for 13 students: 15, 17, 17, 18, 21, 21, 22, 22, 24, 24, 24, 27, 30.

   a. What approach will indicate internal consistency?
   b. What is the reliability value?
   c. What is the standard error of measurement?
   d. With $p = .68$, what range of scores will capture the true score for someone who scores 27?

6. A 10-item math test is designed with items that can have scores from 0–4. The test is administered to 8 students whose scores on the items are as below:

	item1	item2	item3	item4	item5	item6	item7	item8	item9	item10
1.	3	4	4	3	3	3	2	4	4	3
2.	2	3	3	3	2	2	1	2	2	2
3.	2	3	4	4	3	3	4	3	1	3
4.	3	1	2	4	4	2	1	4	3	0
5.	1	4	1	2	4	4	3	2	2	1
6.	2	3	4	4	4	3	3	4	4	2
7.	1	2	2	1	1	1	0	2	2	1
8.	1	3	2	0	1	2	1	0	3	0

   a. Calculate Cronbach's alpha for these scores.
   b. What is the standard error of measurement for this set of scores?
   c. What adjustments would likely decrease the value of the *SEM*?
   d. What would adding another 10 items do for reliability?
   e. Why does the addition of 10 items have such a nominal effect?

7. A test of grammar and usage is created for English learners. The individual items are scored correct (1) or incorrect (0) from left to right for each of 10 test-takers.

1	0	1	1	0	1	0	0	1	0
1	0	0	1	0	1	0	0	0	0
1	1	0	1	1	1	1	0	1	1
1	1	1	1	0	1	1	1	1	0
0	0	0	0	0	1	0	0	1	0
0	1	1	0	0	0	1	1	0	1
1	1	1	1	0	1	1	1	1	1
0	0	0	0	0	0	0	0	1	0
0	1	0	0	1	0	0	0	1	0
1	1	0	1	0	1	0	1	1	0

   a. What is r_{KR20} = reliability?
   b. Determine the boundary within which the true score will occur with $p = .95$ for someone with an observed score of 7.

8. Since Cronbach's alpha, Kuder and Richardson's formulae 20 and 21, and split-half reliability procedures all determine internal consistency, what determines which approach should be used in a particular situation?

9. For a particular 20-item test given to administrators to test their understanding of legal issues, scores are as follows:

17, 14, 19, 11, 14, 13, 16, 15, 18, 20

a. What is r_{KR21} reliability?
b. Why can you calculate neither coefficient α nor r_{KR20} reliability?
c. What can you estimate reliability to become if 10 items of similar quality are added to the instrument?

10. An observation instrument is designed to determine whether candidates are competent to teach music. It is administered to 20 candidates twice. As a result of the first administration, 17 of the candidates are judged competent. When the instrument is repeated, all of those thought competent the first time were once again judged competent, plus one more. What is the index of classification consistency?

11. An instrument used to determine whether students have a reading disability is employed with a group of 45 subjects in a large urban school district. As a result of the first administration, 32 are determined to have a reading disability, and the other 13 are indicated to be "slow readers." A second administration indicates that 37 have a reading disability. That number includes 27 of those who were indicated to be reading disabled the first time. Another 10 were determined not to have a reading disability both times. What is the index of classification consistency?

12. Why is it misleading to speak of "test" rather than "score" reliability?

13. Besides using correlation to determine whether the relationship between test scores and subsequent performance is similar for females and males, how could regression procedures lend themselves to this question?

14. In the chapter we found that a t-test for differences between the scores of males and females yielded nonsignificant results.

a. Why must t-test results that are not statistically significant with small samples be treated cautiously?
b. What type of decision error (Chapter 5) might have occurred with such results?

REFERENCES

Cannell, J. J. (1988). Nationally normed elementary achievement testing in America's public schools: How all 50 states are above the national average. *Educational Measurement: Issues and Practice, 7*(2), 5–9.

Chase, C. I. (1999). *Contemporary assessment for educators.* New York: Longman.

Kincheloe, J. L., & Steinberg, S. R. (2007). *Cutting class: Socioeconomic status and education.* Lanham, MD: Rowman & Littlefield.

Phillips, G. W., & Finn, C. E. Jr. (1988). The Lake Wobegon effect: A skeleton in the testing closet? *Educational Measurement: Issues and Practice, 7*(2), 10–12.

Sandoval, J., Frisby, C. L., Geisinger, K. F., Sheuneman, J. D., & Grenier, J. R. (1998). *Test interpretation* *and diversity: Achieving equity in assessment.* Washington, DC: American Psychological Association.

Skelton, C., Francis, B., & Smulyan, L. (2006). *The Sage handbook on gender and education.* Thousand Oaks, CA: Sage.

THE FORMULAE AND THEIR SYMBOLS

Formula 15.1: $x = t + e$. This formula represents the classical test theory position that any observed score (x) has two components, a true score (t) and some error (e).

Formula 15.2: $r_{sp/br} = \dfrac{(n\,r)}{1 + (n-1)r}$

This is the Spearman-Brown Prophecy Formula, which allows one to predict the impact on reliability of lengthening or abbreviating the number of items on an instrument.

Formula 15.3: $\alpha = \dfrac{k}{k-1}\left(\dfrac{1 - \Sigma s_i^2}{s^2}\right)$

Cronbach's alpha calculates internal consistency reliability for data based on items that can have variable scores.

Formula 15.4: $r_{KR20} = \dfrac{k}{k-1}\left(\dfrac{1 - \Sigma pq}{s^2}\right)$

The Kuder and Richardson's Formula 20 calculates internal consistency reliability when items have only two possible scores.

Formula 15.5: $r_{KR21} = 1 - \dfrac{(.8)(M)(k-M)}{(k)(s^2)}$

Kuder and Richardson's Formula 21 is an alternative to r_{KR20} when only the number of items, the score variance, and the mean are available.

Formula 15.6: $C_i = \dfrac{(P + F)}{T}$

This index of classification consistency provides a measure of agreement among multiple judges. It's a form of inter-rater reliability. With values ranging to 1.0, it's interpreted like other reliability coefficients.

Formula 15.7: $SEM = \sqrt{1 - r}$ The standard error of measurement is the standard deviation of multiple measure of some trait under consistent conditions. It is an estimate of measurement error.

STUDENT STUDY SITE

Visit the Student Study Site at **www.sagepub.com/tanner** for additional learning tools.

Chapter 16

A Brief Introduction to Selected Advanced Topics

THE PROBLEM: USING ANALYSES THAT ACCOMMODATE HUMAN COMPLEXITY

Many educational questions call for fairly simple analyses. Questions about which reading curriculum appears to result in the highest achievement gains, which instructional technique works best for gifted students, and the parents of which groups of students appear to be most supportive of their children's academic work lend themselves to answers based on descriptive statistics, or independent *t*-tests, or analyses of variance, and so on. Human complexity being what it is, however, thse issues are often more involved.

Perhaps the best instructional technique for gifted students is partly a function of the students' ages; that is, maybe differences related to age can become confused with differences related to technique. Maybe the differences in parental support that affect student progress are related to differences in parents' employment. Sometimes the difference between groups is best understood in terms of *multiple* dependent variables, rather than the one that *ANOVA* will accommodate.

Educators and the public generally have worried about economic and social consequences of students' dropping out of school. It would be helpful to predict whether a student is likely to drop out.

QUESTIONS AND ANSWERS

❏ How does one control a variable that isn't the primary focus, but affects an outcome nevertheless?

This is the question that analysis of covariance addresses. It allows one to neutralize the impact that one variable has on an outcome to get a clearer picture of another variable.

❏ When an independent variable such as curriculum appears to prompt differences in multiple, related dependent variables what's the best approach?

This will bring us to multivariate analysis of variance, an extension of analysis of variance that accommodates more than one dependent variable.

❏ Students who leave before graduating are at a perpetual financial disadvantage. There is, therefore, a compelling economic as well as social interest in retention. Can one predict a discrete outcome, rather than predict a score value?

This will bring us to discriminant function analysis.

◆ – ◆ – ◆

As helpful as it is to treat one variable at a time, such univariate approaches often don't reflect this reality: people's behaviors are enormously complicated. Think of the many factors that could be part of any comprehensive explanation of why students perform differently. One must consider aptitude differences, motivational differences, differences in teaching quality, curriculum, parental expectation, social class, and a host of other variables. For *some* questions the answers aren't simple. That notwithstanding, the work we did in the first 15 chapters has paved the way for this chapter, and for topics beyond. Having developed some ability with those initial procedures, no mean accomplishment by the way, we'll approach, on at least a conceptual level, some of the more advanced procedures. In most cases the math is beyond the scope of this book, but the ideas aren't. You're ready for this. The first few procedures are accompanied by SPSS output, the later examples are simply described in general terms. They're designed to let one know the sorts of problems each procedure can address.

Analysis of Covariance

One of the questions posed at the beginning of the chapter asked, how does one control a variable that isn't the variable of interest, but that may affect the outcome in an analysis nevertheless. To use the gifted students example, perhaps all the 9th- through 12th-grade students in honors history classes at a particular high school are randomly divided into three groups.

- One group receives a highly structured instructional program where the teacher makes all of the decisions, keeps to a detailed schedule, and allows for very little student input.
- A second group is assigned to classes where students make most of the decisions about what to study, how much time to spend on a topic, which kinds of assignments to complete, and so on.
- A third group receives a program where the teacher provides the instructional plan, but some modifications are allowed as a result of student input, and student discussion is encouraged.

After 8 weeks, students take a history test. Their scores are analyzed for significant differences between the groups.

To this point, the problem should look like a one-way *ANOVA* problem. There is one nominal scale independent variable that is the student's instructional group, and one (presumably) interval scale dependent variable, the score on the history test. But what if there is some concern that age, years and months old, might be a factor in score variation?

One way to control for age-related differences is to make the problem a factorial *ANOVA*, with age the second independent variable. That might be cumbersome since either each different year/month combination would need its own group, or ranges of ages would need to be collapsed so that there are relatively few age categories. The first option would require a very large sample to begin with so that there could be enough to create one group for 14-year-olds, another for those who are 14 years and 1 month, another for those 14 and 2 months, and so on up to 18 years and however many months.

The second option solves this problem by collapsing the groups according to years, but that ignores all the age differences within the group of those who are 14+, or 15+ and so on. Neither is ideal and besides, age isn't the focus of the study. In **analysis of covariance** (*ANCOVA*), we can solve this problem another way. The procedure is as follows:

- One determines how much of the variation in the dependent variable (history test scores) is related to the potentially confounding variable, age in this example,
- One neutralizes that variance by adjusting the means so that dependent variable (*DV*) differences related to age disappear, and then
- One proceeds with the adjusted scores with what at that point becomes a conventional analysis of variance (Pedhazur & Schmelkin, 1991).

The potentially confounding variable is called the **covariate**. Its name comes from the fact that, like the independent variable, it also "co-varies" with the dependent variable and part of the *DV* score may reflect differences in this variable rather than the independent variable (*IV*). In our example, if some of the differences in student performance are related to age, and age differences aren't accounted for, those differences may confound results. It may be impossible to know when performance differences reflect instructional differences, and when they stem from age differences.

■ **Analysis of covariance** mathematically neutralizes the effect of a potentially confounding variable to clarify the IV/DV relationship.

■ A **covariate** is a variable mathematically controlled in a statistical procedure so that it has a neutral effect on the outcome.

An *ANCOVA* Example

If different age groups of honors students are taught differently and there are corresponding performance differences between the groups, it is difficult to know whether the differences reflect age variability, instructional variability, or both. By way of illustrating *ANCOVA*, we'll do an example on SPSS. Perhaps the (contrived) data are as follows, with numbers indicating the student's instructional group (grp), the student's age in years (age), and the student's score (scr):

grp	age	scr
1	15.0	28
1	15.5	30
1	17.25	33
2	16.0	30
2	16.3	36
2	17.75	38
3	15.75	45
3	16.5	50
3	17.25	55

Having created the file above in SPSS, the commands are:

Analyze→General Linear Model (GLM)→Univariate (indicating that there's just one dependent variable).

Once the window is open:

- Identify the dependent variable, scr.
- "Fixed Factor" is GLM language for the IV, grp.
- The covariate, the variable to be controlled, is age.
- Click "OK."

The output includes an initial table that indicates how many are in each group, but what we're interested in is the figure immediately below titled "Tests of Between Subjects Effects."

Note that this procedure runs under the widely adaptable "General Linear Model" procedure (Chapters 8 and 9). Because the GLM isn't tailored to just one kind of problem, it typically provides more information than we need to answer our particular question so we have to sort through the output for what we want.

Understanding the Results: The Covariate

The focus is the significance values for the covariate (age) and for the *IV* (grp). Age, the covariate, is statistically significant. With a significance value of

Figure 16.1   Analysis of Covariance

Tests of Between-Subjects Effects

Dependent Variable: SCR

Source	Type III Sum of Squares	df	Mean Square	F	Sig.
Corrected Model	708.209 [a]	3	236.070	39.621	.001
Intercept	6.965	1	6.965	1.169	.329
AGE	67.543	1	67.543	11.336	.020
GRP	558.073	2	279.037	46.833	.001
Error	29.791	5	5.958		
Total	13963.000	9			
Corrected Total	738.000	8			

a. R Squared = .960 (Adjusted R Squared = .935)

.020, we have exceeded the $p = .05$ criterion. That tells us that we were right to control this source of variability. If it isn't controlled, then all the variance associated with age shows up as error variance and becomes part of the mean square for error, MS_{error}, or what was MS_w in the one-way ANOVA (Chapter 7). Recall that the mean square error is the denominator for calculating the F statistic in ANOVA $(F = MS_{bet}/MS_{error})$, so if the error term is large relative to the variance explained by the independent variable, chances are that the F value won't be significant.

The Independent Variable

Now the issue is the differences in the DV (the scores) related to instructional differences (the IV, "grp" variable). This source of variance too is statistically significant. It indicates that even after the variance associated with the covariate (students' ages) is controlled, scoring differences related to students' instructional groups are statistically significant. The type of instruction makes a difference in students' performance, even after accounting for age differences.

Another ANCOVA Example

Perhaps a researcher is interested in mathematics performance differences among students from different schools that correlate with students' ethnicity and gender. As it is, the problem looks like a factorial *ANOVA*, with ethnicity and gender the independent variables. But if some of the math difference stems from the fact that some students were able to take more math classes than others, that source of variance ought to be controlled. The number of units taken during high school can serve as a covariate in what would become a *factorial ANCOVA*.

There are many applications for *ANCOVA*. Besides separating the variability related to age from that related to teaching technique in the beginning-of-the-chapter example, class size might be a factor in the performance of students. In that case, the number of students in a class might serve as a covariate in an analysis of how curricular differences impact student achievement. Or, one studying violence as a function of school location (rural, urban, suburban) might need to treat the number of students as a covariate and control school size as a factor in student violence

Some Final Considerations

Since the *ANCOVA* allows one to rule out variance related to one or more potential confounding variables, why not just use it all the time rather than *ANOVA*? There are a couple of reasons for this. First and most obviously, in addition to the data for the *IV* and the *DV*, one must have data for the covariate, and those data must be measured on interval or ratio scale. They aren't always at hand.

Second, for every covariate added to an analysis, a degree of freedom (*df*) is assigned to the covariate, and lost from the MS_{error}. Remember that the various *MS* values in *ANOVA* are all calculated by dividing the *SS* values by their respective degrees of freedom. If the error term loses a degree of freedom, the resulting *MS* value is going to increase and affect the value of *F*. As long as the covariate is statistically significant, the effect of that *df* loss is more than compensated for by the reduction in SS_{error}. This isn't the case if the covariate is not statistically significant, however, so one chooses covariates carefully.

Finally, *ANCOVA* is sometimes used to create after-the-fact equivalence between groups in an analysis. That is, *ANCOVA* is sometimes used as a substitute for random selection in order to make convenience samples mathematically equivalent. Rather than "papering over" a mistake in research design, whenever one has a choice *ANCOVA* is best used to deal with equivalence problems that persist *after* random selection and random assignment.

MULTIVARIATE ANALYSIS OF VARIANCE

When there is more than one dependent variable in what would otherwise be an *ANOVA* problem the procedure is **multivariate analysis of variance**, usually referred to by its acronym, *MANOVA*. There are probably hundreds of studies of how different reading curricula impact students' reading achievement and others that study the impact on students' motivation to read. Since motivation is probably also related to achievement, it seems logical to include both variables in the same analysis.

> ■ *MANOVA* is like ANOVA except that multiple, related dependent variables are combined to explain differences in the IV.

Both *MANOVA* and *ANOVA* answer the same basic research question: Do groups have significantly different scores? The distinction between them is the number of dependent variables. If the question is, do students exposed to the different reading curricula have different levels of reading comprehension, a one-way *ANOVA* will answer because there's just one *DV*, reading comprehension. Add a second *DV*, the motivation to read in our example, and it's a *MANOVA* problem.

Combining the Dependent Variables

Although there are multiple *DV*s in a *MANOVA*, they aren't treated separately. The *DV*s are combined so as to provide the maximum separation between the levels of the independent variable. In our example, a reading comprehension score is combined with a motivation to read measure, with each variable optimally weighted, so that the combination provides the best distinction between the curriculum groups. The issue then is whether the differences are statistically significant. Once the *DV*s are combined, the problem is very much like a conventional *ANOVA*.

A *MANOVA* Example

To use the example from the beginning of the chapter, perhaps five students are randomly selected for each of three different reading programs.

- In the first program there is a great emphasis on reading current events in newspapers and newsweekly magazines.
- The second reading program emphasizes contemporary novels.
- The third curriculum is centered in classic literature.

After 16 weeks, students are given a standardized reading comprehension test. Their motivation to read is gauged by the number of hours per week they choose to read. The data are below with "cur" indicating the student's curricular group, "score" the score on the reading test, and "motiv" indicating the number of hours per week students read.

	cur	score	motiv
1.	1	19	2.0
2.	1	19	1.0
3.	1	20	2.0
4.	1	20	2.0
5.	1	17	1.0
6.	2	19	2.0
7.	2	22	2.5
8.	2	19	2.0
9.	2	22	2.5
10.	2	20	1.5
11.	3	20	1.0
12.	3	20	1.5
13.	3	23	2.5
14.	3	21	1.0
15.	3	22	2.5

The *MANOVA* procedure is to combine "score" and "motiv" into one aggregated dependent variable and then determine whether there are significant differences between any of the three groups on that combined variable.

Once the data file has been created

- Like the *ANCOVA*, this procedure runs under the GLM.
- With "multivariate" rather than "univariate" to indicate multiple *DVs*.
- The sequence in SPSS is: Analyze→General Linear Model→Multivariate

We'll designate both "score" and "motiv" as the *DVs*. The *MANOVA* solution for our data is in Figure 16.2.

Figure 16.2   Multivariate Analysis of Variance

Multivariate Tests[c]

Effect		Value	F	Hypothesis df	Error df	Sig.
Intercept	Pillai's Trace	.998	2492.754[a]	2.000	11.000	.000
	Wilks' Lambda	.002	2492.754[a]	2.000	11.000	.000
	Hotelling's Trace	453.228	2492.754[a]	2.000	11.000	.000
	Roy's Largest Root	453.228	2492.754[a]	2.000	11.000	.000
CUR	Pillai's Trace	.667	3.000	4.000	24.000	.039
	Wilks' Lambda	.408	3.112[a]	4.000	22.000	.036
	Hotelling's Trace	1.269	3.172	4.000	20.000	.036
	Roy's Largest Root	1.103	6.618[b]	2.000	12.000	.012

a. Exact statistic

b. The statistic is an upper bound on F that yields a lower bound on the significance level.

c. Design: Intercept+CUR

Tests of Between-Subjects Effects

Source	Dependent Variable	Type III Sum of Squares	df	Mean Square	F	Sig.
Corrected Model	SCORE	12.400[a]	2	6.200	3.382	.068
	MOTIV	.700[b]	2	.350	1.000	.397
Intercept	SCORE	6120.600	1	6120.600	3338.509	.000
	MOTIV	48.600	1	48.600	138.857	.000
CUR	SCORE	12.400	2	6.200	3.382	.068
	MOTIV	.700	2	.350	1.000	.397
Error	SCORE	22.000	12	1.833		
	MOTIV	4.200	12	.350		
Total	SCORE	6155.000	15			
	MOTIV	53.500	15			
Corrected Total	SCORE	34.400	14			
	MOTIV	4.900	14			

a. R Squared = .360 (Adjusted R Squared = .254)

b. R Squared = .143 (Adjusted R Squared = .000)

Understanding *MANOVA* Results

The issue is whether scores on reading comprehension and motivation *combined* are significantly different for the curriculum groups. The first table, titled "Multivariate Tests," is where this question is answered but the output takes some explanation. There are multiple significance tests for *MANOVA*, each designed to address slightly different circumstances. The most widely used test is called Wilks' *Lambda*, but because *MANOVA* can involve a variety of circumstances, SPSS lists three additional tests, Pillai's Trace, Hotelling's T^2, and Roy's Largest Root.

- If sample sizes are unequal, "Pillai's Trace" is usually the best choice.
- "Wilks' *Lambda*" indicates how much separation between groups the model does ***not*** explain; small *Lambda* values indicate that the *DVs* explain most of the difference between groups.
- If there are just two *IV* groups, "Hotelling's T^2" is the appropriate test. When there are two groups, *MANOVA* is a multivariate equivalent of the independent *t*-test, as the *T* suggests.
- "Roy's Largest Root" compares the first group with a combination of the others.

When there are just two groups, by the way, the *F* will have the same value for all four tests. This problem had three levels and the *F* values ranged from 3.000 for the Pillai's test to 6.618 for Roy's, but note two things:

- Wilks' *Lambda* is the most commonly cited *MANOVA* statistic.
- Even though they may have different values, the four tests generally suggest the same conclusion about statistical significance.

The first table in Figure 16.2 has two sections, one labeled "Intercept" and one labeled "CUR," which is the abbreviation we used for the *IV*. We're focused on just the Wilks' *Lambda* value in the "CUR" section. Note that the significance value is .036, exceeding the traditional standard for statistical significance ($p = .05$). The curriculum groups have significantly different levels of reading scores and motivation to read scores combined.

This GLM procedure also provides the univariate results. They're contained in the second table, labeled "Tests of Between-Subjects Effects." In this table, the "CUR" line indicates what the results would have been if the two *DVs* had been separated and the analyses run as two separate *ANOVAs*. Note that the curriculum groups aren't significantly different for either *DV*. The probability that the *F* values could have occurred by chance are $p = .068$ and $p = .397$ for the comprehension score and the motivation to read score, respectively. In this case, at least, the multivariate analysis has more power than the univariate analyses would have had.

MANOVA Variations

The example here is a **one-way** *MANOVA*—there's just one independent variable, the reading curriculum. With more than one *IV* the procedure becomes a **factorial** *MANOVA* and it's a little more involved. One must examine the differences between the levels of each *IV* for significance, and also the interactions between *IVs* just as we did for factorial *ANOVA* in Chapter 8.

In addition to factorial models, a *MANOVA* problem can also include covariates, making it a *MAN<u>C</u>OVA.* If there are multiple *IVs*, it's a *factorial MANCOVA*. In fact the variations can be quite dizzying. The point of this introduction was just to note that sometimes we need multiple *DVs* to understand how groups differ.

- A **one-way** **MANOVA** has one IV.

- With more than one IV it becomes a **factorial MANOVA**.

Another *MANOVA* Example

A school superintendent wants to know whether female and male teachers have different levels of job satisfaction and different commitments to the "learning communities" within which teachers work and plan together. Not wishing for salary differences to cloud the outcome, he decides on a *MANCOVA.* The *IV* is gender. The *DVs* are job satisfaction, based on attendance, and commitment to one's learning community, gauged by the number of hours during the term committed to voluntary meetings. Salary is the covariate.

Some Final Considerations

The appeal of *MANOVA* is that it allows one to address situations where the difference between groups is best understood as a function of a combination of *DVs*, rather than a solitary variable. That was the case in the problem worked here. The *MANOVA* was significant, the *ANOVAs* were not. Neither the reading score nor the motivation to read are significantly different for the *IV* groups when the *DVs* are treated separately. When the information from both dependent variables is pooled, however, the difference became statistically significant.

It won't always be the case, by the way, that *MANOVA* is more powerful, more likely to detect significance, than *ANOVA*. When the *DVs* are uncorrelated, sometimes selecting just one *DV* and using *ANOVA* provides the more powerful analysis. This can occur because either the *DVs* are uncorrelated, in which case there was no point in attempting to combine them, or they are so highly correlated that they're redundant. There needs to be some reason to combine *DVs*. In our case, it was because the motivation to read appeared to be logically related to reading comprehension scores. The evidence, by the way, is a correlation between the two variables.

Another reason for combining *DVs* goes back to discussions in earlier chapters about inflated type I errors. Recall from Chapter 7 that when multiple tests are run with the same data set, the potential for type I error doesn't remain fixed but creeps upward with each subsequent analysis performed with the same data. Consequently, running a separate *ANOVA* for each *DV* really shouldn't be an option when there is reason to believe that the *DVs* are related to each other as well as to the *IV(s)*.

One of the downsides to *MANOVA* is that explaining the results can be quite complicated. It's one thing to mathematically combine (in our example) a reading comprehension test score with a motivation to read value, and quite another to explain what that new variable is and how it distinguishes between the groups.

DISCRIMINANT FUNCTION ANALYSIS

In the *MANOVA* problem, we asked whether different groups of students have significantly different levels of the reading comprehension/motivation to read combination. Students were assigned to three different reading curriculum groups, and then measured to see if they significantly differed on the combination of dependent variables.

Sometimes the problem is the other way around; the groups exist prior to the research and the task is to understand what prompts individuals to belong to one group or another. This is the case with student dropouts. They aren't assigned to one group or the other. The groups occur naturally, and sometimes the task is to find an interval/ratio scale variable (or variables) that explains the difference between the groups. This is **discriminant function analysis** (*dfa*), and in addition to being like *MANOVA* in reverse, it's also like the regression problems in Chapters 11 and 12 except that instead of an interval/ratio dependent variable, the *DV* is nominal.

First consider how *dfa* is a one-way *MANOVA* in reverse. Rather than assigning people to groups, imposing a treatment, and then checking to see if the groups differ on a combination of interval/ratio measures, *dfa* uses the

■ Discriminant
function analysis
uses interval data
to predict a
subject's group.

interval/ratio variable or variables to predict the group to which an individual case will belong. Although the scale of the independent and dependent variables is swapped, the two analyses are mathematically equivalent. They even employ the same test statistic, Wilks' *Lambda*. Just note that the important conceptual difference between discriminant function analysis (*dfa*) and *MANOVA* is that the groups can't be manipulated or assigned in a *dfa*. They're naturally occurring. You can imagine that someone would chafe a little if the researcher begins by saying, "Okay, you 20 will be the dropouts, and you 20 will remain and graduate."

However, even the best *MANOVA* studies don't always use assigned groups. Those involving gender as an *IV* are a case in point. That's one naturally occurring group for which a *dfa* study has little application (predicting one's gender??).

The interval/ratio *IVs* in *dfa* are sometimes called "discriminating variables" and when they're combined so that they optimally distinguish between the groups they constitute what in both *MANOVA* and *dfa* is called the **discriminant function**.

> ■ The combined predictors constitute a **discriminant function**.

A *dfa* Example

Discriminant function analysis emerged from the health professions where researchers needed a procedure that would predict those who would develop a particular health condition and those who wouldn't. The idea, of course, was to predict soon enough that intervention was feasible.

There are also applications for educators. Consider how valuable it would be to be able to predict which students will attend college or which young people are likely to abuse drugs before either outcome is a reality.

One of the problems at the beginning of the chapter was related to student dropouts. If one could identify those who are most likely to drop out, perhaps one can intervene in behalf of the students who are most at-risk.

If research suggests that those who drop out of school have relatively low 9th-grade math scores and relatively high absentee rates in the 10th grade, perhaps the researcher gathers those data for 12 students, 6 who graduated on time, and 6 who dropped out. The math scores are used as they are. Absentee rates indicate an average of how many days were missed per month during the school year. Whether the student dropped out or not is tabulated "1" for dropped out and "2" for graduated. The data for the 12 students are as follows:

	math	absent	dropt
1.	54	6	1
2.	46	5	1
3.	73	8	1
4.	35	9	1
5.	62	6	1
6.	52	5	1
7.	69	3	2
8.	75	4	2
9.	84	2	2
10.	65	2	2
11.	79	3	2
12.	48	1	2

Using subjects for whom the outcome is known, *dfa* uses the *IV*s to predict an outcome for each. One can then see how consistent the solution is with what is already the known result, but fundamentally the issue will be, can one provide a better-than-chance (a statistically significant) prediction of the outcome.

In spite of its similarity to *MANOVA*, in SPSS *dfa* is under a procedure called "Classify" rather than the GLM. The commands are:

Analyze→Classify→Discriminant

The "Grouping Variable" is the variable that defines the groups we're trying to explain. In that regard, it's like the *IV* was in *ANOVA*, but in *dfa* it's the *DV*. The *IV*s, "math" and "absent" in our example, are moved into the "independents" window. If one selects "classify" and then "casewise results," the solution will indicate the group predicted for each individual. Figure 16.3 contains a partial *dfa* solution for the data set above.

Understanding *dfa* Output

The first table is a *chi*-square test of Wilks' *Lambda*. Note that for our data, the probability that this value could have occurred by chance is $p = .001$. Recall that with Wilks' *Lambda*, smaller is better. The smaller the value, the

Figure 16.3   Discriminant Function Analysis

Discriminant Function Analysis

Wilks' Lambda

Test of Function(s)	Wilks' Lambda	Chi-square	df	Sig.
1	.221	13.571	2	.001

Standardized Canonical Discriminant Function Coefficients

	Function 1
MATH	-.540
ABSENT	.945

Casewise Statistics

Case Number	Actual Group	Highest Group Predicted Group	P(D>d | G=g) p	Df	P(G=g | D=d)	Squared Mahalanobis Distance to Centroid	Second Highest Group Group	P(G=g | D=d)	Squared Mahalanobis Distance to Centroid	Discriminant Scores Function 1
1	1	1	.721	1	.990	.127	2	.010	9.409	1.355
2	1	1	.479	1	.969	.500	2	.031	7.380	1.005
3	1	1	.826	1	.999	.048	2	.001	13.276	1.932
4	1	1	.013	1	1.000	6.218	2	.000	35.019	4.206
5	1	1	.490	1	.971	.478	2	.029	7.469	1.021
6	1	1	.338	1	.930	.918	2	.070	6.080	.754
7	2	2	.701	1	.989	.148	1	.011	9.239	-1.328
8	2	2	.413	1	.955	.671	1	.045	6.787	-.893
9	2	2	.353	1	1.000	.861	1	.000	18.940	-2.640
10	2	2	.894	1	.998	.018	1	.002	12.656	-1.846
11	2	2	.973	1	.997	.001	1	.003	11.956	-1.746
12	2	2	.914	1	.998	.012	1	.002	12.475	-1.820

smaller part of the difference between groups is left unexplained, and the more likely that the result is significant. This means, at least for this sample, if one has 9th-grade math scores and 10th-grade attendance data, the *dfa* solution allows one to make a much better-than-chance prediction of who will drop out.

The prediction is based on something like a regression solution. Similar to regression, coefficients are calculated that indicate how to weight each of the *IVs* for each subject. Those coefficients, called "canonical discriminant function coefficients" in *dfa*, are multipliers applied to each of the *IV* scores (math and absences) for each student. The resulting score for each subject is compared with an average value for each of the two categories (those who dropped and those who graduated in our case). If the score for a student is closer to the average value for those who dropped out (the 1s), then that's the predicted outcome. If the scores is closer to the average for those who graduated (the 2s), graduation is the predicted outcome.

The "Casewise Statistics" table lists each individual and indicates whether that individual actually dropped out or graduated (1 or 2) as well as what the individual was predicted to do, based on the solution. In this example, those who dropped out were all predicted to drop out, and those who graduated were all predicted to graduate—the actual and predicted columns exactly match. Unhappily, this will rarely be the case in an actual research study, but the point is that "Casewise Statistics" give one a quick picture of how successful the solution is for particular cases.

Another *dfa* Example

A researcher wishes to investigate turnover among new teachers. The literature indicates that salary and classroom management issues are the major factors in whether new teachers remain or leave during their first 3 years of employment. There is also some indication that the amount debt resulting from school loans may be a factor. A *dfa* analysis allows one to treat salary, the frequency of student misbehavior, and the amount of load debt as *IVs*. Whether the individual remains or is gone after 3 years are the categories of the *DV.*

Some Final Considerations

So what's the point of developing a solution for students when we already know the outcome? The idea is to use what is known to predict what is unknown. In the example, 12 students for whom the outcome is known are something of a template for a solution that can be applied to students who have yet neither graduated nor dropped out, but for whom the other data are available. When the solution allows a better-than-chance prediction of those most likely to drop, decision makers can direct special attention to the needs of those students.

It's important to recognize that *dfa* isn't a causal model. There's no judgment that low math scores or high absentee rates "cause" students to drop out, although that may be the case. The argument is that those variables are at least correlated with the tendency to drop out. Were they not at least related to that outcome, the Wilks' *Lambda* value wouldn't have been statistically significant. For whatever reason, students with relatively high math scores and low levels of absenteeism tend to remain and graduate, and, according to these (contrived) data, those with low scores and high absenteeism leave early.

OTHER PROCEDURES

It doesn't take much time in the research literature before one bumps into data analyzed with *ANCOVA*, *MANOVA*, or *dfa*. They have become very common data analysis tools because the questions they help answer are so important.

There are some other procedures that have also become staples in quantitative analysis. Except for the regression methods immediately below, some are complicated enough that the details are beyond the scope of this book, but still one should have some general familiarity with the kinds of problems they help address. So after elaborating some regression procedures we'll develop a brief description for a few of the other procedures that educational decision makers and researchers are likely to encounter.

Regression Methods

Recall that multiple regression (Chapter 12) uses two or more variables to predict the value of a criterion variable with which the predictors are correlated. The approach in Chapter 12 was to use all of the predictor variables simultaneously. This is the default procedure in SPSS, which terms it the "Enter" approach (statistics texts sometimes call it the "Direct" method). But the predictor variables *don't* need to be entered simultaneously. Once one has selected

Analyze→Regression→Linear, and entered the *DV* and the *IVs*, there is a "Method" box just below the window for the *IV*. It contains the options for the choices described below.

■ **Forward regression** adds variables to a solution, beginning with one most correlated with the DV.

A Forward *Regression Solution*

An alternative to using all the predictor variables simultaneously is to allow the computer to select them one at a time, beginning with the variable that provides the most information about the variable to be predicted. In the first step the one predictor variable that explains the greatest amount of variance in the criterion variable—the one with the highest r^2 value with the *DV*—is the one selected.

- The *second* variable is whichever has the second highest squared correlation with the criterion variable *when the influence of the variable already included is held constant.*
- The third variable will be that which has the highest squared correlation with the criterion variable, controlling in the predictor whatever it has in common those already in the solution, and so on through the rest of the *IVs.*
- This process ends when including additional variables fails to significantly increase the proportion of variance in the criterion variable explained by the predictors.

A Backward *Regression Solution*

■ **Backward regression** begin with all variables and eliminate those that contribute least.

A **backward regression** solution begins by including all predictor variables, like the default procedure. The computer then removes the predictors one at a time beginning with that variable that contributes the *least* to the total variance explained (R^2). When an additional elimination would result in a significant reduction in the value of R^2, the process ends.

The forward and backward solutions arrive at the "best" solution from opposite directions. Forward builds the regression solution one variable at a time, beginning with the variable most informative of the criterion variable and stops when an additional variable doesn't significantly improve the prediction. Backward begins with all the variables included and then systematically deletes those of least value until an additional deletion significantly decreases the value of the prediction.

A Stepwise *Regression Solution*

■ **Stepwise regression solutions** can add and delete variables in the same step.

Stepwise regression includes features of both forward and backward solutions. Stepwise includes at each step the variable that adds the most to R^2, but in the same step one or more of the *IVs* already in the equation may be deleted if doing so would not significantly reduce the predictive power of the equation. This is an important advantage because sometimes adding or deleting a variable will alter the relationship among those that remain in the solution.

A Hierarchical *Regression Solution*

In **hierarchical regression,** rather than allowing a formula to drive the addition and deletion of variables, the order (the hierarchy) of adding or deleting the variables is specified by the researcher in advance of the procedure. Ideally, the hierarchy is based on the researcher's understanding of the relationships among the variables rather than the purely mathematical considerations that define Forward, Backward, or Stepwise regression procedures.

In addition to what one knows about how the variables are related to one another, this procedure allows one sufficient control to make decisions based upon cost. Variables that are time-consuming or expensive can be set aside if the solution is effective without them.

■ **Hierarchical regression** is multiple regression in which the researcher controls the order in which predictor variables are entered into the solution.

Canonical Correlation

Multiple correlation (R—Chapter 12) transforms a number of predictor variables into an aggregated variable that can be correlated with a criterion variable. The logical next step is to correlate two *sets* of variables. This is what occurs in **canonical correlation** where two composites are formed, one for the independent variables and a second for the dependent variables. The canonical correlation is the maximum correlation possible given the two sets of data. The symbol is R_c and the values, like most correlation values, range from −1.0 to 1.0.

Perhaps a researcher is interested in the degree to which students' attitudes about school correlate with their behaviors. The researcher treats the attitudinal variables as the *IV*s, including:

■ **Canonical correlation** gauges the relationship between two sets of interval or ratio variables.

- Whether the student likes school
- Whether the student has friends at school
- Whether the student has objectives that include attending school

The researcher then correlates the measures of those variables with a set of behavioral variables, treated as the *DV*s, which include the following:

- The student's attendance
- The student's participation in extracurricular activities
- The student's grade average

The variables in each group are individually weighted to provide for maximum correlation. Note that each combination of variables should have theoretical meaning as a set. Otherwise the correlation isn't interpretable and has no value.

■ Factor analysis reduces many scores to fewer underlying "factors" which cause the scores.

Factor Analysis

The key to understanding factor analysis is in the language SPSS uses. Factor analytic procedures occur under the heading "Dimension Reduction" in version 18, "*Data* Reduction" in earlier versions. The point is to reduce the complexity of a data set.

A test score or the response to a test item is supposed to reflect whether the respondent possesses some underlying trait or characteristic the test or the item was designed to measure. In factor analysis these underlying traits are called "factors" and test scores or item responses are the visible manifestation of these elusive underlying factor. There isn't any way, for example, to directly measure something like verbal ability. The best one can do is design a test that calls upon characteristics associated with verbal ability, and then make a judgment about verbal ability based on how individuals respond to the test items.

When scores from separate tests correlate, it indicates that to the degree they're correlated, the tests measure the same thing; they have some factor in common. The task with factor analysis is to take multiple correlated measures, determine how many underlying factors there are, and provide the mathematical information that allows an analyst to at least tentatively identify them. As such, factor analysis serves the cause of parsimony; it's a mechanism for simplifying a data set.

Tests of, say, reading comprehension, vocabulary, spelling ability, word recognition, grammar, and punctuation might be more similar in what they measure than they are unique, in spite of the fact that they're separate tests with, ostensibly at least, separate purposes. To varying degrees, perhaps they all reflect the same underlying factor, maybe something we might call "language ability." Determining whether this *is* the case is the point of factor analysis. Scores, which are called "indicators" for the purpose of factor analysis, are gathered for each subject and then grouped into categories of homogenous measures based on the correlations. Each separate category is thought to be evidence of a specific underlying factor. Factor analysis indicates the number of categories, and so the number of factor that explain the scores.

Besides multiple instruments, factor analysis can also be applied to the items within a single instrument. Perhaps a survey is developed to ask parents questions related to their confidence in the instruction and administration at the local school, their sense of their children's academic progress, their sense of their children's social progress, and their feelings about their children's psychological and physical safety. If the instrument has 40 items, factor analysis might reveal that just one or two underlying factors explain most of the responses, perhaps a factor like "confidence in schools."

The analysis indicates, based initially on correlations between measures, how many factors underlie a set of scores. But factor analysis cannot name the factors. This is where the researcher comes in. It falls to that person to identify what the factors may be, and then verify them through continued analysis.

Recall from Chapter 15 that construct validity is the degree to which one measures what one claims to have measured. Factor analysis is one way to verify construct validity.

Cluster Analysis

Factor analysis examines individuals' scores to see if multiple measures can be reduced to fewer underlying factors while retaining enough basic information about why the scores to reproduce them. Cluster analysis approaches data reduction from the other direction. Patterns in multiple scores are used to cluster individuals, rather than scores, into groups.

■ **Cluster analysis** "clusters" individuals in a data set into subgroups based on similarities in their scores.

Perhaps there are 100 students for whom one has reading comprehension scores, vocabulary scores, math computation scores, and logical reasoning scores. A cluster analysis will look for patterns in the scoring and cluster students accordingly. Perhaps those who do well on the reading comprehension and logical reasoning constitute a cluster and those who do well on vocabulary and computation, but less well on reading comprehension, constitute another cluster, and so on. The point of cluster analysis is to detect consistencies among individuals in a data set and group them accordingly. It can be very helpful when one is trying to organize a great deal of data.

Path Analysis

To this point in the book, we've been careful to maintain some difference between correlation and causation. Although causal relationships can be very difficult to verify, there *are* procedures intended to do exactly that, analyze causal relationships among variables. Path analysis, structural equations

■ **Path analysis** uses regression-like procedures to test hypotheses, represented in a path diagram, about causal relationships.

SOURCE: Created by Suzanna Nielson.

" . . . and by the way Tweed, cluster analysis has nothing to do with grapes."

modeling, analysis of covariance systems, and linear structural relations (*LISREL*) are similar in this purpose. A brief description of path analysis is next.

With path analysis a path diagram depicts relationships among a set of variables. The diagram is a hypothesis to be tested. As an example, perhaps a researcher is interested in understanding achievement motivation among secondary school students. Perhaps her review of the research indicates that the variables that appear to be most associated with achievement motivation are the following:

- The student's past record of achievement
- The student's aptitude for the task
- The student's level of parental support

As a result of reviewing the research and identifying the relevant relationships, the researcher wishes to test a theory based on the following preliminary conclusions:

1. Although parental support and student aptitude are correlated, neither causes the other.

2. But both parental support and student aptitude have a direct, causal effect on achievement motivation.

3. Parental support and student aptitude also have a direct, causal effect on past record of achievement that, in turn, affects achievement motivation.

The **path diagram** specifying these relationships is in Figure 16.4.

- Parental support is indicated as variable 1
- Student aptitude is variable 2
- Past record of achievement is variable 3
- Achievement motivation is variable 4

■ A **path diagram** is a visual representation of the relationships between the variables involved in a path analysis or a structural equations modeling problem. The arrows in a path diagram indicate which variables are dependent, which are independent, and which are correlated with which.

Figure 16.4   A Path Diagram

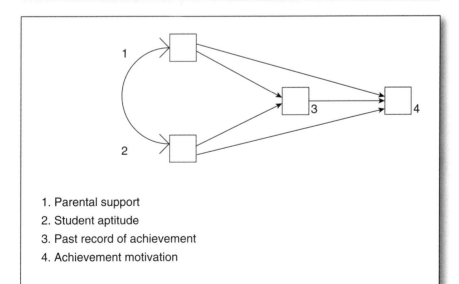

1. Parental support
2. Student aptitude
3. Past record of achievement
4. Achievement motivation

Note that the same variable in a path model can be both a cause and an effect. The arrows indicate that variable 3 (the student's past record of achievement) is the effect of variables 1 (parental support) and 2 (student aptitude). In turn, variable 3, along with variables 1 and 2, is believed to be a cause of variable 4 (achievement motivation).

Not all relationships are causal, of course. Sometimes, as we've noted repeatedly in the book, characteristics vary together because they're both influenced by something else. In the model here parental support and student aptitude are assumed to correlate but there is no assumption of a causal relationship. This is indicated by the curved line between these two variables with arrows on both ends. The other relationships are presumed to be causal and are tested with the analysis. Causal relationships are indicated by unidirectional arrows.

Path analysis produces path coefficients that indicate the effect one variable has on another for which the hypothesis maintains that it is a cause. The path coefficients are essentially standardized partial regression coefficients, the *beta* (β) values calculated in an SPSS multiple regression solution. Viewed as a series of regression problems we would have the following:

- In the first component of the analysis, X_1 and X_2, parental support and student aptitude respectively, are used to predict the past record of achievement, the *Y* variable.
- In the second component, the *Y* variable in the first component becomes one of the *IVs*. Parental support, student achievement, and past record of achievement are the X_1, X_2, and X_3 variables in the analysis of achievement motivation, which is now the *Y* variable.
- Furthermore, X_1 and X_2 affect *Y* directly, and also indirectly because of their impact on the X_3 variable.

Multiple regression analysis won't accommodate both components of this problem simultaneously. Specialized software such as AMOS has been developed because it can examine all of the hypothetical relationships and produce all of the path coefficients in one analysis.

If the analysis is consistent with the path model (Figure 16.4), the theory from which the diagram was constructed is confirmed. If the theory isn't confirmed, the model is revised, new data gathered, and the analysis pursued again.

SUMMARY

From the standpoint of the new statistics student, the one-sample *t*-test, one-way *ANOVA* and bivariate correlation are important for what they help us to understand about the differences between samples and populations, the differences between samples, and relationships between measures. But sometimes educational problems involve more variables than those procedures can accommodate. Failing to include all of the relevant variables in an analysis is one of the reasons that research findings aren't always consistent.

The point of this chapter was to introduce some of the procedures that will accommodate the higher level of complexity that seems to accompany the human subjects research. Hopefully, the reader can know which procedures help one answer some of the more involved questions. We briefly examined the following:

- Analysis of covariance (*ANCOVA*) is an *ANOVA* approach with the added advantage of neutralizing the impact of variables that can obscure the *IV/DV* relationship.
- Multivariate analysis of variance (*MANOVA*) uses multiple dependent variables to understand the differences between groups.
- Discriminant function analysis (*dfa*) produces a solution that can be used to predict the category to which a subject will ultimately belong.
- The different multiple regression procedures allow one to determine the optimal combination of predictor variables in a solution.
- Factor analysis suggests the number and nature of latent characteristics, called factors, for which test scores are the visible evidence.
- Cluster analysis provides a way to detect common elements among the subjects in a large data set.
- Path analysis allows one to quantify the causal impact that independent variables in a complex analysis have on dependent variables.

The material in this chapter is an acknowledgment that understanding people's behavior can be complicated. Complex problems require complex analyses. This shouldn't diminish the importance of the earlier chapters, however. The procedures in those chapters are also critical elements in the decision making necessary to educational improvement, and they're also necessary to understanding the procedures outlined in this chapter.

There's something of a truism in education stating that no one is hired to maintain the status quo. If we don't teach better, administer better, counsel better, than we were taught, administered, and counseled, we have failed because there is no progress. Many of the tools we need to make better decision are here. Now the task is to begin to use them. Your author wishes you the very best of luck!

EXERCISES

1. If one were to examine school-to-school differences on the mathematics portion of a college admissions test but wished to rule out any variance due to differences in the number of mathematics units students had registered for, what statistical procedure fits best?

2. According to the example in item 1, what is the designation for the number of mathematics units for which students had registered?

3. What are the data scales of the *IV(s)* and the *DVs* in a *MANOVA*?

4. What does Wilks' *Lambda* measure?

5. Under what circumstances will all four multivariate tests that *SPSS* reports for a *MANOVA* have the same *F* values?

6. How do *MANOVA* and *dfa* compare? What is different about the groups involved in either analysis?

7. What is the scale of each of the variables involved in a two-way *ANCOVA*?

8. What is the point of the discriminant function in *dfa*?

9. What analytical procedure will reveal the strength of the relationship between a set of behavioral variables and a set of attitudinal variables?

10. Under what circumstances is *ANOVA* more powerful than *ANCOVA*?

11. What procedure will reveal how subjects form subgroups within a data set?

12. In factor analysis the scores that are the subjects of the analysis are assumed to be the visible evidence of what?

13. Why is it accurate to call factor analysis a "data reduction" technique?

14. How is the researcher's theory about how variables are related to one another represented in path analysis?

15. What do the path coefficients indicate in path analysis?

REFERENCES

Pedhazur, E. J., & Schmelkin, L. P. (1991). *Measurement, design, and analysis*. Hillsdale, NJ: Lawrence Erlbaum.

STUDENT STUDY SITE

Visit the Student Study Site at **www.sagepub.com/tanner** for additional learning tools.

GLOSSARY

Actual limits extend the interval in apparent limits up and down 1/2 point.

Alpha errors, also called type I or false positive decision errors, occur when one erroneously concludes that a result is statistically significant.

Alpha level is the probability of incorrectly determining a statistically significant result, a type I error.

Analysis of covariance determines whether there are significant differences among any number of groups, but in addition it allows one to neutralize a variable, the covariate, that may alter the *IV* to *DV* relationship.

Analysis of variance determines whether there are significant differences among any number of groups with one test.

Apparent limits are represented by the lowest and highest integers (whole numbers) in a category.

Attenuated range means that a variable's full range of possible values is artificially limited. Attenuated range can lead to artificially low correlation values.

Backward regression in multiple regression initially selects all variables available in the analysis then deletes them one at a time, beginning with the weakest predictor of the dependent variable. Other predictors are eliminated in order from the weakest until deleting additional variables would significantly diminish the value of R^2.

Bar charts are used to represent proportional differences in data categories with bars of different sizes.

Before/after *t*-test: Rather than the separate groups that the independent *t*-test test employs, the same group is measured twice, once before the treatment and then after.

Beta errors, also called type II or false negative decision errors, occur when, on the basis of statistical analysis, one erroneously concludes that a result is not statistically significant.

Bimodal distribution has two values that occur most frequently and consequently, two peaks.

Bivariate correlation indicates the strength of the relationship between *two* variables.

Bivariate regression is regression with one predictor variable.

Canonical correlation is the correlation of two *sets* of variables with multiple variables in each set.

Canonical discriminant function coefficients are the weighting values applied to each *IV* in a *dfa* solution.

Cartesian coordinates are values along a horzontal **abscissa** and a vertical **ordinate**. The are used to plot **frequency polygons**.

Central limit theorem holds that a distribution made of sample means will be normal even if the original distribution of individual scores was not.

Central tendency measures of indicate what is most typical in a data set.

Chi-**square tests of independence** determine whether two nominal variables are correlated.

Class intervals group data in a frequency distribution rather than list them individually.

Classical test theory maintains that every measure (x) involves some component of error (e) that obscures the true measure (t) of the characteristic.

Cluster analysis is a procedure for detecting the relationships or commonalities *among subjects* in an analysis. Whereas factor analysis detects common elements among measures, cluster analysis reveals how individuals in a data set cluster according to communality among measures.

Coefficient alpha is a measure of internal consistency reliability.

Coefficients of contingency are correlation procedures for nominal data based on the value of chi-square. It is a very conservative measure, with no possibility of reaching a value of 1.0.

Coefficients of determination indicate the proportion of variance in one variable that can be explained by manipulating the other. It is the square of the Pearson Correlation.

Cohen's *d* provides an effect size measure for the independent *t*-test. It indicates the practical importance of a statistically significant *t*.

Confidence intervals used in conjunction with a statistically significant value of z provide an interval (rather than the point estimate that the mean of the sample provides) within which the mean of the population represented by a sample mean will occur with a specified probability.

Confidence intervals for regression solutions indicate, with a specified level of probability, the interval within which the actual value of the criterion variable will occur.

Confidence interval of the difference estimate the difference between the populations means represented by two samples in an independent *t*-test.

Constants are numerical values which never vary. Some statistical formulae include constant values.

Construct validity is the accuracy with which a score represents the quantity of the measured construct or mental characteristic.

Contingency tables are arrangements of data in a *chi*-square test of independence. Rows represent the categories of one variable and columns the categories of the other.

Convenience samples of subjects for a research study are appealing because of their accessibility. But because the individuals in the sample are not randomly selected, there is a substantial probability that they will differ from the population for reasons unrelated to the variable of interest.

Covariate designates the variable whose influence is mathematically controlled in analysis of covariance so as not to obscure or distort the effect of the *IV* on the *DV*.

Criterion variable is the alternate name of "dependent variable".

Data scale refers to the *kind* of information that a particular measure provides. See **nominal**, **ordinal**, **interval**, and **ratio** scale.

Deciles are portions of a distribution containing 10% of the scores. The first decile includes the lowest 10% of scores.

Degrees of freedom refers to the number of values in the calculation of a statistic that are free to vary when the value of the statistic is known.

Dependent samples tests either measure the same group multiple times, or subjects in each group are matched on specified characteristics. Dependent samples tests allow one to control error variance by eliminating initial between-group differences and by keeping within-group differences constant in all sets of scores.

Dependent variable is the consequence variable in a research design or study. It is the variable affected by whatever is manipulated.

Descriptive statistics indicate the characteristics of a group of measures. They usually include measures of central tendency and measures of variability.

Discriminant function analysis is regression with interval/ratio scale independent variables but a nominal scale (categorical) dependent variable. The *IV*s are combined into a **discriminant function,** which distinguishes between the categories of the *DV*.

Distribution of sample means is that theoretical distribution made up of all possible sample means of size *n* in a distribution of raw scores. The concept allows one to answer many of the questions about groups that *z* scores allow one to ask about individuals.

Estimated standard error of the mean, SE_m, estimates the standard deviation of the sample means in the distribution of sample means. Determined by dividing the sample standard deviation by the square root of the number in the sample, it is a measure of data variability in the *t*-tests.

Factor analysis is a data reduction procedure designed to reveal the number of traits or factors that underlie a set of related measures.

Factorial analysis of variance is analysis of variance with more than one independent variable or factor.

Forward regression is a multiple regression procedure that selects the variables to be included in a solution one at a time, beginning with the one that is the best single predictor of the dependent variable. The next variable is that which predicts next best, having accounted for what the first variable already explains, and so on, until additional variables no longer make a significant difference in the value of R^2.

Frequency distributions display data so that their variety and frequency of occurrences are apparent.

Frequency polygons are plotted according to values along a horizontal **abscissa** and a **vertical ordinate** that are **Cartesian coordinates.**

Friedman's *ANOVA* allows one to test for significant differences when there are two or more measures of nonindependent groups and the data are of ordinal scale. The test is the ordinal scale equivalent of the within-subjects *F* test for interval/ratio data.

Gaussian distributions take on a bell shape because they are symmetrical, unimodal, and the standard deviation is about 1/6th of the range.

Goodness of fit *chi*-square procedures test whether nominal data occur in specified groups or categories consistent with the predicted proportions.

Grade equivalent score is a nonstandard score often used to report a student's level of performance in grade-level and month in grade. Prone to overinterpretation, grade-level scores should be treated as a general indicator of the student's performance level compared with others at the same educational level.

Hierarchical regression allows the researcher to specify the variables and the order of the variables to be included in an analysis. Ideally, this reflects the theory that drives the analysis, although other factors such as the cost of collecting certain variables may factor into the decision about the hierarchy.

Histograms are similar to **bar charts** except there is no separation between the bars.

Independent *t*-test is used to determine whether two independent samples are likely drawn from populations with the same mean.

Independent variable is the antecedent variable presumed to explain a consequence or an effect in a research design or study.

Inferential statistics are used to understand the population by viewing the sample.

Interaction occurs in analysis of variance when independent variables in combination have a different effect on a dependent variable than they have individually.

Interdecile range is that part of the distribution between the 10th and 90th deciles.

Interquartile range is the middle half of the distribution containing scores from the 25th to the 75th percentile.

Interval data have constant differences in what is measured between any two consecutive data points.

Kuder and Richardson formulae (r_{KR20}, r_{KR21}) measure internal consistency reliability for test items that are dichotomously scored.

Kruskal-Wallis *H* allows one to test for significant differences when two or more groups are independent and the data are of ordinal scale. The test is the ordinal equivalent of the one-way *ANOVA*.

Kurtosis describes the degree to which data are bunched around the middle of a distribution.

The **law of large numbers** was set down by Jacob Bernoulli and holds that larger samples have a better chance of emulating the population than smaller samples. As sample sizes grow, sampling errors shrink.

Least squares regression means that error is the difference between the predicted and actual values of the criterion variable. When the sum of those squared errors has its lowest possible value, the regression procedure meets the **least squares criterion**.

Leptokurtic describes distributions of data that are too bunched together to be normal.

Mann-Whitney *U* allows one to test for significant differences when two groups are independent and the data are of ordinal scale. The test is the ordinal equivalent of the independent *t*-test for interval/ratio data.

MANOVA, or multivariate analysis of variance, tests whether a combination of dependent variables can significantly distinguish between levels of the independent variable(s). If there is one independent variable, it is a **one-way *MANOVA***. Multiple *IV*s make it a **factorial *MANOVA***.

Matched pairs designs are statistical tests in which each subject in a particular group is matched in the other group(s) with a subject who has the same characteristic. The purpose of matching is to control the effect of the matched variable on the outcome.

Mean denotes the arithmetic average of the numbers in a group.

Mean square is sum of squares divided by degrees of freedom in *ANOVA*.

Measurement is assigning numbers according to rules.

Median is the middle-most number in a group arranged in order.

Mesokurtic data occur when distribution is normal.

Mode is the most frequently occurring value in a set.

Modified standard score is a score for which the mean and standard deviation are specified to have preselected values. It is a variation in this process that allows major test publishers to maintain descriptive statistics that remain constant even while the test is revised to reflect a new length or format.

Multiple correlation, *R,* gauges the strength of the relationship between multiple predictor variables and a criterion variable.

Multiple regression The use of more than one variable to predict the criterion.

Multivariate approach is an analytic approach involving more than one variable. Alternatively, it is any analytic approach involving more than one *dependent* variable.

Nominal data, sometimes called "count" or "categorical data," indicate the category to which an individual subject belongs.

Nonparametric statistical procedures make no assumptions about the normality of the data involved in the analysis.

Normal distribution. See Gaussian distribution.

Normal curve equivalent (*NCE*) is a standard score for which the mean = 50 and the standard deviation = 21.06. These values allow for *NCE* scores from 1 to 99 to range in that area of a normal distribution where scores are most likely to occur.

Omega-squared (ω^2) is an effect size measure for the *t*-test and for analysis of variance. It indicates how much of the variance in the dependent variable can be explained by manipulating the independent variable.

One-sample *t*-test determines whether a sample is likely to have been drawn from a specified population, but unlike the *z* test, it requires no population standard deviation.

One-tailed test is one in which the direction of the significant difference is predicted. In *t*-test, for example, one predicts that the mean of Group 1 will be significantly *greater* or *lesser* than the mean of Group 2, rather than just significantly different from it.

One-way *ANOVA* is *analysis of variance* involving just one independent variable.

Ordinal data allow "more than" or "less than" normative comparisons between individuals in whatever is measured. Ordinal data do not reveal how much more or less than one individual is than another, however.

Outliers are the extreme scores in a distribution. They are uncharacteristic of the other measures.

Overfitted refers to a regression solution when it is accurate only for a particular data set.

Parameters are the characteristics of populations. They are symbolized with Greek letters. The letter mu, μ, indicates the parameter mean of a population, and the lowercase sigma, σ, indicates the parameter standard deviation of a population.

Partial correlation gauges the strength of the relationship between two variables, removing from both the influence of a third variable.

Partial *eta*-squared (η_p^2) is one of several effect size measures that indicate how much of the variance in scores can be explained by the independent variable. It is a more liberal estimate than *omega*-squared.

Partial regression coefficients indicate the influence of a predictor on a criterion variable, controlling for the influence of all other predictors.

Path analysis is one of the statistical procedures designed to verify causal relationships among variables. The procedure begins with a **path diagram,** which represents a hypothesis about relationships and visually represents which variables are believed to have a causal impact on others in the model. A variable that is thought to cause another may also be the effect of an earlier variable in the diagram. Calculated path coefficients prompt one to confirm or revise the initial hypothesis.

Path coefficients are produced by path analysis. They quantify the causal effect a variable has on another. They are similar to the standardized partial regression coefficients (β values) in a regression solution.

Pearson's r is a correlation procedure for two variables which can be either interval or ratio scale.

A **percentile score** is the point below which a particular percentage of all scores occur.

Platykurtic is the term that describes distributions with too much variability.

Point of inflection is where a normal curve moves outward more quickly than downward. It occurs +/– one standard deviation from the mean.

Point of origin designates where the x and y axes intercept, where x = 0 and y = 0, in a frequency polygon.

Population is a group that includes all possible members of a defined group. It is sometimes referred to as a "universe."

***Post-hoc* test** is a test conducted after a significant F in an *ANOVA* to determine which groups are significantly different from which.

Predictive validity is the accuracy with which a particular measure anticipates some future measure.

Predictor variable is another term for the independent variable in linear regression.

Probability of an event indicates the likelihood of its occurrence. It is determined by the proportion of times an event will occur in an infinite number of trials. Probability values range from 0, the event never happens, to 1.0, the event will occur every time.

Quadrant is one of four areas in a frequency polygon resulting from the intersection of the abscissa and the ordinate.

Qualitative variables refer to characteristics like an individual's gender, ethnicity, political affiliation, or school site. Differences are in the quality or nature of the characteristic rather than in the measured amount.

Quantitative variables differ in the amount of the characteristic measured.

Quartiles are intervals of the distribution containing 25% of the scores each. The first quartile contains the lowest 25% of scores.

Range of a data set is the difference between the largest and smallest values in a set.

Ratio scale data are equal interval measures which also allow ratio comparisons in what is measured. One can properly be said to have twice as much of some characteristic as another. They also include a zero that indicates the absence of the quality measured.

Regression line In a scatter plot, a straight line positioned so that it is as close as possible to all the data points in the plot.

Regression coefficient is another name for the slope of the regression line, *b*.

Regression intercept (*a*) is the value of the criterion variable when the predictor variable equals zero. When the regression line is graphed, it is the point where the regression line crosses the y axis.

Reliability of data indicates scoring consistency. It can be established by **testing and retesting** with the same test, by retesting with an **alternate form** of the test, or by the consistency of scoring within a single test, called **internal consistency**.

Research design is a formal plan for gathering and analyzing data in order to answer research questions. If the subjects are randomly assigned to multiple groups the design is **experimental**. If there are multiple groups but no random assignment, the design is **quasi-experimental**. If there are no treatment and control groups the study is **nonexperimental** or **correlational**.

Residual score, in regression, is the difference between the actual and predicted value of a variable.

Sample refers to any subset of the population.

Sampling error is reflected in $M - \mu_M$. It is the difference between the mean of the sample and the mean of the population of sample means.

Sampling error of the mean gauges variability in the distribution of sample means, indicated by σ_M.

Scatter plots are a way to represent the relationship between two variables in a graph. Each point in the scatter plot represents the individual's score on both the *x* and *y* variables.

Semi-interquartile range is the middle half of the interquartile range.

Shrinkage is the reduction in predictive accuracy when a regression solution is applied to new data sets.

Significant main effect in analysis of variance indicates that the particular independent variable is associated with statistically significant changes in the dependent variable.

Skewed describes a data distribution that isn't symmetrical.

Slope of the regression line, *b*, indicates how much the criterion variable changes for every 1.0 increase in the predictor variable. It indicates how radically the regression slope inclines or declines.

Spearman-Brown prophecy formula allows one to predict the impact on score reliability of altering test length.

Spearman's *rho* is a correlation procedure for ordinal scale data.

Split-half reliability is a form of internal consistency reliability in which the scores on one half of the test are compared for consistency with those on the other half.

Standard deviation indicates how much individual cases typically vary from the mean. The sample standard deviation is the square root of the sum of the squared differences between individual measures and the mean of the group, divided by the number of measures, minus one.

Standard error of the difference, SE_d, is the statistic in which the within groups variability is pooled from both samples in an independent *t*-test.

Standard error of the estimate is an estimate of the amount of error in a bivariate regression solution. Theoretically, it is the standard deviation of all possible differences between the actual and predicted values of the criterion variable.

Standard error of the mean, symbolized by σ_M, is an indicator of data variability. It is the standard deviation of the differences between individual sample means and the mean of the distribution of sample means.

Standard error of measurement is an estimate of the measurement error in a test score.

Standard error of the multiple estimate is an estimate of error in a multiple regression solution. See **standard error of the estimate.**

Standard nine-point scale, or stanine, is a standard score consisting of score intervals rather than the discrete points characteristic of z, T, and NCE. Each stanine is ½ standard deviations wide, with the 5th stanine straddling the mean of the distribution.

Standard normal distribution Another term for z distribution.

Standard score refers to one score from a distribution of scores that has constant values for the mean and standard deviation. Prominent examples of standard scores are z, T, the normal curve equivalent.

Statistically significant means that an outcome isn't likely to have occurred by chance.

Stem-and-leaf displays list all values according to stem (the numbers preceding the final value) and leaf (the final digit).

Stepwise regression combines elements of both forward and backward regression in an incremental procedure so that when adding or deleting additional variables changes the relationship among other predictors and the criterion variable the procedure can adjust accordingly to achieve the best solution.

Sum of squares are the sum of the squared deviations of the scores from a mean.

T **score** is, like the z score, a standard score. Its distribution has a mean = 0 and a standard deviation = 10.

Test bias is systematic variance in measurement scores for reasons unrelated to the amount of the construct present.

Two-tailed statistical tests are such that the test statistic is positive or negative doesn't matter. The only issue is whether the test statistic is extreme enough that it isn't likely to have occurred by chance.

Unimodal distribution has many values, but just one value that occurs most frequently. Normal distributions are unimodal.

Univariate approach is an approach with just one variable included in the analysis. It can also describe an analytic approach involving just one dependent variable.

Variables have more than one manifestation; their values change.

Variability statistics gauge the degree to which individuals in a group vary from each other.

Variance indicates how much individual cases typically vary from the mean. The sample variance is the sum of the squared differences between individual measures and the mean of the group, divided by the number of measures, minus one.

Wilcoxon T, also called the **Wilcoxon Signed Ranks Test,** allows one to test for significant differences when one group is measured twice, or two groups are paired, and the data are ordinal scale. The test is the ordinal data equivalent of the before/after t-test for interval/ratio data.

Within-subjects F is the repeated measures equivalent of the one-way $ANOVA$.

z **distribution** is another name for the **standard normal distribution,** a distribution where the mean = 0 and the standard deviation = 1.0. Because its characteristics are well known, once raw scores from any normal distribution are transformed into *z* scores, one can make statements about the percentage of the distribution below a specified point, or the percentage of the distribution between two points, and so on.

z **test** is a test of how closely a sample approximates a population. In *z*-score-like applications, it also allows one to make same judgments about the probability of selecting a sample with a mean above a point, below a point, or between two points, just as is done for individuals with the *z* score.

z **transformation** is $(x - M)/s$. Scores thus transformed scores belong to a distribution for which the mean $= 0$ and the standard deviation $= 1.0$.

APPENDICES

TABLES OF CRITICAL VALUES

Table A   The % of a Normal Population From z to the Mean

z	%	z	%	z	%	z	%	z	%	z	%	z	%	z	%
3	49.87	2.6	49.53	2.2	48.61	1.8	46.41	1.4	41.92	1	34.13	0.6	22.57	0.2	7.93
2.99	49.86	2.59	49.52	2.19	48.57	1.79	46.33	1.39	41.77	0.99	33.89	0.59	22.24	0.19	7.53
2.98	49.86	2.58	49.51	2.18	48.54	1.78	46.25	1.38	41.62	0.98	33.65	0.58	21.9	0.18	7.14
2.97	49.85	2.57	49.49	2.17	48.5	1.77	46.16	1.37	41.47	0.97	33.4	0.57	21.57	0.17	6.75
2.96	49.85	2.56	49.48	2.16	48.46	1.76	46.08	1.36	41.31	0.96	33.15	0.56	21.23	0.16	6.36
2.95	49.84	2.55	40.46	2.15	48.42	1.75	45.99	1.35	41.15	0.95	32.9	0.55	20.88	0.15	5.96
2.94	49.84	2.54	49.45	2.14	48.38	1.74	45.91	1.34	40.99	0.94	32.64	0.54	20.54	0.14	5.57
2.93	49.83	2.53	39.43	2.13	48.34	1.73	45.82	1.33	40.82	0.93	32.38	0.53	20.19	0.13	5.17
2.92	49.82	2.52	49.41	2.12	48.3	1.72	45.73	1.32	40.66	0.92	32.12	0.52	19.85	0.12	4.78
2.91	49.82	2.51	49.4	2.11	48.26	1.71	45.64	1.31	40.49	0.91	31.86	0.51	19.5	0.11	4.38
2.9	49.81	2.5	49.38	2.1	48.21	1.7	45.54	1.3	40.32	0.9	31.59	0.5	19.15	0.1	3.98
2.89	49.81	2.49	49.36	2.09	48.17	1.69	45.45	1.29	40.15	0.89	31.33	0.49	28.79	0.09	3.59
2.88	49.8	2.48	49.34	2.08	48.12	1.68	45.35	1.28	39.97	0.88	31.06	0.48	18.44	0.08	3.19
2.87	49.79	2.47	49.32	2.07	48.08	1.67	45.25	1.27	39.8	0.87	30.78	0.47	18.08	0.07	2.79
2.86	49.79	2.46	49.31	2.06	48.03	1.66	45.15	1.26	39.62	0.86	30.51	0.46	17.72	0.06	2.39
2.85	49.78	2.45	49.29	2.05	47.98	1.65	45.05	1.25	39.44	0.85	30.23	0.45	17.36	0.05	1.99
2.84	49.77	2.44	49.27	2.04	47.93	1.64	44.95	1.24	39.25	0.84	29.95	0.44	17	0.04	1.6
2.83	49.77	2.43	49.25	2.03	47.88	1.63	44.84	1.23	39.07	0.83	29.67	0.43	16.64	0.03	1.2

z	%	z	%	z	%	z	%	z	%	z	%	z	%	z	%
2.82	49.76	2.42	49.2	2.02	47.83	1.62	44.74	1.22	38.88	0.82	29.39	0.42	16.28	0.02	0.8
2.81	79.75	2.41	49.28	2.01	47.78	1.61	44.64	1.21	38.69	0.81	29.1	0.41	15.91	0.01	0.4
2.8	49.74	2.4	49.18	2	47.72	1.6	44.52	1.2	38.49	0.8	28.81	0.4	15.54		
2.79	49.74	2.39	49.16	1.99	47.67	1.59	44.41	1.19	38.3	0.79	28.52	0.39	15.17		
2.78	49.73	2.38	49.13	1.98	47.61	1.58	44.29	1.18	38.1	0.78	228.2	0.38	14.8		
2.77	49.72	2.37	49.11	1.97	47.56	1.57	44.18	1.17	37.9	0.77	27.94	0.37	14.43		
2.76	49.71	2.36	49.09	1.96	47.5	1.56	44.06	1.16	37.7	0.76	27.64	0.36	14.06		
2.75	49.7	2.35	49.06	1.95	47.44	1.55	43.94	1.15	37.49	0.75	27.34	0.35	13.68		
2.74	49.69	2.34	49.04	1.94	47.38	1.54	43.83	1.14	37.29	0.74	27.04	0.34	13.31		
2.73	49.68	2.33	49.01	1.93	47.32	1.53	43.7	1.13	37.08	0.73	26.73	0.33	12.93		
2.72	49.67	2.32	48.98	1.92	47.26	1.52	43.57	1.12	36.86	0.72	26.42	0.32	12.55		
2.71	49.66	2.31	48.96	1.91	47.19	1.51	43.45	1.11	36.65	0.71	26.11	0.31	12.17		
2.7	49.65	2.3	48.93	1.9	47.13	1.5	43.32	1.1	36.43	0.7	25.8	0.3	11.7		
2.69	49.64	2.29	48.9	1.89	47.06	1.49	43.19	1.09	36.21	0.69	25.49	0.29	11.41		
2.68	49.63	2.28	48.87	1.88	46.99	1.48	43.06	1.08	35.99	0.68	25.17	0.28	11.03		
2.67	49.62	2.27	48.84	1.87	46.93	1.47	42.92	1.07	35.77	0.67	24.86	0.27	10.64		
2.66	49.61	2.26	48.81	1.86	46.86	1.46	42.79	1.06	35.54	0.66	24.54	0.26	10.26		
2.65	49.6	2.25	48.78	1.85	46.78	1.45	42.65	1.05	35.31	0.65	24.22	0.25	9.87		
2.64	49.59	2.24	48.75	1.84	46.71	1.44	42.51	1.04	35.08	0.64	23.89	0.24	9.48		
2.63	49.57	2.23	48.71	1.83	46.64	1.43	42.36	1.03	34.85	0.63	23.57	0.23	9.1		
2.62	49.56	2.22	48.68	1.82	46.56	1.42	42.22	1.02	34.61	0.62	23.24	0.22	8.71		
2.61	49.55	2.21	48.64	1.81	46.49	1.41	42.07	1.01	34.38	0.61	22.91	0.21	8.32		

SOURCE: Adapted from Wendy Steinberg's *Statistics Alive!* Appendix A.

Table B *t* Table

df	Level of Significance for One-Tailed Test (%)			
	5	2.5	1	.5
	Level of Significance for Two-Tailed Test (%)			
df	10	5 .05	2	1
1	6.3138	12.7062	31.8207	63.6574
2	2.9200	4.3027	6.9646	9.9248
3	2.3534	3.1824	4.5407	5.8409
4	2.1318	2.7764	3.7469	4.6041
5	2.0150	2.5706	3.3649	4.0322
6	1.9432	2.4469	3.1427	3.7074
7	1.8946	2.3646	2.9980	3.4995
8	1.8595	2.3060	2.8965	3.3554
9	1.8331	2.2622	2.8214	3.2498
10	1.8125	2.2281	2.7638	3.1693
11	1.7959	2.2010	2.7181	3.1058
12	1.7823	2.1788	2.6810	3.0545
13	1.7709	2.1604	2.6503	3.0123
14	1.7613	2.1448	2.6245	2.9768
15	1.7531	2.1315	2.6025	2.9467
16	1.7459	2.1199	2.5835	2.9208
17	1.7396	2.1098	2.5669	2.8982
18	1.7341	2.1009	2.5524	2.8784
19	1.7291	2.0930	2.5395	2.8609
20	1.7247	2.0860	2.5280	2.8453
21	1.7207	2.0796	2.5177	2.8314

df	Level of Significance for One-Tailed Test (%)			
	5	2.5	1	.5
	Level of Significance for Two-Tailed Test (%)			
	10	5	2	1
22	1.7171	2.0739	2.5083	2.8188
23	1.7139	2.0687	2.4999	2.8073
24	1.7109	2.0639	2.4922	2.7969
25	1.7081	2.0595	2.4851	2.7874
26	1.7056	2.0555	2.4786	2.7787
27	1.7033	2.0518	2.4727	2.7707
28	1.7011	2.0484	2.4671	2.7633
29	1.6991	2.0452	2.4620	2.7564
30	1.6973	2.0423	2.4573	2.7500
35	1.6869	2.0301	2.4377	2.7238
40	1.6839	2.0211	2.4233	2.7045
45	1.6794	2.0141	2.4121	2.6896
50	1.6759	2.0086	2.4033	2.6778
60	1.6706	2.0003	2.3901	2.6603
70	1.6669	1.9944	2.3808	2.6479
80	1.6641	1.9901	2.3739	2.6387
90	1.6620	1.9867	2.3685	2.6316
100	1.6602	1.9840	2.3642	2.6259
110	1.6588	1.9818	2.3607	2.6213
120	1.6577	1.9799	2.3598	2.6174
∞	1.6449	1.9600	2.3263	2.5758

SOURCE: Adapted from Wendy Steinberg's *Statistics Alive!* Appendix C.

Table C F Table (ANOVA)

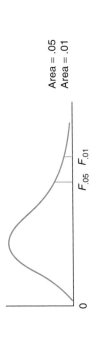

Area = .05
Area = .01

$F_{.05}$ $F_{.01}$

Degrees of Freedom: Numerator

Degrees of Freedom: Denominator	1	2	3	4	5	6	7	8	9	10	11	12	14	16	20	24	30	40	50	75	100	200	500	∞
1	161	200	216	225	230	234	237	239	241	242	243	244	245	246	248	249	250	241	252	255	253	254	254	254
	4052	**4999**	**5403**	**5625**	**5764**	**5859**	**5928**	**5981**	**6022**	**6056**	**6082**	**6106**	**6142**	**6169**	**6208**	**6234**	**6258**	**6286**	**6302**	**6323**	**6334**	**6352**	**6361**	**6366**
2	18.51	19.00	19.16	19.25	19.30	19.33	19.36	19.37	19.38	19.39	19.40	19.41	19.42	19.43	19.44	19.45	19.46	19.47	19.47	19.48	19.49	19.49	19.50	19.50
	98.49	**99.00**	**99.17**	**99.25**	**99.30**	**99.33**	**99.34**	**99.36**	**99.38**	**99.40**	**99.41**	**99.42**	**99.43**	**99.44**	**99.45**	**99.46**	**99.47**	**99.48**	**99.48**	**99.49**	**99.49**	**99.49**	**99.50**	**99.50**
3	10.13	9.55	9.28	9.12	9.01	8.94	8.88	8.84	8.81	8.78	8.76	8.74	8.71	8.69	8.66	8.64	8.62	8.60	8.58	8.57	8.56	8.54	8.54	8.53
	34.12	**30.82**	**29.46**	**28.71**	**28.24**	**27.91**	**27.67**	**27.49**	**27.34**	**27.23**	**27.13**	**27.05**	**26.92**	**26.83**	**26.69**	**26.60**	**26.50**	**26.41**	**26.35**	**26.27**	**26.23**	**26.18**	**26.14**	**26.12**
4	7.71	6.94	6.59	6.39	6.26	6.16	6.09	6.04	6.00	5.96	5.93	5.91	5.87	5.84	5.80	5.77	5.74	5.71	5.70	5.68	5.66	5.65	5.64	5.63
	21.20	**18.00**	**16.69**	**15.98**	**15.52**	**15.21**	**14.98**	**14.80**	**14.66**	**14.54**	**14.45**	**14.37**	**14.24**	**14.15**	**14.02**	**13.93**	**13.83**	**13.74**	**13.69**	**13.61**	**13.57**	**13.52**	**13.48**	**13.46**
5	6.61	5.79	5.41	5.19	5.05	4.95	4.88	4.82	4.78	4.74	4.70	4.68	4.64	4.60	4.56	4.53	4.50	4.46	4.44	4.42	4.40	4.38	4.37	4.36
	16.26	**13.27**	**12.06**	**11.39**	**10.97**	**10.67**	**10.45**	**10.27**	**10.15**	**10.05**	**9.96**	**9.89**	**9.77**	**9.68**	**9.55**	**9.47**	**9.38**	**9.29**	**9.24**	**9.17**	**9.13**	**9.07**	**9.04**	**9.02**
6	5.99	5.14	4.76	4.53	4.39	4.28	4.21	4.15	4.10	4.06	4.03	4.00	3.96	3.92	3.87	3.84	3.81	3.77	3.75	3.72	3.71	3.69	3.68	3.67
	13.74	**10.92**	**9.78**	**9.15**	**8.75**	**8.47**	**8.26**	**8.10**	**7.98**	**7.87**	**7.79**	**7.72**	**7.60**	**7.52**	**7.39**	**7.31**	**7.23**	**7.14**	**7.09**	**7.02**	**6.99**	**6.94**	**6.90**	**6.88**
7	5.59	4.47	4.35	4.12	3.97	3.87	3.79	3.73	3.68	3.63	3.60	3.57	3.52	3.49	3.44	3.41	3.38	3.34	3.32	3.29	3.28	3.25	3.24	3.23
	12.25	**9.55**	**8.45**	**7.85**	**7.46**	**7.19**	**7.00**	**6.84**	**6.71**	**6.62**	**6.54**	**6.47**	**6.35**	**6.27**	**6.15**	**6.07**	**5.98**	**5.90**	**5.85**	**5.78**	**5.75**	**5.70**	**5.67**	**5.65**
8	5.32	4.46	4.07	3.84	3.69	3.58	3.50	3.44	3.39	3.34	3.31	3.28	3.23	3.20	3.15	3.12	3.08	3.05	3.03	3.00	2.98	2.96	2.94	2.93
	11.26	**8.65**	**7.59**	**7.01**	**6.63**	**6.37**	**6.19**	**6.03**	**5.91**	**5.82**	**5.74**	**5.67**	**5.56**	**5.48**	**5.36**	**5.28**	**5.20**	**5.11**	**5.06**	**5.00**	**4.96**	**4.91**	**4.88**	**4.86**
9	5.12	4.26	3.86	3.63	3.48	3.37	3.29	3.23	3.18	3.13	3.10	3.07	3.02	2.98	2.93	2.90	2.86	2.82	2.80	2.77	2.76	2.73	2.72	2.71
	10.56	**8.02**	**6.99**	**6.42**	**6.06**	**5.80**	**5.62**	**5.47**	**5.35**	**5.26**	**5.18**	**5.11**	**5.00**	**4.92**	**4.80**	**4.73**	**4.64**	**4.56**	**4.51**	**4.45**	**4.41**	**4.36**	**4.33**	**4.31**
10	4.96	4.10	3.71	3.48	3.33	3.22	3.14	3.07	3.02	2.97	2.94	2.91	2.86	2.82	2.77	2.74	2.70	2.67	2.64	2.61	2.59	2.56	2.55	2.54
	10.04	**7.56**	**6.55**	**5.99**	**5.64**	**5.39**	**5.21**	**5.06**	**4.95**	**4.85**	**4.78**	**4.71**	**4.60**	**4.52**	**4.41**	**4.33**	**4.25**	**4.17**	**4.12**	**4.05**	**4.01**	**3.96**	**3.93**	**3.91**
11	4.84	3.98	3.59	3.36	3.20	3.09	3.01	2.95	2.90	2.86	2.82	2.79	2.74	2.70	2.65	2.61	2.57	2.53	2.50	2.47	2.45	2.42	2.41	2.40
	9.65	**7.20**	**6.22**	**5.67**	**5.32**	**5.07**	**4.88**	**4.74**	**4.63**	**4.54**	**4.46**	**4.40**	**4.29**	**4.21**	**4.10**	**4.02**	**3.94**	**3.86**	**3.80**	**3.74**	**3.70**	**3.66**	**3.62**	**3.60**

Degrees of Freedom: Denominator	Degrees of Freedom: Numerator																							
	1	2	3	4	5	6	7	8	9	10	11	12	14	16	20	24	30	40	50	75	100	200	500	∞
12	4.75	3.88	3.49	3.26	3.11	3.00	2.92	2.85	2.80	2.76	2.72	2.69	2.64	2.60	2.54	2.50	2.46	2.42	2.40	2.36	2.35	2.32	2.31	2.30
	9.33	**6.93**	**5.95**	**5.41**	**5.06**	**4.82**	**4.65**	**4.50**	**4.39**	**4.30**	**4.22**	**4.16**	**4.05**	**3.98**	**3.86**	**3.78**	**3.70**	**3.61**	**3.56**	**3.49**	**3.46**	**3.41**	**3.38**	**3.36**
13	4.67	3.80	3.41	3.18	3.02	2.92	2.84	2.77	2.72	2.67	2.63	2.60	2.55	2.51	2.46	2.42	2.38	2.34	2.32	2.28	2.26	2.24	2.22	2.21
	9.07	**6.70**	**5.74**	**5.20**	**4.86**	**4.62**	**4.44**	**6.30**	**4.19**	**4.10**	**4.02**	**3.96**	**3.85**	**3.78**	**3.67**	**3.59**	**3.51**	**3.42**	**3.37**	**3.30**	**3.27**	**3.21**	**3.18**	**3.16**
14	4.60	3.74	3.34	3.11	2.96	2.85	2.77	2.70	2.65	2.60	2.56	2.53	2.48	2.44	2.39	2.35	2.31	2.27	2.24	2.21	2.19	2.16	2.14	2.13
	8.86	**6.51**	**5.56**	**5.03**	**4.69**	**4.46**	**4.28**	**4.14**	**4.03**	**3.94**	**3.86**	**3.80**	**3.70**	**3.62**	**3.51**	**3.43**	**3.34**	**3.26**	**3.21**	**3.14**	**3.11**	**3.06**	**3.02**	**3.00**
15	4.54	3.68	3.29	3.06	2.90	2.79	2.70	2.64	2.59	2.55	2.51	2.48	2.43	2.39	2.33	2.29	2.25	2.21	2.18	2.15	2.12	2.10	2.08	2.07
	8.68	**6.36**	**5.42**	**4.89**	**4.56**	**4.32**	**4.14**	**4.00**	**3.89**	**3.80**	**3.73**	**3.67**	**3.56**	**3.48**	**3.36**	**3.29**	**3.20**	**3.12**	**3.07**	**3.00**	**2.97**	**2.92**	**2.89**	**2.87**
16	4.49	3.63	3.24	3.01	2.85	2.74	2.66	2.59	2.54	2.49	2.45	2.42	2.37	2.33	2.28	2.24	2.20	2.16	2.13	2.09	2.07	2.04	2.02	2.01
	8.53	**6.23**	**5.29**	**4.77**	**4.44**	**4.20**	**4.03**	**3.89**	**3.78**	**3.69**	**3.61**	**3.55**	**3.45**	**3.37**	**3.25**	**3.18**	**3.10**	**3.01**	**2.96**	**2.89**	**2.86**	**2.80**	**2.77**	**2.75**
17	4.45	3.59	3.20	2.96	2.81	2.70	2.62	2.55	2.50	2.45	2.41	2.38	2.33	2.29	2.23	2.19	2.15	2.11	2.08	2.04	2.02	1.99	1.97	1.96
	8.40	**6.11**	**5.18**	**4.67**	**4.34**	**4.10**	**3.93**	**3.79**	**3.68**	**3.59**	**3.52**	**3.45**	**3.35**	**3.27**	**3.16**	**3.08**	**3.00**	**2.92**	**2.86**	**2.79**	**2.76**	**2.70**	**2.67**	**2.65**
18	4.41	3.55	3.16	2.93	2.77	2.66	2.58	2.51	2.46	2.41	2.37	2.34	2.29	2.25	2.19	2.15	2.11	2.07	2.04	2.00	1.98	1.95	1.93	1.92
	8.28	**6.01**	**5.09**	**4.58**	**4.25**	**4.01**	**3.85**	**3.71**	**3.60**	**3.51**	**3.44**	**3.37**	**3.27**	**3.19**	**3.07**	**3.00**	**2.91**	**2.83**	**2.78**	**2.71**	**2.68**	**2.62**	**2.59**	**2.57**
19	4.38	3.52	3.13	2.90	2.74	2.63	2.55	2.48	2.43	2.38	2.34	2.31	2.26	2.21	2.15	2.11	2.07	2.02	2.00	1.96	1.94	1.91	1.90	1.88
	8.18	**5.93**	**5.01**	**4.50**	**4.17**	**3.94**	**3.77**	**3.63**	**3.52**	**3.43**	**3.36**	**3.30**	**3.19**	**3.12**	**3.00**	**2.92**	**2.84**	**2.76**	**2.70**	**2.63**	**2.60**	**2.54**	**2.51**	**2.49**
20	4.35	3.49	3.10	2.87	2.71	2.60	2.52	2.45	2.40	2.35	2.31	2.28	2.23	2.18	2.12	2.08	2.04	1.99	1.96	1.92	1.90	1.87	1.85	1.84
	8.10	**5.85**	**4.94**	**4.43**	**4.10**	**3.87**	**3.71**	**3.56**	**3.45**	**3.37**	**3.30**	**3.23**	**3.13**	**3.05**	**2.94**	**2.86**	**2.77**	**2.69**	**2.63**	**2.56**	**2.53**	**2.47**	**2.44**	**2.42**
21	4.32	3.47	3.07	2.84	2.68	2.57	2.49	2.42	2.37	2.32	2.28	2.25	2.20	2.15	2.09	2.05	2.00	1.96	1.93	1.89	1.87	1.84	1.82	1.81
	8.02	**5.78**	**4.87**	**4.37**	**4.04**	**3.81**	**3.65**	**3.51**	**3.40**	**3.31**	**3.24**	**3.17**	**3.07**	**2.99**	**2.88**	**2.80**	**2.72**	**2.63**	**2.58**	**2.51**	**2.47**	**2.42**	**2.38**	**2.36**
22	4.30	3.44	3.05	2.82	2.66	2.55	2.47	2.40	2.35	2.30	2.26	2.23	2.18	2.13	2.07	2.03	1.98	1.93	1.91	1.87	1.84	1.81	1.80	1.78
	7.94	**5.72**	**4.82**	**4.31**	**3.99**	**3.76**	**3.59**	**3.45**	**3.35**	**3.26**	**3.18**	**3.12**	**3.02**	**2.94**	**2.83**	**2.75**	**2.67**	**2.58**	**2.53**	**2.46**	**2.42**	**2.37**	**2.33**	**2.31**
23	4.28	3.42	3.03	2.80	2.04	2.53	2.45	2.38	2.32	2.28	2.24	2.20	2.14	2.10	2.04	2.00	1.96	1.91	1.88	1.84	1.82	1.79	1.77	1.76
	7.88	**5.66**	**4.76**	**4.26**	**3.94**	**3.71**	**3.54**	**3.41**	**3.30**	**3.21**	**3.14**	**3.07**	**2.97**	**2.89**	**2.78**	**2.70**	**2.62**	**2.53**	**2.48**	**2.41**	**2.37**	**2.32**	**2.28**	**2.26**
24	4.26	3.40	3.01	2.78	2.62	2.51	2.43	2.36	2.30	2.26	2.22	2.18	2.13	2.09	2.02	1.98	1.94	1.89	1.86	1.82	1.80	1.76	1.74	1.73
	7.82	**5.61**	**4.72**	**4.22**	**3.90**	**3.67**	**3.50**	**3.36**	**3.25**	**3.17**	**3.09**	**3.03**	**2.93**	**2.85**	**2.74**	**2.66**	**2.58**	**2.49**	**2.44**	**2.36**	**2.33**	**2.27**	**2.23**	**2.21**
25	4.24	3.38	2.99	2.76	2.60	2.49	2.41	2.34	2.28	2.24	2.20	2.16	2.11	2.06	2.00	1.96	1.92	1.87	1.84	1.80	1.77	1.74	1.72	1.71
	7.77	**5.57**	**4.68**	**4.18**	**3.86**	**3.63**	**3.46**	**3.32**	**3.21**	**3.13**	**3.05**	**2.99**	**2.89**	**2.81**	**2.70**	**2.62**	**2.54**	**2.45**	**2.40**	**2.32**	**2.29**	**2.23**	**2.19**	**2.17**
26	4.22	3.37	2.98	2.74	2.59	2.47	2.39	2.32	2.27	2.22	2.18	2.15	2.10	2.05	1.99	1.95	1.90	1.85	1.82	1.78	1.76	1.72	1.70	1.69

(Continued)

Table C (Continued)

Degrees of Freedom: Numerator

Degrees of Freedom: Denominator	1	2	3	4	5	6	7	8	9	10	11	12	14	16	20	24	30	40	50	75	100	200	500	∞
27	**7.72**	**5.53**	**4.64**	**4.14**	**3.82**	**3.59**	**3.42**	**3.29**	**3.17**	**3.09**	**3.02**	**2.96**	**2.86**	**2.77**	**2.66**	**2.58**	**2.50**	**2.41**	**2.36**	**2.28**	**2.25**	**2.19**	**2.15**	**2.13**
	4.21	3.35	2.96	2.73	2.57	2.46	2.37	2.30	2.25	2.20	2.16	2.13	2.08	2.03	1.97	1.93	1.88	1.84	1.80	1.76	1.74	1.71	1.68	1.67
28	**7.68**	**5.49**	**4.60**	**4.11**	**3.79**	**3.56**	**3.39**	**3.26**	**3.14**	**3.0€**	**2.98**	**2.93**	**2.83**	**2.74**	**2.63**	**2.55**	**2.47**	**2.38**	**2.33**	**2.25**	**2.21**	**2.16**	**2.12**	**2.10**
	4.20	3.34	2.95	2.71	2.56	2.44	2.36	2.29	2.24	2.19	2.15	2.12	2.06	2.02	1.96	1.91	1.87	1.81	1.78	1.75	1.72	1.69	1.67	1.65
29	**7.64**	**5.45**	**4.57**	**4.07**	**3.76**	**3.53**	**3.36**	**3.23**	**3.11**	**3.03**	**2.95**	**2.90**	**2.80**	**2.71**	**2.60**	**2.52**	**2.44**	**2.35**	**2.30**	**2.22**	**2.18**	**2.13**	**2.09**	**2.06**
	4.18	3.33	2.93	2.70	2.54	2.43	2.35	2.28	2.22	2.18	2.14	2.10	2.05	2.00	1.94	1.90	1.85	1.80	1.77	1.73	1.71	1.68	1.65	1.64
30	**7.60**	**5.42**	**4.54**	**4.04**	**3.73**	**3.50**	**3.33**	**3.20**	**3.08**	**3.00**	**2.92**	**2.87**	**2.77**	**2.68**	**2.57**	**2.49**	**2.41**	**2.32**	**2.27**	**2.19**	**2.15**	**2.10**	**2.06**	**2.03**
	4.17	3.32	2.92	2.69	2.53	2.42	2.34	2.27	2.21	2.16	2.12	2.09	2.04	1.99	1.93	1.89	1.84	1.79	1.76	1.72	1.69	1.66	1.64	1.62
32	**7.56**	**5.39**	**4.51**	**4.02**	**3.70**	**3.47**	**3.30**	**3.17**	**3.06**	**2.98**	**2.90**	**2.84**	**2.74**	**2.66**	**2.55**	**2.47**	**2.38**	**2.29**	**2.24**	**2.16**	**2.13**	**2.07**	**2.03**	**2.01**
	4.15	3.30	2.90	2.67	2.51	2.40	2.32	2.25	2.19	2.14	2.10	2.07	2.02	1.97	1.91	1.86	1.82	1.76	1.74	1.69	1.67	1.64	1.61	1.59
34	**7.50**	**5.34**	**4.46**	**3.97**	**3.66**	**3.42**	**3.25**	**3.12**	**3.01**	**2.94**	**2.86**	**2.80**	**2.70**	**2.62**	**2.51**	**2.42**	**2.34**	**2.25**	**2.20**	**2.12**	**2.08**	**2.02**	**1.98**	**1.96**
	4.13	3.28	2.88	2.65	2.49	2.38	2.30	2.23	2.17	2.12	2.08	2.05	2.00	1.95	1.89	1.84	1.80	1.74	1.71	1.67	1.64	1.61	1.59	1.57
36	**7.44**	**5.29**	**4.42**	**3.93**	**3.61**	**3.38**	**3.21**	**3.08**	**2.97**	**2.89**	**2.82**	**2.76**	**2.66**	**2.58**	**2.47**	**2.38**	**2.30**	**2.21**	**2.15**	**2.08**	**2.04**	**1.98**	**1.94**	**1.91**
	4.11	3.26	2.86	2.63	2.48	2.36	2.28	2.21	2.15	2.10	2.06	2.03	1.98	1.93	1.87	1.82	1.78	1.72	1.69	1.65	1.62	1.59	1.56	1.55
38	**7.39**	**5.25**	**4.38**	**3.89**	**3.58**	**3.35**	**3.18**	**3.04**	**2.94**	**2.86**	**2.78**	**2.72**	**2.62**	**2.54**	**2.43**	**2.35**	**2.26**	**2.17**	**2.12**	**2.04**	**2.00**	**1.94**	**1.90**	**1.87**
	4.10	3.25	2.85	2.62	2.46	2.35	2.26	2.19	2.14	2.09	2.05	2.02	1.96	1.92	1.85	1.80	1.76	1.71	1.67	1.63	1.60	1.57	1.54	1.53
40	**7.35**	**5.21**	**4.34**	**3.86**	**3.54**	**3.32**	**3.15**	**3.02**	**2.91**	**2.82**	**2.75**	**2.69**	**2.59**	**2.51**	**2.40**	**2.32**	**2.22**	**2.14**	**2.08**	**2.00**	**1.97**	**1.90**	**1.86**	**1.84**
	4.08	3.23	2.84	2.61	2.45	2.34	2.25	2.18	2.12	2.07	2.04	2.00	1.95	1.90	1.84	1.79	1.74	1.69	1.66	1.61	1.59	1.55	1.53	1.51
42	**7.31**	**5.18**	**4.31**	**3.83**	**3.51**	**3.29**	**3.12**	**2.99**	**2.88**	**2.80**	**2.73**	**2.66**	**2.56**	**2.49**	**2.37**	**2.29**	**2.20**	**2.11**	**2.05**	**1.97**	**1.94**	**1.88**	**1.84**	**1.81**
	4.07	3.22	2.83	2.59	2.44	2.32	2.24	2.17	2.11	2.06	2.02	1.99	1.94	1.89	1.82	1.78	1.73	1.68	1.64	1.60	1.57	1.54	1.51	1.49
44	**7.27**	**5.15**	**4.29**	**3.80**	**3.49**	**3.26**	**3.10**	**2.96**	**2.86**	**2.77**	**2.70**	**2.64**	**2.54**	**2.46**	**2.35**	**2.26**	**2.17**	**2.08**	**2.02**	**1.94**	**1.91**	**1.85**	**1.80**	**1.78**
	4.06	3.21	2.82	2.58	2.43	2.31	2.23	2.16	2.10	2.05	2.01	1.98	1.92	1.88	1.81	1.76	1.72	1.66	1.63	1.58	1.56	1.52	1.50	1.48
46	**7.24**	**5.12**	**4.26**	**3.78**	**3.46**	**3.24**	**3.07**	**2.94**	**2.84**	**2.75**	**2.68**	**2.62**	**2.52**	**2.44**	**2.32**	**2.24**	**2.15**	**2.06**	**2.00**	**1.92**	**1.88**	**1.82**	**1.78**	**1.75**
	4.05	3.20	2.81	2.57	2.42	2.30	2.22	2.14	2.09	2.04	2.00	1.97	1.91	1.87	1.80	1.75	1.71	1.65	1.62	1.57	1.54	1.51	1.48	1.46
48	**7.21**	**5.10**	**4.24**	**3.76**	**3.44**	**3.22**	**3.05**	**2.92**	**2.82**	**2.73**	**2.66**	**2.60**	**2.50**	**2.42**	**2.30**	**2.22**	**2.13**	**2.04**	**1.98**	**1.90**	**1.86**	**1.80**	**1.76**	**1.72**
	4.04	3.19	2.80	2.56	2.41	2.30	2.21	2.14	2.08	2.03	1.99	1.96	1.90	1.86	1.79	1.74	1.70	1.64	1.61	1.56	1.53	1.50	1.47	1.45
50	**7.19**	**5.08**	**4.22**	**3.74**	**3.42**	**3.20**	**3.04**	**2.90**	**2.80**	**2.71**	**2.64**	**2.58**	**2.48**	**2.40**	**2.28**	**2.20**	**2.11**	**2.02**	**1.96**	**1.88**	**1.84**	**1.78**	**1.73**	**1.70**
	4.03	3.18	2.79	2.56	2.40	2.29	2.20	2.13	2.07	2.02	1.98	1.95	1.90	1.85	1.78	1.74	1.69	1.63	1.60	1.55	1.52	1.48	1.46	1.44
55	**7.17**	**5.06**	**4.20**	**3.72**	**3.41**	**3.18**	**3.02**	**2.88**	**2.78**	**2.70**	**2.62**	**2.56**	**2.46**	**2.39**	**2.26**	**2.18**	**2.10**	**2.00**	**1.94**	**1.86**	**1.82**	**1.76**	**1.71**	**1.68**
	4.02	3.17	2.78	2.54	2.38	2.27	2.18	2.11	2.05	2.00	1.97	1.93	1.88	1.83	1.76	1.72	1.67	1.61	1.58	1.52	1.50	1.46	1.43	1.41

Degrees of Freedom: Numerator

The table below gives critical values of the F distribution. Within each denominator group the upper (roman) value corresponds to 5% and the lower (boldface) value to 1% of the area in the upper tail.

Degrees of Freedom: Denominator	1	2	3	4	5	6	7	8	9	10	11	12	14	16	20	24	30	40	50	75	100	200	500	∞
(continued, 1%)	**7.12**	**5.01**	**4.16**	**3.68**	**3.37**	**3.15**	**2.98**	**2.85**	**2.75**	**2.66**	**2.59**	**2.53**	**2.43**	**2.35**	**2.23**	**2.15**	**2.06**	**1.96**	**1.90**	**1.82**	**1.78**	**1.71**	**1.66**	**1.64**
60 (5%)	4.00	3.15	2.76	2.52	2.37	2.25	2.17	2.10	2.04	1.99	1.95	1.92	1.86	1.81	1.75	1.70	1.65	1.59	1.56	1.50	1.48	1.44	1.41	1.39
60 (1%)	**7.08**	**4.98**	**4.13**	**3.65**	**3.34**	**3.12**	**2.95**	**2.82**	**2.72**	**2.63**	**2.56**	**2.50**	**2.40**	**2.32**	**2.20**	**2.12**	**2.03**	**1.93**	**1.87**	**1.79**	**1.74**	**1.68**	**1.63**	**1.60**
65 (5%)	3.99	3.14	2.75	2.51	2.36	2.24	2.15	2.08	2.02	1.98	1.94	1.90	1.85	1.80	1.73	1.68	1.63	1.57	1.54	1.49	1.46	1.42	1.39	1.37
65 (1%)	**7.04**	**4.95**	**4.10**	**3.62**	**3.31**	**3.09**	**2.93**	**2.79**	**2.70**	**2.61**	**2.54**	**2.47**	**2.37**	**2.30**	**2.18**	**2.09**	**2.00**	**1.90**	**1.84**	**1.76**	**1.71**	**1.64**	**1.60**	**1.56**
70 (5%)	3.98	3.13	2.74	2.50	2.35	2.23	2.14	2.07	2.01	1.97	1.93	1.89	1.84	1.79	1.72	1.67	1.62	1.56	1.53	1.47	1.45	1.40	1.37	1.35
70 (1%)	**7.01**	**4.92**	**4.08**	**3.60**	**3.29**	**3.07**	**2.91**	**2.77**	**2.67**	**2.59**	**2.51**	**2.45**	**2.35**	**2.28**	**2.15**	**2.07**	**1.98**	**1.88**	**1.82**	**1.74**	**1.69**	**1.62**	**1.56**	**1.53**
80 (5%)	3.96	3.11	2.72	2.48	2.33	2.21	2.12	2.05	1.99	1.95	1.91	1.88	1.82	1.77	1.70	1.65	1.60	1.54	1.51	1.45	1.42	1.38	1.35	1.32
80 (1%)	**6.96**	**4.88**	**4.04**	**3.56**	**3.25**	**3.04**	**2.87**	**2.74**	**2.64**	**2.55**	**2.48**	**2.41**	**2.32**	**2.24**	**2.11**	**2.03**	**1.94**	**1.84**	**1.78**	**1.70**	**1.65**	**1.57**	**1.52**	**1.49**
100 (5%)	3.94	3.09	2.70	2.46	2.30	2.19	2.10	2.03	1.97	1.92	1.88	1.85	1.79	1.75	1.68	1.63	1.57	1.51	1.48	1.42	1.39	1.34	1.30	1.28
100 (1%)	**6.90**	**4.82**	**3.98**	**3.51**	**3.20**	**2.99**	**2.82**	**2.69**	**2.59**	**2.51**	**2.43**	**2.36**	**2.26**	**2.19**	**2.06**	**1.98**	**1.89**	**1.79**	**1.73**	**1.64**	**1.59**	**1.51**	**1.46**	**1.43**
125 (5%)	3.92	3.07	2.68	2.44	2.29	2.17	2.08	2.01	1.95	1.90	1.86	1.83	1.77	1.72	1.65	1.60	1.55	1.49	1.45	1.39	1.36	1.31	1.27	1.25
125 (1%)	**6.84**	**4.78**	**3.94**	**3.47**	**3.17**	**2.95**	**2.79**	**2.65**	**2.56**	**2.47**	**2.40**	**2.33**	**2.23**	**2.15**	**2.03**	**1.94**	**1.85**	**1.75**	**1.68**	**1.59**	**1.54**	**1.46**	**1.40**	**1.37**
150 (5%)	3.91	3.06	2.67	2.43	2.27	2.16	2.07	2.00	1.94	1.89	1.85	1.82	1.76	1.71	1.64	1.59	1.54	1.47	1.44	1.37	1.34	1.29	1.25	1.22
150 (1%)	**6.81**	**4.75**	**3.91**	**3.44**	**3.14**	**2.92**	**2.76**	**2.62**	**2.53**	**2.44**	**2.37**	**2.30**	**2.20**	**2.12**	**2.00**	**1.91**	**1.83**	**1.72**	**1.66**	**1.56**	**1.51**	**1.43**	**1.37**	**1.33**
200 (5%)	3.89	3.04	2.65	2.41	2.26	2.14	2.05	1.98	1.92	1.87	1.83	1.80	1.74	1.69	1.62	1.57	1.52	1.45	1.42	1.35	1.32	1.26	1.22	1.19
200 (1%)	**6.76**	**4.71**	**3.88**	**3.41**	**3.11**	**2.90**	**2.73**	**2.60**	**2.50**	**2.41**	**2.34**	**2.28**	**2.17**	**2.09**	**1.97**	**1.88**	**1.79**	**1.69**	**1.62**	**1.53**	**1.48**	**1.39**	**1.33**	**1.28**
400 (5%)	3.86	3.02	2.62	2.39	2.23	2.12	2.03	1.96	1.90	1.85	1.81	1.78	1.72	1.67	1.60	1.54	1.49	1.42	1.38	1.32	1.28	1.22	1.16	1.13
400 (1%)	**6.70**	**4.66**	**3.83**	**3.36**	**3.06**	**2.85**	**2.69**	**2.55**	**2.46**	**2.37**	**2.29**	**2.23**	**2.12**	**2.04**	**1.92**	**1.84**	**1.74**	**1.64**	**1.57**	**1.47**	**1.42**	**1.32**	**1.24**	**1.19**
1000 (5%)	3.85	3.00	2.61	2.38	2.22	2.10	2.02	1.95	1.89	1.84	1.80	1.76	1.70	1.65	1.58	1.53	1.47	1.41	1.36	1.30	1.26	1.19	1.13	1.08
1000 (1%)	**6.66**	**4.62**	**3.80**	**3.34**	**3.04**	**2.82**	**2.66**	**2.53**	**2.43**	**2.34**	**2.26**	**2.20**	**2.09**	**2.01**	**1.89**	**1.81**	**1.71**	**1.61**	**1.54**	**1.44**	**1.38**	**1.28**	**1.19**	**1.11**
∞ (5%)	3.84	2.99	2.60	2.37	2.21	2.09	2.01	1.94	1.88	1.83	1.79	1.75	1.69	1.64	1.57	1.52	1.46	1.40	1.35	1.28	1.24	1.17	1.11	1.00
∞ (1%)	**6.64**	**4.60**	**3.78**	**3.32**	**3.02**	**2.80**	**2.64**	**2.51**	**2.41**	**2.32**	**2.24**	**2.18**	**2.07**	**1.99**	**1.87**	**1.79**	**1.69**	**1.59**	**1.52**	**1.41**	**1.36**	**1.25**	**1.15**	**1.00**

NOTE: The specific F distribution must be identified by the number of degrees of freedom characterizing the numerator and the denominator of F. The values of F corresponding to 5% of the area in the upper tail are shown in roman type and those corresponding to 1%, in boldface type.

SOURCE: Adapted from Wendy Steinberg's *Statistics Alive!* Appendix D.

Only for the post-hoc test

Table D Studentized Range Statistic (for Tukey *HSD*)

df_{with}	α	2	3	4	5	6	7	8	9	10
5	.05	3.64	4.60	5.22	5.67	6.03	6.33	6.58	6.80	6.99
	.01	5.70	6.98	7.80	8.42	8.91	9.32	9.67	9.97	10.24
6	.05	3.46	4.34	4.90	5.30	5.63	5.90	6.12	6.32	6.49
	.01	5.24	6.33	7.03	7.56	7.97	8.32	8.61	8.87	9.10
7	.05	3.34	4.16	4.68	5.06	5.36	5.61	5.82	6.00	6.16
	.01	4.95	5.92	6.54	7.01	7.37	7.68	7.94	8.17	8.37
8	.05	3.26	4.04	4.53	4.89	5.17	5.40	5.60	5.77	5.92
	.01	4.75	5.64	6.20	6.62	6.96	7.24	7.47	7.68	7.86
9	.05	3.20	3.95	4.41	4.76	5.02	5.24	5.43	5.59	5.74
	.01	4.60	5.43	5.96	6.35	6.66	6.91	7.13	7.33	7.49
10	.05	3.15	3.88	4.33	4.65	4.91	5.12	5.30	5.46	5.60
	.01	4.48	5.27	5.77	6.14	6.43	6.67	6.87	7.05	7.21
11	.05	3.11	3.82	4.26	4.57	4.82	5.03	5.20	5.35	5.49
	.01	4.39	5.15	5.62	5.97	6.25	6.48	6.67	6.84	6.99
12	.05	3.08	3.77	4.20	4.51	4.75	4.95	5.12	5.27	5.39
	.01	4.32	5.05	5.50	5.84	6.10	6.32	6.51	6.67	6.81
13	.05	3.06	3.73	4.15	4.45	4.69	4.88	5.05	5.19	5.32
	.01	4.26	4.96	5.40	5.73	5.98	6.19	6.37	6.53	6.67
14	.05	3.03	3.70	4.11	4.41	4.64	4.83	4.99	5.13	5.25
	.01	4.21	4.89	5.32	5.63	5.88	6.08	6.26	6.41	6.54
15	.05	3.01	3.67	4.08	4.37	4.59	4.78	4.94	5.08	5.20
	.01	4.17	4.84	5.25	5.56	5.80	5.99	6.16	6.31	6.44
16	.05	3.00	3.65	4.05	4.33	4.56	4.74	4.90	5.03	5.15
	.01	4.13	4.79	5.19	5.49	5.72	5.92	6.08	6.22	6.35
17	.05	2.98	3.63	4.02	4.30	4.52	4.70	4.86	4.99	5.11
	.01	4.10	4.74	5.14	5.43	5.66	5.85	6.01	6.15	6.27
18	.05	2.97	3.61	4.00	4.28	4.49	4.67	4.82	4.96	5.07
	.01	4.07	4.70	5.09	5.38	5.60	5.79	5.94	6.08	6.20
19	.05	2.96	3.59	3.98	4.25	4.47	4.65	4.79	4.92	5.04
	.01	4.05	4.67	5.05	5.33	5.55	5.73	5.89	6.02	6.14

k = Number of Groups

| df_{with} | α | \multicolumn{9}{c}{k = Number of Groups} |
		2	3	4	5	6	7	8	9	10
20	.05	2.95	3.58	3.96	4.23	4.45	4.62	4.77	4.90	5.01
	.01	4.02	4.64	5.02	5.29	5.51	5.69	5.84	5.97	6.09
24	.05	2.92	3.53	3.90	4.17	4.37	4.54	4.68	4.81	4.92
	.01	3.96	4.55	4.91	5.17	5.37	5.54	5.69	5.81	5.92
30	.05	2.89	3.49	3.85	4.10	4.30	4.46	4.60	4.72	4.82
	.01	3.89	4.45	4.80	5.05	5.24	5.40	5.54	5.65	5.76
40	.05	2.86	3.44	3.79	4.04	4.23	4.39	4.52	4.63	4.73
	.01	3.82	4.37	4.70	4.93	5.11	5.26	5.39	5.50	5.60
60	.05	2.83	3.40	3.74	3.98	4.16	4.31	4.44	4.55	4.65
	.01	3.76	4.28	4.59	4.82	4.99	5.13	5.25	5.36	5.45
120	.05	2.80	3.36	3.68	3.92	4.10	4.24	4.36	4.47	4.56
	.01	3.70	4.20	4.50	4.71	4.87	5.01	5.12	5.21	5.30
∞	.05	2.77	3.31	3.63	3.86	4.03	4.17	4.29	4.39	4.47
	.01	3.64	4.12	4.40	4.60	4.76	4.88	4.99	5.08	5.16

SOURCE: Adapted from Wendy Steinberg's *Statistics Alive!* Appendix E.

Table E Correlation Table

Critical Values for the Pearson Product Moment Correlation			Critical Values for Spearman's rho		
df	0.05	0.01			
1	0.977	0.9999	n = no. of pairs		
2	0.95	0.99	n	0.05	0.01
3	0.878	0.959	4	*	*
4	0.811	0.917	5	1	*
5	0.754	0.874	6	0.886	1
6	0.707	0.834	7	0.786	0.929
7	0.666	0.798	8	0.738	0.881
8	0.632	0.765	9	0.7	0.883
9	0.602	0.735	10	0.648	0.794
10	0.576	0.708	11	0.618	0.755
11	0.553	0.684	12	0.587	0.727
12	0.532	0.661	13	0.56	0.703
13	0.514	0.641	14	0.538	0.679
14	0.497	0.623	15	0.521	0.654
15	0.482	0.606	16	0.503	0.635
16	0.468	0.59	17	0.488	0.618
17	0.456	0.575	18	0.472	0.6
18	0.444	0.561	19	0.46	0.584
19	0.433	0.549	20	0.447	0.57
20	0.423	0.537	21	0.436	0.556
21	0.413	0.526	22	0.425	0.544
22	0.404	0.515	23	0.416	0.532

df	0.05	0.01			
23	0.396	0.505	24	0.407	0.521
24	0.388	0.496	25	0.389	0.511
25	0.381	0.487	26	0.39	0.501
26	0.374	0.479	27	0.383	0.492
27	0.367	0.471	28	0.375	0.483
28	0.361	0.463	29	0.368	0.475
29	0.355	0.456	30	0.362	0.467
30	0.349	0.449			

SOURCE: Adapted from Wendy Steinberg's *Statistics Alive!* Appendix G.

Table F *Chi*-Square Table

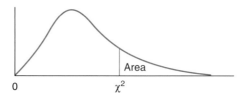

Area

0   χ^2

df	Area in the Upper Tail				
	.10	*.05*	*.025*	*.01*	*.005*
1	2.71	3.84	5.02	6.63	7.88
2	4.61	5.99	7.38	9.21	10.60
3	6.25	7.81	9.35	11.34	12.84
4	7.78	9.49	11.14	13.28	14.86
5	9.24	11.07	12.83	15.09	16.75
6	10.64	12.59	14.45	16.81	18.55
7	12.02	14.07	16.01	18.48	20.28
8	13.36	15.51	17.53	20.09	21.96
9	14.68	16.92	19.02	21.67	23.59
10	15.99	18.31	20.48	23.21	25.19
11	17.28	19.68	21.92	24.72	26.76
12	18.55	21.03	23.34	26.22	28.30
13	19.81	22.36	24.74	27.69	29.82
14	21.06	23.68	26.12	29.14	31.32
15	22.31	25.00	27.49	30.58	32.80
16	23.54	26.30	28.85	32.00	34.27
17	24.77	27.59	30.19	33.41	35.72
18	25.99	28.87	31.53	34.81	37.15
19	27.20	30.14	32.85	36.19	38.58
20	28.41	31.41	34.17	37.57	40.00
21	29.62	32.67	35.48	38.93	41.40
22	30.81	33.92	36.78	40.29	42.80
23	32.01	35.17	38.08	41.64	44.18
24	33.20	36.42	39.36	42.98	45.56
25	34.38	37.65	40.65	44.31	46.93
26	35.56	38.89	41.92	45.64	48.29

df	Area in the Upper Tail				
	.10	.05	.025	.01	.005
27	36.74	40.11	43.19	46.96	49.64
28	37.92	41.34	44.46	48.28	50.99
29	39.09	42.56	45.72	49.59	52.34
30	40.26	43.77	46.98	50.89	53.67
40	51.81	55.76	59.34	63.69	66.77
50	63.17	67.50	71.42	76.15	79.49
60	74.40	79.08	83.30	88.38	91.95
70	85.53	90.53	95.02	100.42	104.22
80	96.58	101.88	106.63	112.33	116.32
90	107.56	113.14	118.14	124.12	128.30
100	118.50	124.34	129.56	135.81	140.17
120	140.23	146.57	152.21	158.95	163.64

NOTE: The first column identifies the specific χ^2 distribution according to its number of degrees of freedom. Other columns give the proportion of the area under the entire curve that falls above the tabled value of χ^2.

SOURCE: Adapted from Wendy Steinberg's *Statistics Alive!* Appendix F.

A PRIMER IN SPSS

To use SPSS to calculate descriptive statistics for the data in Figure 2.2, proceed as follows:

1. Once SPSS is loaded, select "Type in Data." You'll have a spreadsheet-type display. In the lower left corner, there are two options, Data View (the default) and Variable View. Click "Variable View" and under the column heading "Name:" type "science."

2. Return to Data View.

3. Enter the data in the column as they are in Figure 2.2 under what now is "science." Your screen will look this way:

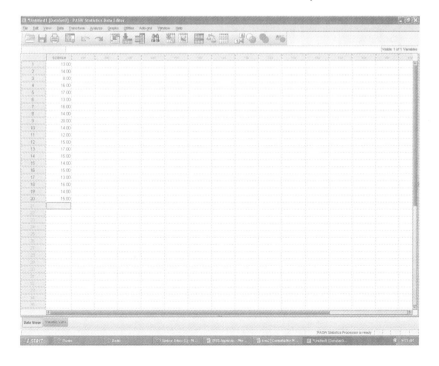

4. Click "Analyze" in the task bar across the top of your screen, and then the following selections in the menus that subsequently open;

5. Click "Descriptive Statistics."

6. Click "Descriptives."

7. Click the arrow to move "science" from the left to the right box.

8. To change the defaults, click "Options."

9. Click "Range."

10. Unclick "minimum" and "maximum" (we don't need to be told what the lowest and highest numbers in the set are when the group is n = 20).

11. Click "Continue."

12. Click "OK." The resulting table looks this way, indicating the number of science scores as well as the range (20–8), the sample mean, and the sample standard deviation.

Descriptive Statistics

	N	Range	Mean	Std. Deviation
Science	20	12.00	14.5500	2.37254
Valid N (listwise)	20			

A Histogram—Chapter 3

Once the data are entered in a data file, the commands are:
Graphs→ Legacy Dialogs→Histogram
Move the variable from the left window to the window marked "variable" and click "OK."

Descriptive Statistics—Chapter 3

You did descriptive statistics in Chapter 2, but here we'll add skewness, kurtosis, and the quartile values.

1. Once SPSS is loaded, choose the option to enter your own data.

2. Create a data file using the data in item 10 from the Exercises.

3. If you wish, you can go to "Variable View" (lower left-hand corner) and name the variable something such as "normality." You can also get rid of the decimals by changing the value in column 4 from the default of 2 to 0.

4. The commands are:

Analyze→Descriptive Statistics→Descriptives

Move the variable into the "Variable" window. Select as Options "Skew" and "Kurtosis," unselect "Minimum" and "Maximum." Click "Continue" and then "OK."

Descriptive Statistics

	N	Mean	Std.	Skewness		Kurtosis	
	Statistic	Statistic	Statistic	Statistic	Std. Error	Statistic	Std. Error
normality	12	19.83	4.914	−.348	.637	−1.354	1.232
Valid N (listwise)	12						

Note that from left to right we have the name of the variable, the number of values, *M* and *s* values. "We'll ignore the standard error value for now."

Interpreting Skewness and Kurtosis—Chapter 3

For skewness calculations:

- Positive values ($sk+$) indicate right, or positive skew.
- Negative values ($sk-$) indicate left or negative skew.
- A zero indicates that the distribution is symmetrical.

For kurtosis calculations:

- Negative values indicate that the data are platykurtic (too flat).
- Positive values indicate leptokurtic distributions (too bunched together).
- Zero indicates that the data are mesokurtic, which is the way data in normal distributions are distributed.

Skewness and kurtosis values that are +/− 2.0 are within useable limits; they don't violate normality requirements too severely. Values within +/− 1.0 are ideal.

For quartiles the commands are:

Analyze→Descriptive Statistics→Frequencies—move the variable into the "Variable" window.

Select as Statistics→Quartiles→Continue→K

Along with a Frequencies table indicating what the individual scores were and how many times they are repeated, this table is the result. Note that Q_1 = 15.25 and Q_3 = 24.75.

Statistics

normality

N	Valid	12
	Missing	0
Percentiles	25	15.25
	50	21.00
	75	24.75

Note that SPSS doesn't take the midpoint between two scores for Q_1 or Q_3, although this is the case for Q_2 (M_{dn}). Rather for Q_1, it is 1/4th of the way from the third score to the fourth and for Q_3 it is 3/4th of the interval between the 9th score and the 10th.

Creating Cross-Tabular Presentations—Chapter 3

To complete the display that is Figure 3.1, one must enter the data in two columns, one for the student's gender, the second for the level of reading proficiency. Just as with the descriptive statistics example immediately above:

1. Go to "Variable View" and name the variables, perhaps "gender" and "performance."

2. In the "Labels" column to right of each variable name, one can enter a "key" explaining what the different values mean. Since in the example "1" indicated female and "2" indicated male, we noted that in the Label section where we simply typed in "1 = female," "2 = male." The label for the performance variable indicates "1 = advanced," and so on.

3. Return to Data View and enter the data so that they appear as below.

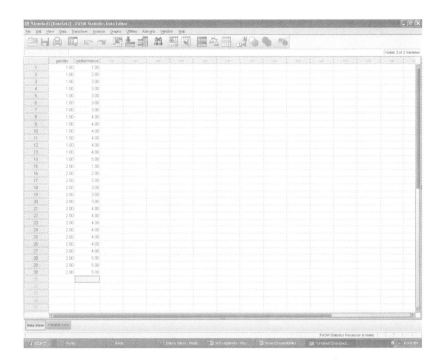

4. The commands are then:

   Analyze→Descriptive Statistics→Crosstabs

5. Indicate which variable will constitute Rows, and which will be Columns. In Figure 3.1 they are **gender** and **performance,** respectively.

6. Select "OK."

The output will be as it is in Figure 3.1.

Transforming Raw Scores Into z Scores—Chapter 4

SPSS makes it easy to transform scores into z scores. Perhaps Ms. Washington organizes a tutoring club. For 20 classrooms, the number of hours committed to the tutoring project is noted below. Ms. Washington wishes to transform them to z scores.

4, 5, 6, 6, 7, 7, 8, 10, 11, 11, 11, 13, 13, 14, 15, 15, 18, 18, 19, 20

1. Load SPSS.

2. Create a data file by typing in the scores in one column.

   a. Click "Variable View" in the lower left and name the file, if you wish.

   b. Reduce the number of decimals to 0 if you wish.

3. Click Analyze→ Descriptive Statistics→ Descriptives.

4. Move the name of your variable to the Variables window via the arrow.

5. In the lower left of this display, click "Save Standardized Values as Variables."

6. Click "OK"—the initial result is the following:

Descriptive Statistics

	N	Minimum	Maximum	Mean	Std. Deviation
Project	20	4	20	11.55	4.936
Valid N (listwise)	20				

But in Data View, there is now a second column named z, plus whatever name you used. Here, Project became ZProject. The z equivalent of 4 is -1.52953, and so on.

Project	ZProject
4	−1.52953
5	−1.32694
6	−1.12435
6	−1.12435
.	.
.	.
.	.
.	.

The One-Sample *t*-test—Chapter 6

The procedure for completing a one-sample *t*-test SPSS, is the following:

1. Create a data file with the scores in one column.

2. Once the data are in, the commands are:

   Analyze→Compare Means→ One-sample *t*-test

3. Move your variable to the **Test Variable** window.

4. In the **Test Value** window near the bottom, change the value from "0" to the value of the population mean.

5. Click "OK."

T-test

One-Sample Statistics

	N	Mean	Std. Deviation	Std. Error Mean
SATM	8	456.88	57.44	20.31

One-Sample Test

	Test Value = 500					
					95% Confidence Interval of the Difference	
	t	df	Sig. (2-tailed)	Mean Difference	Lower	Upper
SATM	-2.123	7	.071	-43.13	-91.15	4.90

- This is the output for problem 2 at the end of Chapter 6.
- The variable name and the descriptive statistics are in the first table.
- The calculated value of t, the degrees of freedom $(n-1)$, the level of significance (.071), and the difference between the mean of the sample (456.88) and the mean of the population (500) are in the second table as well as the Confidence Interval.
- Rather than indicating whether the result is significant at $p = .05$, SPSS indicates the probability that this t value (-2.123) occurred by chance. If "Sig." is .05 *or less*, the result is statistically significant. Here it isn't.

The Independent *t*-test—Chapter 6

1. Set up a data file using the scores in end-of-chapter exercises 1 and 3.

   - Use two columns, one indicating the group to which the subject belongs, and a second for all subjects' scores.
   - In "Variable View" label the columns "group" and "reading." To indicate the subjects' groups, 1s and 2s will do.

2. Enter the data so that the first *line* in Data View reads 1 under "group" and 67 under "reading." Line 16 will read 2 under "group" and 71 under "reading."

3. Once the data are in, the commands are:

Analyze→Compare Means→Independent-samples *t*-test

4. *Reading* is the Test Variable.

5. *Group* is the Grouping Variable.
   - To *define the groups,* click that button, and indicate that 1 designates group 1 and 2 indicates group 2.

6. Click "Continue." The data should look as they do below.

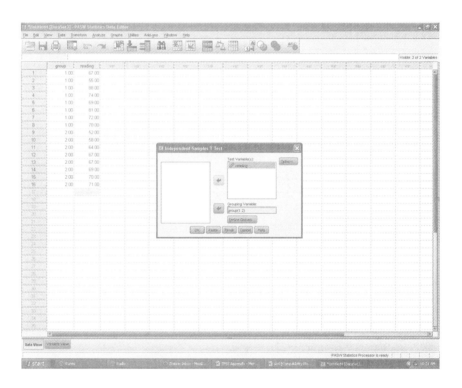

7. Click "OK."

8. The output looks much like the one-sample *t* except that it includes Levene's test for equality of variances explained in the chapter.

9. The *t* value, degrees of freedom, and standard error of the differences will match the calculated values from exercise 3. The "Sig. (2-tailed)" value is interpreted the same as it was for the one-tailed *t* above. Review the chapter for an explanation of the confidence interval.

T-test

Group Statistics

	1=honors, 2= not	N	Mean	Std. Deviation	Std. Error Mean
READING	1	8	72.00	9.77	3.45
	2	8	64.75	6.58	2.33

Independent Samples Test

		Levene's Test for Equality of Variances		t-test for Equality of Means						
									95% Confidence Interval of the Difference	
		F	Sig.	t	df	Sig. (2-tailed)	Mean Difference	Std. Error Difference	Lower	Upper
READING	Equal variances assumed	.397	.539	1.741	14	.104	7.25	4.17	-1.68	16.18
	Equal variances not assumed			1.741	12.272	.107	7.25	4.17	-1.80	16.30

One-Way *ANOVA*—Chapter 7

We'll complete problem 7 from the exercises at the end of Chapter 7.

1. Load SPSS and create a data file with the scores in the exercise. Since there are two variables (one *IV*, one *DV*), you will need two columns. Call them "minutes" and "scores," and enter them in Variable View (lower left corner). You may also wish to reset the decimals to 0 since the scores are all whole numbers.

2. Return to Data View.
   - Since we have five scores for each group, in the "minutes" column, we'll need five 1s, followed by five 2s, and then five 3s.
   - In the "scores" column, enter the scores that correspond to the 1s, 2s, and 3s.

3. Once the data are in, the commands are:

Analyze→Compare Means→One-way *ANOVA*

4. Indicate the dependent variable by moving "score" to the Dependent list window.

5. Indicate the independent variable by moving "minutes" to the Factor window.

6. Click the "Post Hoc" button, and select Tukey→ Continue→ OK.

The output is as follows:

One-way—This table is very much the same as what you produced longhand except that total sum of squares are last. The other difference is that instead of listing the critical value from the table, SPSS indicates the probability that this value of F could have occurred by chance. At $p = .033$, it's less likely to have occurred by chance than the usual criterion, $p < .05$). The result is statistically significant. Note that SPSS indicates the name of the DV above the table "score."

ANOVA

score

	Sum of Squares	df	Mean Square	F	Sig.
Between Groups	1533.733	2	766.867	4.570	.033
Within Groups	2013.600	12	167.800		
Total	3547.333	14			

Post Hoc Tests—This table can be interpreted simply. Each row is devoted to one group where that one group is compared with all others, and the probability that the difference is a random difference is indicated in the Sig. column. Group 1, for example is not significantly different from Group 2 ($p = .209$), but it *is* significantly different from Group 3 ($p = .028$). Group 2 is not significantly different from Group 3 ($p = .478$). Ignore the other columns.

Multiple Comparisons

Dependent Variable: score

Tukey HSD

(I) minutes	(J) minutes	Mean Difference (I-J)	Std. Error	Sig.	95% Confidence Interval Lower Bound	95% Confidence Interval Upper Bound
1	2	-14.800	8.193	.209	-36.66	7.06
	3	-24.600*	8.193	.028	-46.46	-2.74
2	1	14.800	8.193	.209	-7.06	36.66
	3	-9.800	8.193	.478	-31.66	12.06
3	1	24.600*	8.193	.028	2.74	46.46
	2	9.800	8.193	.478	-12.06	31.66

*The mean difference is significant at the .05 level.

Homogeneous Subsets—In this table, we get the same results as above presented a little differently. The two "subset" columns are intended to indicate that Groups 1 and 2 are not significantly different, nor are Groups 2 and 3. By default, 1 and 3 *are* significantly different.

score

Tukey HSD[a]

minutes	N	Subset for alpha = .05	
		1	2
1	5	53.20	
2	5	68.00	68.00
3	5		77.80
Sig.		.209	.478

Means for groups in homogeneous subsets are displayed.

a. Uses Harmonic Mean Sample Size = 5.000.

The Factorial *ANOVA*—Chapter 8

Factorial *ANOVA*s must be completed under a separate SPSS procedure called the General Linear Model.

- Once the data file exists, with each *IV* and the *DV* in separate columns, the commands are:
  - Analyze→General Linear Model→Univariate

Dependent Groups Tests for Interval Data—Chapter 9

The Before/After t-test

The before/after *t*, the paired *t,* and the Within-Subjects *F* all must be set up so that the related measures occur on the same row. As an example, we'll do the first problem in Chapter 9, the problem on students' self-esteem.

- If it helps, go into Variable View first and name the variables. Your instructor (who is devoid of imagination) just calls the first measure the "before" measure and the second measure the "after" measure.
- Return to Data View and enter the data. Once data for all 10 students have been entered, the commands are:

Analyze→Compare Means→Paired-Samples T-test

(Your author takes exception to SPSS's use of an uppercase "T" here. In statistics, independent and paired *t* statistics are usually indicated by the lowercase *t*. Your instructor's assumption is that the probability that his raising the issue with the powers that be would be followed by an adjustment is something like $p < .0001$.)

At this point, the variables you've named (or elected not to name) will be in the left window.

- Move the pair of variable names that represent before and after scores to the window marked "Paired Variables." Because the variables must be paired, SPSS won't let you move them one at a time. Highlight them both, click the arrow, and then click "OK." The output are the following tables:

SPSS uses the correlation value above to calculate t. We have used a different approach, but to the same effect. Note that the mean of the difference scores in the table below is the same -1.70 value we calculated, and the value of t (-2.940) is likewise the same, except for rounding differences.

Paired Samples Statistics

		Mean	N	Std. Deviation	Std. Error Mean
Pair 1	Before	5.50	10	1.581	.500
	After	7.20	10	1.687	.533

Paired Samples Correlations

		N	Correlation	Sig.
Pair 1	Before & After	10	.375	.286

The significance value ($p = .016$) indicates that this result is statistically significant at $p = .05$, just as we concluded.

Paired Samples Test

		Paired Differences					t	df	Sig. (2-tailed)
		Mean	Std. Deviation	Std. Error Mean	95% Confidence Interval of the Difference Lower	Upper			
Pair 1	Before - After	-1.700	1.829	.578	-3.008	-.392	-2.940	9	.016

The Within-Subjects F—Chapter 9

We'll work the problem in the chapter dealing with the number of hours studied per week over 3 months. In Variable View, name the variables (perhaps "first," "second," and "third" for the months) and then enter them in Data View with one column for each set of scores. Once the data are in, the commands are as follows:

Analyze→General Linear Model→Repeated Measures
This page will prompt you to do several things.

- It will ask you to name the within-subjects factor. We'll use "hours."
- Indicate the number or levels, "3."
- Click "Add" so that the three levels are included.
- Click "Define" after which you highlight a set of measures, and then click the arrow so that a set of scores is associated with each level of the variable.
- Clicking "Options" allows one to add "Estimates of Effect Size," which in this case is *eta*-squared, η^2. We've been calculating *partial eta*-squared, but in this instance, the two statistics produce the same value.

Click "OK."

As we noted in Chapter 8 when we did a factorial *ANOVA* , the General Linear Model is used for a variety of different analyses, and here it's going to provide more information than we need to answer the question. We're interested just the Tests of Within-Subjects Effects, below.

- The "factor1" line in the table refers to the independent variable. Note that the sum of squares value and the degrees of freedom are the same that we calculated for the month.

Tests of Within-Subjects Effects

Measure: MEASURE_1

Source		Type III Sum of Squares	df	Mean Square	F	Sig.	Partial Eta Squared
factor1	Sphericity Assumed	277.800	2	138.900	25.634	.000	.740
	Greenhouse-Geisser	277.800	1.086	255.688	25.634	.000	.740
	Huynh-Feldt	277.800	1.120	247.989	25.634	.000	.740
	Lower-bound	277.800	1.000	277.800	25.634	.001	.740
Error(factor1)	Sphericity Assumed	97.533	18	5.419			
	Greenhouse-Geisser	97.533	9.778	9.974			
	Huynh-Feldt	97.533	10.082	9.674			
	Lower-bound	97.533	9.000	10.837			

- The Error(factor1) line is the error term, what we called "residual variance." Note that the value of F is very similar to what we calculated.
- The *eta*-squared value indicates that 74% of the variance amount of time studied is a function of the month.

Correlation—Chapter 10

A. For the Pearson's *r* problem in Chapter 10 dealing with the relationship between homework and grades:

1. Once SPSS is loaded, create the data set with two columns.

2. In "Variable View" (lower left corner of the screen), name the two variables "hmwrk" and "grades."

3. Enter the data.

4. The commands are: Analyze→Correlate→Bivariate

5. Move "hmwrk" and "grades" from the left window to the "Variables" window.

6. Click "OK."

This table will be the result:

Correlations

		hmwrk	grades
hmwrk	Pearson Correlation	1	.755*
	Sig. (2-tailed)		.030
	N	8	8
grades	Pearson Correlation	.755*	1
	Sig. (2-tailed)	.030	
	N	8	8

*Correlation is significant at the 0.05 level (2-tailed).

The table is a **correlation matrix** in which each of the variables is correlated with each of the other variables in the analysis. Here there are just two variables. Because any variable is perfectly correlated with itself the *hmwrk* × *hmwrk* correlation gives us the "1.0" in the upper left square. It's the *hmwrk* with *grades* correlation in the upper right that we're interested in. The lower half of the matrix provides the same correlations in reverse, first the *grades* with *hmwrk* correlation and then *grades* with *grades*.

- The first line in the cell indicates the correlation coefficient.
- The second indicates the probability that the correlation occurred by chance.
  - For *hmwrk* and *grades* it is $p = .030$. Since the probability is less than $p = .05$, the correlation is significant at that level, which is what the asterisk and the footnote indicate.

Simple Regression—Chapter 11

To complete the problem in Chapter 11 that's presented just before the chapter summary:

1. Enter the data in parallel columns. I've used the same names for the variables we used in the chapter, although SPSS won't allow the use of hyphens (it treats a hyphen as a minus sign and calls it an "illegal character").

2. The commands are Analyze→Regression→Linear
   a. Enter "probsa," the variable whose value we're trying to predict in the little window at the top right titled "Dependent Variable."
   b. Enter "tape," the task persistence predictor variable in the larger window just below titled "Independent Variable(s)."

3. Click "OK."

The tables below are what we're interested in at this point:

Regression

Model Summary

Model	R	R Square	Adjusted R Square	Std. Error of the Estimate
	.819[a]	.670	.616	1.344

a. Predictors: (Constant), tape

ANOVA[b]

Model		Sum of Squares	df	Mean Square	F	Sig.
1	Regression	22.042	1	22.042	12.208	.013[a]
	Residual	10.833	6	1.806		
	Total	32.875	7			

a. Predictors: (Constant), tape

b. Dependent Variable: probsa

Coefficients[a]

Model		Unstandardized Coefficients		Standardized Coefficients	t	Sig.
		B	Std. Error	Beta		
1	(Constant)	-.944	1.80 1		- .524	.6 19
	tape	1.278	.366	.819	3.4 94	.0 13

a. Dependent Variable: probsa

- The first table provides values for the correlation (R), the square of the correlation, an adjustment based on sample size that we didn't make, and then an SE_{est} value *based on the adjusted squared correlation*.
- The second table is the significance test for the correlation. The null hypothesis is that there is no relationship between the two variables (*ta-pe* and *probsa*). The fact that F is significant means that there is a statistically significant relationship between the predictor and criterion variables so regression procedures make sense.
- The third table is the regression output. The "constant" value is what we calculated for a, the intercept which is slightly different from the longhand calculation in the chapter, and the B value is the regression coefficient, b, which matches our calculation. The significance test of the predictor matches the significance value in the *ANOVA* table, which will always be the case when there is just one predictor.

Multiple Regression—Chapter 12

1. Once in SPSS, choose to enter data and enter those below.

2. If you wish to name the variables as they are named here, select "Variable View" in the lower left corner and enter the names of the 6 variables in the first column. At this point you may also select 0 decimals for the data.

3. Return to "Data View" by selecting that option in the lower left corner of the screen. The data set should look as they do here.

	SATV	SATM	GREV	GREQ	RDG	MATH
1.	300	230	280	310	33	35
2.	400	430	460	340	47	45
3.	500	490	540	510	57	55
4.	480	430	450	510	55	52
5.	230	280	290	270	27	29
6.	330	350	350	420	43	39
7.	510	500	520	440	71	59
8.	430	460	420	530	55	56
9.	440	520	460	470	51	66
10.	430	520	450	470	54	57
11.	590	570	520	510	68	70
12.	500	400	420	430	59	41
13.	570	520	710	540	68	74
14.	420	400	490	410	52	39
15.	520	570	620	690	48	74
16.	430	630	570	730	54	75
17.	360	520	360	560	49	71
18.	280	380	360	400	32	31
19.	490	500	460	540	59	61
20.	550	670	580	620	73	68

4. We want to use the computer to regress the math score on the SAT-M (X_1) and GRE-Q (X_2) scores. The commands are:

Analyze→Regression→Linear

Select the dependent variable—math

Select the independent variables—SAT-M and GRE-Q

5. The default method is Enter, which we will use—Click "OK," which ends the setup.

Regression

Variable Entered/Removed

Regression

Variable Entered/Removed

Model	Variables Entered	Variables Removed	Method
1	GRE-Q SAT-M		Enter

a. All requested variables entered

b. Dependent Variable: MATH

Model Summary

Model	R	$Rsquare$	Adjusted R Square	Std. Error of Est.
1	.910	.828	.807	6.694

a. Predictors: (Constant), GREQ, SAT-M

ANOVA

Model	Sum of Squares	df	Mean Square	F	Sig
1.Regression	3656.628	2	1828.314	40.793	.000
Residual	761.922	17	44.819		
Total	4418.550	19			

a. Predictors : (Constant), GRE-Q, SAT-M

b. Dependent Variable: MATH
Coefficients

Model	Unstandardized Coefficients		Standardized Coefficients	t	Sig.
	B	Std. Error	Beta		
1(Constant)	−6.079	6.915		−.879	.392
SAT-M	8.604E-02	.027	.617	3.155	.006
GRE-Q	4.251E-02	.026	.324	1.656	.116

a. Dependent Variable: MATH

a. Dependent Variable: MATH

- The first table indicates the predictors used (GRE-Q, SAT-M) and the method used (Enter).
- In the second table where there are statistics for R, R^2, and an *Adjusted R^2* value. They allow one to determine how well a combination of the predictors correlates with the criterion variable, and the two R^2 values give some indication of shrinkage.
- The *ANOVA* table tests whether there is a linear relationship between the predictors and the criterion variable. The significance value for F indicates that the probability that this is a chance relationship is less than 1 in 1,000.
- In the last table the unstandardized coefficients are the longhand results. The coefficient for SAT-M, for example, is .08604—don't be distracted by the scientific notation. If that coefficient were based on standard scores it would be .617. The significance column indicates that most of the predictive power in this solution is provided by SAT-M.

Chi-Square Problems—Chapter 13

The setups for the goodness-of-fit and the test of independence are different in SPSS.

The Goodness-of-Fit *Chi*-Square

To complete the problem in Table 13.1, we need just one variable (column), the county of the student's origin. The code will indicate the county. Code Card County 1, Mountain County 2, and so on. In that column that we'll name "county," we'll have 18 "1s," 8 "2s," and so on to the last 15 "5s." (Note that in the Label tab in Variable View, you can enter your code so that you can remember the number you've used for each county.)

Once the data are entered, the commands are:

Analyze→Nonparametric tests→*Chi*-Square

Move the "county" variable to the "Test Variable" window.

Note that the default is that all expected values are equal. If this isn't the case (Table 11.2), the default must be changed.

Click "OK."

The first just indicates the f_o and f_e values and the difference. The second indicates the value of χ^2, and whether it's significant. With a significance value > .05, it isn't.

1=Card, 2=Mountain, 3=Stirling, 4=Garden, 5=Welling

	Observed N	Expected N	Residual
1	15	12.0	3.0
2	8	12.0	-4.0
3	12	12.0	.0
4	10	12.0	-2.0
5	15	12.0	3.0
Total	60		

Test Statistics

	1=Card, 2=Mountain, 3=Stirling, 4=Garden, 5=Welling
Chi-Square[a]	3.167
df	4
Asymp. Sig.	.530

a. 0 cells (.0%) have expected frequencies less than 5. The minimum expected cell frequency is 12.0.

The *Chi*-Square Test of Independence

Using Table 13.3, create columns for economic category (**lunch**): 1 = qualified for free lunch, 2 = did not qualify, and a second column for **shot**: 1 = received flu shot, 2 = did not receive flu shot.

- The first column (econ) has 15 "1s" (qualified for free lunch) and then 15 "2s" (did not qualify).
- From the top, the second column has 2 "1s" (shot) followed by 13 "2s" (no shot), and then
- 7 "1s" (shot) followed by 8 "2s" (no shot).

Once the data are in, the commands are:
Analyze→Descriptive Statistics→Crosstabs—designate **lunch** and **shot**.

Click "Statistics" and choose "*Chi*-square" and "*Phi* Coefficient."

Click "Continue."

Click "OK."

The first two tables are summaries of the cases and they've been omitted here. In the next table, you can see the "Pearson *chi*-square" value similar to what we calculated, and its significance level ($p = .046$).

Chi-Square Tests

	Value	df	Asymp. Sig. (2-sided)	Exact Sig. (2-sided)	Exact Sig. (1-sided)
Pearson *Chi*-Square	3.968[b]	1	.046		
Continuity Correction[a]	2.540	1	.111		
Likelihood Ratio	4.144	1	.042		
Fisher's Exact Test				.109	.054
Linear-by-Linear Association	3.836	1	.050		
N of Valid Cases	30				

a. Computed only for a 2x2 table

b. 2 cells (50.0%) have expected count less than 5. The minimum expected count is 4.50.

Tests for Ordinal Data—Chapter 14

Spearman's **rho:** We'll run the analysis for the end-of-chapter exercise 4 above.

Create a data set with two columns for each of the two measures for each subject. The "Variable View" option in the lower left corner of the screen will let you name your variables. In the example, they're "tutor" and "college." Return to "Data View" and enter the data in the two columns.

Once the data are entered the commands are:

Analyze→Correlate→Bivariate

Move the variables to the "Variables" window. Change the default correlation to "Spearman." If you don't unclick "Pearson," it will provide both coefficients.

Click "OK."

Nonparametric Correlations

Correlations

			tutor	college
Spearman's rho	tutor	Correlation Coefficient	1.000	.650
		Sig. (2-tailed)	.	.081
		N	8	8
	college	Correlation Coefficient	.650	1.000
		Sig. (2-tailed)	.081	.
		N	8	8

The output is the matrix above which indicates the correlation for each variable entered with all the others that were entered. Since we only entered two, it's quite simple. The correlation coefficient is indicated where the two variables intersect. The bottom half of the matrix is just the same result repeated in reverse. Note that SPSS calculates the probability that this relationship could have occurred by chance. At $p = .081$, that probability is too high to conclude that the result is statistically significant. We can't reject the null hypothesis.

Mann-Whitney U: We'll run the analysis for the end-of-chapter exercise 3 above.

Create a data set with two columns, one to identify the subject's group, the second for the subject's score. In "Variable View" they're named "agegroup" and "dogscore."

Once the data are entered the commands are:

Analyze→Nonparametric Tests→2 Independent Samples

Note that default is Mann-Whitney. Move the two variables to their relevant windows, "dogscore" (in our example here) to the "Test Variable List" window and "agegroup" to the "Grouping Variable" window. You'll need to "Define Groups." Just click the button and indicate that "1" indicates Group 1 and "2" indicates Group 2. Click "Continue" and then "OK."

Mann-Whitney Test

Ranks

	agegroup	N	Mean Rank	Sum of Ranks
dogscore	1	10	8.30	83.00
	2	10	12.70	127.00
	Total	20		

Test Statistics[b]

	dogscore
Mann-Whitney U	28.000
Wilcoxon W	83.000
Z	-1.676
Asymp. Sig. (2-tailed)	.094
Exact Sig. [2*(1-tailed Sig.)]	.105[a]

a. Not corrected for ties.

b. Grouping Variable: agegroup

What we're interested in is the value of z. If it's greater than $+/- 1.96$, it's statistically significant at $p = .05$. At -1.676 the difference isn't significant here, indicated by a significance value of .094. We fail to reject.

If we had selected K Independent Samples rather than 2, the default would have been Kruskal-Wallis H. We would need to define Groups to reflect the number range that identifies however many groups were involved, and the procedure would have produced a *chi*-square value, but otherwise the two approaches are very similar.

Wilcoxon *T*: We'll run the analysis for the end-of-chapter exercise 2 above.

Since this is a repeated measures design, create a data file with two columns, one for each set of measures. Make sure that the data are lined up so that the 53rd percentile and the 55th percentile scores for subject #1 appear on the same row. If you wish to, select "Data View" and name the variables, perhaps aptA and aptB.

Once the data are entered the commands are:

Analyze→Nonparametric Tests→2 Related samples

Move the two variables to the "Test Pairs List" window.

Click "OK."

Wilcoxon Signed Ranks Test

Ranks

		N	Mean Rank	Sum of Ranks
aptB - aptA	Negative Ranks	2[a]	3.50	7.00
	Positive Ranks	8[b]	6.00	48.00
	Ties	0[c]		
	Total	10		

a. aptB < aptA

b. aptB > aptA

c. aptB = aptA

Test Statistics[b]

	aptB - aptA
Z	-2.094[a]
Asymp. Sig. (2-tailed)	.036

a. Based on negative ranks.

b. Wilcoxon Signed Ranks Test

It's the calculated value of z we're interested in. The fact that it exceeds $z = 1.96$, indicates that there is a statistically significant difference between the two sets of scores. Don't be distracted by its negative value. SPSS does it a little differently, subtracting the second column from the first. It makes the test statistic negative.

If we had selected "K Related samples" instead of "2 Related samples," the default test would have been Friedman's, by the way, and SPSS would have produced a *chi*-square value.

Cronbach's Alpha—Chapter 15

When individual items aren't scored right/wrong, yes/no and the test is given once, the most common reliability approach is Cronbach's alpha. Enter the data so that the rows are the individuals who completed the instrument, and the columns are their responses to each item as they are here:

	item1	item2	item3	item4	item5	item6	item7	item8	item9	item10
1.	3	4	4	3	3	3	2	4	4	3
2.	2	3	3	3	2	2	1	2	2	2
3.	2	3	4	4	3	3	4	3	1	3
4.	3	1	2	4	4	2	1	4	3	0
5.	1	4	1	2	4	4	3	2	2	1
6.	2	3	4	4	4	3	3	4	4	2
7.	1	2	2	1	1	1	0	2	2	1
8.	1	3	2	0	1	2	1	0	3	0

Once the data are entered, the commands are:
Analyze→Scale→Reliability Analysis
Move the items to the "items" window.
Click "OK."
The output is as follows:

Reliability

Scale: ALL VARIABLES

Case Processing Summary

		N	%
C a s e s	Valiases	8	10 0.0
	Excluded[a]	0	.0
	Total	8	10 0.0

a. Listwise deletion based on all variables in the procedure.

Reliability Statistics

Cronbach's Alpha	N of Items
.863	10

SOLUTIONS TO SELECTED PROBLEMS

Chapter 1:

None

Chapter 2:

1. Nominal scale

3. Ratio

5.

    a. The mean = 14.333
    b. The median = 15
    c. The mode = 15
    d. The range = 7.0
    e. The standard deviation = 2.060

7.

    a. If another score is added near the mean of the group, the standard deviation will shrink since s measures the "standard," or typical deviation from the mean.
    b. If a "5" is added, the standard deviation will increase since the effect of adding a score that is relatively distant from the mean is to increase the typical deviation from the mean.

9. For the ANGST data, $n = 15$, $M = 19.80$, $M_{dn} = 20.0$, $s = 4.109$

11. For the history data:

    a. As a measure of the number of items answered correctly, the data are ratio scale
    b. $R = 22$

c. $M = 33.90$
d. $s = 6.208$
e. $M_{dn} = 34$

Chapter 3:

1.

a. The groups must have equal ranges.
b. A particular score or observation can fit into just one group.

3. The data in item 2 represent an "ordered array."

5. The bar chart will have gaps between the vertical bars. The histogram has no gaps, which indicates that the data are continuous from one value to the next.

7. This distribution has positive skew.

9. In a mesokurtic distribution $6s = R$. If $s = 3.756$ and $R = 43$, 11.448 $s = R$ in this instance. The standard deviation is too small for a mesokurtic distribution. This distribution is leptokurtic.

11.

a. $M_{dn} = 21.0$; $Q_1 = 15.5$; $Q_3 = 24.5$; $IQR = 24.5 - 15.5 = 9.0$
b. *The* $Q_1 - (1.5 \times IQR) = 15.5 - (1.5 \times 9) =$ any score lower than 2, and
c. $Q_3 + (1.5 \times IQR) = 24.5 + (1.5 \times 9) =$ any score higher than 38. According to Lockhart's criteria, there are no outliers in this group.

13. From the stem-and-leaf display in item 2:

a. $Q_1 = 295$
b. $Q_2 (M_{dn}) = 450$
c. $Q_3 = 620$

15. If the data were normal, from **307.477** ($M - s$, 459.688 – 152.211) to **611.899** ($M + s$, 459.688 + 152.211) would include about 68% of the distribution.

Chapter 4:

1. The percentage of the distribution

a. Lower than 34?

$z = (x - M)/s = (34 - 29.6)/6.512 = .68$ (25.17) 25.17 + 50 = **75.17%**

b. Lower than 26?

$z_{26} = (x - M)/s = (26 - 29.6)/6.512 = -.55 \ (20.88) \ 50 - 20.88 =$ **29.12%**

c. Between 30 and 38?

$z_{30} = .06 \ (2.39); \ z_{38} = 1.29 \ (40.15); \ 40.15 - 1.29 = $ **38.86%**

3.

$z_{RAT} = .67$

$z_{CAT} = 1.032.$ This person did better on the CAT.

5. For

$z_{RAT} = .67, \ T_{RAT} = 56.70 \ (z * 10) + 50$

$z_{CAT} = 1.032. \ T_{CAT} = 60.32$

7. The probability of ANGST scores:

a. Lower than 50: $p = $ **.19**
b. Higher than 65: $p = $ **.31**
c. Between 40 and 85: $p = $ **.95**

9.

a. Outside $z = -1.0$ to $z = 1.0 = $ **31.74%**
b. Outside $z = 1.17$ to $z = 2.15 = $ **89.48%**
c. Outside $z = -1.35$ to $z = -.35 = $ **72.53%**

T, NCE, and the stanine are all standard scores; they have equal intervals between consecutive data points. Percentile scores do not.

11.

a. Those expected to do poorly = **21.77%**
b. Those expected to excel = **23.89%**
c. 12 occurs at the **76th percentile**

13.

a. $z_{15} = -1.189, \ M_{spec} = 20$ and $s_{spec} = 2.50$, so MSS = $2.50 \times -1.189 + 20 = $ **17.028**
b. $z_{22} = .509, \ M_{spec} = 20$ and $s_{spec} = 2.50$, so MSS = $2.50 \times .509 + 20 = $ **21.274**

Chapter 5:

1. Since $\mu = \mu_M$, μ_M also $= 37.5$.

3. $z_{35} = .345$, or $.35(13.68)$; $50 - 13.68 = 36.32$; $p = \textbf{.36}$

5. $\sigma_M = \sigma/\sqrt{n} = 13.755/\sqrt{65} = \textbf{1.706}$

7. $n = 384.16$ or $\textbf{384,}$ at $.95$ probability

   $n = 1584.04$ or $\textbf{1584}$ at $.99$ probability

9. $\sigma_M = 1.581$; $z = 1.752$. At $p = .05$, their ages are not significantly different from the ages of students at the university generally.

11. $z = 1.990$, at $p = .05$ the sample is significantly different from the population.

    $.95$ CI $= 14.505, 7.629$

Chapter 6:

1. $SE_M = 3.454$

   $t = 1.737$; $t_{.05(7)} = 2.365$. At $p = .05$, the sample is **not significantly different** from the population.

3. $SE_d = 4.165$; $t = 1.741$; $t_{.05(14)} = 2.145$, the samples are **probably not** drawn from populations with significantly different means.

5. When testing at $p = .05$, if the null hypothesis is rejected, the probability of type I error is $.05$. The probability of type II error when rejecting is zero.

7. The IV is the classroom

   The DV is spelling performance

   The IV must be nominal scale

   The DV must be at least interval scale

9. $SE_d = 1.081$; $t = 3.443$; $t_{.05(17)} = 1.740$

   This is a one-tailed test.
   H_A: $m_1 > m_2$
   The difference is statistically significant.
   $d = 1.250$, a relatively large effect
   With $.95$ confidence, the difference between the population means which these two samples represent is between 6.003 and 1.441.

Chapter 7:

1. $SS = 83.625$

3. $F = 8.232$ and is statistically significant at $p = .05$

5. With only two groups, the first must be significantly different from the second.

7. $F = 8.142$ and is significant at $p = .05$

   Group 1 (15 minutes) is significantly different from Group 3 (90 minutes)

   $\eta_p^2 = .576$; about 58% of the variance in scores is explained by study time

9. $N = 40$ and $k = 4$ so $df_{bet} = 3$ and $df_{within} = 36$

   Therefore, $MS_{bet} = 24/3 = 8.0$ and $MS_{within} = 72/36 = 2.0$; $F = 8.0/2.0 =$ **4.0**; $F.05(3,36) = 2.86$ and is significant.

Chapter 8:

1. The *GLM* provides partial *eta*-squared (η_p^2).

3. *df* for *IV* #1 will be 2 (levels -1) and *df* for the interaction will be 4 $(3-1)(3-1)$

5. A significant interaction indicates that the independent variables have a combined effect that is different than either variable operating independently. Analyzing the separate effects of the *IVs* won't reveal that combined effect.

7. There are 2 *IVs*.

   df for the *IV* with 2 levels will be 1; the *df* for the *IV* with 3 levels will be 2

   there will be 6 groups—2 levels of one times 3 levels of the other *IV*.

Chapter 9:

1.
   a. The standard deviation of the difference scores = 2.714
   b. The standard error of the mean for the difference scores = 1.108

  c. $t = -1.053$ and
  d. is not significant ($t_{.05(5)} = 2.571$)
  e. Asking whether students miss significantly more school makes it a one-tailed test,
  f. and the critical value of t becomes $t = 2.015$

3.

  a. The *IV* is type of reinforcement
  b. The *IV* is ratio scale
  c. The differences are significant, $F = 59.267$.
  d. All groups are significantly different from each other.
  e. $\eta_p^2 = .894$; about 89% of the variance in response rate is explained by the type of reinforcement.

5. In a one-way *ANOVA*, subject-to-subject differences are more difficult to isolate because they're different for each group.

7.

  a. The *DV* is the biology final score.
  b. The standard error of the mean for the difference scores $= 2.55.3$.
  c. The differences are not statistically significant ($t = -1.910$; $t_{.05(7)} = 2.365$).
  d. Although those who take the lab do better, the difference is not significant and may reflect a random difference.

9.

  a. There are significant differences related to the month.
  b. The month is the IV.
  c. $\eta_p^2 = .707$; about 71% of the days missed is related to the month.

11. Effect sizes are greater for within-subjects designs than in a one-way *ANOVA* design because the latter leaves more of the variance uncontrolled; there is more error variance involved.

Chapter 10:

1. Pearson values can range from -1 to $+1$.

3. Absent some variability in the data, there can't be correlation since correlation gauges how variable "co-vary."

5.

  a. The time of retirement, grades correlation is $r = -647$.

  b. The correlation isn't statistically significant at $p = .05$.

  c. Technically, none of it since the correlation isn't statistically significant.

7.

  a. The minutes/score relationship is $r = -.060$ and not significant, so

  b. time spent in the seminars doesn't explain any of the variance in scores.

9. At $p = .05$, the $r = .504$ persistency/attendance relationship is not statistically significant.

11.

  a. This problem calls for a point-biserial correlation.

  b. Those reporting no stress had higher levels of performance.

  c. However, at $p = .05$ the $r = .415$ correlation is *not* statistically significant.

Chapter 11:

1. For someone with SAT-V of 490, the predicted reading score is $y' = 58.210$.

  a. For a 1.0 increase in SAT-V, the reading score will increase by .105

  b. If SAT-V = 0, reading = 6.76

  c. The reading score when SAT-V = 0 represents the y intercept, a.

3. A .99 CI = 68.112, 48.308

  a. The CI contains the actual value of y.

  b. The CI will be wrong approximately 1% of the time.

  c. Any of a lower level of confidence, a higher correlation between x and y, or less variability in y will shrink the CI.

5. A negative correlation indicates a downward slope in the regression line from left to right.

7. The variable that will provide the best prediction of GRE-V scores is the variable that has the highest correlation with GRE-V, SAT-V.

9. If reading = 60, GRE-V = 511.98

Chapter 12:

1. $R_{y.x1,x2} = .910$

3.

    a. If SAT-V = 490 and Reading = 46, GRE-V = 534.651
    b. When scores have very different ranges of values, the magnitude of the regression coefficient may reflect the size of the scores more than the strength of the prediction.

5. Samples are overfitted when the regression solution predicts better for the original sample than it will for other data sets.

7. $CI_{95} = 22.979, 10.511$

9.

    a. If Reading = 60, Math = 62, GREQ = 529.088
    b. As long as there's a significant correlation, one can make a better-than-chance prediction.
    c. A CI_{95} with $n = 32 = 652.479, 405.697$

11. The standard error of the estimate, or of the multiple estimate, is affected by the value of R and the variability in the DV, y.

Chapter 13:

1. Difference in the preferences are not significant, $\chi^2 = 2.923$.

3. The f_e values for part-time workers is 10.667 and for full-time workers is 8.0.

5. Differences *are* significant, $\chi^2 = 6.303$.

7. The relationship between tutoring and other charitable service is not significant $\chi^2 = 2.286$.

    a. The null hypothesis predicts no relationship between family observances and substance abuse.
    b. Here the null hypothesis is rejected.
    c. $\chi^2 = 6.357$

9.

    a. There appears to be no relationship between the reading curriculum and whether students met the standard, $\chi^2 = 4.518$.
    b. From these data, the particular curriculum doesn't matter.

Chapter 14:

1.
- a. Kruskal-Wallis H
- b. Wilcoxon T
- c. Spearman's *rho*

3.
- a. Mann-Whitney U
- b. Dogmatism is *not* significantly different by age, according to these data.

5.
- a. Friedman's *ANOVA*
- b. The *IV* is nominal scale
- c. The *DV* is ordinal scales
- d. The differences are *not* statistically significant

7. $\Sigma R_1 = 47.5$.

9.
- a. The null hypothesis is that the rankings in the two distributions are the same, $H_o: R_1 = R_2$.
- b. The groups are dependent—either matched, or one group measured twice.
- c. The *DV* is ordinal scale.

11. The correlation between reading ability and introversion is $r_s = -.530$ and, at $p = .05$ is *not* statistically significant.

Chapter 15:

1.
- a. Test-retest reliability is $r = .947$
- b. If the test were doubled, the Spearman-Brown formula predicts that reliability would likely become $r = .973$.

3.
- a. $r = .884$
- b. If $n = 1.5$, Spearman Brown predicts reliability will be $r = .920$.

5.

    a. Without individual item data, r_{KR21} will provide an estimate of reliability.

    b. In this case, the estimate is $r_{KR21} = .635$.

    c. $SEM = 2.568$

    d. $27 +/- 2.568 = 29.568, 24.432$

7.

    a. $r_{KR20} = .791$

    b. For $p = .95$, we need $+/- 2 \ SEM$ around x, which is 7. $SEM = 1.257$. With $p = .95$, $t = 9.514, 4.486$

9.

    a. $r_{KR21} = .663$

    b. There are no individual item data available, which both α and r_{KR20} require.

    c. If test length is increased by half, Spearman-Brown predicts $r = .747$.

11. $C_i = .822$

13. Rather than just correlation, perhaps the more compelling issue is whether the scores predict future performance equally well for males and for females. Regression analysis would allow one to compare the regression coefficients for each gender group to see if the prediction is equally well for both groups.

Chapter 16:

1. Analysis of covariance.

3. For *MANOVA*, the *IV*s are nominal, and the *DV*s are interval/ratio.

5. When there are two *IV* groups.

7. In a two-way *ANCOVA*, the *IV*s will be nominal, the covariate interval/ratio, and the *DV* interval/ratio.

9. Canonical correlation

11. Cluster analysis

13. The task is to explain a greater number of visual indicators (scores) with fewer underlying factors.

15. The causal effect of an independent variable on a dependent variable

INDEX

ABOUT THE AUTHOR

David Tanner is a Professor in the Department of Educational Research and Administration at California State University, Fresno, where he was the Department Chair from 1990–1995. He received his PhD in Curriculum and Instruction/Measurement from Texas A&M University, and his areas of interest include educational psychology; statistics and measurement; educational research; quantitative and qualitative evaluation; assessing student achievement; evaluating classroom assessment instruments; and evaluating the performance of teachers and teacher candidates. He has authored several journal articles and the textbook *Assessing Academic Achievement* (©2001).